Queensbury, NY 12804

ARCHITECTURE, LANDSCAPE, AND AMERICAN CULTURE SERIES

Katherine Solomonson, University of Minnesota

Series Editor

ARCHITECTURE, LANDSCAPE, AND AMERICAN CULTURE

A MANUFACTURED WILDERNESS

Summer Camps and the Shaping of American Youth, 1890–1960

ABIGAIL A. VAN SLYCK

UNIVERSITY OF MINNESOTA PRESS *Minneapolis & London*

A version of chapter 3 appeared as "Housing the Happy Camper," *Minnesota History* 58 (Summer 2002): 68–83. An earlier version of chapter 4 was published as "Kitchen Technologies and Mealtime Rituals: Interpreting the Food Axis at American Summer Camps, 1890–1950," *Technology and Culture* 43 (October 2002): 668–92. Parts of chapter 6 appeared as "Connecting with the Landscape: Campfires and Youth Culture at American Summer Camps, 1890–1950," in Marta Gutman and Ning de Coninck-Smith, eds., *Designing Modern Childhoods: History, Space, and the Material Culture of Children / An International Reader* (New Brunswick, N.J.: Rutgers University Press, forthcoming); reprinted with permission of Rutgers University Press.

Every effort has been made to obtain permission to reproduce the illustrations in this book. If any acknowledgment has not been included, we encourage copyright holders to notify the publisher.

Copyright 2006 by the Regents of the University of Minnesota

All rights reserved. No part of this publication may be reproduced, stored in a retrieval system, or transmitted, in any form or by any means, electronic, mechanical, photocopying, recording, or otherwise, without the prior written permission of the publisher.

Published by the University of Minnesota Press
111 Third Avenue South, Suite 290
Minneapolis, MN 55401-2520
http://www.upress.umn.edu

LIBRARY OF CONGRESS
CATALOGING-IN-PUBLICATION DATA

Van Slyck, Abigail Ayres.
  A manufactured wilderness : summer camps and the shaping of American youth, 1890–1960 / Abigail A. Van Slyck.
      p. cm. — (Architecture, landscape, and American culture series)
Includes bibliographical references and index.
ISBN-13: 978-0-8166-4876-4 (hc/j : alk. paper)
ISBN-10: 0-8166-4876-X (hc/j : alk. paper)
ISBN-13: 978-0-8166-4877-1 (pb : alk. paper)
ISBN-10: 0-8166-4877-8 (pb : alk. paper)
  1. Camps—United States—History. I. Title.
GV193.V37 2006
796.540973—dc22   2006019019

Printed in Canada
on acid-free paper

The University of Minnesota is an equal-opportunity educator and employer.

12 11 10 09 08 07 06   10 9 8 7 6 5 4 3 2 1

For E. J. V. S. and A. W. V. S.

who sent me to camp
until I liked it

Camp Onontio, Shelter Lake, Vermont,
1933. The author's father is seated in
the third chair from the right.

CONTENTS

ILLUSTRATIONS

ACKNOWLEDGMENTS

THE PROCESS OF RESEARCHING AND WRITING A BOOK ON summer camps has certainly had its share of pleasant moments, but some of the most enjoyable have been spent reflecting on the range of institutions and individuals who have helped me with this project in one way or another during the past nine years. I have been particularly fortunate to receive financial support from the Schlesinger Library at the Radcliffe Institute for Advanced Study, the Graham Foundation for Advanced Studies in the Visual Arts, and the Spencer Foundation. I would especially like to acknowledge Debbie Miller, the able and creative administrator of an exciting, and now sadly defunct, research grant program at the Minnesota Historical Society, which offered important early support.

My research also brought me into contact with dozens of people who own, run, and staff camps. They are a special breed, a fact that—as a failed camper myself—I had not fully appreciated in my youth. Thus, it is with a certain sense of awe that I acknowledge the help of all of those who interrupted their very busy days—often in the midst of the camp season—to give me tours, share with me their views of the camping endeavor, let me dig through their records, and allow me to tie up their copiers. Several devoted an unusual amount of time and energy to this project and deserve extra thanks: Steve

Purdum at Camp Mishawaka, Fred Rogers at Camp Lincoln, Pat Krol at Camp Becket, Fran McIntyre at Camp Jeanne d'Arc, Margaret Lyle Jones and Charlotte Page at Rockbrook Camp, Fritz Orr III at Camp Merrie-Woode, Laurie Strayhorn at Camp Illahee, Bernie Ruf at the Fresh Air Foundation camps, and Taylor C. Statten at Camp Ahmek.

I am equally grateful for the assistance of archivists and librarians at the American Camp Association, Billy Graham Center Archives at Wheaton College, Prints and Photographs Division of the Library of Congress, Minnesota Historical Society, National Archives, Philmont Museum–Seton Memorial Library, Schlesinger Library at Radcliffe Institute for Advanced Study, Special Collections at the Frances Loeb Library of the Harvard Graduate School of Design, and Social Welfare History Archives at the University of Minnesota. Special thanks go to Marylène Altieri, formerly of the Gutman Library at Harvard University; Mary Degenhardt, archivist at the Girl Scouts of the USA; and especially Dagmar Getz at the Kautz Family YMCA Archives at the University of Minnesota. I am also indebted to Richard B. Salomon, who shared with me documents related to the career of his father, Julian Harris Salomon.

As I traveled from camp to camp, I enjoyed the hospitality of many friends, who took me into their homes often for weeks at a time. Their friendship, good cooking, and interest in this project made the research all the more enjoyable. Thanks to Catherine and John Bishir, Mike and Heather Koop, Sally McMurry and Barry Kernfeld, Brenda Reishus, and Sally and John Roach. Special thanks go to Vanessa Reid, a traveling companion *sans pareil*.

I would like to acknowledge colleagues who supported this research in any number of ways, including sharing their professional expertise on summer camps, pushing me to think more critically about race, supporting my research grants, giving me thoughtful criticism on earlier articles on this work, or modeling an approach to architectural history that I find particularly inspiring. They include Jacqui Alexander, Ning de Coninck-Smith, Betsy Cromley, Deborah Dietrich-Smith, Alice Friedman, Rebecca Ginsburg, Sandy Grande, Paul Groth, Marta Gutman, Dianne Harris, Dolores Hayden, Kim Hoagland, Richard Longstreth, David M. Malatzky, Jennifer Martin, W. Barksdale Maynard, Sally McMurry, Will Moore, Tim Orwig, Joy Parr, Martin Perdue, Mary Corbin Sies, David Sloane, and Dell Upton. Special thanks to those who read the entire manuscript: the two anonymous readers for the University of Minnesota Press, Annmarie Adams, Lisa Wilson, and especially Kate Solomonson, an extraordinarily insightful editor. I am enormously grateful for the time and energy she devoted to helping me shape the final version of this book.

A number of colleagues, students, and former students helped me prepare the manuscript for publication: Mark Braunstein and Frank Fulchiero, who offered much-needed scanning advice; Allison Park, who translated my nearly illegible field notes into measured drawings; Ian Clifford, who prepared the appendix; and the amazing Liz Marwell, who took on the daunting task of getting my illustrations in order. Her calm efficiency and gentle sense of humor were much appreciated.

No one completes such a project without the indirect but nonetheless invaluable support of friends and colleagues who make life and work both stimulating and enjoyable. Many people in my life fall into this category, but I feel compelled to mention a few by name. From my days in Arizona, Renée Cheng, Mary Graham, Paul Ivey, Brooks Jeffery, David Klanderman, and Eric Olson deserve special mention. In Connecticut and environs, I would particularly like to acknowledge Joe Alchermes, Jon Dahlberg, Candace Howes, Dave Kanen, Brenda Reishus, Chris Steiner, Rebecca Steiner, Stuart Vyse, Lisa Wilson, Barbara Zabel, and those who pursued their own writing projects around my kitchen table at the Home for Lonely Scholars: Tristan Borer, Jenny Fredricks, Sandy Grande, and Andy Lanoux.

Finally, I count myself unusually fortunate to have been born into such a supportive family. Although bemused that their youngest child—whose homesickness resulted in so many tear-stained missives from camp—would choose to write a book on this topic, my mom and dad have also demonstrated genuine interest in the project and pride in my achievements. I bask in their love and support and continue to rely heavily on my mother's sharp editorial eye. Even more important to my sense of well-being is my husband, Mitch Favreau, who endured my absences, fixed my computer, scanned my images, listened to my worries, drove me to the oncologist, shaved my head when chemotherapy killed my hair follicles, quieted my fears, and continues to celebrate my return to good health. He may be my biggest fan, but I know I am his.

Summer Camps and the Problem of Modern Childhood

THIS SUMMER MORE THAN TEN MILLION NORTH AMERICAN children will experience the simple pleasures of summer camp: the feel of pine needles underfoot, the smell of the campfire, the taste of s'mores. Many will attend day camps, but a significant number will enroll in residential camps, swelling the ranks of those who have spent some part of each summer living away from home in a rustic setting with other children their own age. Whether privately run, supported by a charitable foundation, affiliated with a religious enterprise, or sponsored by a youth organization (such as the YMCA or the Girl Scouts), summer camps have become a common feature of North American life. Among social institutions, only public schools have touched the lives of more youngsters.[1]

From a historical perspective, however, summer camps are anything but simple. First introduced to the North American landscape in the 1880s, camps were part of a back-to-nature trend that had been developing on both sides of the Atlantic since the middle of the nineteenth century. In this respect, they are like urban parks, residential suburbs, resort hotels, and national parks, all institutions aimed at providing respite from what were regarded as the moral and physical degradations of urban life, evils to which women and children were understood to be particularly prone.[2]

Figure I.1. *Snap-the-Whip,* engraving by Winslow Homer. Published in *Harper's Weekly,* September 20, 1873.

Yet, the search for pastoral relaxation and rejuvenation was rarely uncomplicated. Instead, it often involved the wholesale commodification of the countryside to meet the needs and desires of tourists who consumed the very idea of country life, as well as the goods and services offered there. Typically, this process was aimed at giving urban dwellers a supposedly authentic encounter with folk life—itself a cultural construction of the late nineteenth century. As historian Ian McKay has demonstrated in his study of Nova Scotia, once the particular visual tropes of folk life have been established, the role of the rural "tourism plant" is to simulate what the tourist expects to see.[3] Like other rural sites that catered to city people, summer camps manufactured a version of the wilderness that would meet the expectations of campers and their parents. By the 1920s and 1930s, they began to mimic the material trappings of Native Americans and rural mountain folk with almost as much gusto as other tourist destinations.

Unlike other tourist landscapes, however, the summer camps discussed in this book were designed specifically to serve youngsters and thus intersected with another important trend in twentieth-century life in North America, namely, the provision of more and more places outside the home catering exclusively to the needs of children. Some of these settings—such as rustic Boy Scout huts designed for troop meetings—were brand-new building types. Others—like schools—had been common features of the nineteenth-century landscape. In the twentieth century, however, existing subtypes (such as the high school) were more fully elaborated and become more distinct, whereas a range of new subtypes—for example, the junior high school and the public school kindergarten—sprang into being. Other building types that had been established primarily for adults spawned separate children's sections that became commonplace in the twentieth century: playgrounds in urban parks, children's reading rooms in public libraries, children's hospitals, and even children's sections in cemeteries. In the postwar period, this trend extended into larger and larger components of the North American landscape, notably in residential suburbs that used superblock planning to give pupils an automobile-free walk to the elementary school that served as the organizing core of each neighborhood.[4]

At each of these sites, the middle-class professionals in charge—Scout leaders, teachers, play directors, librarians, doctors, undertakers, city planners—arranged the building and its environs to meet the needs of children. Or so they would have said. What they did not say—what they could not say—was that, in articulating their understanding of children's needs, they helped invent a particular version of childhood that suited their time and place. In other words, their actions were deeply involved in the social construction of modern childhood, a process that Marta Gutman and Ning de Coninck-Smith have characterized as "threaded with hopes and aspirations for children, as well as the dreams and fears of adults."[5]

At summer camps, those dreams and fears were initially defined by late-nineteenth-century social and demographic changes that seemed to threaten the dominant position within American society of a native-born middle class, largely of northern European descent. While camping was eventually taken up by other groups for their own purposes, this was the segment of society most actively involved in developing a new notion of childhood (which centered on the figure of the carefree child who joined the nonworking wife as a key signifier of middle-class identity) and whose interests and values were most directly advanced at what have come to be called traditional camps. Indeed, summer camps provided an important means for this group to address anxieties about gender roles, race relations, class tensions, and particularly about modernity and its impact on the lives of children—particularly their own children.

From the perspective of these adults, the modern world deprived youngsters of essential childhood experiences, and camps were one means to compensate for those losses. To get an idea of what was at stake, consider *Snap-the-Whip*, Winslow Homer's depiction of nine boys engaged in a vigorous version of the time-honored game named in the work's title (Figure I.1). White, sturdy, and barefoot, the boys are evidently the sons of farm families. Having emerged into the clear sunlight from the one-room schoolhouse in the background, they are playing in a field without adult supervision. Although they are neither neat nor clean, they are healthy and their play is innocent—that is, joyful, spontaneous, and not dependent on consumer goods. Wildflowers in the foreground highlight the rural setting, which, Homer implies, contributes to the purity of these boys. Painted in 1872 and published the next year as an engraving in *Harper's Weekly*, the image drew upon Homer's memories of his own pleasant boyhood in the decades before the cataclysmic events of the Civil War. It is, in short, an idyll of childhood that resonated with Homer's Victorian audience.[6]

If this mode of childhood was fading when Homer represented it in the 1870s, within another twenty years the forces of modernization had eradicated it entirely, or such was the fear of middle-class, native-born Americans. In their eyes, the rise of large cities deprived modern children of wide-open, sun-filled spaces for active play, while overcrowded tenements and substandard sanitation threatened the very health and vitality of the young. Massive European immigration made these developments particularly troubling, flooding American cities with children who were not just culturally different from Anglo-Saxons, but understood to be racially inferior to them as well. How, these native-born Americans wondered, would immigrant children learn the cherished values of the American republic in congested cities? What was to prevent urban youths from becoming hollow-chested toughs who would rather haunt the nickelodeon than engage in wholesome play? And what would happen to American society when these supposedly inferior specimens, who were reproducing at alarming rates, exercised the rights of citizenship?[7]

As troubling as native-born Americans found urban neighborhoods, pastoral suburbs were little better. True, such suburbs had been established in the Victorian era to insulate their middle-class inhabitants from the degradation of the city, but these bucolic settings offered none of the character-building opportunities increasingly associated with the American frontier. Indeed, for many late Victorians, the frontier's particular hardships—confronting the untamed elements of the natural environment, battling the indigenous population for possession of the continent, and bringing the land under cultivation through force of will and hard physical labor—were responsible for transforming the Anglo-Saxon race into a new stock that was stronger and distinctly American.[8]

Instead of facing these challenges, suburban children (and their middle-class counterparts living in cities) were subject to the cultural norms of the parlor, supervised by doting mothers who (according to some late-Victorian commentators) limited the activities of their offspring in the name of cleanliness and good manners. Fearing that the sons of such households were becoming "sissies," many worried that this erosion of manliness would undermine the military might required to pursue the all but imperial aspirations of the United States.[9]

Adding to these concerns were other changes in the lives of American children. Protective labor legislation and compulsory school attendance laws were, of course, aimed at safeguarding children from workplace hazards and providing them with a basic education. But they also ensured that boys and girls (especially those whose parents did not need them to be wage earners) were spending more time than ever before in the regimented atmosphere of the schoolroom, without the opportunity to apply their book knowledge to the real world. For children of the leisured classes (the middle- and upper-class youngsters who most concerned camp organizers), the long summer vacation offered a respite from this regimentation, but a school break unconnected to farm chores was still a relatively new—and worrisome—phenomenon in the 1890s. Camp director Henry W. Gibson characterized it as "a period of moral deterioration with most boys . . . who have heretofore wasted the glorious summer time loafing on the city streets, or as disastrously at summer hotels or amusements places." [10] Given that middle-class men often visited their summering families only for brief intervals during the season, Gibson's criticism of summer hotels is linked to anxieties about too much female influence.

This book investigates summer camps as a response to these issues, tracing the development of both the issues and the camps themselves from the last decade of the nineteenth century through about 1960, when special skills camps and day camps began to challenge the dominance of traditional camps. Even for readers familiar with camp life, a bit of background is in order: an overview of the social and cultural trends that informed the summer camp phenomenon; some general information about who owned and operated camps, who designed and built them, and who staffed and attended them; and a discussion of methodology with particular attention to how the methods of architectural history can be adapted to interpret summer camps.

THE RISE OF SUMMER CAMPS AND BEYOND

The decades between 1890 and 1920 saw several attempts to address the problem of modern childhood. The movement to build and supervise urban playgrounds and the establishment of youth organizations like the Boy Scouts and the Camp Fire Girls spring immediately to mind. [11] But summer camps (whose champions included men and women associated with both the playground and scouting movements) offered perhaps the most comprehensive response. Not only were their natural settings inherently healthy (or at least initially seemed to be so), but they also helped fill the long summer vacation without subjecting children to the resort hotel.

Despite their differences, camps were overtly antimodernist, self-consciously celebrating the past in a search for authenticity that ultimately (according to historian Jackson Lears) prepared individuals to function more effectively in the bureaucratic structures of the modern world.[12] At summer camps, these antimodern impulses took many forms, but a romanticized emulation of frontier life was chief among them. Installed in a rustic setting devoid of modern technologies of comfort (at least in these early decades of the twentieth century), campers could learn some of the survival skills that had sustained their pioneering forebears: fishing, building fires, cooking over an open flame, engaging in handicrafts, and—eventually—living in log cabins. (Although some camps taught youngsters to track animals, hunting was not a part of the camp program.) The same antimodernist sentiments that prompted middle-class Americans to build Colonial Revival houses or to equip their bungalows with Arts and Crafts furnishings (made by machine to look hand-crafted) also impelled them to send their children to camp.[13]

Remaking gender roles was integral to this process. Early boys' camps—and the earliest camps were exclusively for boys—were understood to offer a potent antidote to the feminized homes that threatened to undermine American manliness. In addition to distancing boys from their mothers' influence, camps also immersed them in an all-male environment in which adult role models were carefully vetted. One manifestation of Theodore Roosevelt's cult of the strenuous life, early camps sought to toughen boys through long hikes, competitive sports, calisthenics, and rough-and-tumble games. Reinforcing the gendered meaning of the camp experience, the military layout used at many early camps blurred the boundaries between war and play, thus preparing boys to be enthusiastic participants someday in their own "bully little war" (TR's fond nickname for the sort of military adventure he enjoyed in Cuba in 1898).

World War I did not prove to be so "bully," but it did intensify the military practices at boys' camps, while also providing a powerful rationale for extending the summer camp experience to girls. Private girls' camps had been established in the early years of the twentieth century, but the war effort encouraged newly formed groups like the Camp Fire Girls and the Girl Scouts to enter the camping field in a big way. In addition to teaching useful skills like first aid and canning, camps gave girls the chance to experience military discipline on a daily basis, thus preparing them (in a generic way) for their patriotic duties.[14]

Organized camping (the industry's term for the sort of residential children's camps that are the focus of this book) seemed an ideal way to address growing concerns about girls—concerns that had prompted TR to associate the rise of the New Woman with the falling birthrate (specifically among the white middle class) and so-called race suicide.[15] The champions of camping for girls were hardly radical in their thinking and often explicitly stated their conviction that a girl's destiny lay in marriage and motherhood. Nonetheless, they had become disenchanted by Victorian conventions of femininity (which they associated with helplessness and hysteria) and embraced camping as a means to create a new generation of happy and capable women who would be vivacious companions to their husbands and energetic mothers to the next generation of boys. While the organizers of girls' camps were wary of pleasure-seeking flappers, the camp experience itself encouraged self-confidence, independence, and a taste for an active life beyond the confines of the domestic sphere, and thus may have played a role in reproducing such freedom-loving females.

In the aftermath of World War I, the realities of modern warfare undermined the appeal of militarism in North American camps. Rather than playing soldier, campers were more likely to play Indian, historian Philip Deloria's phrase for a long-standing practice among whites to adopt Indian personae.[16] Like Buffalo Bill's Wild West Show (which started in the late nineteenth century) and other, twentieth-century, representations of Indian life, playing Indian at summer camp reinforced the idea of the Vanishing Indian, pushing Native American culture safely into the past and forestalling any consideration of Native American realities in the present. By the time racial issues were addressed explicitly in the aftermath of World War II, supporters of interracial camps identified their mission as improving relations between whites and African Americans. As campers continued to play Indian, the status of actual Native Americans faded from their consciousness.

Camps have never been an exclusively North American phenomenon; by the 1930s, New Zealanders had established health camps to serve "disadvantaged" children, Communist-governed municipalities had established *colonies de vacances* in France, and *colonie* in Fascist Italy aided the cause of political indoctrination.[17] But American summer camps worked their way more deeply into the fabric of the nation. Indeed, during the Depression summer camps were considered so essential to the production of good citizens that the federal government used New Deal programs to sponsor the construction of state-of-the-art campgrounds earmarked for the use of charitable agencies serving poor children. De-emphasizing differences between the sexes, these camps highlighted instead their potential for easing class tensions heightened by the economic crisis.

If summer camps had become integral to what the dominant culture considered the American way of life, they could also offer resistance to mainstream values. In the 1930s and 1940s, the radical Left embraced summer camps as "ideal locations for putting into practice the visionary aspects of Communist culture"; in New York State alone there were twenty-seven Communist camps for so-called red diaper babies by 1956.[18] Jewish camps (including some affiliated with the radical movement) enjoyed a surge of popularity between the 1920s and the 1950s, as they sought to maintain ethnic practices threatened by modernization and assimilation.[19] Like other camps organized around ethnic or religious affiliations, these were typically coeducational camps that encouraged young people to marry one of their own.[20] Other camps—like Camp Atwater, established in 1921 in North Brookfield, Massachusetts—offered sex-segregated sessions for the sons and daughters of elite African American families, providing them with a camp experience that was comparable in most respects to that enjoyed by white children.[21]

At the start of World War II, public discourse often positioned summer camps as experiments in democratic living, although what exactly this entailed could vary widely. Sometimes it involved attempts to give campers a vote on every aspect of camp life. In other cases, democracy was invoked in conjunction with interracial camps, which were touted as a means "to broaden the racial attitudes of the next generation."[22] Although such attempts to bridge social divisions based on race were groundbreaking within the summer camp movement, their tendency to locate the roots of racial inequality in individual prejudice did little to challenge the systemic inequalities that plagued—and continue to plague—American culture.

In the postwar era, the focus returned to traditional camps, thanks in large part to the "intensive parenting" that historian Elaine Tyler May has associated with the baby boom.[23] Like ballet lessons and Little League, summer camp became an increasingly common enhancement activity for middle-class children, as well as a welcome break for their parents, who were devoting so much of their time and energy to child-rearing responsibilities. If anything, the cold war exacerbated the importance of the camp experience. In contrast to the treeless gray streets of Moscow, the lush, green, natural environment of summer camp helped introduce American children to the sensation of freedom that was understood as a hallmark of Western democracies.

By about 1960, however, traditional camps seemed to be on the decline, outpaced by camps teaching special skills and eventually outnumbered by day camps (which often functioned as summertime day care centers for school-age children). Although traditional camps began to enjoy a renaissance in the late twentieth century, camp—a term now used to describe any summer experience for youngsters—plays a somewhat different role in American life. Thus, 1960 serves as the end point for this study of the older camp type.

THE BUSINESS OF CAMPING

If this brief overview explains why summer camps were integral to white, middle-class American culture, it also begs the question of how—in a concrete way—such camps came into being. Who sponsored them? Who built them? Who staffed them? To what extent did these people share ideas about what they were doing? In short, to what extent does it make sense to talk of a camping industry?

Answers to these questions depend to a degree on the kind of camp under consideration. Private camps, for instance, were usually founded, owned, and operated by one or two individuals (sometimes a married couple) who were often educators at private schools. They tended to treat camp like an extension of boarding school, hiring leaders from the ranks of private school teachers and attracting campers from a relatively small circle of well-to-do families who could afford both the transportation to a distant campsite and the fees for an eight-week camping season. Like boarding schools, these camps emphasized the reinforcement of elite social ties among a relatively small number of families. Not only did siblings and cousins camp together, but former campers also tended to send sons and daughters, grandsons and granddaughters to the same camp. Such camps relied heavily on personal recommendations to attract new campers, although they supplemented this approach with others familiar from the world of private schools. In the 1910s, private camps were listed in their own section of Porter Sargent's *A Handbook of American Private Schools*. Beginning in 1924, a separate Porter Sargent publication, *A Handbook of Summer Camps*, provided parents with a comprehensive listing of private camps.[24] In the same years, *Red Book* magazine "adopted an editorial policy which consistently sought to promote the work and influence of the private school and the cultural camp," and began publishing guides of its own.[25] By the 1930s, some camp directors visited the homes of prospective campers, armed with slide shows.

In contrast, organizational camps—those sponsored by YMCA, Girl Scouts, Boy Scouts, Camp Fire Girls, or any one of the many youth organizations that sprang up in the early twentieth century—had different goals and a different structure. Aimed at middle-class children from cities and suburbs, these camps were more affordable, offering shorter sessions (two weeks was a common length) at campsites that could be reached cheaply and easily by train or trolley. At early YMCA camps, the mission was explicitly evangelical, with camp directors measuring their success by the number of boys who "expressed a desire to live for Christ."[26] At these camps, responsibility for the day-to-day operations fell to the local boys' work secretary, a full-time YMCA employee. At least early on, these camps were staffed by YMCA members, young men who stayed at camp only a week or two during their own vacations from office jobs. Camp rallies—where boys saw lantern slides of camp and reminisced about the good times they had enjoyed there—were held at YMCA headquarters each spring and proved effective means of promoting these opportunities to boys and leaders alike. (A slightly later development, church-based camps shared the YMCA's evangelical goals, but functioned for the most part without state or national coordination.)

Camps sponsored by the newer youth organizations were less overtly Christian in their orientation, defining their goal as the building of character. Like YMCA camps, however, they were sponsored by local chapters of the national organization—called *councils* in scouting. Also like YMCA camps, these camps turned to the national office for support, which could take a range of forms. The YMCA encouraged the camping activities of boys' work secretaries by publishing detailed practical advice in the pages of *Association Boys*, a periodical introduced in 1901. The Boy Scouts generated enthusiasm for camping among youngsters through the well-illustrated articles in *Boys' Life*, first published by the national office in 1912. The Girl Scouts established Camp Edith Macy, near Briarcliff Manor, New York, in 1926; here the Scouts ran national leader training programs for the adult volunteers who would help run their camps.

Different still were agency camps, sponsored by social service agencies and aimed at providing camping excursions for the urban poor. Settlement houses, orphan asylums, fresh air societies, welfare associations, church-based charities, boys' and girls' homes—all of them provided summer vacation sites that the Playground and Recreation Association of America (PRAA) recognized as offering "some of the essential environmental features of camping"; established initially as the Playground Association of America, the PRAA advocated camping for children of all classes.[27] While the tone of these camps could vary somewhat, they were typically overseen by boards of white, middle-class volunteers who established policies and raised the funds to subsidize campers' fees, either in part or in whole. An employee of the board, the camp director was sometimes a social worker without extensive camping experience. In any case, these camps rarely had the funds to buy their own camp facilities; for the first four decades of the twentieth century, they often borrowed campsites from other organizations. After about 1940, many were able to rent fully equipped campsites that had been built for the purpose at federal Recreational Demonstration Areas (RDAs) as part of the New Deal.

The impact of the RDA program was felt far beyond the realm of agency camps. Designed by teams of professional landscape architects and recreational specialists, and carrying the federal imprimatur, these campsites introduced a new level of professionalism into camp planning. They also set new standards for camp design, thanks in large part to *Park and Recreation Structures*, a handsome three-volume work that celebrated the New Deal achievements of the Park Service. The program not only prompted the major camping organizations to publish their own guidelines in the 1940s, it also launched the careers of professional camp planners, such as Julian Harris Salomon, who went on to design some one thousand individual recreation sites by 1960.[28]

Before the 1930s, however, few camps of any type were touched by professional design expertise. Responsibility for camp layout typically fell to camp directors, who were guided by their own varied experiences with other rural compounds, such as hunting and fishing camps of the well-to-do, Chautauquas, military encampments, and even rural resort hotels. Individual buildings were only rarely designed by professional architects; the majority were vernacular buildings, imagined and built by camp personnel, sometimes with the aid of local craftspeople.

This is not to say that early-twentieth-century camp organizers were unconcerned about the camp's physical plant. The character of the camp landscape was a major concern for camp directors, who increasingly associated the ability to control the environment and to use it to enhance camp program as important signs of their own professional expertise.

Nonetheless, attempts to identify the best practices in the field were complicated by a number of factors, including the emergence of a commercial camp industry promising to enhance the effectiveness and attractiveness of camp life—for a fee. Advertisements that filled the pages of *Camping* magazine (launched in 1926 as the official organ of the Camp Directors Association) give some sense of the breadth of commercial products and services available. Photographers, employment agencies, and accounting firms offered their services to camp directors, while Condé Nast touted *Vogue, Vanity Fair*, and *House and Garden* for their ability to bring camp advertisements to "360,000 *well-to-do, socially active* families—the best kind of prospects for camp enrollments" (emphasis in the original). Woven name tags, medals and pins, middies and bloomers, arts and crafts materials, chemical toilets, kitchen equipment, tents, prefabricated camp buildings, and real estate (including entire camps) were all regularly offered for sale before 1930.[29]

While strong professional guidance might have helped camp directors navigate this sea of options, the fledgling profession of camp directing was fractured into a number of competing organizations: a professional organization of boys' work secretaries, established in 1906 for YMCA camp directors; the Camp Directors Association of America (CDAA), established in 1910 to serve a membership limited to male directors of private camps; and the National Association of Directors of Girls' Camps (NADGC), founded in 1916 and dominated by men and women who directed New England's many private girls' camps. In 1924 the CDAA and NADGC merged into the Camp Directors Association (CDA) in an attempt to represent the entire profession, but regional differences and tensions between private camps and agency camps continued to plague the organization.[30] These factional differences were largely overcome by 1935, at which time the organization became the American Camping Association (ACA); it has recently been renamed the American Camp Association.

Thus, throughout the first four decades of the twentieth century, camp directors were bombarded with a dizzying array of advice. The CDA (and later the ACA) offered camp-planning suggestions in the pages of *Camping*. The YMCA likewise relied heavily on published advice; in addition to articles in *Association Boys*, the YMCA published Henry Gibson's 1911 book, *Camping for Boys*, a work that quickly became the bible of the organized camping movement. The Girl Scouts' Camp Department (established in 1922) experimented with a range of ways to advise local councils: making personal visits, offering plans for sale, and in 1932 developing an Architectural Loan File composed of photographs and plans of the best camp buildings constructed by local councils.[31] The Boy Scouts also established a Department of Camping, which in 1927 issued *Camp Site Development Plans*, a combination of idealized plans and plans of existing buildings. After World War II, organization camps came out with new manuals, modeled on *Park and Recreation Structures*. These publications circulated well beyond their sponsoring organizations, creating a lively discourse on how best to plan a summer camp, a discourse that plays an important role in this book.

A CULTURAL LANDSCAPE APPROACH

An architectural history of North American summer camps, *A Manufactured Wilderness* is different from conventional works in the field in two important ways. First, it focuses on the cultural landscape, a term used to describe the intersection of the natural landscape with built forms and social life. Rather than considering individual buildings in isolation, it looks at the camp landscape as a whole: natural environment, outdoor areas, individual structures, and the relationships among them. It also takes seriously what architectural historian Elizabeth Cromley has called "activity arenas," spaces not necessarily defined by walls and roofs, but created by human action.[32] The place where campers wash dishes, for instance, is an activity arena—whether it is an open-air area that will soon be used for another function or the corner of a large kitchen in a space devoted to the purpose. Both kinds of settings are equally important in understanding the relationship between the camp environment and camp life.

A second difference has to do with the understanding of architecture that drives this work. Architectural historians have tended implicitly to see architecture as the result of architects' efforts to generate new aesthetically pleasing forms. In contrast, this book defines architecture as a process in which institutional priorities are translated into material form. Instead of giving architects the starring roles, the approach used here considers a wide range of actors, shifting the focus to the decision makers who hired the architects or—as was often the case at summer camps—who decided to forgo their services entirely. The conceptual shift is important for many reasons, but perhaps chief among them is that it allows architectural history to engage a broader range of questions about the spaces and places we encounter every day.

In this case, the specific questions center on the role of summer camps in the social construction of modern childhood. To what extent did camp organizers see children as fundamentally different from adults? How did they define the physical, educational, social, and spiritual needs of children? What factors affected the ability of the nuclear family to meet those needs? What kinds of men and women were camps trying to produce? How did the answers to these questions change during the first sixty years of the twentieth century?

The cultural landscape is a particularly good venue for addressing the complexities of this process. On one hand, it provides us with insights into the minds of the adults who made the major decisions about camp life, while allowing us to see how these camp organizers put those ideas into action. On the other, it gives us an opportunity to investigate how campers actually inhabited the spaces created for their use and the extent to which they subverted their leaders' intentions. In short, it is an approach that lets us see both the ways that institutional priorities shaped the landscape and also how the landscape attempted to shape children—who may have resisted those efforts.

A close consideration of the built environment is essential to this process, in that there is often a significant gap between the written word and the physical reality. The evolution of the waterfront (discussed in detail in chapter 2) is a case in point. Although camp organizers have always stated clearly and explicitly their commitment to ensuring the safety of swimmers, the unimproved waterfronts of the early twentieth century (with campers diving into the water directly from a rocky shoreline) reveal an openness to camper risk taking that is entirely absent from the swimming cribs of the 1920s and 1930s and the H-shaped docks installed in the postwar period (with swimmers penned into finite swimming areas).

Understanding the physical layout of the camp landscape and knowing what it meant—to camp organizers as well as to campers—are two different things, however. Even the most thorough investigation of the built fabric is useless unless we can also begin to see it through the eyes of its users. Getting a sense of the issues on the minds of camp directors is an important starting point and also a relatively easy matter, given the bounty of theoretical writing about children and childhood produced in the twentieth century. Child-rearing advice, educational treatises, health guidelines, child-study journals, and an expansive body of camping literature all serve as essential background for this study.

The more challenging task is to understand how campers and camp organizers saw their own camps. Here period photographs are informative for many reasons, not the least of which is because they often capture furnishings and fittings—now long gone—that provide important traces of the actual human habitation of these intensively used places.

Photographs, however, are much more than dispassionate reflections of historical facts. One of the arguments of this book is that photographs played an active role in producing meaning in the camp landscape. While campers' memoirs suggest that youngsters tended to experience camp most vividly through their other senses, their parents—who made the decisions and wrote the checks—had to be swayed largely through the visual evidence offered in brochures. The increasing reliance on photographs to demonstrate the benefits of camping prompted camp organizers to create settings and encourage activities that would photograph well. By framing particular views of camps, the photograph became a crucial tool for communicating the meaning of the camp landscape to parents and others.

Thus, this book draws heavily upon a range of period photographs—snapshots taken by amateurs and sometimes assembled into albums, as well as more formal images produced for promotional purposes and sometimes assembled with texts into brochures. These brochures have proved especially rich sources for understanding what the camp landscape meant to the adults in charge. Their carefully staged images convey a great deal about officially approved uses of the landscape, while their captions and other texts reveal additional layers of meaning.

These period words and images communicate a great deal about how camps constructed a version of childhood that was inevitably complicated by interrelated ideas about gender, class, and race. Gender is perhaps the easiest of these to grasp, given that most private and organizational camps served either boys or girls. Some of them, however, leased their facilities to social service agencies or churches that brought children of the other gender to camp. Even after they purchased their own sites, agency and church camps typically accommodated both males and females on the same campsite, albeit in different sessions. As a result, it is difficult to discern formal differences between boys' and girls' camps. Nonetheless, camp organizers encouraged their charges to use the camp landscape in highly gendered ways.

However temporary, this gendered use of the landscape was integral to the camp experience.

Ideas about class and race were also reproduced in the camp landscape in the sense that most camps practiced some form of racial segregation, while camp fees served to sort campers by class as well. Paying attention to the differences between camps aimed at campers of different classes, however significant, is only one aspect of the issue. It is perhaps even more important to recognize the ways in which summer camps—all of them—served as incubators of the middle class, instilling middle-class values (faith in the existence of a meritocracy and a commitment to fair play) and encouraging middle-class behaviors in youngsters from every walk of life.

Likewise, when we consider race, the issue is not just—or even primarily—the race of the kids allowed to camp here but not there. Rather the question is how summer camps reinforced and naturalized ideas about race—particularly understandings of whiteness—that were in flux in the first half of the twentieth century. As historian Matthew Frye Jacobson has argued, nineteenth-century Americans considered Celts, Slavs, Hebrews, and Mediterraneans (to use the terms of the day) to be racially distinct from and biologically inferior to Anglo-Saxons. These groups were only consolidated under the rubric of Caucasians in the twentieth century, partly in response to the internal migration of African Americans that changed the racial dynamics of northern and western cities.[33] In this sense, the pervasive use of Indian motifs is significant, both in reinforcing white privilege and in contributing to the larger cultural project of redrawing the boundaries between those who were considered white and those who were not. Thus, one of the major arguments of this book is that summer camps contributed directly to this cultural work of creating a more inclusive definition of whiteness that was exclusive in new ways.

This is also the aspect of the book that might initially disconcert some former campers, a few of whom have tried to convince me that playing Indian was never a tool for supporting white privilege, but simply a means of demonstrating respect for Native American culture. The hard truth is that racism and good intentions can coexist; it is one of the things that makes racism so difficult to eradicate. I ask readers to move beyond their preconceptions about summer camps in order to join me in considering the ways in which camps and their own camp experiences reinforced racial hierarchies that continue to structure American society.

SCOPE AND STRUCTURE OF THE STUDY

The camps that I have studied are a heterogeneous lot, including private camps, camps with a religious affiliation, camps organized by social service agencies, and camps sponsored by youth organizations. In addition to archival and library research into camp records and brochures, construction documents, period photographs, and the prescriptive literature on camp planning, I have studied firsthand camps in three major camping regions: the Northeast and the neighboring sections of Canada (where many of the earliest camps were located); the Southeast, and especially the Blue Ridge Mountains (whose high altitudes offered cooler summertime temperatures); and the upper Midwest, with particular emphasis on Minnesota (where many of the state's fabled ten thousand lakes provided waterfront facilities for summer camps).

The study, however, does not pretend to offer an exhaustive coverage of all camps. For one thing, I have deliberately excluded family camps and well-baby camps, which also served adult campers and thus required very different living arrangements. Nor does it consider special needs camps or skill-based camps that flourished after 1960. Even within these restrictions, the sheer number of residential camps in North America—more than seven thousand functioning in 2005 and many other historical examples no longer in operation—makes a comprehensive history impossible.[34]

While it would have been possible to impose geographical limitations on the topic or to restrict my focus to the camp activities of a single youth organization (e.g., the YMCA or the Girl Scouts), my research convinced me that such approaches would diminish the effectiveness of this study. From my first forays into the archives of the YMCA, it became clear that the organizational boundaries between youth organizations were extremely permeable, as camping advocates associated with one group readily lent their expertise to another.[35] Equally important, discussions of camp planning between organizations and across regional boundaries took place for decades, and especially after the establishment of the ACA in 1935. In short, theorizing about the camp landscape and its impact on camp program was widespread; a study that looked at a discrete subset of camps ran the risk of overstating their singularity.

Instead of attempting to construct a chronological narrative that would inevitably be incomplete, this book investigates the major trends in camp-planning practices between 1890 and 1960 in light of their impact on the construction of childhood. Six chapters dissect the camp landscape into its major functional components, the better to identify the range of factors that affected each one.

The first chapter addresses the camp layout as a whole, tracing both the manipulation of the natural landscape and the introduction of built forms to create settings that encouraged campers to enact a range of adult roles: soldier, frontiersman (or -woman), Indian. By the postwar period, pastoral settings akin to contemporary suburbs encouraged campers to forgo those roles in favor of another that adults were increasingly eager to see them play—namely, the carefree child.

Chapter 2 considers the program activities that are the heart of the camp experience, noting that most program activities at the earliest camps were carried out in natural settings where human intervention was minimal. Not only is the provision of specially designed program areas (including playing fields, nature and crafts cabins, and the waterfront) a relatively recent development, it is also a sign of a broader cultural trend to protect child life at all costs.

Chapter 3 examines the sites associated with sleeping, areas considered particularly important in maintaining campers' good health. While the first part of the story traces the transition from tents to cabins, the narrative is complicated by conflicting theories of disease prevention. Eventually a new focus on campers' psychological well-being prompted the construction of elaborate cabins with integral socializing space that allowed counselors to assess campers' emotional health. Featured in the camp-planning manuals published by the YMCA, Camp Fire Girls, and Girl Scouts in the late 1940s, such cabins became common features of the camp landscape in the postwar camp-building boom.

Sites associated with cooking and eating were equally important to any well-run camp. Not only were wholesome meals essential for building up the physical strength of campers, but mealtime rituals were also important mechanisms for camp socialization. Chapter 4 traces the development of these facilities from the military-style mess hall (where campers of both sexes were deeply involved in food preparation, albeit in gender-specific ways) to the dining lodge, a new building type that was less highly charged in terms of gender. While campers of both sexes continued to be responsible for some alimentary chores, these later buildings attempted to isolate them from the adult world of labor.

Chapter 5 delves deeper into the gendered practices of summer camp by looking more closely at the issue of camp sanitation and campers' different roles in keeping the camp landscape free from disease. By midcentury, ideas about camp cleanliness shifted from the camp environment to campers' bodies, but they remained highly gendered. Indeed, throughout the twentieth century, girls carried a double burden at American summer camps: in addition to taking on new, more self-sufficient roles at camp, they were simultaneously expected to maintain high standards of cleanliness—both for their surroundings and for themselves.

Chapter 6 considers the introduction of Native American motifs into the camp landscape, with a particular focus on the Indian council rings that became a widespread feature of camp life in the interwar period. Popularized by naturalist Ernest Thompson Seton as the material expression of the orderliness and community orientation of Indian life, the council ring fostered a new appreciation for Indian culture, even as it supported the idea of Indians as a dying race, denying contemporary realities of Native American life and reinforcing white dominance. At the same time, its rituals allowed children from different European ethnicities to assume—at least temporarily—a common racial identity; once campers removed their feather headdresses and war paint, their shared whiteness may also have seemed more evident.

Summer camps continue to be a central feature of North American life—for the children who attend them, for the adults who work at them, and even for the former campers of all ages who cherish vivid (if not exclusively pleasant) memories of their camp experiences.[36] The buildings that comprise the camp landscape may be rudimentary in form; indeed, that is a key component of their appeal. Yet, they are also fertile sites for examining a constellation of concerns that have informed—that continue to inform—conceptions of modern childhood.

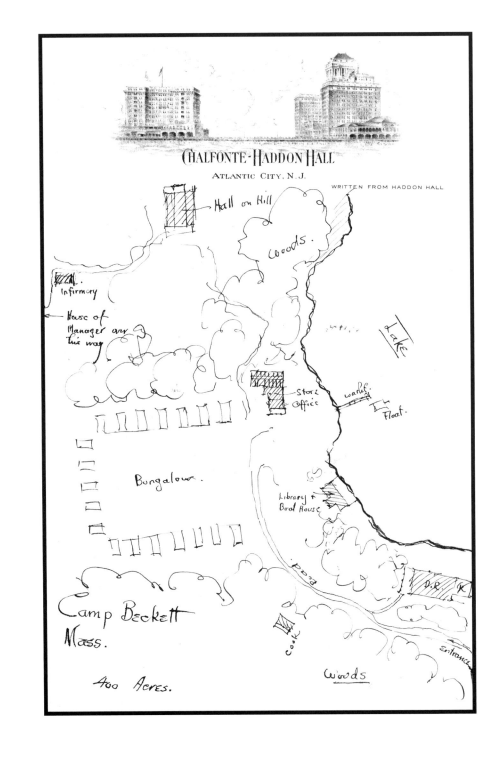

CHALFONTE-HADDON HALL

ATLANTIC CITY, N.J.

WRITTEN FROM HADDON HALL

Hall on Hill

Woods.

Infirmary

House of
Manager are
this way

Lake

Store
Office

wharf

Float.

Bungalows.

Library &
Boat House

Camp Beckett
Mass.

Road

D.R. K

Cook

Entrance

400 Acres.

Woods

CHAPTER 1

Putting Campers in Their Place
Camp Landscapes and Changing Ideas of Childhood

IN THE SUMMER OF 1931, ARCHITECT ARTHUR B. HEATON VISITED Camp Becket, a YMCA camp in the Berkshire Mountains of western Massachusetts. In his pocket, he carried a letter of introduction from the general secretary of the Washington, D.C., YMCA, which explained that Heaton was visiting "some of our leading boys' camps . . . gathering information that we trust will be helpful to us in our contemplated program of expansion" at Camp Letts, the district's YMCA camp in Edgewater, Maryland. Heaton also had with him hotel stationery from Atlantic City, New Jersey—undoubtedly picked up en route—on which he sketched the layout of Camp Becket (Figure 1.1). The campgrounds were dominated by a hollow square, defined on three sides by rows of small cabins that Heaton identified as "bungalows." Along the fourth side ran the only road, which paralleled the lakeshore and went past the dining hall and kitchen, cook's quarters, and the combination library and boathouse, before petering out in front of the camp office. These last two buildings framed the vista from the bungalows to the waterfront, while the infirmary and Gibson Hall (a building that housed a stage, nature museum, and hobby rooms) were situated in the woods farther inland. Heaton's sure pen strokes captured very well the major components of the Becket landscape.[1]

Heaton's engaging drawing also attests—although unwittingly—to the

Figure 1.1. Camp Becket, Becket, Massachusetts. Site plan sketched by Arthur B. Heaton in 1931.

Figure 1.2. Camp Becket. Parade ground, circa 1910.

BIRD'S EYE VIEW OF CAMP BECKET. 45

mutability of the camp landscape, both in practice and in theory. A comparison of Heaton's sketch with photographs published in 1911 reveals that Camp Becket had once related to its site in a very different way (Figure 1.2). Rather than addressing the lake, its hollow square—defined by tents instead of bungalows—had focused inward on a flagpole, its fourth side closed by a dining pavilion. What is more, when Heaton returned to Washington, he soon discovered that attitudes toward camp layout were in flux more generally. Although he provided his clients with the option of arranging the cabins at Camp Letts around three sides of a hollow square, they rejected that plan in favor of one that arranged the cabins in a gentle arc along the lakeshore. What Heaton could not have known was that by the end of the 1930s, Camp Becket's arrangements would seem hopelessly out of date.

This chapter will consider the cultural meaning of the camp landscape in two realms. First, it will look briefly at the role of camps in a wholesale transformation of the rural landscape that took place as North Americans began to value the wilderness at least as highly as cultivated land. Second, it will examine at greater length changing theories of camp planning and their impact on actual camps. While acknowledging that some changes were driven by functional requirements (like Becket's Gibson Hall, built to house an expanding range of camp activities), this discussion will give special attention to the metaphors embedded in the camp landscape. After all, there is always more than one way to address programmatic needs, and the choice between those different possibilities has meaning. At summer camps, these metaphors illuminate a host of concerns: about the state of American manhood, about the effectiveness of modern parenting skills, and about the proper relationship between home and camp.

MANUFACTURING THE WILDERNESS

The cultural landscape of North America was in flux in the late nineteenth century, both physically and conceptually. Perhaps the best-known interpretation of these changes is historian Frederick Jackson Turner's 1893 assertion that the western frontier had closed, that the continent had been settled, and that it was no longer possible to identify what Turner himself called "the hither edge of free land." Turner's understanding of the process of landscape change was flawed in a number of ways, as environmental historian William Cronon has demonstrated; it ignored Native American claims to this supposedly "free" land and overlooked the economic relationships between the frontier and the city.[2] Nonetheless, Turner's frontier thesis (especially his contention that the frontier experience was responsible for giving American democracy its particular form and spirit) and its corollary (that the closing of the frontier was cause for alarm) suggest the extent of the conceptual shift taking place.

Throughout most of the century, the goal of western expansion had been to make the frontier—that line between civilization and wilderness—obsolete. The ideal was to bring the landscape firmly under human control and to make it visibly productive. Indeed, the very rationale for claiming territory inhabited by indigenous people had been that they had failed to turn the land to productive uses. The Jeffersonian grid offered the promise of a land in which no place was outside the conceptual grasp of the human mind. Popular images celebrated the progress of civilization, a process in which technology—in the form of the ax, the plow, the railroad, and the telegraph—steadily eradicated any vestiges of an untamed wilderness.

By the late nineteenth century, this understanding of the landscape was increasingly turned on its head by figures like John Muir, who embraced the wilderness as "the hope of the world," a precious thing, a site unsullied by civilization, where weary urban dwellers could experience physical and spiritual rejuvenation.[3] This change in philosophy had a great impact on the physical landscape as well, as Muir, Theodore Roosevelt, and others led the movement to designate large swaths of land as wilderness in order to preserve them from logging, farming, mining, or other productive exploitation. Some of the more notable examples—Adirondack Forest Preserve (later subsumed by the even larger Adirondack Park), Sequoia National Park, Yosemite National Park, and Grand Canyon National Monument—were established between 1885 and 1908.[4]

Summer camps, of course, grew out of this new appreciation for the wilderness and out of turn-of-the-century anxieties about the disappearance of the wilder parts of nature. Such concerns help explain why the summer camp phenomenon began in the East, and why eastern camps outnumber the many camps established in the Midwest, while western camps remain comparatively few. In the areas where nineteenth-century urbanism was most intensive, middle-class parents embraced the opportunity to buy for their children an experience of the wilderness without having to confront the fact that their own actions were helping to eradicate the real thing. These were, after all, the same people who commuted between houses in burgeoning suburbs and jobs in increasingly crowded cities, thus supporting the expansion of both. In this sense, summer camps are like the eighteenth-century English pastoral landscape paintings that art historian Ann Bermingham has described as products of "actual loss and imagined recovery."[5]

Camps were also active contributors to the process of reshaping the landscape—albeit often in different ways. While parks were the result of well-organized and state-sanctioned efforts to preserve the wilderness, children's summer camps (along with Chautauquas, resort hotels, family camps, and summer cottages) were part of a widespread but largely uncoordinated process—what we might consider a vernacular process—by which private enterprise reclaimed large tracts of productive land, transforming them into a version of the wilderness and rededicating them to recreational use.

In manufacturing a new type of wilderness out of what—in many cases—had been farmland, summer camps (and to some extent, other rural resorts) seemed to turn back the clock, reversing the westward motion of the advancing frontier and (particularly at eastern camps) returning the landscape to something that evoked its pristine natural form. Indian names suggested that the land had passed into the hands of camp organizers directly from its indigenous inhabitants, and thus worked conceptually to scrub the land clean of its earlier productive manifestations, even in landscapes like that of Camp Siwanoy near Wingdale, New York, where a remodeled barn and straight rock walls were visible vestiges of the site's agricultural past (Figure 1.3). The ready availability of land untouched by white settlement was a fiction, but a powerful fiction that appealed to the antiquarian impulses of the early twentieth century.

In fact, summer camps were embedded in a landscape in which recreational, agricultural, industrial, and public lands were often in close proximity. Camp Mishawaka, a private camp for boys established in 1910 near Grand Rapids, Minnesota, is a case in point. Situated near an Indian reservation on Lake Winnibigoshish, Mishawaka was also in the vicinity of logging operations and surface iron mines at Coleraine. Rather than ignoring these jarring contrasts to the camp's advertised location "in the wilds of Minnesota," Director George F. Green incorporated outings to all three sites into the camp program. While visits to the reservation reinforced the wilderness quality of Mishawaka's setting, trips to the industrial sites allowed campers to enjoy a somewhat romanticized spectacle of hard physical labor. Logging landscapes seem to have made a particular impact on campers, as evidenced by a poem written by Dave Kimball who attended camp in 1920. Titled "The Booming of the Logs," the poem was punctuated by a refrain that urged:

Oh! Harken Mishawaka, to that ancient logging chant
Can't you hear the saw a-screaming,
Can't you hear the engine pant,
Hear the lumber jacks a-fighting
In their bloody wolfish way?
Oh! it's great to hear that booming
From Cohasset up the bay.[6]

As the poem makes clear, campers from privileged families were encouraged to see themselves in spiritual communion with the lumberjack, a figure who had become a larger-than-life symbol of robust, working-class manhood in the 1910s, with the first publication of the Paul Bunyan myth.[7] Thus, these excursions helped reinforce the camp's larger mission of remaking middle-class masculinity.

Equally important, camps were often enmeshed in economic relationships with these other rural sites—although these relationships were not always easy. Consider, for instance, the tensions between summer camps and resort

Figure 1.3. Camp Siwanoy, Wingdale, New York. Site plan, circa 1925. From Boy Scouts of America Department of Camping, *Camp Site Development Plans*, 6.

hotels. Not only did camp organizers argue that children were better off at camp than in the morally dubious environments of resort hotels, but they also found proximity to such resorts problematic. Hotel guests might inadvertently wander into camp and disrupt its activities, while campers, it seemed, found the lure of resorts irresistible. According to Camp Becket's director, Henry W. Gibson, "Nothing demoralizes a boys' camp so quickly as proximity to a summer resort."[8]

Nonetheless, early camps benefited enormously from the presence of hotel guests, not only from their direct custom, but also because their positive reports did much to spread the word of this social experiment.[9] Likewise, hotel proprietors appreciated the fact that a nearby summer camp would attract visiting parents. In many cases, camp organizers opted to profit from this connection themselves. Charles Cobb, for instance, established Camps Winona and Wyonegonic (brother and sister camps) near Bridgton, Maine, and also ran various hotels in the area at different times, including the Denmark Inn and Camp for Adults, which he advertised on Wyonegonic and Winona flyers.[10] Similarly, by the 1930s, brochures for Camp Lincoln for Boys and Camp Lake Hubert for Girls reminded parents that "Inwood Lodge and Grand View Lodge, two of Minnesota's finest summer resorts located on nearby Gull Lake, are now owned and operated by our camps."[11]

Equally important, this new rural landscape—summer camps included—was dependent upon an extensive transportation network to bring urbanites to the so-called wilderness. Before World War II, camping would not have been possible were it not for the existence of an extensive system of rail lines. The trip to a private camp catering to the children of well-to-do families often extended overnight. Early Mishawaka campers, for instance, took the train to either Chicago or Milwaukee, where in the evening they embarked for Duluth in special cars chartered from the Chicago and Northwestern Railway. In Duluth, their coaches were attached to a Great Northern train that delivered them to Grand Rapids the next day at noon.[12] In contrast, the YMCA kept camps affordable by minimizing transportation costs. At Camp Becket, this involved selecting a site that could be reached easily by train, negotiating special fares with the Boston and Albany Railroad (in 1910, these varied from $4.50 round-trip from Boston to a mere $.40 round-trip from nearby Pittsfield), and having the boys hike the four and one-half miles from Becket Station to camp.[13]

After World War II, most children arrived at summer camp by bus or car along new and improved highways. Both the roads and a massive increase in the number of privately owned automobiles were outgrowths of the intensive suburbanization that threatened the once-bucolic settings of older camps. Camp Mary Day in Natick, Massachusetts, is a case in point. Established in 1923, this Girl Scout camp was situated on Nonesuch Pond, a desirable site in that it stood near the end of a streetcar line that could carry scouts to camp.[14] As early as the 1930s, however, camp brochures no longer mentioned the streetcar and provided only driving directions.[15] In the postwar period, the needs of automobiles—particularly those carrying suburban commuters into and out of Boston—became paramount; in 1955, the Massachusetts Turnpike divided the property, taking the tennis court, reducing the program area, and introducing an all-pervasive mechanized hum. These changes prompted the local Girl Scout council to discontinue overnight camping on the site in 1956, although it continued to use Mary Day as a day camp until 1979.[16] Even more distant camps found their activities increasingly disturbed by weekend campers carried farther afield in private autos, and many relocated their entrances in the postwar period to minimize these disruptions.

As much as camp organizers and campers' parents may have liked to think it was possible to let children experience the wilderness, summer camps were just one component of complex cultural landscape that was in the process of rapid change. They may have purported to offer respite from the modern world, but they were in fact very much a part of that world. It was a contradictory situation and one that made it particularly important to shape the camp landscape itself to manage—if not to disguise—the summer camp's inherently modern character.

REMAKING GENDER ROLES

From its the earliest years, the camping movement was informed by a cluster of late-Victorian concerns about child rearing. While the importance of getting children out of the city was recognized in the nineteenth century, new scientific theories gave an added urgency to the idea in the early twentieth century.[17] The germ theory of disease, for instance, heightened awareness of urban crowding as a menace to physical health, while child psychology hinted at the city's dire threat to the child's mental well-being. The recapitulation theory advanced by psychologist G. Stanley Hall held that each child (although he really meant each Anglo-Saxon child) repeated (or recapitulated) the evolution of the human race from savagery through barbarism to civilization. Thus, children were not only closer to nature than their parents, but thrusting them too soon into modern urban civilization could derail their normal development.[18] In fact, Hall's theory offered striking parallels to Turner's frontier thesis, which maintained that each wave of western settlement also recapitulated the social evolution of human civilization.[19] If anything, these theories reinforced one another, redoubling anxieties about the loss of the wilderness.

For Hall and his contemporaries, these theories had great import for privileged white boys, whose incipient manhood seemed particularly threatened by what came to be called overcivilization.[20] The scientific community, for instance, understood the male body as more prone than the female to neurasthenia, a neurological illness discovered by physician George M. Beard and defined by him in 1881 as "a lack of nervous force" caused by modern civilization.[21] More generally, overcivilization was linked to effeminacy and racial decadence, prompting intellectuals throughout Europe, England, and North America to worry about the "emasculating tendencies of higher civilization."[22] As historian Gail Bederman has demonstrated, these anxieties prompted a wholesale shift in middle-class ideals of male identity. Although Victorian culture had valued high-minded self-restraint (the chief quality in what they called manliness), middle-class men at the end of the nineteenth century came to consider such conduct effeminate and sought to temper it with more aggressive behaviors associated with masculinity, itself a new term in the late-Victorian period.[23]

If these anxieties about overcivilization challenged Victorian notions of manliness, they also called into question the value of institutions established to civilize young boys. The feminized home and Victorian motherhood were favorite targets for censure in the late nineteenth century. Middle-class men who may have once praised doting mothers for their maternal dedication increasingly accused them of coddling their sons and thus failing to develop in them the self-reliance that many critics believed had been the hallmark of earlier generations.[24] For some, such mothering practices were responsible for thwarting military preparedness. The Boy Scouts—one of the first youth organizations to endorse summer camps in the United States—had been founded in England in 1908 by Robert Baden-Powell, who was motivated in large part by the poor quality of soldiering he had encountered during the Boer War.[25] Whereas Baden-Powell placed the blame on the ignorance of working-class home life, his American contemporaries made it clear that they considered middle-class mothers equally guilty of undermining robust manhood. Hall was among them. In a 1908 article titled "Feminization in School and Home," he stated flatly that "the callow fledgling in the pin-feather stage of the earliest 'teens whom the lady teacher and the fond mother can truly call a perfect gentleman has something the matter with him."[26]

For many Americans, the solution lay in instituting a new kind of summer experience for boys, one that would remove them from the feminized home for some period of time and send them out into nature in the company of the right kind of men. There could be some difference of opinion about the attributes of the ideal role model—the YMCA emphasized religious feeling, for instance, while many private camps placed greater store in athletic prowess or knowledge of the out-of-doors. What was beyond dispute was the close connection between a natural setting and the fostering of a new mode of manliness. American clergyman and author Edward Everett Hale made this connection explicit when he stated that "a boy must learn to sleep under the open sky and to tramp ten miles through the rain if he wants to be strong. He must learn what sort of men it was who made America, and he must not get into this fuss and flurry of our American civilization and think that patent leather shoes and white kid gloves are necessary for the salvation of his life."[27] In short, the summer camp as an institution was called into being by modern anxieties about boys—particularly white, privileged ones—and their needs dominated the public discussion about the form and role of the summer camp.

While extending the benefits of summer camp to girls may now seem inevitable, that was not the case. Indeed, the first camps for girls were not established until around 1900, almost twenty years after the earliest boys' camps, and the endeavor remained controversial for another twenty years. Hall, a great supporter of boys' camps, was much less sanguine about encouraging girls to develop the same kind of self-sufficiency. Haunted by the same concerns that had prompted Theodore Roosevelt to equate the rise of the New Woman with the falling birthrate among white, middle-class women and so-called race suicide, Hall expressed dismay at what he saw as "the new love of freedom which women have lately felt," which, he complained, "inclines a girl to abandon the home for the office."[28] Nor were the directors of boys' camps always sympathetic to the cause. The fact that a rival group, the National Association of Directors of Girls' Camps—officially established in 1916—welcomed both men and women suggests that the difference between this group and the all-male Camp Directors Association of America had as much to do with the sex of the campers as with the sex of the camp directors involved.

Even those who championed camping for girls were not interested in encouraging female campers to act like boys. To be sure, girls' youth organizations disliked conventional definitions of femininity; in Camp Fire Girl novels, women of the older generation were portrayed as helpless and sometimes hysterical.[29] But both the Girl Scouts and the Camp Fire Girls still upheld the importance of gender differentiation and continued to see marriage and motherhood as each girl's ultimate goal. According to *The Book of the Camp Fire Girls,* "The foundation of Camp Fire is the Home . . . The tasks of making the home should be kept from becoming drudgery, and *this* Camp Fire does for its girls" (emphasis in the original).[30] This commitment to policing the line between male and female behavior could manifest itself in even the smallest details. The Camp Fire Girls encouraged members to dress in an interpretation of Native American garb, but forbade them to wear upright feathers in their headbands, a practice associated exclusively with Indian braves.[31] Such prohibitions may seem inconsequential, but as Bederman has pointed out, gender differentiation and civilization were closely interconnected. In the early part of the century, to give up on the former inevitably meant the demise of the latter.[32] Thus, girls' camps could not merely imitate the form and function of boys' camps.

RUSTIC GENTILITY AT EARLY PRIVATE CAMPS

If early converts to the cause of camping espoused a common faith in the benefits of bringing privileged white boys (and later their sisters) into contact with nature, there was relatively little consensus on what form the camp landscape should take. A strong preference for a lakeside site, however, was all but universal. A natural body of water met pressing daily requirements for drinking, cooking, and bathing, and was also essential for swimming and boating, activities that were integral to camp life from the very beginning.[33] Riverside sites were sometimes used, although strong currents could make them somewhat more dangerous venues for waterfront activities.

Lakes also offered other advantages, as they typically provided a greater and more visible distance from adjacent land and an enhanced degree of isolation from recreating neighbors. The frequency with which open-air chapels

Figure 1.4. Camp Pasquaney, New Hampshire. View of Squam Lake from camp, 1899.

were oriented to provide worshippers with a view of the water suggests that the calm surface of the lake became a metaphor for spiritual rejuvenation as well.

The choice and treatment of other aspects of the natural landscape varied greatly between private camps and those run by youth organizations. Some of the earliest private camps for boys clustered around Squam Lake in New Hampshire, on sites that combined wooded seclusion and a good view of the lake. Founded in 1881, Camp Chocorua stood on a small wooded island; although such island sites complicated the delivery of campers and supplies, many private camps opted for this mode of achieving seclusion. Camp Asquam (established in 1885 as Camp Harvard and renamed in 1887) sat on a forested hilltop overlooking the lake, a setting that delighted Director Winthrop T. Talbot, who was convinced that "boys behave better when they have beautiful views to look at." In contrast, Camp Pasquaney was started in 1895 in the hayfield of a farm owned by the director's father. What the site lacked in trees, it made up for in sweeping vistas of the lake some 370 feet below (Figure 1.4).[34]

All three camps sought to complement nature by scattering rustic lodges in an irregular arrangement throughout their wooded sites. At heart, such an approach relied heavily on the picturesque aesthetic tradition that had first emerged in eighteenth-century England as an alternative to beauty. Celebrating the quaint over the grand, the rustic over the polished, and the irregular over the symmetrical, the Picturesque had long been associated with rural retreats of the aristocracy, a trend that continued into the second half of the nineteenth century, when wealthy New Yorkers used picturesque principles in the design and layout of their own summer retreats in the Adirondacks. [35] These "camps" (as these elaborate private estates were known) offered an appropriate model for summer camps catering to the sons of elite families.

Private camps for girls established in the early years of the twentieth century followed a similar approach to the landscape. Consider the camp that Charlotte and Luther Halsey Gulick began in Maine in 1907, where they worked out the program activities that they used to establish the Camp Fire Girls in 1912. First called Camp Gulick but soon renamed Camp Wohelo, the camp perched high among the trees atop a rocky outcropping on the shores of Lake Sebago. Initially, the only permanent building was the "shack," which combined living accommodation for the Gulicks, the kitchen and dining room for the camp, an ice house, and darkroom (Figure 1.5). Vistas were important here as well; the "shack" (despite its name) was sited with care and offered,

Figure 1.5. Camp Wohelo, Sebago Lake, Maine. The "shack," built circa 1909.

in Charlotte Gulick's words, "an unobstructed view across the placid lake and the wooded hills beyond to where the distant White Mountains lift their lofty summits against the sky." The girls slept in tents, which were "grouped close by in cosy spots." [36] Early photographs reveal that these were platform tents set close to the water, thus providing natural vistas akin to those available to the Gulicks. As the camp grew, the tent clusters took on names that reflected their close connection to the landscape: the Boulders and the Heavenlies, which sat upon a tall rock outcropping, closer to heaven.

MILITARY ARRANGEMENTS AT ORGANIZATION CAMPS

If such picturesque arrangements seemed natural, they were nonetheless the product of the relative wealth of these private camps, which were able to purchase land outright. In contrast, early YMCA camps operated on small budgets, relying on sites borrowed from supporters or rented cheaply from farmers. Camp Dudley, for instance, was first held in 1885 on Orange Lake, near Newburgh, New York, before moving the next year to Wawayanda Lake, some thirty-seven miles away. In 1891, it relocated to the shores of Lake Champlain, using rented or borrowed land until 1908, when the New York State Committee of the YMCA purchased one of the sites. At such peripatetic camps, there was no opportunity to create the kind of wooded retreats favored in private camps; as short-term renters, these camps were forced to take the landscape as they found it, choosing only where on the site to pitch their tents. Yet, even in these decisions, aesthetic considerations seem to have been minimal, with little concern for providing a view of the water. At one early YMCA camp in Pennsylvania, the director cited health reasons for situating the camp a full ten minutes' walk from a small artificial lake—an indication that he took seriously the risk involved in locating the latrine too close to the camp's water supply.[37]

Similarly, permanent buildings were a waste of resources at such camps; movable canvas tents provided the only protection from the elements. Even when a camp returned to a familiar site, tents were pitched anew each year, placed according to the whims of the leaders and campers who provided the labor for setting up camp. Throughout the first twenty-three years of Dudley's existence, its layout changed from year to year. A photograph of Dudley taken before the turn of the century shows an informal arrangement that nonethe-

Figure 1.6. Camp Dudley, Lake Champlain, New York. Tents set up on rented land, circa 1895.

less lacks the careful attention to the natural setting that characterizes picturesque planning (Figure 1.6).[38]

Such ad hoc camping arrangements, however, were rather short lived, and by the early twentieth century YMCA camp directors began to develop a new approach to camp layout that mimicked the arrangements of military encampments. Camp Becket (discussed at the beginning of this chapter) was dominated by a square parade ground lined on three sides with tents, with a mess hall (albeit in the form of a rustic pavilion) enclosing the fourth side and a flagpole in the middle.[39] After Becket's director, Henry W. Gibson, featured images of the camp in his influential 1911 book, *Camping for Boys*, such military layouts were widely adopted both within the YMCA and by other camping organizations, although the precise form varied somewhat with the site conditions of a particular camp. Some camps—like an early YMCA camp on Catalina Island, on the California coast—took greater advantage of their waterfronts by arranging tents in a semicircle open to the beach. Those in more wooded sites—like Camp Ranachqua, a Boy Scout camp established in 1917 on the Kanohwahke Lakes in New York's Harriman State Park—arranged tents in long rows called "company streets" (Figure 1.7).[40]

By the 1910s, military layouts were spreading even farther afield. Newly established private camps for boys were also likely to adopt military

Figure 1.7. Camp Ranachqua, Harriman State Park, New York. Tents arranged as a company street, 1919. Photograph by W. D. Hassler, New York.

arrangements. Camp Mishawaka housed campers in tightly aligned sleeping tents bordering a parade ground, while the bungalow (a horizontal log building built by the founding director with the help of local farmers) served as a mess hall of sorts. Even camps established by the Girl Scouts and Camp Fire Girls used military arrangements. A photograph of a "typical Camp Fire Girls' Camp" reproduced in the 1913 edition of *The Book of Camp Fire Girls* (which was reprinted for the tenth time in 1922) showed two rows of tents facing one another across a company street, while *Campward Ho!* (published in 1920 by the Girl Scouts) included an image of an unnamed Girl Scout camp in Colorado, with girls standing at attention in front of their tents during inspection (Figure 1.8).[41]

At all of these camps, the parade ground served as the setting for a host of military practices that structured the day's tightly packed schedule. The 1910 brochure for Camp Becket set out a daily program that began with reveille at 6:30 AM followed by flag raising, a cannon salute, and setting-up exercises. Tent inspection took place at 5 PM, followed by "Colors" at 5:45. After dinner, an hour of Bible study, and the evening campfire, the bugler blew "Tattoo" at 8:45 and "Taps" (indicating lights out) fifteen minutes later.[42] Ten years later, the Girl Scouts advocated a comparable daily program, while also specifying a special schedule for the "housekeeping squad," whose members were required to report for duty five times in a twenty-four-hour period. At the fifth meeting, they were officially "relieved of duty" and allowed an early swim before rejoining the regular camp program.[43] At many camps, particularly those operated by the Boy Scouts and Girl Scouts, uniforms modeled on military drab reinforced the martial flavor of camp.

The appeal of such arrangements was multifaceted. Gibson's text, for instance, emphasized the practical advantages of the Becket arrangement over a picturesque grouping of camp facilities, warning, "When tents are scattered the difficulty of control is increased."[44] Most military arrangements were also easy to expand, an important consideration for YMCA camps, whose financial health depended on attracting larger numbers of campers. Camp Dudley, for instance, grew from 23 campers in 1886 to 83 in 1891 and 226 in 1902. (In contrast, private camps could remain more selective; Pasquaney in New Hampshire opened in 1895 with 18 campers, served only 43 boys in 1900, and 101 boys in 1997.)[45] Conceptually simple, such layouts were also

Figure 1.8. Unidentified Girl Scout camp. Tents arranged in a military fashion, circa 1920. From Girl Scouts, *Campward Ho! A Manual for Girl Scout Camps,* 20.

particularly practical at camps on borrowed or leased land, where the layout had to be renewed each year without the benefit of professional on-site guidance. Given that its geometrical form ignored the natural features of the site, the hollow square required no picturesque imagination, no flair for composing vignettes from a combination of plants and buildings. In this respect, the hollow square used at Becket and advocated in *Camping for Boys* is a modern descendant of the ancient Roman *castrum* plan, the Spanish Laws of the Indies town, and other gridded city plans used by colonizing powers to claim new territory; built with great speed, such new settlements also signaled the colonizer's control of the natural and human landscape.

These military layouts had an added appeal at boys' camps in that they immersed campers in an all-male environment that gave boys an opportunity to practice roles they would carry out as men. In this respect, the camp landscape marked a decisive break with feminized homes of nineteenth- and twentieth-century suburbs, sites that used asymmetry, varied textures, and curving paths to emphasize their submissiveness to the natural world. At the same time, it brought campers closer to the imaginary world created in contemporary boys' novels, in which young protagonists spent their summers in the company of manly men doing men's work: lumberjacks, forest rangers, miners, and—especially with America's entry in 1917 into World War I—soldiers.[46] The attempt to help campers make the transition to manhood was nothing new at boys' camps. Like other aspects of nineteenth-century male youth culture studied by historian E. Anthony Rotundo, even the earliest camp programs had combined "elements of the boys' world they had left behind with aspects of the men's life they had not yet attained."[47] What is distinctive about these early-twentieth-century camps is their attempt to enhance their effectiveness by giving material expression to this social function.

The use of military layouts at girls' camps was more directly related to World War I. Established only in 1912, both the Girl Scouts and Camp Fire Girls were relatively new organizations when the United States entered the war. By organizing highly visible demonstrations of female patriotism, they helped the war effort while building greater awareness of their programs. The Camp Fire Girls were particularly eager to prove that girls could be as patriotic as their brothers and even renamed *The Camp Fire Girl Book* in 1917 to reflect this change. Called *War Call to the Girls of America*, it outlined the Minute Girl program that Luther Gulick had created as a means of mobilizing some ninety-four thousand Camp Fire Girls for the war effort. While the Girl Scouts published camp songs that encouraged girls to see themselves as potential soldiers ("So, if you want some others / To take the place of our brothers / America we're prepared"), most leaders thought girls would contribute to the war effort in other ways—cooking meatless and wheatless meals, growing and canning food, selling war bonds. All of them embraced military discipline lived on a daily basis at camp as the best way to prepare girls for their patriotic duties, and to counteract the effects of Khaki Fever—the tendency for a girl to forget her moral code when confronted by a man in uniform.[48]

Yet, the fact that middle-class girls' camps continued to use military layouts well into the 1920s suggests that they were more than a wartime expedient. After all, these organizations were attempting to create a new kind of girl—one who embraced her role as wife and mother, without imposing Victorian standards of gentility (now condemned as overcivilization) on her husband and children. In the age of companionate marriage (exemplified by camp-directing couples like the Gulicks), summer camps prepared girls to be better pals to both their husbands and their sons by giving them a camping experience akin—although not identical—to that of their brothers. Like boys' camps, then, girls' camps ultimately sought to address the sissy problem by forging a new generation of middle-class white women who knew the value of discipline, while enjoying the hardy outdoors activities that their sons would need to grow into manly men.

THE DEMISE OF THE MILITARY PLAN

By the 1920s, however, the growth of the summer camp movement brought new pressures to bear on the camp landscape. Not only did the number of camps increase dramatically in this decade, but publications like *Red Book* magazine also provided parents with greater opportunities to compare their features. In the summers of 1923 and 1924, the associate director of the magazine's Camp Department, Henry Wellington Wack, made a personal inspection tour of about a third of his estimated total of 1,200 private camps. The result was the publication of two books. *Summer Camps—Boys and Girls* detailed his visits to 243 New England camps, while *The Camping Ideal: The New Human Race* offered both a eugenics argument for summer camps in general as well as his impressions of 121 camps in New York, Pennsylvania, Michigan, Wisconsin, and Minnesota.[49]

Both trends increased competition between camps, a competition in which the camp landscape—a camp's most visible component—played an important role. Gone were the days of ad hoc encampments on borrowed land. Camp organizers increasingly required dedicated campsites on which to erect a wide range of permanent buildings that provided the visible, photographable evidence of a well-rounded program. Once ubiquitous features of the camp landscape, tents were quickly becoming a thing of the past, at least for program activities. Some camps retained tents as camper housing, but even this practice had begun to fall out of favor.

The military layout that had dominated the 1910s also came into question in the 1920s. When the Girl Scout National Camp Committee sent its secretary, Louise M. Price, on a tour of about two dozen summer camps in 1923, change was already in the air. Price went into the field armed with questions, including "whether or not we were military or non-military in layout and rigidity and stress of program"; rather than associating military order with welcome discipline, she had begun to equate it with inflexibility. Given the frequent teaming of the parade ground with military routines that required strict control of campers' bodies and facilitated punctuality, the concern had some merit. Yet even when Price respected a camp's staff and program, as she did at Gales Ferry, Connecticut, she maintained that its military arrangement alone was enough to "handicap" the camp's overall effectiveness. In Price's view, camp layouts that worked in harmony with "beautiful woodsy natural surroundings" were the best for producing "a sort of expanse of the soul" that she hoped campers would experience.[50]

Even the Boy Scouts, an organization with a long history of mimicking army encampments, came out against the practice in 1927. In that year, the director of the Boy Scouts Department of Camping warned camp organizers against "improvements which give the appearance of a town site, summer resort or military cantonment." Like his counterpart in the Girl Scouts, he argued instead for giving campers "the full benefit of the *natural* advantages offered by the site" (emphasis in the original).[51]

In practice, not every camp organizer heeded this advice, but even at camps that retained vestiges of a military layout, there was a growing concern with creating charming views of the natural landscape and particularly with bringing camp activities closer to the water. Both tendencies are apparent in Arthur Heaton's 1931 sketch of Camp Becket (see Figure 1.1). Although it retained the hollow square of its initial military layout, the dining pavilion

Figure 1.9. Camp Alleghany, Greenbriar County, West Virginia. View of the lodge from the parade ground, from camp brochure for the 1934 season.

had been moved in order to open one side to lake views. A library on the upper floor of the boathouse gave campers the chance to enjoy periods of quiet contemplation at the water's edge, while the new dining hall was also located near the lake. Likewise, a 1934 brochure for Camp Alleghany for Girls revealed that this West Virginia camp still housed campers in tents "arranged in a rectangle parallel to the river bank," an area used for calisthenics and tent inspection.[52] The camp also included a rustic lodge that was carefully sited to provide vistas from the camp across the water (Figure 1.9). While Alleghany campers used their parade ground for tent inspection and mass calisthenics, they also engaged in aesthetic dance to highlight their connection with nature.

Even at new camps, however, the call for a more natural camp landscape rarely resulted in the kind of wooded seclusion that had characterized early private camps, at least in part because camp populations were on the rise and camp organizers found it difficult to do without a large all-purpose activity area like the parade ground. Many camps maintained a demilitarized

Figure 1.10. Camp Wigwam, Waterford, Maine. Site plan, from camp brochure for the 1930 season.
Harrison, noted on the map, was the location of the nearest post office in 1930.

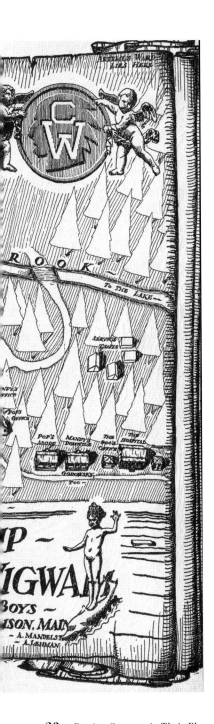

version of this landscape feature—often called a campus—into the 1930s and beyond. At Camp Wigwam, a private camp for boys in Waterford, Maine, the campus was a literal transformation of an old parade ground whose sharp corners were still visible in 1930 (Figure 1.10). At new camps, such as Camp Mary Day, the campus had more irregular borders, although it was still lined with camper cabins, as was the practice with parade grounds (Figure 1.11). Despite the rhetoric of naturalism in the interwar period, most camps maintained large expanses of lawn—perhaps the quintessential marker of human control and cultivation.

EVOKING PIONEERS AND INDIANS IN INTERWAR CAMPS

At many camps, the demise of military symbolism was more apparent in the buildings constructed in the interwar years, structures that evoked more overtly historical settings: the log buildings of the American frontier and the tipi and council ring associated with Indian life (a phenomenon covered in greater detail in chapter 6). At many camps, the two motifs were used simultaneously. Although both had played a role in youth organizations in the early twentieth century, they became permanent components of the camp landscape—and thus durable backdrops for camp life—only after World War I. The timing may be significant, as historical distance would allow campers to "recapitulate" the primitiveness of Indian or pioneer life without either glorifying or minimizing the horrors of the Great War, an inherent risk in camps that evoked army life. Used in different ways at boys' camps and girls' camps, both motifs contributed to the ongoing work of reshaping gender relations, albeit in ways that reinforced the racial dominance of Anglo-Saxons.

In the early years of the twentieth century, a number of youth organizations used pioneer life (which Turner had linked inexorably to American nationalism) as the basis for their activities, most notably the Sons of Daniel Boone. Established by Daniel Carter Beard in 1905, this early competitor to the Boy Scouts encouraged boys—implicitly white boys—"to emulate our great American forebears in lofty aims and iron character."[53] In the 1910s, Beard's sisters, Lina and Adelia Beard, founded the Girl Pioneers of America, offering pioneer women as exemplars of character traits suitable for the modern (presumably white) girl: strength, honesty, and self-sacrifice.[54] Both boys and girls had much to learn from the pioneers, these organizations suggested, but

Figure 1.11. Camp Mary Day, Natick, Massachusetts. Site plan, circa 1925.

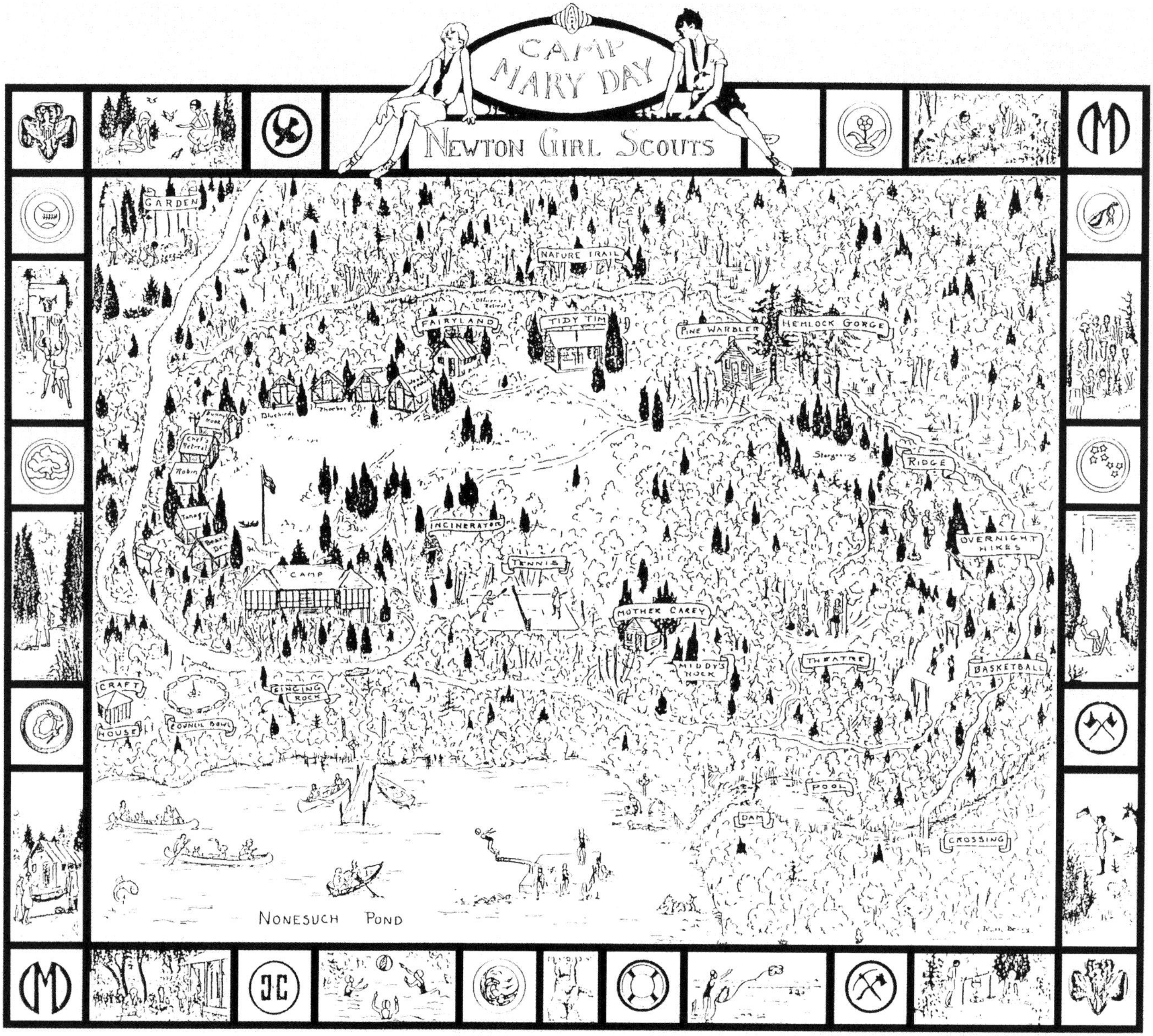

Figure 1.12. Camp Warren, Eveleth, Minnesota. Camper cabin in the cub unit, built circa 1936.

their lessons were different in important ways; boys were never called upon to be unselfish and self-sacrificing.

Only in the 1920s, however, were frontier motifs regularly incorporated into the camp landscape. The most common form was the log cabin, which, according to the 1931 brochure for Blazing Trail Camp in Maine, "typifies early American life on the frontier."[55] Used extensively at both boys' camps and girls' camps, it was adapted to almost every camp building type: camper cabins, woodcraft shops, infirmaries, and dining lodges. Log camper cabins erected at YMCA Camp Warren in the 1920s reveal the degree to which such buildings were romantic interpretations of the past (Figure 1.12). Each cabin was fitted out with a porch, while the log ends extended well beyond the walls in carefully composed arrangements that helped give each building an individual character. Minus their porches, these log cabins are also somewhat reminiscent of bunkhouses built at logging camps in the late nineteenth and early twentieth centuries, and so may have had special resonance at boys' camps where the lumberjack had become something of a cult figure.[56]

Other log structures—like the stockade and the Adirondack lean-to—appeared almost exclusively at boys' camps, suggesting that not all aspects of pioneer life were suitable for modern girls. Both forms were featured in

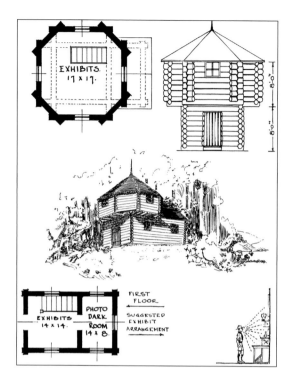

Figure 1.13. Boy Scout camp museum, 1925. From Boy Scouts of America Department of Camping, *Camp Site Development Plans*, 31.

the 1927 Boy Scout publication, *Camp Site Development Plans*, where the stockade housed a museum and darkroom (Figure 1.13).[57] While Beard's association with the Boys Scouts may account in part for their enthusiasm for the form, it is worth noting that in the 1920s and 1930s, frontier buildings sprang up in camps sponsored by a wide range of organizations. The frontier stockade, for instance, was the inspiration for an enclosure at the private Adirondack Woodcraft Camps in New York, described in a 1935 brochure as the setting for their youngest campers—boys between the ages of five and seven. Likewise, younger boys at Maine's Camp Idlewild lived in a "fort" made from vertical logs.[58]

The Adirondack lean-to was a form with particularly fluid historical associations. By the 1920s the Boy Scouts saw it as a close relative of the frontier log cabin and pictured them both on the same page of *Camp Site Development Plans*, but in the nineteenth century the lean-to was used in a variety of settings. The earliest were shelters made of poles covered with bark, often erected quickly by professional guides for the temporary use of wilderness tourists of both sexes. Later, when the practice of girdling trees for their bark

Figure 1.14. Open camp on the grounds of the Hotel Glenmore, Big Moose Lake, New York, circa 1895.

had begun to devastate popular campsites, lean-tos were made of logs. Built over a few days by carpenters, these more permanent structures were used at sanitariums, at permanent Adirondack camps (where they were considered a particularly good venue for exposing children and adolescents to the fresh air), and on the grounds of resort hotels, where they served as destinations for hikers of both sexes.[59] When furnished with rocking chairs, embroidered pillows, and Asian lanterns, and softened (and made fragrant) with plant materials (as was an open camp at the Hotel Glenmore on Big Moose Lake in New York), such lean-tos approximated the comforts of the Victorian parlor (Figure 1.14).

In popular imagination, however, the lean-to became closely associated with more rugged experiences of nature, and particularly with all-male hunting expeditions during which middle-class sportsmen ventured deep into the Adirondacks in the company of knowledgeable local guides. Currier and Ives were among those who celebrated such expeditions in prints like *Camping in the Woods.* "*A Good Time Coming.*" Issued in 1863, after a painting by A. F. Tait, the scene highlights the open camp as the setting for male companionship that is as much the purpose of the day's outing as is catching fish for the evening meal (Figure 1.15). After the 1869 publication of William Henry Harrison Murray's *Adventures in the Wilderness; or, Camp-Life in the Adirondacks*, interest in the Adirondacks as a tourist destination reached fever

Figure 1.15. *Camping in the Woods.*
"A Good Time Coming," Currier and
Ives, after a painting by A. F. Tait, 1863.

Figure 1.16. Medomak Camp,
Washington, Maine. Boys cooking
over an open fire in front of an
Adirondack lean-to, from camp
brochure for the 1933 season.

pitch, prompting illustrated newspapers to publish images of male bonding in front of the lean-to for decades. As late as 1892, *Harper's Weekly* printed Frederick Remington's depiction of male friends gathered around a lean-to in *A Good Day's Hunting in the Adirondacks*.[60]

This association between the lean-to and elite male sociability had first reached summer camps in the 1910s, when boys' camps like the YMCA's Camp Durrell were building such "shacks" deep in the woods, to offer small groups of boys what camp brochures called "a real camping experience."[61] But by the 1920s, the form began to figure more prominently in advice literature; *Camp Site Development Plans* included detailed instructions on how to build a log version of the Adirondack lean-to.[62] More telling still are staged images from camp brochures, which hint at the different meanings associated with the form. Those from boys' camps (such as the 1933 brochure for Medomak Camp in Maine) show campers in the lean-to and around the campfire in positions very similar to those captured by Currier and Ives seventy years earlier (Figure 1.16). In contrast, brochures from girls' camps rarely depict lean-tos. A 1933 brochure for Blazing Trail Camp included one picture of a lean-to, but it was located on Mt. Katahdin (rather than on camp property) and the people using it were the camp directors: Miss Eugenia Parker, whom the brochure identified as "one of three women to have the distinction of being a licensed Maine guide," and Mr. Harry E. Jordan, who "knows the woods like an Indian."[63] In short, while boys' camps favored the lean-to as a setting for male camaraderie, at girls' camps it functioned on a more symbolic level, signifying the organizers' woodcraft expertise.

THE UNIT PLAN AND THE MASTER PLAN

By the end of the 1930s, the camp landscape was reshaped in more fundamental ways, as New Deal initiatives involved the federal government directly in the camping movement. The key agency was the National Park Service (NPS), which built organized camp facilities in thirty-four of forty-three Recreational Demonstration Areas (RDAs), pilot projects aimed at converting submarginal agricultural lands into parks.[64] Initially operated through State Emergency Relief Administrations and later converted into state parks, these RDAs provided social service agencies with affordable camp facilities based on the most up-to-date thinking about camp planning. According to Julian Salomon, a camp-planning consultant who worked on the RDAs: "There

Figure 1.17. Layout for a large
organized camp on a lakefront site at
a Recreational Demonstration Area,
1938. From Albert H. Good, *Park and
Recreation Structures,* 3:116.

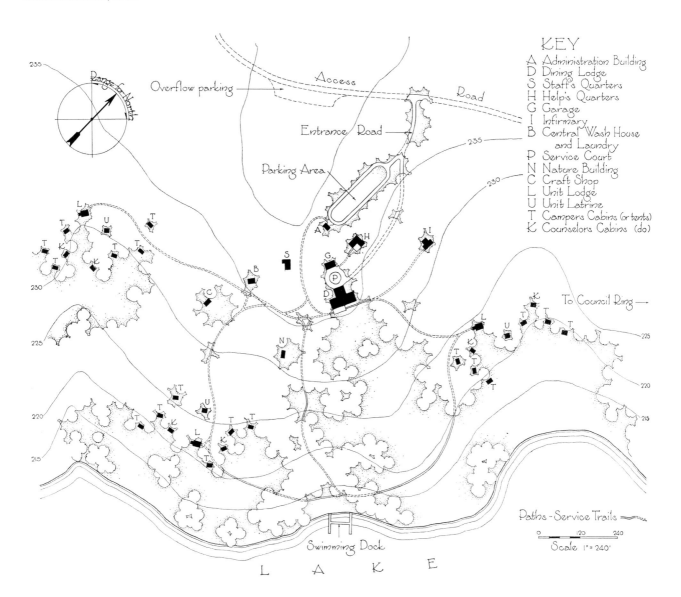

KEY
A Administration Building
D Dining Lodge
S Staff's Quarters
H Help's Quarters
G Garage
I Infirmary
B Central Wash House
    and Laundry
P Service Court
N Nature Building
C Craft Shop
L Unit Lodge
U Unit Latrine
T Campers Cabins (or tents)
K Counselors Cabins (do)

Overflow parking

Access Road

Entrance Road

Parking Area

Range for North

To Council Ring

Paths - Service Trails

Scale 1" = 240'
0   120   240

Swimming Dock

L A K E

surely never was a time before that when so many well-trained, experienced architects, landscape architects, and engineers had an opportunity to play with anything as small and unimportant as a children's camp so that naturally all of these people made tremendous contributions and all kinds of new ideas were developed. The camps built were far in advance of their times."[65]

The most significant aspect of these camps was their use of the unit plan, a decentralized arrangement of camp structures similar in concept to the neighborhood unit being promoted by the Federal Housing Administration (FHA) for residential suburbs. Inspired by the new field of child study and its concern for identifying the phases of human development through which every well-adjusted child should pass, the unit plan subdivided the camp into age-based units, each of which consisted of a unit lodge surrounded by four to eight tents or cabins. All of the units shared a single dining hall, infirmary, craft house, waterfront area, and other recreation facilities.

As important as it was for the camp program, the unit plan represented a radically new approach to the camp landscape as well (Figure 1.17). Not only was it the product of professional design expertise, it was also an approach that required substantial manipulation of the natural landscape—precisely because it was intended to appear absolutely natural. From its inception in 1917, the NPS had worked to develop landscape designs that would balance visitor use with stewardship of the natural environment. By the 1930s, NPS landscape architects had ample experience with "landscape naturalization," a range of techniques that erased the scars of construction and (in the words of landscape historian Linda McClelland) "created the illusion in the minds of visitors that the landscape had never been disturbed."[66]

At RDA campgrounds, this approach was particularly evident in the calculated use of trees and plantings of other native species to reinforce the visual and auditory isolation that separated shared facilities from units and individual units from one another; these plantings even provided a degree of privacy between tent-cabins within a single unit. Circulation was also carefully planned, with roads located to minimize the incursion of automobiles and paths designed to direct pedestrians easily to unit latrines and to encourage them to wend their way through a landscape that offered a series of carefully framed vistas.

The form and placement of buildings were also affected by this approach. Except for boathouses, buildings were to be kept well back from the water's edge, especially at artificial lakes, which were naturalized by "re-creating naturally occurring zones of vegetation."[67] Likewise, Herbert Maier (an NPS employee who was already one of the most accomplished park architects of the day) wrote design guidelines that advised architects to "steer clear of the 'twig' type of architecture which flourishes under the name of 'rustic.'" In its place, Maier encouraged NPS designers to use native materials, references to older construction techniques, and a color palette that would allow the buildings to "blend" into their natural surroundings.[68]

These new camp-planning ideas were codified in the third volume of *Park and Recreation Structures*; although NPS architectural consultant Albert H. Good is listed as the author on the book's title page, in his "Apologia," he readily identified Salomon as the primary contributor to the section on organized camping.[69] Here readers encountered a clear and persuasive endorsement of the unit plan, which was described in terms of suburban planning: the units are akin to "outlying 'hamlets' suburban to a 'village' in which the mutual interests of all the units in orderly government, food supply, medical care, and recreation and cultural pursuits center."[70] With its consistent graphic style and its clean plans drawn to a uniform scale, *Park and Recreation Structures* set the standard that the major middle-class camping organizations would strive to meet.

As soon as the war was over, the YMCA, Camp Fire Girls, and Girl Scouts rushed to update their published camp-planning advice. In 1946, the Camp Fire Girls issued *When You Plan Your Camp*, a typescript prepared in the Camping Department of the headquarters of the national council in New York. The designs included were based on real buildings constructed by local councils, who submitted blueprints and sketches of their "successful building adventures." The staff of the Camping Department selected designs they deemed "typical of their kind," while Mrs. Kenneth H. Brigham redrew the plans to a somewhat rudimentary graphic consistency.

In the same year, the YMCA published *Layout, Building Designs, and Equipment for Y.M.C.A. Camps*. The material for this publication had been prepared under the direction of John A. Ledlie, director of New Jersey's YMCA Camp Wawayanda from 1930 to 1944, and a recent addition to the program service staff of the National Board of YMCAs. An advocate for camping standards, Ledlie was undoubtedly responsible for setting the tone of the YMCA publication; a slender but beautifully designed pamphlet illustrated with elegant drawings provided by the Architectural and Engineering Bureau

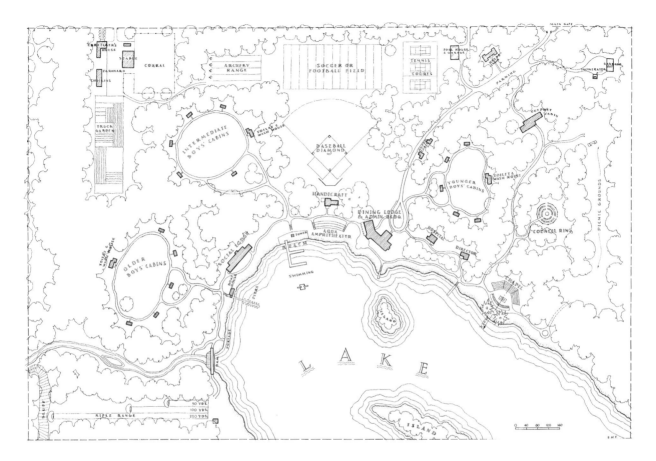

Figure 1.18. Layout for a YMCA camp with a capacity of 125, 1946. From John A. Ledlie, ed., *Layout, Building Designs, and Equipment for Y.M.C.A. Camps,* 11.

of the Chicago YMCA, it offered a limited number of idealized plans rather than a large compilation of realized projects.

In 1948, the Girl Scouts issued *Camp Site Development*, written by Julian Salomon. Given Salomon's involvement with RDA camp facilities and *Park and Recreation Structures*, it is not surprising that the first edition of *Camp Site Development* had much in common with that earlier book, something that is especially evident in the graphic style used to convey principles of camp planning, complete with isobars and stippling to distinguish the site's ground plane from its dense foliage.[71]

Despite their differences in style, these publications offered quite similar advice. All three publications, for example, endorsed the unit plan, which was also illustrated in both the YMCA and Girl Scout publications (Figure 1.18). These similarities are to be expected: not only were camp professionals for different organizations conferring regularly on camp planning, but their emerging professional identities depended on being able to articulate scientifically determined and consistent camping standards.

More remarkable is the degree to which the ideal camp landscape described in these 1940s publications was understood as a highly contrived environment; like the eighteenth-century picturesque garden, the nineteenth-century suburb, or its twentieth-century counterpart, the camp was carefully planned to look natural. Camp environments had always been artificial, of course, but in the 1940s that artificiality was acknowledged more openly, something that is especially apparent in a new emphasis on master planning. Both YMCA and Girl Scout publications used that modern term—*master plan*—the Girl Scouts to encourage camp committees to think about the phased development of a camp site, the YMCA to "prevent costly and regrettable mistakes in lay-out and construction." Other advantages of the master plan, according to Ledlie, were to "provide for a consistent architectural style in keeping with the natural environment," as well as for "landscaping, reforestation, the prevention of erosion, the restocking of a lake."[72]

That last phrase is particularly telling in that it suggests the extent to which environmental issues were coming to the fore in the thinking of camp organizers. At the same time, it also points to a fundamental change in attitude toward nature itself. Once seen as a constant and ever-vital resource, standing ready to envelop the camp and its campers in an all-encompassing embrace, nature was here understood as somewhat fragile, depleted by its relationship with camp, ultimately consumable. The goal of these postwar manuals was not just to demonstrate how to fashion camp buildings to fit into the natural environment; they also provided professional advice on design and maintenance procedures through which camp directors could manipulate nature itself in order to make it available for the consumption of subsequent generations of campers. Nature was increasingly treated as one of the commodities included in the camp fee.

If nature seemed to have lost some of its potency, the built components of the camp landscape became ever more elaborate, relying heavily on technologies of comfort. Advice manuals of the 1940s took for granted the necessity of providing electricity to the dining hall, infirmary, administration building, the pump house, and (in the Girl Scout publication) to a caretaker's house as well. The pump house helped supply the ample water that was piped to the flushing toilets, hot showers, and drinking fountains depicted in these plans.

In the 1940s there was also a decisive shift to permanent cabins as the preferred camper sleeping accommodation (a development also associated with changing ideas of health taken up in chapter 3). Increasingly, camp professionals recommended building one "winterized" building—that is, an insulated building with heat and a small cooking unit.[73]

In part, these technological changes were driven by an economic rationale. Electrification, plumbing, and enclosed cabins extended the usefulness of a summer camp into fall, winter, and spring, and gave the camp committee the chance to amortize construction and maintenance costs over a longer camping season. When combined with the decentralization of the unit plan, these technologies created a camp landscape that, in the words of the YMCA publication, "lends itself admirably to group camping and conferences." Indeed, the YMCA headquarters seems to have envisioned a fairly intensive use of camp facilities; author Ledlie noted cheerfully that in the off-season, "two or three conference groups can use the property at the same time," while an outpost cabin near the main gate could be used for group camping or as the base for a day camp during the season "with a minimum of interference with the regular camp program."[74]

The financial benefit of off-season camping, however, was only one reason that camp professionals allowed and even encouraged the introduction of technologies of comfort. Increasingly, they explained the decision on the basis of the campers' needs. In a memo of August 1945, for instance, the Girl Scout Camp Bureau observed that because campers came from homes that pampered them, they "must be protected from the rigors of the out-of-doors" and supplied with camp buildings that provide "freedom from dampness, fresh air without drafts, . . . [and] protection against sudden changes in temperature." The observation that children were coddled at home is nothing new. Camping professionals in the early twentieth century often commented upon the softness of the modern home environment, citing it as one of the main reasons children needed to go to camp. What is different in the postwar period is the sense that camp should not attempt to counteract the softness of modern home life, but should instead take into account the standards of comfort considered normal at home.[75]

This new willingness to bend the camp to the campers' desires may have been exacerbated by new modes of parenting that gave children a greater say in their summer plans, and by the postwar camp boom itself. With the number of competitors growing steadily, camp directors could not always afford to offer a rugged sort of camp experience that might not appeal to campers accustomed to the comforts of home. Another factor might have been the target age for campers, which had dropped significantly over the course of the twentieth century. Camp Becket, for instance, admitted boys between the ages of twelve and eighteen for its 1910 season.[76] By the 1930s, however, it was increasingly acknowledged that "teenagers" (who had only been recently recognized as comprising a distinct phase of human development) considered themselves too old for camp. Many camps responded by establishing counselor-in-training programs, which allowed sixteen-year-olds to pay a reduced rate in exchange for helping full-time counselors guide the camp experience for preadolescents, who became the primary audience for camp activities.[77]

A closer look at these camp-planning manuals of the 1940s reveals that camps were taking on characteristics of the postwar suburb—from their overall fit in the larger landscape to the particular details of their buildings. Camp-planning manuals of the 1940s, for instance, exhorted camp organizers to buy more land than required for their programs, the better to buffer the campus from encroaching development—the very idea that had given greenbelt cities their name during the 1930s.

Likewise, there are remarkable similarities between these camp layouts and suburbs, particularly superblock planning, a 1920s idea that came to dominate postwar suburban development. Vehicular roads were limited to the periphery of the site and functions requiring easy automotive access placed relatively close to the entrance. Like the kitchen in postwar suburban houses, the camp kitchen and dining hall were located at the end of the entrance road for easy delivery of food supplies. In the decentralized units, individual living cabins (like houses in those postwar suburbs that maintained the neighborhood concept) were turned inward toward small communal green spaces, which were connected by pedestrian paths to centrally located recreation facilities.

To be sure, these postwar camp-planning manuals featured a range of architectural styles, including lightweight buildings of dimensioned lumber (a mode of building that had been common in summer camps in the 1910s), as well as the heavier log buildings that had become increasingly popular in the 1920s and that had predominated in *Park and Recreation Structures*. Yet, there were also designs that sought to express the camp's rustic nature in a distinctly modern way. A dining hall designed by Albert Kahn Associates and illustrated in *Camp Site Development* is a case in point. A modern building with a shed roof and expansive use of glass, its prominent stone chimney stack and exposed roof structure marked its rustic character. In other designs, the rustic modern style was even more clearly related to the postwar suburban ranch house. The dining hall that Satre and Senescall designed for a Sheboygan, Wisconsin, Girl Scout Camp could be easily confused for a single-family home, given its relationship to its site (with its horizontal massing filling the visitor's view), its long, low proportions, and even its jalousie windows—all rendered in a graphic style familiar from postwar shelter magazines. Like those magazines, these manuals both anticipated and fueled the postwar building boom by teaching local camp organizers to desire a more elaborate camp environment than they really needed.

At first glance, these picturesque plans of the postwar period seem to suggest that camp planning was simply returning to its nineteenth-century roots after a brief flirtation with military discipline. The picturesque features of the postwar camp were less about fitting camp buildings neatly into their natural surroundings, however, and more about shaping both buildings and nature to provide an environment in which campers could enjoy "the semblance of autonomy or freedom within limits set by adults," to borrow historian Gary Cross's apt description of the purpose of educational toys.[78] This semblance of freedom is one of the most remarkable characteristics of postwar environments for children—although it is usually couched in terms of securing the child's safety, foreclosing further analysis. Certainly, superblock planning (with cars relegated to the periphery of the site) protected children from the dangers of automobile traffic, but it also freed child pedestrians from more regimented behaviors—walking in straight lines, waiting at traffic lights, curbing the impulse to chase a ball into the street—that could be equally effective in keeping them safe from passing cars. At the same time, these picturesque layouts disguised the boundaries of both environments and reduced young pedestrians' awareness of the extent to which their unimpeded rambles through the landscape were in fact the product of careful planning. If the open-plan suburban house was the ideal domestic setting for the intuitive parenting popularized by Dr. Benjamin Spock—sites where mother could respond immediately to every whimper—the postwar camp and the child-centered suburb were its public counterparts: sites where children could act on their impulses without endangering their lives.[79]

Instituted in the nineteenth century in response to concerns about the disappearance of wilderness lands deemed essential to the physical, psychological, and social development of American children, summer camps were involved in the wholesale reshaping of the rural landscape. Paralleling state-sponsored initiatives to preserve the wilder parts of nature in national (and, later, state) parks, a host of individual decisions to establish summer camps, resort hotels, and cottages redirected productive land to recreational purposes. The process was uneven, leaving many camps in close proximity to other recreational sites, as well as to farms, logging and mining operations, and, in some parts of the country, Indian reservations. It was also a dynamic process, which meant that camps found themselves not in timeless forests primeval but in changing landscapes subject to the forces of modern capitalism.

While camps themselves originated in the Victorian era, the type was constantly reinvented throughout the first half of the twentieth century. What had started, at least at middle-class camps, as an ad hoc arrangement of tents sitting lightly on the land had been transformed by midcentury into a professionally planned environment that required enduring changes to the landscape. Permanent buildings appeared in increasing numbers, some of them supplied with electricity and running water. While interwar camps were nostalgic in tone—using log buildings to evoke a time when pioneers were still taming the wilderness on the westward-moving frontier—midcentury camps enveloped campers in an environment akin to the modern suburb: safe, bucolic, and somewhat artificial.

To a certain extent, the transformation seems an almost natural outcome of the growing strength of the camp movement. As the number of camps increased, so did competition among them. As camp enrollments climbed and individual camps commanded greater financial resources, camp organizers were able to buy land and invest in permanent structures. With increasing professionalism among their peers, camp directors became more concerned that the physical plant meet accepted standards.

Yet, these changes also represented an important philosophical shift, as camp organizers tempered a desire to toughen youngsters with a growing concern for ensuring comfort and safety. This attitude affected many components of the camp landscape, but had a particularly visible impact on areas associated with recreation. While early campers had tended to do what they pleased, when they pleased, and how they pleased, camp organizers became more and more invested in directing the camp program. Not only did they determine what campers should do for fun and when, they also used the camp landscape to influence how campers should recreate.

CHAPTER 2

Fun and Games

The Serious Work of Play

IN THE FALL OF 1926, THE GIRL SCOUTS CAMP COMMITTEE MET in the organization's New York headquarters to discuss the previous summer's site visits. One of the camps visited by Professor L. D. Cox elicited considerable discussion. Near Glens Falls, New York, the camp enjoyed the use of "a site of exceptional beauty on Lake George." Two things, however, gave Cox pause. One was the camp's location on a main road, a factor that had prompted him to advise the director against purchasing the site, despite its beauty. The other was the camp program, which included "baseball and other activities not particular [*sic*] 'camp-y.'" While the rest of the committee shared both of Cox's concerns, the issue of camp recreation merited more serious attention. Dismayed that camps might become nothing more than "schools or playgrounds transferred to the woods," the committee agreed that its "policy nationally should be one of encouragement for really 'camp-y' camps."[1]

At first glance, these minutes seem to confirm a consensus about which recreational activities were appropriate for summer camp. The members of this committee, at least, were in sufficient agreement about the type of summer camps they wanted to encourage that they felt comfortable shaping national Girl Scout policy to accommodate their shared vision. Yet, their call for "really 'camp-y' camps" offered little firm guidance to a camp director trying

Figure 2.1. Camp Mishawaka, Grand Rapids, Minnesota. Boys playing baseball, from brochure for the 1938 season.

to decide which activities to encourage her Girl Scouts to pursue. Did tennis constitute a campy activity? What about aesthetic dance? Or productions of Gilbert and Sullivan? The wider circle of camp professionals, the greater the difficulties in identifying appropriate activities for camps. Baseball, the only supposedly noncampy activity the Girl Scout committee mentioned by name, had been played at summer camps as early as the 1890s and was an important part of many camp traditions (Figure 2.1). The pronouncements of the Girl Scout committee notwithstanding, the character of camp recreation was not self-evident in 1926.

Nor had it ever been. At heart, the issue was a new appreciation for the importance of play in child development, a pedagogical revolution started in the middle of the nineteenth century with the kindergarten movement. In fact, camps themselves were a product of this sea change; the camping movement's earliest supporters hailed the summer camp as an alternative to the stultifying schoolroom and its abstract approach to learning.[2] But by the 1910s, the growing consensus about play's importance was splintered by a range of theories about why play was important and how precisely it contributed to child development. Physiological, cognitive, social, even moral explanations all had their adherents in the early twentieth century. Cognizant of these competing theories, but also confronted with the practicalities of resources and personalities, camp organizers forged recreational programs that often varied dramatically in character from one to the next.

Rather than attempt to identify the full range of activities pursued at different kinds of camps at various historical moments, this chapter will focus on the priorities of camp organizers, while highlighting how their favored activities were conducted, that is, when and where they took place and with what degree of adult supervision. The goal of this approach is to consider summer camps in light of play theorist Brian Sutton-Smith's assertion that "the major play event of the past three hundred years has been the ever-increasing domestication of children's play," defined not simply as the tendency for children to play inside the family home, but rather as "the increasing control and supervision of play to get rid of its physical dangers and its emotional licenses."[3] Since camps were developed to counteract the domestication of boys' play within the feminized home of the Victorian era, we might expect little evidence of domesticated play at camp. Indeed, the earliest camps offered boys (in this case, older adolescents) ample opportunity for rough-and-tumble play. Summer camps were always embedded within their cultural contexts, however, and often participated in the cultural practices they sought to critique. Thus, the opportunities for dangerous physical play faced increasing limitations throughout the first half of the twentieth century. This consideration of when, where, and how campers played will reveal ample evidence of the domestication of play at summer camp.

Especially significant is the extent to which space became the favorite means of encouraging domesticated play. When the camp landscape had a great deal of conceptually empty space, campers were able to play more or less as they pleased. When camp organizers attempted to control campers' play, they initially tried to control their time (through strict schedules) and their bodies (through instruction). Eventually, they attempted to constrain children's play spatially, first by filling—conceptually, at least—all the available space at camp and then by communicating this conceptual landscape to campers through maps and naming practices. When organized according to the picturesque design principles popular in the postwar era, this conceptually full landscape simultaneously enforced and disguised adult control over children's "free time."

THE RECREATION REVOLUTION

The late nineteenth and early twentieth centuries witnessed a recreation revolution that transformed American life for men, women, and children of all classes (albeit in different ways). With an unprecedented amount of leisure on their hands, urban dwellers pursued now-common recreational activities with an almost maniacal zeal. Some of these were new activities (like bicycling), while others (like shooting and fishing) were older ones newly converted from subsistence strategies to leisure time pursuits. Still others (like football and baseball) were popular for players and spectators alike.[4]

It was not just that Americans were recreating more than ever, but also that they were beginning to look at leisure and recreation in a new light. No longer a luxury or an indulgence, adult leisure was increasingly accepted as a necessity. Most commonly defined as the opposite of work, it came to be understood as the only effective antidote to "Americanitis," the overdeveloped work ethic that seemed to pervade the offices and factories of industrial cities.[5]

The issue of children's recreation, and particularly play, was even more fraught with significance. To be sure, play long had been recognized as an inherent component of child behavior. But while earlier theories had tended to tolerate play as a means for expending excess energy, later approaches came to see play as a positive force in the child's development. The pioneer in this way of thinking was Friedrich Froebel, the founder of the kindergarten movement, which flourished after his death in 1852. Convinced that education could begin from the earliest moments of life, Froebel created a series of play objects—his "gifts" and "occupations"—that would give expression to children's "self-activity" (that is, their spontaneous actions), while imparting both metaphysical concepts and moral lessons to preliterate children.[6]

By the turn of the twentieth century, kindergarten methods came under attack by child psychologist G. Stanley Hall, the proponent of the recapitulation theory. Although he agreed that play was essential to child development, Hall found the Froebelian approach unscientific and sometimes dangerous. Kindergarten methods, for instance, tended to exercise accessory muscles, which only developed in later stages of childhood, while the "gifts" caused fatigue and actually contributed to "Americanitis." Not only did Hall seek to put the understanding of play on a more scientific footing, he also acknowledged its importance for the development of older children, including those in adolescence, a term he coined. For Hall and his followers in the child-study movement, play was an important instrument in the individual's recapitulation of the species, serving as "the medium through which the child received the biological and intellectual 'equipment' peculiar to that stage" of development. According to Joseph Lee, who incorporated Hall's theories into his own 1915 treatise, *Play in Education,* children between the ages of six and eleven had entered the "Big Injun" phase, when their anarchistic play paralleled the nomadic phase of human evolution, while those between eleven and their midtwenties tended toward games that depended upon a fierce loyalty to their peer group, something Lee associated with tribalism.[7]

Luther Gulick, a cofounder of the Camp Fire Girls, took Hall's theories even further. Not content merely to provide play experiences appropriate to naturally ordained stages of development, Gulick was convinced that muscular development could be deployed strategically to enhance and direct moral and intellectual growth. For Gulick, team sports (rather than individual calisthenics) were important for imparting not just physical skills but also the mental attitudes that would help youngsters adapt to modern society.[8]

This recognition of recreation's importance also fostered a sense of crisis. When defined as an antidote to the hectic pace of modern life, recreation was abruptly transformed into a required activity, and adults who failed to find recreational outlets were understood to endanger their own health and the well-being of society at large. Even worse, many commentators worried that American city dwellers were unwilling to take a break from their busy work lives and that their work habits had, in fact, caused them to lose the very ability to recreate. As historian Steven Gelber has demonstrated, hobby enthusiasts promoted handicrafts and collecting as leisure-time activities that could help adults take their minds off their paying occupations.[9]

In contrast, children were in no danger of forgetting how to play; the city streets teemed with playing children. Yet, play theory heightened worries that children were misusing their leisure time, thus undermining the development of cognitive and moral functions that the right kind of play could inspire. In many cities, social workers set out to measure the extent of the problem. Those in Cleveland, Ohio, interviewed fifteen thousand boys and girls to find out how they were using their spare time in the summer of 1913. More than half spent their time on the streets, sometimes playing baseball and jacks or flying kites, but mostly "doing nothing," or rather engaging in activities that social workers did not consider proper play: pitching pennies, shooting craps, teasing, stealing fruit, starting fires, writing on walls, or fighting. Indeed, according to historian Bernard Mergen, boys' play in particular was becoming rougher in the early twentieth century, fueled by a male subculture fostered in sex-segregated schoolyards. Even seemingly peaceful occupations, however, caused concern. Going to the nickelodeon was especially suspect, given that producers typically catered to children's taste for vulgar excitement.[10]

For those most concerned with children's play, the issue was not just what children did for recreation, but also where they spent their leisure time. Like their Victorian predecessors, middle-class adults continued to see the countryside as an idyll for childhood, a place where—they felt—the purity of nature would protect and preserve the purity of childhood. In contrast, the urban settings in which many children spent their leisure time were particularly troubling. The environment of the nickelodeon—a darkened room in which boys "slyly embrace the girls near them and offer certain indignities," according to the 1909 report of New York's Society for the Prevention of Cruelty to Children—alarmed observers at least as much as the lurid content of the films themselves. Playing in the streets was somewhat less risky in moral terms, but in the early twentieth century the street had become axiomatically associated with physical danger, particularly from motorized vehicles. Thus, activities that might have seemed tame enough in another setting were deemed pernicious when practiced on the city street or in an empty lot, perceptions that extended to the children themselves. In the country, angelic children might stretch out on the riverbank or against a tree trunk; on the street, children engaged in similar activities were demonized, their relaxation characterized as "loafing."[11]

What was new at the turn of the twentieth century was a related concern about how children played. As historian Elliott West notes, "Playtime has usually been the part of life in which boys and girls found their greatest independence, when they have been most on their own."[12] By 1900, however, that freedom came to seem problematic and adults developed a range of strategies for supervising children's play. Some of these were legalistic and not very effective, such as municipal and state laws that precluded children from attending movies without an adult guardian.[13] Others attempted to make children willing participants in adult-directed play. One such strategy involved book-length compendiums of gender-specific games and activities, something that began as early as the 1880s with tomes like Daniel Beard's *The American Boys Handy Book: What to Do and How to Do It*, and the *American Girls Handy Book: How to Amuse Yourself and Others*, written by Beard's sisters, Lina and Adelia.[14] After 1900, the impulse to control children's play led these authors and their contemporaries to found youth organizations. The Boy Scouts, the Camp Fire Girls, and the Girl Scouts are the best known, but early in the century they competed with a host of others.[15]

Perhaps more important than these self-conscious strategies was what sociologist Viviana Zelizer has characterized as "a dramatic reorganization of child space and child time," sequestering children from adults, removing them from the street, and enclosing their activities in playgrounds and in the home—increasingly in their own rooms.[16] Although Zelizer's interest in the question of children's accidental deaths prompts her to focus on spatial changes in the 1920s, this dramatic reorganization of child space and time began a few decades earlier, especially with the campaign to create urban playgrounds spearheaded by the Playground Association of America (PAA), established in 1906. Informed by the play theories of Luther Gulick and Joseph Lee—the PAA's first and second presidents, respectively—the playground movement took a multipronged approach to the problem of children's play. Not only did it remove urban children from the street, it also used adult leaders to ensure that suitable games would be played in appropriate ways. By de-emphasizing individual competition in favor of group cooperation, organized play promised to reduce delinquency, increase industrial efficiency, and promote good citizenship. To the extent that it targeted working-class children, particularly those from immigrant families, it would also help maintain the kind of public decorum valued by middle-class adults. As historian Dominic Cavallo puts it, Gulick, Lee, and their ilk were convinced that "play was too serious a business to be left to children and parents."[17]

Like their contemporaries, camp organizers were fully cognizant of the crisis in recreation and were eager to do their part to address it. In 1907, Walter M. Wood, the superintendent of educational work at the Chicago YMCA, listed recreation as one of the ten objectives of camp, noting that "the cultivation of the habit of wholesome recreation" is "an important duty . . . increasingly neglected in cities," where many boys have "never learned how to have fun." Echoing the sentiments of social workers and play organizers, he asserted that this neglect led inevitably to delinquency, as "the only kind of fun [the city boy] knows is some form of deviltry which involves an infringement upon the rights of other people." Given this situation, Wood argued that the "camp experience ought to be practically a summer course on how to really recreate," in which leaders "deliberately plan to educate the boy campers as to how to have a good time in physical, educational, social and religious ways."[18] A practical adjunct to the church, summer camp promised to turn little devils back into little angels.

To many observers, summer camps seemed ideally suited to teaching children how to recreate properly. They shared some traits with organized playgrounds, especially in their ability to influence (if not control) where, what, and how campers played. But in many ways, they offered substantial advantages over the organized playground. Camps not only removed campers from the dangers of the city streets on a round-the-clock basis for the duration of the camping period, but their natural settings were related to the countryside that had been construed from the late nineteenth century on as an ideal setting for childhood. Better still, their distance from the city made camps more effective than playgrounds in divorcing children from their economic roles as consumers of cheap commercial entertainment. More than just sports grounds, camps might also interest children in other kinds of recreational activities, including crafts that could serve as hobbies for their future overworked adult selves.

Despite these inherent advantages of the summer camp environment, questions remained. If the value of the summer camp was in offering children a kind of return to the idyll of the countryside, was the model of the organized playground too regimented, especially at camps that catered to middle-class children? Was camp an opportunity to give children a degree of independence that was no longer possible in the city, letting them play as they liked according to the rhythms of the day, rather than the strictures of the clock? If children were inherently drawn to nature, to what extent did camps need to structure their interactions with the natural world? In short, what sorts of recreational activities should campers pursue?

RECREATIONAL FREEDOM AT EARLY BOYS' CAMPS

At the very earliest camps for boys, recreation was an ad hoc affair, with campers allowed a great deal of freedom in what they did and when they did it. At Camp Pasquaney, boys were required to complete camp chores each morning, but afterward were "absolutely free to do anything they want to do," except once or twice a week when their attendance was required at an informal lecture on natural history. The afternoon, however, was always "absolutely free" and boys were allowed to "play tennis, golf, boat—to do anything the boys care to do."[19]

Early YMCA camps offered a similarly loose structure to the day, with set times only for rising and retiring, meals, swimming, and devotions. Before 1909, the daily routine at Camp Dudley was what one camp historian characterized as "a go-as-you-please affair," with the daylight hours devoted to "impromptu games, sporadic tennis matches, and boating at pleasure."[20] Likewise, in his reflections on his experience as the first director of Camp Couchiching (established by the Toronto YMCA in 1905), Taylor Statten recalled that "we planned for considerable fun and good times, but we did not have any such thing as an organized program."[21]

Although such ad hoc arrangements often appealed to adult leaders who used the unstructured time to pursue their own recreational agendas, these practices were more carefully considered than they might appear. The director of Pasquaney told a conference of his colleagues in 1903 that he was "very strongly of the opinion" that boys should be free to do as they liked.[22] Likewise, when Edgar M. Robinson (the YMCA's first international secretary of boys' work) published advice to YMCA camp directors in 1902, he urged them to "let the boys arrange their own sports and amusements as far as possible. Encourage spontaneity in this direction." Although he agreed with Wood that city boys tend to have more difficulty in amusing themselves for any length of time, he nonetheless instructed directors to help the "campers understand that they are at perfect liberty to indulge in every kind of innocent fun, taking care only that their fun does not bring unhappiness to any one else."[23] Even the William Carey Camp of the Boys' Club, which served working-class boys from New York's East Side, attributed its success at teaching a love for country life to the fact that "the boys have been free to amuse themselves (only with due regard to their safety) as they pleased . . . all has been spontaneous, free, joyous, and informal."[24]

By arguing that campers needed "perfect liberty" and "absolute freedom," these camp directors revealed that they sought to provide campers with a respite from their normal routines, an approach to recreation common among adults and one appropriate for these "boys," who were, after all, older adolescents on the cusp of adulthood. At the same time, this commitment to recreational freedom speaks to the directors' perception of camp landscapes as "pure," that is, inherently healthy and safe. In contrast to the impure spaces of the city, where every pastime was suspect, in the natural setting of the countryside all pastimes seemed wholesome. In truth, the natural setting of camp did place some natural limitations on camp recreation. With no sidewalks on which campers could pitch pennies, with neither fruit stands for them to plunder nor darkened nickelodeons for them to haunt, camps simply did not offer the environmental props for the urban diversions that middle-class adults found most alarming.

Convinced that nature was a sufficient backdrop for wholesome play, camp leaders felt little need to provide specialized places for camp recreation and made few permanent interventions in the landscape for this purpose. Early photographs confirm that campers simply used the surroundings more or less as they found them, playing games in a clearing in the woods, entertaining themselves in a sleeping tent on a rainy day, or swimming near a natural shoreline.

Unaltered lakeshores—so different from the carefully structured waterfronts that have dominated the camp landscape since the 1930s—highlight this take-it-as-you-find-it approach to recreation. At Camp Dudley, for instance, campers in the 1890s (some in bathing costumes, some not) dove into Lake Champlain directly from the rocky coastline, either from the rocks

Figure 2.2. Camp Dudley, Lake Champlain, New York. Unimproved waterfront, circa 1895.

themselves, from an improvised diving board, or from a spindly tower (Figure 2.2). Camp directors tended to see their role as establishing policies for campers to follow—deciding which waters were shallow enough for nonswimmers, limiting boat use to boys who could demonstrate that they knew how to swim, and establishing strict times for swimming. By the turn of the century, leaders in the field had begun to advocate what they considered intense waterfront supervision—with leaders stationed both in the water and in a patrol boat during swim periods—but they did not attempt to teach campers to swim.[25]

For all their emphasis on freedom, early camps developed remarkably similar practices for organizing campers' activities. Mornings were typically devoted to individual activities. At Asquam, after a morning talk on natural history or handicraft, "the boys scatter . . . either work[ing] down in the shops or out in the field in natural history."[26] Although early YMCA camps often started the day with Bible study in lieu of natural history lectures, the balance of the morning was devoted to solitary activities. As an early camper described it, the boy "may write letters, play games, explore, fish or row as he pleases or dares."[27] In most camps, a swim preceded lunch, while the afternoon was devoted to team games, including baseball, basketball, and tennis. While many camps encouraged another swim before dinner, most used the time between dinner and the evening campfire for group games (such as tag, ante over, red rover, or policeman and thieves) or other group activities (like a mock trial, circus, Wild West show, or political convention). Some of the group games played at camp (including white man and Indian and nigger-in-the-hole) suggest the extent to which play activities served to embed ideas about race into children's daily lives.[28]

Particularly striking is how many of the activities at early camps were ones that campers and their leaders enjoyed at home. In addition to playing baseball, they devoted their evenings to familiar schoolyard games, which were often decades old even in the late nineteenth century. Although they typically needed a great deal of space, such games required little specialized equipment, and play could be adjusted to a variety of physical environments. Short in duration, these games were highly physical, albeit stressing agility and shrewdness over brute strength. They could accommodate any number of players and could be played simultaneously by all ages and abilities without diminishing the effectiveness of the play. There were no teams per se. Many games began by pitting a single player against the larger group; when that player caught or tagged another player, the latter was required to change sides and help the first catch others, a process that eventually led to everyone changing sides, which marked the end of the game. Perhaps most important of all, they had easy rules that passed from child to child, rather than being imparted by adults. Indeed, directors found it impossible to describe these games to their peers. Asquam's director, Winthrop Talbot, gave a very muddled description of ante over to his fellow camp directors, finally concluding that "there are no rules except as handed down by tradition."[29] The products of what historian Elliott West has characterized as "a common culture of play throughout the United States," these games encouraged vigorous exercise and gave players the chance to express aggression, while also providing "a mechanism for creating and keeping bonds among children, even if they were strangers."[30]

Perhaps more surprising than the presence of these familiar games is the absence of other activities that later became synonymous with summer camp, particularly those that encouraged campers to engage directly with the natural environment. As noted earlier, private camps like Asquam and Pasquaney did provide periodic talks on nature, although only the semiweekly presentations at Pasquaney were compulsory. In both cases, boys were expected to follow through on these talks on their own. In early YMCA camps, nature study received even less emphasis, despite rhetorical emphasis on nature's ability to "speak to the boys of God as the generous and good builder of the world."[31] At a camp directors' conference, directors of YMCA camps expressed interest in Talbot's description of Asquam's exhibit of native wood species, but had to admit that they offered little (if any) direct nature study; Henry Gibson (who was associated with a YMCA camp at Mt. Gretna in Pennsylvania before assuming the directorship of Camp Becket in the fall of 1903) noted that his camp offered only flower and bird walks, leaving campers to peruse nature books on their own in the camp library. W. Armstrong Perry, boys' secretary in Salem, Massachusetts, admitted that his camp provided no systematic study of nature, but that older boys instructed the younger ones "as best they can." Opportunities for handicraft were equally scarce at early YMCA camps, with Gibson quipping that in his experience in Pennsylvania the only woodwork campers did was chopping wood for the fire.[32]

SUNDAYS AT CAMP

If freedom was the watchword most of the week, Sundays were the exception, at least at camps with an overtly or implicitly Christian orientation. Many camp organizers felt that most camp activities were simply too boisterous for the Sabbath, and they worked to establish a different tone on this day of rest. At some camps, campers were allowed to get up later than usual and were then required to spend the day in quiet pursuits. Typically organizers arranged some kind of worship service in the morning, which was followed by a special meal at noon. Campers were expected to spend much of the afternoon writing letters home and reading. At Camp Pasquaney, boys used part of the afternoon to walk "to some definite point, where they rest[ed], and the counselor of the day [spoke] to them on some subject that [gave] them some thought that would be useful in their camp life." At Camp Idlewild, another private boys' camp established by the Reverend John M. Dick on Lake Winnipesaukee (also in New Hampshire), the day ended with "an illustrated stereopticon religious service, largely song, on some topic." At another private boys' camp organized by the Reverend William T. McElveen, the evening stereopticon program was more secular in tone; in 1902, the Sunday evening program focused on "rivers of the world."[33] At most camps, youngsters donned more formal attire—at boys' camps, long white trousers and white shirts—to discourage active forms of recreation.

Figure 2.3. Camp Chocorua, Squam Lake, New Hampshire. Open-air chapel, built 1881. Photograph circa 1888.

Even in the early twentieth century, camp directors found it challenging to enforce the rules to keep Sundays quiet. In 1903, Dick admitted to his fellow camp directors that "Sunday has been the most difficult day . . . Most of the punishments we had to give was [*sic*] the result of the Sunday experience rather than the rest of the week." He addressed the problem by having campers attend a worship service at a country church a half mile down the road; the great advantage of this arrangement was that it "used up about half the day." At other camps, organizers reluctantly allowed campers to take a morning dip or even—as at Camp Algonquin, also on Lake Winnipesaukee—to enjoy their usual four o'clock swim.[34]

Another response to the Sunday challenge was to incorporate worship services into the camp landscape itself. Many early private camps followed the lead of Camp Chocorua, which in 1881 established an outdoor chapel to serve the spiritual needs of the camp community. Situated within a grove of aspens, the chapel accommodated worshippers on rustic pews that faced an altar stone, a stone lectern, and—by 1888—a large birch cross (Figure 2.3). Contemporary commentators were impressed by this "open-air cathedral," which tapped into what architectural historian W. Barksdale Maynard has pointed out was a long-standing Romantic idea of the forests as "God's first temples."[35] So widespread was the appreciation for the spiritual aspect of nature that neighboring farmers often accepted the invitation to participate in Sunday morning services at Camp Pasquaney's outdoor chapel.[36] In this sense, open-air chapels were ideologically, if not formally, related to the camp meetings that were such a noticeable aspect of American Protestantism in the nineteenth century. (One indication of the specifically Protestant nature of this connection is that open-air chapels are rare at Roman Catholic camps, which favored instead fully enclosed buildings, like Our Lady of the Pines built in the 1920s at Camp Jeanne d'Arc on Lake Chateaugay in New York.)[37]

Such outdoor chapels were a somewhat later phenomenon at YMCA camps, despite their explicitly religious orientation. Indeed, in the early twentieth century YMCA camp organizers measured their success by the number of boys who "decided during the month [at camp] to live for Christ."[38] Adult leaders recognized that such conversions were greatly facilitated by bringing youngsters "in contact with athletic Christian young men who are full to the brim of fun and sport," but they also incorporated Bible study and other explicitly religious activities into the daily routine.[39] Camp Wawayanda, in New Jersey, marked the beginning and the end of each day with prayer; a fifteen-minute "morning watch" was set aside for "private devotions," while individual tent groups participated in "family prayers" just before campers went to sleep.[40]

Even within such an overtly religious routine, Sundays were special. In his description of best practices at early YMCA camps, Edgar M. Robinson noted that it was "customary to have a morning preaching service [that was] generally more formal than the ordinary camp fire service." This formality was expressed in both the dress and the deportment of campers, who were expected to "come to the service in as good attire as they happen to have at camp, and to sit under the trees or upon the grass, rather than to lounge about as they do in the week day service." Campers then spent some part of the day

Figure 2.4. Unidentified YMCA camp. Outdoor chapel service, circa 1905.

writing letters and perhaps taking a long walk in the woods, while the afternoon was devoted to "Sunday-school."[41]

All of these events took place in the open air, if the weather allowed. Robinson, for instance, recommended that at the morning service "a stump draped with a flag" could serve as a pulpit. Likewise, period photographs show well-dressed boys sitting in neat rows on a natural rise and listening intently to a leader who stands with a Bible in hand (Figure 2.4). Sunday school classes could be held on the lake itself, with each class occupying a boat and "the boats being lashed together for the opening and closing exercises."[42] Easily dismantled after each use, such ad hoc settings were ideal for YMCA camps situated on borrowed land.

Once settled permanently on sites of their own in the 1910s and 1920s, YMCA camps often established open-air chapels similar in character to the rustic outdoor chapels built at private camps decades earlier. At larger camps, this might involve enhancing a natural hillside amphitheater with terracing to give every worshipper a good view of the rustic pulpit. At the Robert Montgomery Chapel at Camp Hazen in Connecticut, such terraces were fitted out with some forty-eight long rustic benches of similar design (Figure 2.5). At the front was a stone pulpit, roughly shaped from a natural boulder, and rustic seats—some quite fantastic in form—for leaders. At other chapels the

Figure 2.5. Camp Hazen, Chester, Connecticut. Robert Montgomery Chapel, dedicated 1925.

landscape manipulation took a different form. At the chapel at a Galesburg, Illinois, YMCA camp, the boys sat directly on the ground, many of them on a large boulder sloping down toward the pulpit (Figure 2.6). Yet their prospect was highly contrived: behind the pulpit was a rustic version of a traceried window, which both framed a vista across the lake and was itself flanked by trees that prevented worshippers from seeing the diving tower.

Many things made these chapels memorable, including services like those at Camp Becket led by Henry Gibson, who tailored his message to his audience. In 1924, for instance, the camp paper reported that he gave "one of his famous talks on 'Some Boys I Have Met,' and in his inimitable way told us about Billy Blue, Georgie Giveup, Tommy Tomorrow, Willie Waitawhile, Timothy Talkmuch, Ikey Impulse," and others. Lectures notwithstanding, the natural views these chapels provided—whether of lake or forest—were central to accomplishing their spiritual goals. Gibson himself made this connection clear when he reflected on Camp Becket's Chapel-by-the-Lake in the pages of the camp newspaper in 1913:

Figure 2.6. YMCA camp, Galesburg, Illinois. Open-air chapel, 1925.

As we sit and look at the sun slowly sinking in the west in all its gorgeousness, our thoughts naturally turn toward the better things in life, and there is a wholesome introspection which leaps to decision, forever changing our lives. God does seem real to us, we feel His presence, and in the coming years the realness of the creator will become even more apparent as we think back upon the Sundays spent in this outdoor Cathedral.

When Gibson's ashes were interred at the Becket chapel in 1941, the site received an added layer of meaning—as a memorial to a longtime director and as a reminder of the kind of fun-loving Christian man Camp Becket was founded to produce.[43]

GUIDING CAMPER RECREATION AT EARLY-TWENTIETH-CENTURY CAMPS

When it came to more purely recreational activities, a conference of private camp organizers in 1903 offered evidence that attitudes had begun to change. As many directors described with pride the perfect freedom they extended to boys at camp, there was a strong dissenting voice. According to Virgil Prettyman, who was in the process of establishing Camp Moosilauke in New Hampshire:

> Absolute definite plans must be made for systematic occupation of the boys' time. It is entirely too easy to feel that because here are so many inviting things, that things will work themselves out—a boy will keep busy . . . but one boy who loafs while the others are busy is an infernal nuisance. If it goes on for two weeks, he will have other boys loafing with him. The hardest thing for a man to deal with in camp is to keep every boy busy.

Prettyman's attitude and especially his use of the word *loafing*—a term commonly associated with lower-class men whose seemingly purposeless use of public space incensed middle-class observers—shocked his fellow camp directors, who refused to see the sons of "good" families as loafers. Elias Brown attempted to get Prettyman to qualify his statement by suggesting that there was a distinction between boys who "loaf in an orderly way" and those who "perniciously loaf," but Prettyman would not budge. When Brown asked him if he considered studying nature and reading as loafing, Prettyman admitted that he considered those activities as "exercise." "If he sat quietly talking to a friend?" Brown asked. "I'd put a question mark there," responded Prettyman.[44]

While the exchange confirms the continued commitment to an unstructured approach to program on the part of many private camp directors, Prettyman's comments also suggest that some camp organizers were beginning to question whether the natural environment of camp was sufficient inducement to wholesome recreation. Although not everyone was as adamant as Prettyman about the dangers of loafing at camp, there was a new tendency for adults to take a more active role in guiding camper recreation during the first two decades of the twentieth century.

Perhaps the most noticeable change was a greater attention to time and time keeping. Schedules became more clearly articulated, with many camps specifying the hour and sometimes the quarter hour at which various activities were to begin. In fact, many camps continued to follow the general pattern established in the late nineteenth century, with individual activities in the morning, followed by a late-morning swim, team sports in the afternoon, and school yard games after dinner. In the early twentieth century, however, these activities were assigned specific times. Printed in brochures, such schedules served an important symbolic function—assuring parents of a well-run camp—even as bugles, bells, and whistles helped graft the abstract schedule onto the lived experience within camp.[45]

Adults took a bigger role in deciding when campers would recreate and also began to assert a greater influence over what campers would do for fun. The range of activities at early-twentieth-century camps was wide and might include sports and games such as baseball, tennis, basketball, quoits, tetherball, and shuffleboard, as well as boating, swimming, and new, nature-based occupations. While this range gave campers a degree of choice, the nature of camp recreation had changed decisively. Camp activities were no longer the products of the campers' imagination and their ability to improvise games that suited the existing conditions and available equipment; instead, camp activities were determined by what camp organizers decided to offer and how adults envisioned what increasingly became known as the camp program.

Some aspects of this camp program were new, especially active attempts to encourage campers to engage more directly with the natural world. While private camps had introduced nature talks at the end of the nineteenth century, the YMCA soon caught up by establishing a range of nature study "clubs," a nomenclature that allowed directors to feel they were simply providing an outlet for campers' inherent interest in nature. To be sure, there was a long-standing connection between children and collecting natural artifacts. Mid-nineteenth-century commentators, including preeminent domestic advice author Catharine Beecher, recommended collecting natural history specimens as an ideal pastime for children, an activity that developed skills and attitudes of discipline and orderliness, while bringing them into contact with the benefits of nature. By the 1890s, G. Stanley Hall identified collecting as an innate phase of human development, particularly pronounced in boys and peaking around age ten.[46] Building on this theory, Camps Becket and Durrell each organized a club for studying flora and fauna by 1906, while Camp Dudley offered three clubs: one for studying the geology and geography of Lake Champlain; one for identifying trees and birds; and another for field surveying.[47]

Woodworking and other forms of handicraft also became increasingly popular in the first decade of the twentieth century, as boys' camps participated in the turn-of-the-century handicraft renaissance in which men played a significant role for the first time. In contrast to "fancywork" (an exclusively female endeavor aimed at protecting leisured Victorian women from idleness), the more masculine field of "craft" developed out of the manual-training movement of the late nineteenth century. Although many American manual-training classes were specifically vocational in intent, others were influenced by the Swedish sloyd system, which, as Steven Gelber points out, "emphasized the broad developmental benefits of learning manual skills." According to this view, boys did not engage in crafts because they were expected to use them on the job later in life, but because crafts enhanced their mental development through muscular coordination and digital dexterity, while helping them appreciate "the relationship between man and production." Equally important, crafts introduced boys to hobbies that might help prevent delinquency in adolescence and that could help restore mental and physical health in adulthood.[48]

At the earliest camps, the line between manual training and manual labor was fine indeed. At Camp Algonquin, a private facility outside Boston, campers worked on projects determined by the director, helping to build roads, clear paths, and construct an extension to the wharf.[49] At other camps, however, construction projects originated with campers. At Dudley, four boys built a workshop for the use of the whole camp in 1904, while at another YMCA camp, boys built "a shack" for their own use in a secret place in the woods and only allowed their leader to see it a year later.[50] Camp organizers encouraged such projects—and continued to do so into the 1920s—not just because they enhanced the campus, but also because they enabled boys to reconnect with preindustrial skills associated with masculinity. According to Algonquin founder, Edwin DeMerritte, "The boys like it. They like to handle an axe or a pick—to hoe, rake, etc. It is outdoor life, which has been advocated as coming nearest to farm life."[51] Far from useless remnants of a far-gone age, such manual skills also helped prepare boys for "domestic masculinity," Gelber's term for the early-twentieth-century tendency for middle-class men to take on domestic tasks that had once been the purview of professional craftsmen, tasks that "retained the aura of preindustrial vocational masculinity," while providing "a masculine alternative to effete office work."[52] The gendered nature of these projects become clear when we realize that DeMerritte only required boys to do certain kinds of manual labor. As he explained to a conference of his peers, "I have never myself felt other than guilty if I asked a boy to go up there and help wash dishes or wait on the table." Kitchen drudgery—assigned to women in the middle-class home—was carried out by Algonquin's "colored help."[53]

Early-twentieth-century camps also encouraged small-scale crafts, initially avoiding those that required specialized tools. At Camp Wawayanda, the first crafts involved braiding lanyards from shoelaces and using jackknives to carve napkin rings, pen handles, toothpick holders, and pencil trays.[54] Likewise, at Camps Becket and Durrell, organizers were happy to have campers take part in the pyrography craze—undoubtedly because wooden postcards and letter openers with patterns or pictures burned into their surfaces had a suitably unpolished appearance; nonetheless, they required boys to bring their own wood-burning sets from home.[55] Within a few years, however, campers were eager to attempt more ambitious projects, and camp organizers began providing shop space in which boys could try their hands at building rustic furniture and metalworking. Yet, purpose-built shops (like the one constructed by Dudley campers in 1904) remained the exception. At Camp Becket, campers used a forge that was protected from the elements only by a tent fly, while at many other camps, early workshops were ad hoc affairs shoehorned into buildings designed for other purposes. In 1906, the shop at Wawayanda moved into a building that had once served as the kitchen, and four years later relocated to the area beneath the lodge porch. At Hayo-Went-Ha, a YMCA camp in Michigan, the manual-training shop was in the basement of the clubhouse (built in 1907), in a space used during the winter to store boats.[56]

TRANSFORMING BASEBALL

Adult intervention in camp recreation also manifested itself in attempts to control how campers played, even when they were pursuing familiar games and activities. A case in point is baseball, a game that was ubiquitous at early boys' camps and featured prominently in every description of camp program. Indeed, in the late nineteenth century, the game was well on its way to becoming a national obsession among adults, as well as among children who eagerly accepted the game as their own. At Camp Dudley, a man named Hyson helped cultivate a culture of baseball. A former player with the Cuban Giants, a Negro team founded in 1885, Hyson worked as Dudley's camp cook in the 1890s, often organizing games in which he and the younger campers played—and frequently beat—a team composed of the best players in camp.[57] According to one camp historian, "At the conclusion of a victorious game it was the custom for Hyson to lead his players in a triumphant march to the provision tent, where he freely dispensed white-washed cookies to the winners. This procession did not take place when the opposing team won."[58] Although almost invisible in official representations of camp life (that is, in prescriptive literature or in brochures and articles describing actual camp practices), black cooks had an impact on the campers' experience that extended well beyond the cook tent.

Hyson's contests also suggest that baseball could be more than just a game; it was a ritual of community as well. By involving himself on the youngsters' team, he gave them courage to challenge older players. They were thus positioned to earn the respect of the older team. In structuring radically unequal teams, Hyson encouraged spectators to cheer for the younger boys, rather than the camp all-stars, who would normally receive the greatest accolades. Hyson's rewarding of the younger boys when they won publicly acknowledged the magnitude of their effort. Depriving the older boys of similar rewards when they won reminded them to be modest about their advantages in age and size. Such rituals of community continued at Dudley in the practice of opening each camp season with a game between the advance party and new arrivals, followed by games between old campers and new campers, and a Fourth of July game between leaders and the youngest campers.[59]

In the 1910s, however, baseball had become subject to adult supervision, thanks in large part to the importance assigned to the game by child psychologists and play organizers in the first decades of the twentieth century. Hall argued that baseball was "racially familiar," in the sense that "it represents activities that were once and for a long time necessary for survival" for all human beings and are "still necessary for perfecting the organism," by which he meant the supposedly more highly evolved white races.[60] Play organizers were equally enthusiastic about baseball, but particularly because of its potential for teaching good citizenship. Although any team sport could serve this purpose in theory, baseball was the game that most often sprang to mind. PAA founder Henry Curtis described the impact of team games on the individual player in 1915:

> The boy must come out and practice when he wants to go fishing. He must bat out in order that the man on third may run in. Many a time he must sacrifice himself to the team. This type of loyalty is the same thing we call good citizenship as applied to the city, that we call patriotism as applied to the country. The team game is undoubtedly the best training school for these civic virtues.[61]

By minimizing the kind of individual competition that might undermine group solidarity, baseball emerged in this period as the team game par excellence.

Camp organizers not only shared play organizers' enthusiasm for baseball, they also adopted their suspicions of "unhealthy" (that is, individual) competition. By encouraging campers to try their hardest, "good natured contest" helped build character, while enhancing camp morale. When taken too far, however, competition might create hard feelings and prompt less skilled boys to retreat to the sidelines. As Henry W. Gibson put it in *Camping for Boys,* "The spirit of camping is too frequently destroyed by over-emphasis on competitive games." Indeed, Gibson feared that more was at stake than a happy camp season; he linked competition to the rise of spectator sports played by semiprofessional athletes, a situation that in his estimation had led to the downfall of ancient Greece.[62]

Thus, published advice and camp practice encouraged a modicum of competition in individual sports, but also urged leaders to exercise care in organizing team games. Gibson himself admitted that awarding ribbons at special meets for track and field helped "in fostering the true spirit of clean athletics and wholesome sport." Yet, he also argued that team games, like "the good old American game of baseball," needed to be organized with care so that all campers would participate. In addition to recommending separate "Midget" teams for the younger boys, he also reported with approval on an unnamed camp that organized baseball games within a "Food League," with teams named after (supposedly) popular camp dishes like "Prunes," "Beans," "Hash," "Mush," and "Chipped Beef."[63] The Berry League, the Mountain League, and even the Toothpaste League graced the baseball field at Camp Dudley, while at Wawayanda, the four baseball teams were named for colleges one year, for Indian tribes another, and for nations of the world in yet another.[64] According to Gibson, such names encouraged amusing accounts in the camp newspaper, which helped keep the tone of baseball games light.[65]

Initially, at least, these games had little impact on the camp landscape. Baseball required a large area, of course, but on temporary playing fields, baselines could be adjusted to existing conditions. In contrast, when regulation fields became the norm in the 1920s, the strict geometries of the baseball diamond were a jarring note in the camp landscape that otherwise embraced naturalness.

In other areas of camper recreation, early camp organizers paid relatively little attention to shaping the spaces in which campers played, and the camp landscape remained largely unencumbered by permanent buildings devoted to play purposes. At many camps (both YMCA and private), the only permanent structure was a large multipurpose building that housed the kitchen, dining room, and a recreational space. Called either "the camp living room" or "the assembly room," this recreational space was typically required to fulfill two contradictory functions. On one hand, it was the place where the whole camp could gather in the evenings or on rainy days. On the other, it was intended to provide a feeling of intimacy for small groups that might stop in during the day.

At many early camps, intimacy won out. At Camp Becket, a rustic pavilion built in 1905 by John E. "Pops" Gibson (the camp director's father) housed the dining room and kitchen, as well as a "camp living room," a large space that was made more intimate by its fittings: "a big stone fireplace, cosy nook, writing tables, library, and reading room," in addition to a piano. According to brochures, the room was heavily used on rainy days as a place for campers to read books or to write letters and in the evenings for "popular music sung around the piano."[66] Eventually it was also pressed into service for the annual minstrel show, in which white campers adopted blackface and took part in performances that served to reinforce their own sense of racial superiority.

The pavilion's exterior—with decorative log work gracing the gables and the area between ground and floor—has much in common with the rustic retreats (also called camps) built in the Adirondacks in the late nineteenth century; the younger Gibson's characterization of this building as "a mountain lodge" suggests that this was a conscious reference (Figure 2.7). Although there are no extant photographs of the camp living room itself, written descriptions of its furniture and fittings also evoke the informal, rough hunting lodges to which adult men were eager to retreat. Indeed, the centrally located pavilion served as the backdrop for multiple performances of middle-class masculinity. Leaders—some in varsity sweaters—posed for group portraits on the steps of the pavilion holding the college pennants that identified both their particular collegiate affiliations and their membership in the more generic category "college man." Even adolescent campers were introduced to

Figure 2.7. Camp Becket, Becket, Massachusetts. The pavilion, built in 1905 by John E. "Pops" Gibson.

selected aspects of campus culture when they gathered around the piano in the evening to sing "the jolly college airs" that Gibson described as "a special feature of the camp life."[67]

Camp Arcadia, a private girls' camp established in Maine in 1916, followed a similar pattern, with a main lodge containing "a large attractive assembly room, an open-air dining room, a 'rest' porch, the offices of the director and counselors, the Hand-Craft Balcony and the kitchen."[68] Although its assembly room could hold the entire camp population, its architecture and fittings—including a loft supported by twin tree trunks, a fireplace, and window seats—emphasized coziness (Figure 2.8). At Camp Mishawaka, the multipurpose building was a log structure called the bungalow, perhaps because of the broad porches where campers took their meals. Inside, the space was dominated by a large "living room . . . equipped with a piano, a Victrola, writing facilities, and a large fireplace, making it cozy and homelike," although period photographs reveal that the relatively intimate space was the setting for camp theatricals as well (Figure 2.9).[69]

At other early camps—especially those operated by the YMCA—the emphasis was on providing ample space, with the dining room itself doing double duty as an assembly hall. At Camp Wawayanda, for instance, the thirty-

Figure 2.8. Camp Arcadia, Casco, Maine. Assembly room, main lodge, from brochure for the 1921 season.

Corner of the Assembly Room of the Main Lodge

Figure 2.9. Camp Mishawaka. Living room in the bungalow, built 1910, from brochure for the 1938 season.

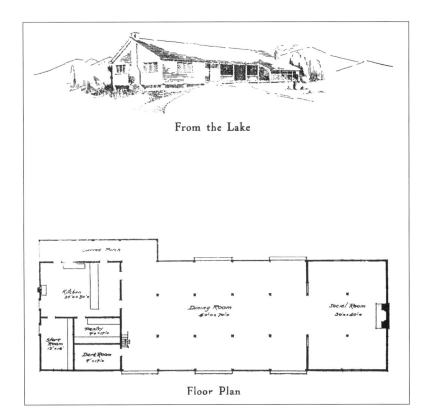

From the Lake

Floor Plan

Figure 2.10. Camp Dudley, Westport, New York. Perspective view and plan of dining lodge, from brochure for the 1908 season.

by-sixty-foot dining room included a stage with a drop curtain in one corner; a fireplace at the other end of the room was the only concession to coziness.[70] Likewise, Camp Durrell had a pavilion with one large room (equipped with a "huge old-fashioned fireplace" and a grand piano) used for dining, indoor games, social gatherings, and gymnastic work, and six smaller rooms used for a store, library, tool room, and guest rooms.[71] At Camp Dudley, the dining lodge included a thirty-by-forty-foot "social room" dominated by a large fireplace, while pocket doors on the opposite wall connected the room to the forty-by-seventy-foot dining room (Figure 2.10).[72]

During the interwar period, however, such arrangements came into conflict with new ideas about camp program. As meal preparation and cleanup were redefined as labor, there was a growing tendency to remove more purely recreational activities from the dining hall and to house them in a freestanding building, sometimes called a social lodge. At the heart of the social lodge was an assembly room, where campers and staff staged increasingly ambitious

Figure 2.11. Camp Becket. Library on second floor of boathouse, designed by Walter Atherton, dedicated August 1910.

Figure 2.12. Camp Becket. Gibson Hall (originally known as Pah-hah-ta), designed by Walter Atherton, 1917.

Figure 2.13. Camp Becket. Interior of Gibson Hall.

productions. Not only were campers of these decades likely to tackle Shakespearean plays or Gilbert and Sullivan operettas, they also often invited townspeople to join the audience. To accommodate such lavish theatrical events, these newer assembly rooms were large buildings that matched—and sometimes exceeded—the scale of the dining lodge.

At Camp Becket, divorcing recreation from dining was a two-step process that began in 1910 when a camp library was installed on the second floor of the boathouse not far from the pavilion. A rustic interior provided tables for writing and an alcove lined with bookshelves, while a porch overlooking the waterfront afforded a protected area for reading (Figure 2.11). Seven years later, there was a more decisive break from the pavilion when an elaborate new building was constructed on the highest point in camp (Figure 2.12). Initially called Pah-hah-ta, the Sioux word for "hilltop," the building was situated some distance from the traditional core of camp, where it formed a node of activity at least as important as the dining pavilion. The core of the building was a double-height assembly hall (measuring forty by sixty feet) planned to hold one hundred campers at play or three hundred seated for entertainment. A raised platform at one end was fitted out with a large fireplace flanked by windows. Thus, it could serve as a stage, but with its lower ceiling (thanks to the second-floor balcony that lined the perimeter of the room) and its domestic fittings, it also served as a camp living room. Period photographs taken

Figure 2.14. Camp Becket. Plans of Gibson Hall, sketched by Arthur B. Heaton in 1931.

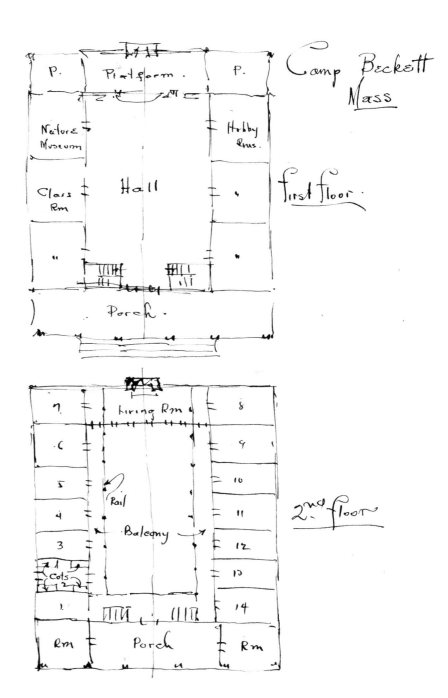

soon after the building's completion show Windsor rocking chairs—icons of Colonial Revival domesticity—on either side of the fireplace (Figure 2.13).

Yet, Gibson Hall (as Pah-hah-ta was renamed in 1927 in honor of Becket's longtime director) was much more than an enlarged version of the camp living room once housed in the pavilion. Indeed, the building was touted in fund-raising materials as the "Proposed Recreational Educational Building" and included space for most camp program activities (Figure 2.14). Flanking the assembly hall were rooms identified in promotional brochures as the printing room, woodworking room, iron-forging room (although there is no indication that a forge was ever installed), lecture room for first aid, and nature library-cum-museum, while the brochure's text mentioned "additional facilities for laboratory work in agriculture, chemistry, and nature study."[73] Above these program rooms were fourteen twenty-by-twenty-foot bedrooms, which would allow Camp Becket to host retreats for YMCA leaders and conferences for high school and college students. More than simply providing space for recreational activities, Gibson Hall set new priorities for camp program.

Such social lodges were built throughout the 1920s and 1930s, although adjunct spaces were kept to a minimum in these later examples, leaving only the assembly hall itself. Some—like Camp Dudley's 1925 Walter C. Witherbee Memorial Hall—were primarily theatrical facilities, complete with sliding curtains, electric lights, baby spotlights, and dimmers. Others—like the Castle built around 1935 at Camp Merrie-Woode, a private girls' camp in North Carolina—accommodated a stage but were also used for informal camp assemblies that reinforced community spirit at the start of each day (Figure 2.15).[74]

Many of the activities that had been included in Gibson Hall were increasingly given their own architectural containers in this period. In part, this change went hand in hand with the decentralization of camp life that eventually culminated in the unit plan. The close physical proximity of campers engaged in different activities might have seemed desirable when the camp population was perceived as a unified whole, but the notion lost much of its appeal when camp was reconceived as a collection of distinct, age-based units.

Equally important, purpose-built facilities were perceived as an effective means of stimulating camper interest in nature study and handicraft, a concession that children were not as inherently interested in nature-oriented activities as adults had once assumed. In 1938, the author of *Park and Recreation Structures* stated the case baldly when he urged camp directors "to

Figure 2.15. Camp Merrie-Woode, Sapphire, North Carolina. Interior of the Castle, built circa 1935.

place the craft and nature buildings so that they will be passed by the campers in the day's routine travel." As he explained:

> Young people, particularly, will not be inclined to seek out these facilities when located off the beaten track, yet their indifference can be broken down, and an enthusiasm can be created, if they are given opportunities for frequent and casual observation of the interest of fellow campers in craft and nature hobbies.[75]

Brochures for Camp Mishawaka cast the situation in a more positive light, but still made it clear that the new nature study museum (a log cabin built with the help of campers in the summer of 1931) was intended to "make Nature Study activities hum around the Camp in the future."[76] The brochure for 1934 confirmed this outcome, assuring prospective campers and their parents that "with the building of the Nature Study Cabin three years ago, the work [of nature study] received fresh impetus." The proof—according to the brochure's author—lay in the trappings of the building, which had been "thoroughly equipped with tables, book cases, filing cabinets, and show cases," as well as "many gifts of books, mounted specimens, and other furnishings."[77]

Finally, freestanding buildings provided greater opportunities for emphasizing the symbolic meaning of camp activities, a trend that reached its peak around 1930. Early manual-training buildings had tended to be utilitarian structures that provided the space, light, and equipment needed for making sometimes quite ambitious furniture projects. But their architectural forms were not expected to contribute to the special character of the camp landscape, and they were often sited unobtrusively. Even though Camp Dudley's Post Manual Training Building was named in honor of its donor, this 1913 structure was built on the back side of the dining lodge, near the office, garage, and other service buildings (Figure 2.16).

By the late 1920s, however, "manual training" was giving way to "crafts" or "handicrafts," a name change of some significance. For one thing, it signaled a shift in technique, with older skills like basketry and weaving coming to the fore. At the same time, it indicated a new attitude as well. Manual training had tended to be oriented toward the future, sending campers into adulthood with greater muscular dexterity as well as a greater appreciation for various steps of the modern production process. In contrast, crafts were part of an international "quest of the Folk," to use Ian McKay's apt phrase—a desire to embrace what was perceived as "the essential and unchanging solidarity of traditional society" in order to counteract the entropy of the modern world.[78] A fundamentally nostalgic endeavor, crafts encouraged campers to see themselves as "recapturing vanishing arts," as a 1933 brochure for Blazing Trail Camp put it.[79]

In this respect, summer camps participated in a widespread interest in preindustrial crafts that had started with the Arts and Crafts movement at the turn of the century, gaining new momentum in the 1920s in the work of social settlements aimed at the uplift of the poor. At Hull House in Chicago, the Labor Museum sought to show the children of immigrant families that their elders possessed substantial craft skills, albeit ones that had been made suddenly obsolete when they relocated to the industrial cities of North America. In rural areas, however, social settlements took a different tack. On one hand, they were strongly antiquarian in their orientation, seeking out almost forgotten songs, stories, and crafts, while ignoring more recent cultural practices. So focused were settlement workers on older forms that they felt compelled to "re-create" a culture of crafts, even to the point of introducing techniques they had observed in Europe. What is more, while mountain children were deeply involved with the crafts revival at folk schools like the one Olive Dame Campbell established in 1925 at Brasstown, North Carolina, they were not the primary audience. Rather their crafts became part of a performance of folk life aimed at distant urban audiences, who bought the crafts and donated funds to support the schools.[80]

Summer camps represent yet a third approach, teaching urban children invented crafts traditions to serve as a portal to the preindustrial world. Informed by Gulick's ideas about learning through the use of muscles, such an approach was also still connected to Hall's theories that children needed to mimic human and cultural evolution. Thus, crafts could transport campers for a time into a golden age of self-sufficiency, wordlessly teaching them character lessons while supplying them with an important stage in their development.

Especially in the mountains of western North Carolina, a log cabin emerged as the preferred setting for this nostalgic approach to crafts. Some were new buildings, while others were older log structures dedicated to new purposes. Rockbrook Camp, a private girls' camp founded in 1921 near Brevard, had both. A brochure for the 1924 season featured interior and exterior views of a log building with a porch along one long side "erected for the benefit of those who are 'hand-minded' . . . [where] skilled instructors teach basketry,

Figure 2.17. Rockbrook Camp, Brevard, North Carolina. Cur'os'ty, built circa 1930.

Figure 2.18. Rockbrook Camp. Interior of Cur'os'ty with looms, circa 1930.

embroidery, and work in metals and ivory."[81] By 1935, two other log buildings had been moved to the site, purportedly from Goodwill Plantation near Charleston, South Carolina. One—still called Goodwill—was used as a welcome center, where a camp hostess greeted visitors. The other was named Cur'os'ty—a mountain term for know-how—and was described in brochures as the place where "the lore of the mountains is preserved in the indigenous craft of weaving" (Figures 2.17 and 2.18).[82]

If log cabins evoked appropriate symbolic associations for camp crafts, they were not always ideally suited to this function. Their limited window openings, for instance, did not always provide sufficient light for detailed craftwork. Many older log buildings (including Rockbrook's Cur'os'ty) consequently received additions of large porches, while newer log structures (like that at another North Carolina camp, Chimney Rock Camp for boys) were designed with large wall openings that came close to undermining the romantic image of the snug log cabin (Figure 2.19).

Camper-produced newspapers suggest that some youngsters at least interpreted their crafts activities as a means of connecting with their forebears. Betty Fuller, who attended Camp Hillaway near Hackensack, Minnesota, in 1934, wrote that "weaving is especially interesting because the articles one

Figure 2.20. Camp Mishawaka. Nature study cabin, built with the help of campers in 1931.

can make on the loom are so pretty and so useful." In fact, the products she mentioned—finger towels, little bags, and mats of different lengths that she deemed "perfect for small tables in a living room"—were largely ornamental adjuncts to modern life. Yet, according to Betty, "when we weave beautiful things we feel like our great-great grandparents who made all such things for themselves."[83] In other words, camp crafts and the settings in which campers pursued them allowed Betty and her friends to experience pioneer conditions that (according to the frontier myth) would temper their Anglo-Saxon heritage into a truly American character.

Nature museums were also given special attention in the 1920s and 1930s. The one pictured in the Boy Scouts' 1927 *Campsite Development Plans* was a two-story log structure modeled on "the old pioneer blockhouse," with a small room for exhibits and a darkroom on the first floor, and an octagonal exhibit space above (see Figure 1.13). Not only would boys enjoy building the museum, according to the text, but the "unusual construction [also] lends glamour to the building," thus attracting boys first as viewers of its carefully arranged exhibits and then, presumably, as contributors to them.[84]

In practice, nature museums of the 1920s and 1930s were less complicated

affairs in form, although equally rich in symbolism. The functional requirements of the type were few and could be met by a small, single-cell building fitted out with simple shelves. Even the plainest nature cabins, however, tended to be constructed of logs, a material that triggered symbolic associations with able frontiersmen. At Camp Hayo-Went-Ha, the eight-by-ten-foot log building that housed the nature museum had once served as the Turner homestead before being disassembled and moved to the campsite in about 1936.[85] Mishawaka's camper-built nature museum went a step further, allowing campers to experience the process of hewing, notching, and fitting the logs into place themselves (Figure 2.20). The Treasure Trove, the 1937 nature cabin at Chimney Corners Camp in the Berkshires, reveals the malleability of the symbolism; window boxes helped domesticate this log cabin that stood near the center of a private camp for girls (Figure 2.21).

MAPPING THE ELABORATED CAMP LANDSCAPE

This tendency to shape the spaces of camper recreation soon extended to larger components of the camp landscape, embracing activity areas as well as camp buildings. Camp brochures of the period often describe the installation of running tracks and other single-purpose playing fields, which were increasingly laid out according to the precise measurements required for regulation play; Gibson's 1923 book, *Camp Management,* included detailed information for constructing regulation baseball diamonds and tennis courts.[86] The Camp Becket newspaper, *Seen and Heard,* reported with enthusiasm on the installation of two regulation marble courts in August 1924 (Figure 2.22). After noting that "many battle royals have already been waged and the courts are always in demand," the young reporter asked, "shall Becket develop a national champion in this typical boy sport?"[87]

By the end of the decade, this approach to recreation began to threaten the conceptual clarity of early camp layouts in which all structures (either tents or permanent buildings) faced the parade ground. At first, there were attempts to continue this pattern, maximizing the limited parade ground frontage with closely packed activity areas. At Camp Mishawaka, the manual-training shop, basketball court, and archery range were wedged together in one corner of the campus. Once the entire parade ground frontage had been

Figure 2.22. Camp Becket. Regulation marble courts, installed 1924.

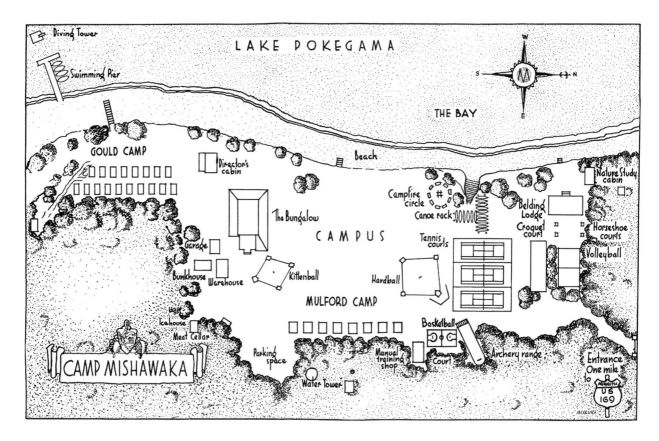

Figure 2.23. Camp Mishawaka.
Site plan, from brochure for the
1938 season.

claimed, new single-purpose playing fields and program buildings spilled over in both directions (Figure 2.23). At many camps, baseball diamonds were permanently installed on the parade ground itself in a place of honor, while other recreation areas formed a second and sometimes a third tier of activity on what had been the back side of the original camp buildings.

At the same time, camp maps began to appear in brochures. In part, no doubt, such plans served to impress parents and prospective campers with the wide range of activities offered at a given camp. Yet, such maps also helped highlight a conceptual order that was no long readily apparent from any single vantage point at camp itself. Although such maps typically showed only the small part of the camp landscape on which permanent buildings stood, they suggest that the core of the summer camp landscape was alive with activity, crowded with recreating campers.

In this context, the New Deal camp-planning practices of the National

Figure 2.24. Norway Point Group Camp, St. Croix River Recreational Demonstration Area (now St. Croix State Park), Minnesota. Craft house, built 1937.

Figure 2.25. Norway Point Group Camp. Interior of craft house.

Park Service were particularly timely. More than just a by-product of the unit plan and the decentralization of camper cabins, the aggressively picturesque planning Albert Good advocated in *Park and Recreation Structures* constituted an abrupt reversal of the tendency to fill the camp landscape with hard-edged program areas (see Figure 1.17). In fact, single-purpose recreation areas were kept to a minimum in these plans, with baseball diamonds completely absent from recommended plans. Even the equipment for "campy" activities was kept to a minimum. While Good noted that "a loom, a small forge, a photographic dark room, a potter's wheel, and a small printing press are among the many possibilities" for a craft house, these facilities were "generally held desirable but less than essential."[88] Devoid of the romantic connotations of 1920s craft buildings, Recreational Demonstration Area craft houses (like the one at Norway Point Group Camp in what is now Minnesota's St. Croix State Park) were small structures that emphasized efficiency, with narrow workbenches lining their perimeters (Figures 2.24 and 2.25).

Figure 2.26. Kamp Kiamesha, Newton, New Jersey. Diving tower, circa 1920.

DESIGNING WATERFRONT SAFETY

This tendency to guide camper recreation through carefully designed play spaces had a particularly noticeable impact on the waterfront, which underwent profound changes in the first forty years of the twentieth century. Early on, campers and leaders alike continued to see the waterfront as a site for frolicking and derring-do; formal instruction in swimming was of little concern. When camp directors invested in permanent equipment, it was often a waterslide, diving tower, rope swing, or some other mechanism that campers could use to effect a dramatic entry into the water. Often there was a physical risk involved, particularly as campers and counselors sought out increasingly ingenious ways to interact with the device. Far from banning such daredevilry, camp directors were happy to abet these demonstrations of camper courage. When a Shoot-the-Chute (probably inspired by a common amusement park ride of the same name) was installed at Camp Dudley in 1904, the director proudly described both its form and its impact to the readers of *Association Boys:* a twenty-five-foot-long chute, lined with oil cloth and set at a thirty-degree angle, it shot campers into the water "at a velocity of something short of a mile a minute."[89] Another favorite stunt was to have multiple divers launch themselves simultaneously from a diving tower, a feat that was attempted at exhibitions on Parents' Day and captured on film well into the 1920s (Figure 2.26).

Camp directors were not indifferent to camper safety; far from it. As Zelizer has demonstrated, Americans were coming to consider children "emotionally priceless" and to see the accidental death a of child not merely as a private tragedy but as a public outrage as well.[90] At least in the early years of the twentieth century, however, adult fears were centered on the urban environment and particularly on the threat that motorized vehicles posed to child life. To the extent that they removed children from an inherently dangerous environment, summer camps seemed—in comparison—remarkably safe. Some camps established branches of the U.S. Life Saving Corps to supervise swimming periods; the one at Camp Dudley was established the same year that the water chute first appeared.[91] But while these groups were ready to react to accidents, they stopped short of seeing waterfront mishaps as inevitable events that could only be reduced through proactive intervention. These corps included campers who had passed tests in swimming, boating, and rescue work, but they did not attempt to teach swimming to those who had not already mastered the skill.

This laissez-faire approach to swim instruction changed dramatically in the 1920s, as summer camps began cooperating with the lifesaving and water safety program of the American Red Cross. First introduced in 1914 and dramatically expanded after its reorganization in 1921, the program was one of a number of attempts to translate intense, but initially diffuse, community outrage about accidental child deaths into official action.[92] Rather than regulate adult behaviors that endangered child life, these initiatives typically took one of two tacks. Some (like street safety lectures in public schools) were aimed at teaching children to protect themselves in a dangerous environment, while others (like the playground movement) placed physical barriers between children and immediate danger.[93] The Red Cross water safety program did both, promoting swimming lessons for everyone and pushing for physical changes that would make swimming areas safer.

The summer camp waterfront was transformed by both strategies. Tailoring the Red Cross slogan to the summer camp situation, camp directors increasingly sought to make "every camper a swimmer and every swimmer a life saver."[94] No longer was it sufficient simply to accommodate campers' swimming skills, allowing experienced swimmers access to deep water while restricting nonswimmers to shallow coves. Camps began to offer swimming lessons to campers at all skill levels and to mandate these lessons for every youngster, often using staff trained at Red Cross National Aquatic Schools.[95] More advanced swimmers could also train in lifesaving skills, and by the late 1920s they could demonstrate their mastery of such skills in examinations administered at camp by Red Cross field representatives.

These lessons certainly had a substantial impact on camp life, with at least part of the first day of camp devoted to swimming tests that many former campers remembered as rites of passage. In her recollections of her first day in 1926 at Camp Wapomeo (a private girls' camp in Ontario), Merle S. Storey recalled being "very nervous about trying my swimming test." Although she failed the fifty-yard test, she persevered. "It was not long before I was proudly sporting a red [swim] cap, indication that I could swim the required number of yards."[96]

From the perspective of the Red Cross, the importance of site visits extended well beyond awarding lifesaving certificates; they also gave Red Cross water safety experts the chance to educate camp leaders about all aspects of waterfront layout and administration. In the summer of 1931, for instance, a Red Cross official visited Camp Thayer, a Camp Fire Girl facility in Cazadero, California, and followed through with a series of suggestions: dividing the swimming area into three parts instead of two; placing metal flags on the floats; supplementing the sand in the beginners' area; adding the Red Cross beginners' test to the other tests in the program; stationing a guard upon the hill; establishing a junior lifesaving crew; having additional lifesaving and "All Out" drills; and purchasing and practicing the use of grappling hooks.[97] When another field representative visited the Boy Scouts' Camp Burton in Adamston, New Jersey, in July 1928, he "helped lay out the plans for the water front."[98]

Resistance to such advice seems to have been rare. During a 1934 visit to Camp Dixie in Clayton, Georgia, for instance, the Red Cross field representative was "very poorly received," especially when he pointed out "the quite apparent danger of their beginners' area as it was then constructed."[99] For the most part, however, camp directors embraced Red Cross expertise as consistent with their own drive to introduce greater professionalism into camp administration. In 1929, for instance, W. E. Longfellow (assistant national director, First Aid and Life Saving) provided waterfront training at Boy Scout Training Camp for Camp Directors and Water Front Men at Camp Bert

Figure 2.27. Unidentified Girl Scout camp. Swimming crib, circa 1920. From Girl Scouts, *Campward Ho! A Manual for Girl Scout Camps*, 69.

Adams, outside of Atlanta, Georgia. The next year, Longfellow attended a camp directors' conference for the YMCA of New Jersey and Pennsylvania, where he talked about water safety and "then conduct[ed] a quiz period on the waterfront, discussing waterfront layouts."[100] In 1931, the Camp Directors' Association passed a resolution at its annual meeting "accepting the standards of the Red Cross as its official minimum standards in swimming, lifesaving, diving, swimming pool leadership, boating, canoeing, camp waterfront leadership, and first aid."[101] By 1933, Red Cross standards were in place in 1,748 summer camps.[102]

Thus, during the interwar years, Red Cross advisers were in a position to encourage camp directors to implement substantial changes to the waterfront layout. Some of the recommended changes were aimed at facilitating formal swimming instruction. In shallow waters this might be something as simple as the installation of a kick rail. In deeper lakes and ponds, however, water safety experts recommended the construction of a beginners' crib, a log or plank structure with end pockets that could be filled with stones to sink it into place (Figure 2.27). A crib not only limited the depth of the water but also provided a sturdy handhold for beginners learning to kick.[103]

Most of the changes, however, involved giving physical form to existing

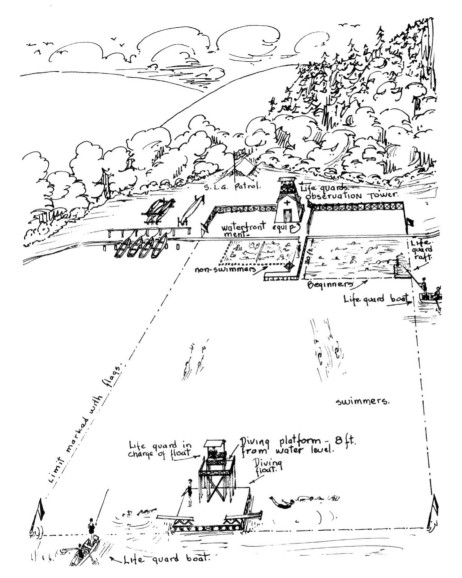

Figure 2.28. Waterfront layout for a Boy Scout camp, 1927. From Boy Scouts of America Department of Camping, *Camp Site Development Plans*, 55.

safety policies, by creating carefully bounded zones to remind campers of their limitations—both their own and the ones imposed upon them. As illustrated in the camp waterfront layout published in the Boy Scouts' *Camp Site Development Plans* of 1927, this zoning started on land, with fencing used to separate campers who had checked in for their swimming period and those who were at the waterfront to use boats, including canoes, which were

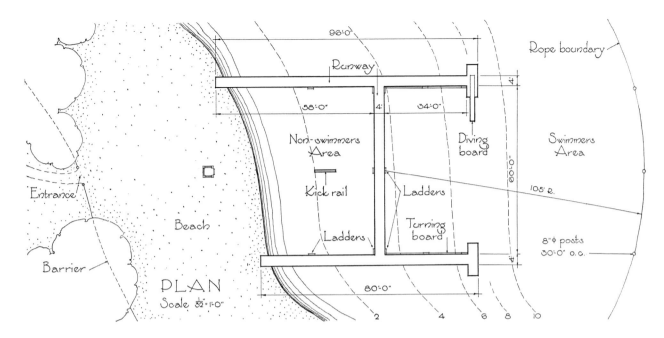

Figure 2.29. Hard Labor Creek Recreational Demonstration Area, Georgia. Waterfront layout, circa 1936. From Albert H. Good, *Park and Recreation Structures*, 3:156.

increasing in popularity in the interwar period along with other Indian motifs at camp (Figure 2.28). Another fence subdivided the beach into an area for nonswimmers and one for beginners. In the water, an L-shaped dock segregated the two groups. The nonswimmers' area was further marked by ropes and buoys, while the limits of the beginners' area were defined conceptually by the edge of the dock and a lifeguard raft. Swimmers were given greater compass, but still found themselves limited to an area clearly marked by the flags. Initially at least, these safety measures were superimposed over the vestiges of the older, daring waterfront. Diving towers, for instance, remained an integral part of many camp waterfronts, and both the Boy Scouts and the Girl Scouts continued to recommend attaching such towers to floats in the deeper water.[104]

By the 1930s, however, professionally designed swimming areas had taken on a new look, thanks in part to the tendency to forgo the play equipment that had characterized the daring waterfront of the early twentieth century. Diving towers and water chutes had no place in newly built campsites. Those built under the auspices of the National Park Service and published in *Park and Recreation Structures* are remarkably flat; only lifeguards enjoyed the privilege of an elevated position (Figure 2.29). At the same time, the tendency to translate safety policy into physical form became even more acute in the 1930s. The F- and H-shaped docks introduced in this period provided exact and highly visible boundaries between the various zones of the swimming area. The author of *Park and Recreation Structures* praised the H-plan as the "ideal development" precisely because its "definitely prescribed limits . . . [served] to restrain the rash and unwary from venturing beyond the bounds of rescue."[105]

Throughout the postwar period, the Red Cross ethos of water safety continued to hold sway at summer camps, prompting the introduction of further refinements to the waterfront system introduced in the 1930s. A notable addition was the buddy board, a physical manifestation of the buddy system. A Red Cross innovation of the late 1920s, the buddy system required campers to swim within easy reach of their assigned swimming buddies—close enough, in fact, to be able to grasp hands over head during buddy drills.[106] Situated at the entrance to the waterfront area, the buddy board facilitated the administration of the system by keeping track of buddy assignments and (through color-coded tags) providing a quick survey of who was still in the water. Since campers were required to turn over their own tags to indicate their position, the buddy board also helped reinforce the sense that each camper had a proper—and publicly acknowledged—place at the waterfront.

If the midcentury waterfront was safer than its predecessors, it was also a landscape that privileged conformity over daring. With its docks and ropes, it regularized a natural body of water, providing campers with rectangular boxes in which to practice approved swim strokes they had learned from certified instructors. Everywhere they went they encountered the physical reminders of their own limitations—or at least of the limitations that others had determined for them. While early waterfront activities had encouraged campers to look within themselves to find the courage and strength required to test their physical and emotional limits, the safe waterfront required campers to look to others for an external sign that they were ready to take the next step. Daring had its price, but so too did safety.

CAMP RECREATION FOR GIRLS

While much of the earliest discussions of camp recreation centered on the needs of male campers, girls' camps did not ignore gender differences when establishing their recreational programs. Although early studies of children's play (such as an 1898 survey of four thousand children in South Carolina) suggested that unsupervised play was gender-specific (with girls playing dolls, jump rope, croquet, clap in-clap out, and drop the handkerchief, while boys preferred baseball, football, swimming, marbles, and fox and geese), many early girls' camps bucked that trend.[107] Evidently eager to demonstrate that girls were every bit as able as boys, many early girls' camps encouraged young women to take on conventionally male activities. Into the 1920s, brochures often featured pictures of pretty campers firing rifles or hoisting logs into place in a camper-built cabin.

From the 1920s on, however, gender differences in play were beginning to change both at home and at camp. Indeed, another study of children's play (this one a 1921 survey of 474 children in San Francisco) revealed a greater overlap in the games of girls and boys, albeit with important differences in emphasis. Boys named baseball, kites, tag, and bicycling as their favorite pastimes, while girls offered a longer list of activities, with different favorites: tag, sewing, bicycling, baseball, hide-and-seek, and basketball.[108]

Likewise, girls' camps offered many of the activities common at boys' camps, but began to differentiate their program in subtle ways. In the field of crafts (rarely called manual arts at girls' camps), for instance, girls were encouraged to take on a wide range of mediums. Published by the Girls Scouts in 1920, *Campward Ho!* recommended not only wood, metal, and leather—the favorite crafts materials in boys' camp—but also dyeing, batiking, stenciling, woodblock printing, pottery, basketry, weaving, and rugmaking. What is more, Girl Scouts were encouraged to put their crafts activities to different ends. As the anonymous author of *Campward Ho!* explained, "Delightful problems in the interior decoration of a camp living room can be worked out by combining the efforts of all the craft workers. The carpenters build the furniture; the weavers make the rugs and materials; the dyers dip the materials and carry out the color scheme and other workers supply the accessories."[109] Fifteen years later, the *Handbook for Leaders of Camp Fire Girls* suggested a comparable connection between camp crafts and the performance of womanly roles:

> But is there anything more worthwhile than to build up taste and discrimination about things that can be made with the hands? It means more attractive clothes, for Hand Craft has to do with fabric and color, design and line. It means more attractive houses, for Hand Craft has to do with many phases of interior decoration and the planning and making of accessories for the house.[110]

While boys were expected to use craftwork to build muscular coordination and to understand production, girls were encouraged to make themselves and their homes more attractive.

Writing for the *Hillaway Wave* in 1931, camper Cherry Koch confirmed the gendered nature of these projects. Although her article was titled "Girls Build Log Cabin and Make Its Simple Furniture," she revealed that "Arnold does the chopping and the sawing," while "the girls have carried all the poplar logs, placed them and nailed them." Although Koch briefly mentioned plans "to make crude, simple furniture for it," she described at length a series of projects for the following summer, when "Hillaway campers will weave the window curtains, bedcovers, and rugs, and make pewter into dishes and into candlesticks just the way the pioneers did. They will even make dyes from berries and roots to color what they are going to weave, and they will mold their own candles."[111]

This emphasis on the aesthetic qualities of the camp experience ran throughout the literature on camp recreation for girls in the 1920s and 1930s, as girls were encouraged to discipline their bodies in order to enhance the natural beauty of the site. For Camp Fire Girls, singing—and especially the "tiresome parodying of popular tunes"—was an important area of concern. As the *Handbook for Leaders* noted, "Such beautiful songs have been written about the woods and nature and all they mean to those who really love them, that it seems almost sacrilegious to profane a beautiful campsite and make old trees and flowers listen to some of the horrible shouting which passes for singing in some camps."[112] Many girls' camps featured rhythmic or aesthetic dance—the one camp activity never offered to boys—encouraging female campers to develop and exhibit bodily grace, while expressing their appreciation for and enhancing the beauty of their natural environment.

As the organizers of girls' camps began to articulate their vision of a gender-specific recreational program, they came to question some of the time-honored practices of boys' camps. Baseball was chief among these, perhaps because organizers considered it too masculine a game. Although advocates of organized play waxed poetic about baseball as a training ground for good (that is, loyal, self-sacrificing, authority-obeying) citizens, geographer Elizabeth Gagen has pointed out that their notions of citizenship were gender specific. Even after women won the vote—perhaps because so many arguments for suffrage had emphasized the need for a distinctly feminine approach to political issues—citizenship remained closely linked with conventionally male qualities. Equally important, the outward performance of good citizenship was understood to derive "naturally" from the male self; encouraging girls to engage in parallel performances not only undermined the femininity of individual girls but also called into question "the apparent naturalness of gender and its attendant performance." In Gagen's view, girls playing baseball (or at least playing baseball with the same gusto and intensity as boys) threatened the whole gender system.[113]

Yet the leaders of girls' camps rarely discussed baseball in such overtly gendered terms, but instead used their critique of the game to express a more general uneasiness with the recreational programs pursued at boys' camps. According to the deliberations of the Girl Scout Camp Committee described in the introduction to this chapter, baseball was not inherently problematic for girls; it was just out of place at camp. The 1935 *Handbook for Leaders of Camp Fire Girls* took a similar stance, describing both baseball and basketball as "over-worked, over-organized games" and encouraging camp leaders to embrace camp as an opportunity "to get your girls away" from them. In their place, the *Handbook* encouraged leaders to "star gaze in the evenings, ramble around the country on exploring trips, poke up and down brooks, little valleys or canyons," activities aimed at fostering in campers an "appreciation of the *real* things about them, without which camping is but a poor substitute for the hectic, dashing life of the town or city" (emphasis in the original).[114] In fact, these approved camp activities contrasted sharply with baseball. Not only was baseball an artificially structured use of time, it also required intense concentration, taut body postures, and coordinated movements that were a far cry from gazing, rambling, and poking up and down. Running around the bases, at least to some eyes, was too much like dashing around town.

THINKING LIKE A CHILD AGAIN: CHILD-CENTERED RECREATION

By the 1940s, the debate about camper recreation was complicated as camping leaders—particularly those associated with girls' camps—began to articulate a radically new approach to camp program. One of the strongest voices in this shift was Abbie Graham, who enjoyed a long association with the YWCA. Her 1941 book, *Working at Play in Summer Camps*, was unprecedented in the camping literature. Instead of a thick compendium of camp games and activities, it was a slim volume that articulated a philosophy of camp program based on fun. The use of the term *fun* was itself significant. Although it had been used since the eighteenth century to describe an amusement or diversion, its older meaning of a cheat or a trick gave it a negative connotation; well into the twentieth century, fun connoted amusement that was frivolous, if not downright mindless. In this sense of the word, fun had little place at early summer camps. Yet, Graham used the word fun in a new way, connoting a joyful, but otherwise somewhat indefinable, quality that only children were able to judge. According to Graham, fun defined in this way was an integral component of a camp's recreation program. Without it, campers would simply not embrace even the most worthwhile activities.

This focus on fun turned earlier camp recreation practices on their head. While adults had spent the first forty years of the twentieth century attempting to guide and influence camper recreation, camp organizers like Graham came to interpret such attempts as ineffective. As she put it, "The fun of campers rather skillfully eludes adult-made blueprints. No one can say, 'This is what every camper enjoys.' No sooner does an adult say this than he discovers a camper inventing an entirely unheard-of-way of enjoying himself." Worse yet, adults were apt to hinder fun, and Graham exhorted camp counselors (the intended audience of her book) to begin their work by confronting their own subconscious resentments of campers' fun.[115]

In Graham's view of things, campers were best suited to determine their recreational program. The role of the camp counselor lay in "finding out what campers have come to camp to do and to enjoy and putting all the resources of adults at the service of such activities and enjoyments." To be sure, she felt that adults had a responsibility to help campers evaluate their recreational goals and that some areas of the camp program deserved special consideration. In this regard, Graham highlighted "social interests" (by which she meant conversations that helped campers confront their own class and race prejudices); engagement with natural resources (which promised to stir the imagination and arouse curiosity); and arts of all kinds (because any experience was incomplete "until we have sung it, danced it, painted it, written it or carved it"). Yet, she maintained that the evaluation of campers' goals was best accomplished "in the give-and-take of skillful discussion between adults and campers."[116] Like Benjamin Spock, whose ideas about "permissive parenting" would soon revolutionize child-rearing discourse, Graham encouraged counselors to put children's interests and desires first.

At first glance, this emphasis on a child-centered program seems to be a throwback to the ad hoc recreation of the 1890s, when boys were free to do what they wanted, when they wanted. In fact, Graham's vision of camp program was quite different in that it promoted the importance of "being" as well as "doing." In order to get to know themselves and their desires, campers needed to lie under a tree, sit near the river, watch grass grow. Other kinds of activities would derive from ideas that sprang up in such quiet times.

THE CHANGING LANDSCAPE FOR FUN AND GAMES

Seen against this background, postwar camp-planning advice is less cohesive than it first appears. The Girl Scouts, for instance, continued to pursue a camper-centered approach to program and accepted the planning practices codified by the National Park Service as compatible with their program philosophy. Thus, when it came time to hire a new camp consultant, they chose Julian Harris Salomon, the planner responsible for the organized camp portions of *Park and Recreation Structures*. In addition to writing *Camp Site Development* in 1948 and revising it in 1959, Salomon traveled the country advising local councils on their camp-building projects. By 1960, he reported that he had designed at least one major camp in every state of the United States, as well as examples in Canada and Mexico. (Since his relationship with the Girl Scouts was not exclusive, these included YWCA, YMCA, and Boy Scout camps.) Staking his claim to professional expertise on his ability "to think like a child again," Salomon was indeed the perfect choice to provide camp plans for an organization intent on providing child-centered camp programs.[117]

In fact, the child-centered plans that Salomon produced for the Girl Scouts are remarkably similar to those published in *Park and Recreation Structures* (see Figure 1.18). Naturalistic clumps of trees subdivide the landscape into distinct living units connected by curving paths. Hard-edged playing fields for baseball and tennis are completely absent. Indeed, the only permanent activity area is the accident-proof waterfront. Far from offering a smorgasbord of things to do, these plans provide a range of intimate places to be.

The camp layout published by the YMCA in 1946 was similarly based on picturesque planning principles, yet these principles are put to different ends (see Figure 1.18). The goal was not to offer an alternative to the elaborated camp landscape of about 1930, but to provide a naturalistic package for a comparable range of activities. The hard edges of the archery range, soccer/football field, and tennis courts may have been disguised by carefully positioned plantings, but they were still there, as were the baseball diamond and handicrafts buildings literally at the center of camp. Nearby was an aqua amphitheater from which to watch waterfront stunts that had been so popular in the interwar period. This core was flanked by the dining hall and social lodge, large buildings that formed two major nodes of activity. In short, the approach to planning was new, but the conception of program had changed very little.

THE SERIOUS WORK OF PLAY

For all its pleasures, camper recreation was serious business, especially for the adults charged with camp program. While they had once been willing to leave campers to spend their days more or less as they pleased, camp organizers increasingly saw it as their duty to guide the play of their charges. In part, this guidance helped ensure that campers would participate in nature-based activities that adults thought should be inherently interesting to children—who did not necessarily agree. In part, this guidance encouraged children to play familiar games in ways that adults deemed appropriate. This was particularly true of baseball, which play theorists considered central to teaching boys the teamwork and "healthy" competition that would make them responsible citizens.

Guided recreation was also an important means for encouraging campers to interpret the camp experience itself as their leaders intended. This is especially apparent in the area of crafts, where the particular projects—so often related to building and furnishing a log cabin—helped children understand that camp life was meant to evoke, however romantically, life on the frontier. The frequency with which campers reported that weaving (or molding candles or making pewter plates) made them feel like their great-great-grandparents suggests that guided recreation was integral in conveying camp's fundamental messages.

Adult involvement in directing recreation was also entwined with other concerns, especially with securing camper health and safety. Early camps had encouraged boys especially to test both their physical and emotional limits, but those risks became increasingly unacceptable as American society redefined child life as priceless. The camp waterfront in particular was transformed by the larger cultural imperative to domesticate children's play.

If these adult concerns shaped activity areas devoted explicitly to camp program, they also affected other aspects of the camp landscape as well. Indeed, adults paid attention to every corner of the landscape—even the most mundane—and to every moment of the campers' day—even when they were asleep.

CHAPTER 3

Housing the Healthy Camper

Tents, Cabins, and Attitudes toward Health

IN THE SUMMER OF 1904, A GROUP OF ABOUT SEVENTY-FIVE boys and girls boarded a train in Chicago. Their destination—the suburbs of Glencoe and Ravinia—was not geographically distant, but the experience that awaited them was intended to be far from their normal routine. These children were beginning a two-week stay at a Fresh Air camp sponsored by the Moody Sunday School, a branch of the evangelical church established on the north side of Chicago by Dwight L. Moody in 1859. Handpicked by the wife of the Sunday school superintendent, these "needy" children were to be taken from the fetid atmosphere of their bleak home neighborhoods to the health-giving air of the leafy suburbs. While building stronger bodies was important, religious instruction topped the agenda. As one Fresh Air worker explained, the superintendent "insisted that the spiritual work should come first."[1]

The settings for these Fresh Air camps were suburban estates lent to the church by well-heeled supporters. While the adult leaders basked in the genteel surroundings of the parlor, the children spent most of their time on the grounds, benefiting from the clean environment lacking in their home neighborhoods. The time was full: daily calisthenics and a splash in the lake; a long hike at least once a week; and occasionally a taffy pull or hayride to Fort

Figure 3.1. Moody Church Fresh Air Home, Glencoe or Ravinia, Illinois. Improvised washing area in basement of suburban house, circa 1904.

Sheridan. Ever present was Bible study in the open air and evening devotions before going to bed. After two weeks, this group would return home, only to be replaced by another, and so on throughout the summer.

A photograph album assembled by G. P. Rockwell, the superintendent of fresh air work for the Moody Sunday School, offers an unparalleled glimpse of life in an early Fresh Air camp, right down to the makeshift washroom in the basement of one suburban house, a grim space where bold letters barked out the order: "Love" (Figure 3.1). Perhaps the most striking thing about Rockwell's album, however, is its documentation of the fact that suburban estates rarely provided the kinds of spaces that Fresh Air camps needed to house dozens of children. At one house, the girls slept in a crowded bedroom, while in another, boys were relegated to cots in the attic (Figure 3.2). Neither space offered the kind of fresh air that organizers sought to provide. Why, then, were suburban estates deemed appropriate sites for early Fresh Air camps?

Like all early summer camps, Fresh Air camps were the product of a Victorian perception that celebrated the natural world as inherently salubrious. Considered the ideal setting for the single-family house and other sites devoted to child nurture, nature was also understood as the best environment for hospitals, asylums, houses of refuge, and other institutions dedicated to protecting and rebuilding moral, physical, and psychological health. Home, health, and nature were strongly linked and mutually supportive concepts. Thus, the decision to house a Fresh Air camp seems motivated by the sense that the material trappings of genteel home life enhanced the health-restoring mission of the camp.

Yet, twentieth-century summer camps quickly moved away from their Victorian roots. Early in the century, the Victorian triad of home, health, and nature began to unravel as two scientific fields helped convince camp organizers that a natural setting, while beneficial, was insufficient to guarantee good health. First, in the 1910s and 1920s, the new field of public health highlighted the dangers associated with bringing together any group of people for extended periods of time—even in camp—and focused concern on the transmission of communicable diseases such as tuberculosis and, later, polio. In the 1930s and 1940s, child psychology had an even bigger impact on the camp environment, shifting concern away from the ills that affected all modern children and toward specific behavior problems caused, it was believed, by the unscientific parenting campers received at home. In short, home had lost its undisputed status as the best setting for the nurture of healthy children, and the summer camp was claiming a place as an effective substitute.

In the process, the camp landscape was fundamentally reimagined. Early camps had offered antidotes to modern life in settings that celebrated martial vigor and, in historian T. J. Jackson Lears's terms, facilitated a quest for authentic selfhood in order to ease American anxieties about modern technocratic culture.[2] By the middle of the twentieth century, camps—for all their rusticity—were conceptually closer to child-study laboratories and closely aligned with the scientifically therapeutic environments celebrated in modern culture.

THE TENT DEBATE

Many elements of the camp landscape played a role in producing healthy campers, but camper sleeping accommodations were seen as particularly important. Given inherited Victorian convictions about the vulnerability of the sleeping body, the tent or cabin was potentially the most treacherous site in

Figure 3.3. Camp Becket, Becket, Massachusetts. "The Sardines," campers in their platform tent, circa 1910.

camp. It is the element that was transformed most dramatically by changing ideas about what constituted a healthy camper.[3]

In the earliest decades of organized camping, tents were the rule. Although some early private camps (like Pasquaney) housed campers in rustic dormitories in the 1880s and 1890s, few camps followed their lead. Even other private camps relied on tents to house campers. In the first seasons at Camp Mishawaka, campers slept in tents that lined the parade ground. In 1916, Director George F. "Doc" Green established a separate sleeping area, the Junior Camp, for younger boys (between nine and eleven years of age), but tents were still the rule. Older boys slept two to a tent, while the juniors were deemed "so little that it is necessary that a counsellor sleep in each tent with the two boys."[4]

Tents were ubiquitous at boys' and girls' camps sponsored by the YMCA and other youth organizations, although they could take many forms. Turn-of-the-century photographs of Camp Dudley show pup tents with flies, while Camp Becket used wall tents, rectangular tents with a ridge pole supported by upright poles front and back and having low side walls of canvas secured by guy ropes (Figure 3.3). Wall tents also appear in published photographs of early Girl Scout and Camp Fire Girl camps, although other photographs show conical wall tents—albeit with a warning from the Girl Scouts that they were "not easy to put up and give little head room." [5] Many camps, including the Boys Scouts' Camp Ranachqua in New York, used a mix of tent types, suggesting that the stock of tents grew over time (see Figure 1.7).

The appeal of tents is clear, at least from the organizers' point of view. Tents were cheap, particularly if procured from military surplus. They were movable, an important consideration for summer encampments that began on borrowed land. They provided for flexibility, because they could be added quickly as camp enrollments grew. Echoing a military encampment, tents were a natural choice for camp organizers bent on introducing campers to the military discipline lacking in feminized homes.

For campers tents were an abrupt departure from the comforts of home. Boys at the YMCA's Camp Couchiching in Ontario slept on homemade ticks stuffed with straw, while those at Camp Dudley retired on hemlock boughs on the earthen floor of their tents, with only their ponchos and blankets between them and their natural bedding. Although it required campers to "become inured to the topographical peculiarities of the terrain," this system was in use for more than fifteen years. It was only in 1911 that Dudley installed tent

Figure 3.4. Unidentified Camp Fire Girl camp. Campers ready for inspection in front of their wall tent, circa 1920. From Playground and Recreation Association of America, *Camping Out: A Manual on Organized Camping,* opposite 48.

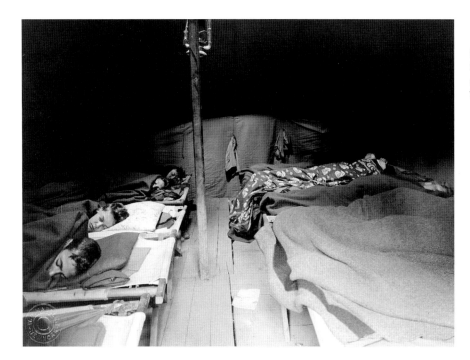

Figure 3.5. Camp Ranachqua, Harriman State Park, New York. Tent 9 before reveille, August 1919. Photograph by W. D. Hassler, New York.

platforms and double-deck cots of canvas supported on frames of dimensioned lumber. This was also the system used at Camp Becket, where the bunks lined the tent's side walls, leaving the higher area under the ridgepole as a place where campers could stand, although they had to give up some of the space for the storage of personal effects. This arrangement of tent equipment was commonplace in wall tents, even in camps that used mass-produced cots of iron or wood, as in the Camp Fire Girl tent pictured in *Camping Out: A Manual of Organized Camping,* published by the Playground and Recreation Association of America (PRAA) in 1924 (Figure 3.4). Conical tents did not lend themselves to this tidy arrangement; at Camp Ranachqua, nine campers slept on closely packed canvas cots that pointed into the center of their tent (Figure 3.5).[6]

As far as early camp leaders were concerned, even small, crowded tents were a perfectly acceptable way of housing campers. Based on his involvement with YMCA camps in the 1880s and 1890s, George Peck advocated "small tents, holding from five to ten in all [because] this plan provides for the best control and care of the boys." Henry W. Gibson concurred. In *Camping for Boys,* he recommended wall tents, describing in detail how to erect them, commenting on guying the tents, trenching around them, the right and the wrong ways of driving stakes into the ground, and other elements of what he called "peg wisdom." But he did not consider the tent a potential health hazard. On the contrary, the caption to one illustration, "'The Sardines'—Eight Boys in a 12 × 14 Tent," suggests that Gibson looked with a fond eye on tents crowded with happy campers (see Figure 3.3).[7]

It is not that early camp directors were unconcerned with issues of health; they were. Mishawaka's Doc Green worked during the school year as athletic director at St. Alban's School in Washington, D.C., and considered athletics "the most important department of Camp life." In addition to swimming, baseball, track, and tennis, Mishawaka emphasized "systematic" physical training, which Green supervised himself, assigning special exercises to individual campers to correct curvature of the spine, flat chest, or round shoulders. As a 1913 brochure explained it, "The results of this system of training, combined with the healthful outdoor life, has [sic] been most gratifying."[8] Far from being problematic, tents promised to minimize the boundary between sleeping campers and the camp's healthy, natural setting.

This easy acceptance of the tent began to change in the 1920s as camp directors began to assert their claims to professional status through a heightened concern with camper health, a move that simultaneously gave their vocation a scientific basis and related camp directing to the profession of medicine. Borrowing techniques used in pediatric hospitals, camp directors (including Green) turned their attention to quantifying the positive impact of camp on campers' health. As described in 1925 by Leonard G. "Pop" Schneller (who would himself become director of Mishawaka in 1933), "The matter [of developing boys' bodies] is gone about in a most systematic manner":

> On the second day in camp, every boy is given a very careful physical examination by men experienced in this kind of work. Approximately twenty measurements are taken, of all important parts of the body. These are recorded upon cards which are kept accessible to those having charge of the physical side of camp work. A photograph is also taken of each boy, and which is kept on hand, unretouched, to show the general condition of the boy.
>
> Then, on the very last days of the season, all of this work is duplicated, so that a comparative record is made of every boy, showing his condition and measurements at the beginning and at the close of the season.[9]

By 1935, Schneller published several of these before-and-after photographs in "The Improvement Shown in Eight Weeks at Camp Mishawaka," a flyer

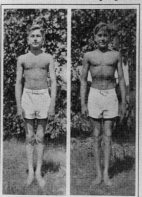
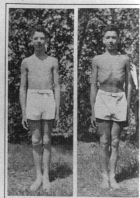

These are pictures of boys taken when the Camp opened and again when it closed

NOTE THE MUSCULAR FIRMNESS, GENERAL POSTURE, AND MENTAL ATTITUDE OF THESE BOYS AFTER EIGHT WEEKS IN CAMP

Figure 3.6. Camp Mishawaka, Grand Rapids, Minnesota. Before-and-after photographs of campers from "The Improvement Shown in Eight Weeks at Camp Mishawaka," a supplement to the brochure for the 1935 season.

sent to parents with the brochure for the upcoming season (Figure 3.6). Urging parents to note improvements in "muscular firmness, general posture, and mental attitude," the text also assured them that "these photographs have not been retouched."[10]

This concern with objectively demonstrating a camp's health-giving qualities also had a great impact on the camp landscape. As directors began to scour public-health literature for guidance, the tent was an early casualty. Having reviewed both U.S. Army regulations and those of the California Commission on Immigration and Housing, the PRAA recommended at least fifty square feet of floor space and five hundred cubic feet of air space per capita, which became the often-invoked camping-industry standard. Equally important, the study revealed that, of the 163 camps surveyed, only 31 met the standard, and another 32 housed campers in half the recommended amount of space or less.[11]

Despite the exactitude of the standard, the rationale behind it remained a rather vague concern about the increase in relative humidity that resulted from moisture emanating from the human body. According to the PRAA, this high relative humidity was "injurious to the health" and could only be relieved by providing sufficient ventilation "to maintain the same relative humidity of the inside air as obtains in the outside atmosphere." Since air movement was the primary concern, the floor space could be reduced with sufficient ventilation, although if campers slept too close together they risked breathing in "massive doses of air-borne germs of respiratory diseases." Nonetheless, worries about this method of transmitting disease remained secondary; the PRAA even approved the practice of relocating double-deck bunks to the center of the tent—an arrangement that allowed "better ventilation and over-head room for occupants of the upper bunks," but also made it easier for campers to breathe in air-borne germs from tent mates in adjacent bunks.[12]

Some camp organizers were loath to abandon tents entirely (and many camps continue to use them today), but in the 1920s, their use became problematic. While it might have been possible to continue to use tents by housing fewer campers in each, there were other hazards. Expensive to maintain (despite their low initial cost), tents were also difficult to keep dry; they dripped during storms wherever campers touched them on the inside. Camp directors who staked their professional reputations on keeping campers healthy, warm, and dry needed something more foolproof.

SLEEPING CABINS AND THE FIGHT AGAINST DISEASE

The advice literature that emerged in the 1920s offered a number of alternatives to the tent and often presented detailed plans of even the most rudimentary structures, presumably to lend them the cachet of scientific exactitude. At this time, "cottages . . . built along plans approved by the National Camp Directors' Association" gradually replaced the tents at Camp Mishawaka (Figure 3.7). According to Pop Schneller, not only did these cottages "allow

Figure 3.7. Camp Mishawaka. Cottages in the senior camp, circa 1923.

Figure 3.8. Camp Icaghowan, Chisago County, Minnesota. Campers posed before tent-houses, circa 1920.

opening of almost the entire side and rear for ventilation purposes," they were also "easier to keep clean . . . more stable in high wind, and . . . drier in case of rain." Housing three campers, the cottages were "proving popular with the boys."[13]

Another common alternative was a structure variously called the tent-house, tent-cottage, or canvas cabin, which retained canvas walls but facilitated ventilation by expanding the building's dimensions. These tent-houses appeared in the early 1920s at the YMCA's Camp Icaghowan in Minnesota and were undoubtedly still in use when Minneapolis landscape architect Charles H. Ramsdell redesigned the site in 1927 (Figures 3.8 and 3.9). Rife with military symbolism, Ramsdell's plan centered on a "camp parade" with tent-houses arranged so that "Headquarters" at the reception lodge "should command every situation by day and by night." Tent-houses also resembled the makeshift lodgings common at mines in the late nineteenth century, and perhaps their association with the manly work of taming the West appealed to camp organizers.[14]

Other variations on the tent-house model attest to its popularity. Gibson, who in 1911 had cheerfully described crowded tent conditions, published his own version a decade later. Called the Strader-Becket tent-house, it had a fourteen-by-sixteen-foot wooden floor supporting a light frame of dimensioned

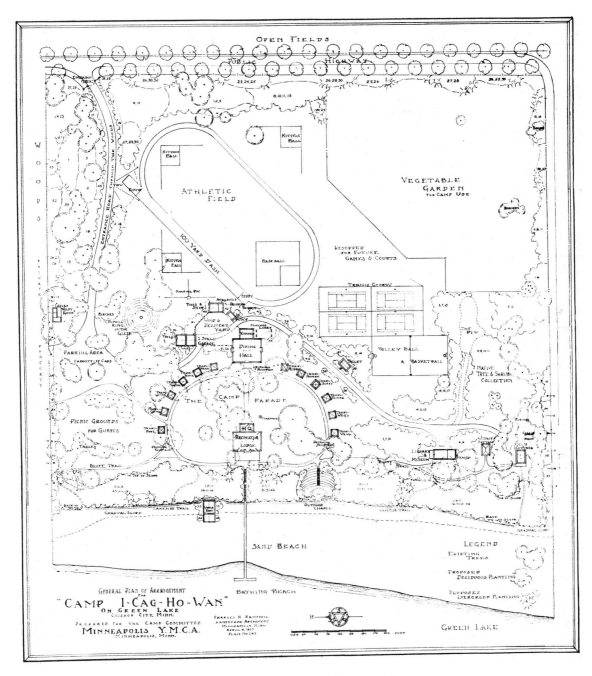

Figure 3.9. Camp Icaghowan. Site plan designed by landscape architect Charles H. Ramsdell, 1927.
From *Parks and Recreation* 15 (March 1932): 414.

lumber and canvas walls that could be rolled up in good weather (Figure 3.10). The entire thing was topped by a hipped roof covered in red rubberoid; readers could secure blueprints by sending Gibson one dollar. The next year the PRAA published a similar scheme, drawn by Major William A. Welch for the Palisades Interstate Park in New York. Measuring eighteen by eighteen feet, this version included a ventilator at the peak of its pyramidal roof. This design was reproduced (without attribution) in the Boys Scouts' 1927 *Camp Site Development Plans.*[15]

In the 1930s, concerns about the transmission of disease through direct contact outweighed vague worries about relative humidity. As a result, overall building dimensions (which played an important role in determining standards for adequate ventilation) became less important than the spacing

Figure 3.10. Strader-Becket tent-house, 1920. From H. W. Gibson, *Camp Management: A Manual for Camp Directors,* 37.

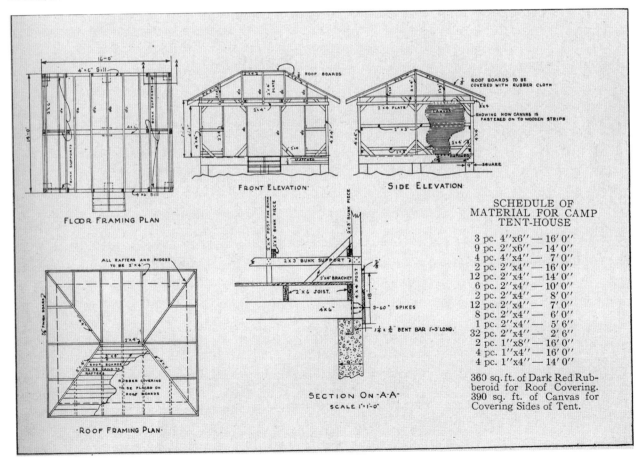

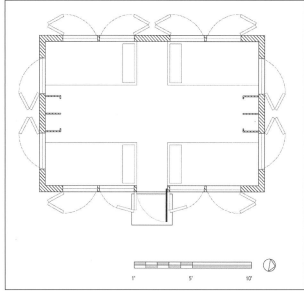

Figure 3.11. Norway Point Group Camp, St. Croix River Recreational Demonstration Area (now St. Croix State Park), Minnesota. Unit cabin, designed by E. T. Waley, 1937.

Figure 3.12. Norway Point Group Camp. Plan of unit cabin.

between beds, and the size of the sleeping quarters could be greatly reduced. Working under the auspices of the New Deal and with the blessing of the U.S. Public Health Service, National Park Service planners built a series of small wooden cabins at organized camps in Recreational Demonstration Areas (RDAs). These structures mimicked the proportions of the beloved tent; indeed, Albert H. Good, the Park Service architectural consultant, called them "wooden tents." Those at Norway Point in Minnesota's St. Croix River Area (now St. Croix State Park) measured approximately twelve by eighteen feet (Figures 3.11 and 3.12). All of them featured a cot in each of the four corners with closets in between. According to Good, the wooden tent was also an aesthetic improvement over the tent-house of the 1920s, which seemed to him "a cross between a corncrib and a cricket box of heroic proportions." At the same time, these nearly indestructible structures worked well in organized campgrounds that would receive hard wear at the hands of renting organizations. Their wood shutters not only helped deflect rain in the summer, they could also be closed and locked during winter months, another advantage for camp buildings on public lands.[16]

Throughout the 1930s, tents still had their advocates. Even Park Service architect Good admitted that "the [canvas] tent stands as an inherited symbol of high adventure, especially to youth." His sympathy was with the "youthful reincarnation of Daniel Boone or Marco Polo [who] finds to his horror that he is expected to sleep in other than a tent . . . and . . . is forever convinced that [he] was born too late." Some camping leaders, Good noted, "will not lightly sacrifice the psychological advantage of the tent," despite the high cost of maintenance or replacement and the difficulty of "screening them against insects."[17]

CAMPING AND CHARACTER

By the 1940s, however, the tent-versus-cabin debate had faded into the background. Camp-planning manuals published just after World War II either reduced the decision to a question of preference or ignored tents altogether. Even more significant, the tent-house and the simple "wooden tents" popularized by the National Park Service had also disappeared from YMCA literature. In their place were relatively elaborate cabins, often with a room for counselors as well as a social area for campers (Figure 3.13). With their more substantial forms, porches, fireplaces, and accommodations for one or more parental figures, these cabins are more reminiscent of domestic architecture than earlier camp structures. Rather than seeking to emulate homes, however, these cabins were integral to a critique of modern parenting fueled by camp professionals' deepening involvement with child psychology.

A knowledge of child psychology was not new to camps in the 1940s. Not only were camp directors used to quoting psychologist G. Stanley Hall, they also made a practice of shaping the camp landscape to fit their somewhat literal interpretation of his recapitulation theory. If the feminized home was forcing children prematurely into civilized behaviors, then why not let them inhabit the wilderness? If children were savages, then why not let them camp among tipis and totem poles?[18]

By the 1930s, professional camp directors had already begun to use child psychology and progressive educational theory to reassess many aspects of their operation. The unit plan was the earliest visible manifestation of this shift, with its small clusters of cabins for campers in distinct and scientifically predictable phases of development. In fact, some camps introduced age-based programming as early as the 1920s, while the most progressive among them also attempted scientific (that is, quantifiable) assessments of their own programs.

The best known of these camp experiments took place at Camp Ahmek,

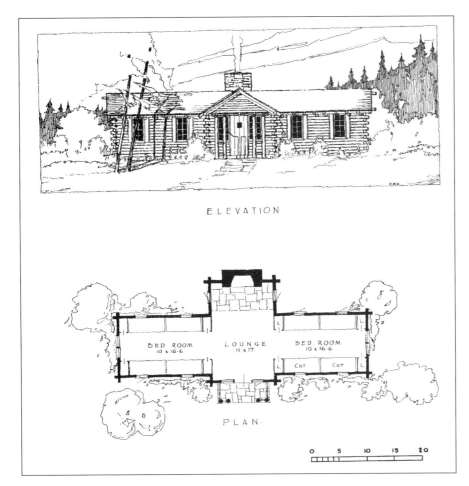

Figure 3.13. Sleeping cabin for older boys, complete with social area, 1946. From John A. Ledlie, ed., *Layout, Building Designs, and Equipment for Y.M.C.A. Camps*, 15.

ELEVATION

BED ROOM
10 x 16·6

LOUNGE
11 x 17

BED ROOM
10 x 16·6

COT COT

·PLAN·

0   5   10   15   20

a private boys' camp founded by Taylor Statten. By the time he established Ahmek in 1921, Statten was the secretary of the National Boys' Work Board of the Religious Education Council of Canada, but he had spent the previous sixteen years with the YMCA, initially as the first full-time boys' work secretary for the Central YMCA of Toronto, and later as boys' work secretary for the National Council of the YMCA in Canada. Influenced by the writings of Ernest Thompson Seton, Statten emphasized camping, woodcraft, and Indian lore as effective ways of interesting boys in the spiritual message of the YMCA. In 1905, his first year with the Toronto YMCA, he organized Camp Couchiching, a YMCA camp with tents pitched military style. During the 1910s, Statten became involved with the development of the Canadian

Standard Efficiency Tests (CSET), which awarded points, certificates, and badges to boys who met "objective standards" of development along intellectual, physical, devotional, and social lines. When leaders in the CSET program expressed their sense that the program was too cold to reach its potential audience, Statten encouraged merging the CSET with woodcraft and Indian lore to form two new programs, Trail Rangers (for older boys) and Tuxis (for younger ones). So involved did Statten become with the program that in 1920 and 1921, he hosted a ten-day leader training camp for men involved in the movement; the site for Camp Tuxis was on the shores of Canoe Lake in Algonquin Park, near Little Wapomeo, the island on which Statten and his wife, Ethel, had built a summer cabin. In 1939, Statten became the founding president of the Canadian Camping Association, and in 1941 he was elected president of the American Camping Association as well.[19]

While Statten had ample camping experience when he started Ahmek, some of it had been of the wrong kind, or so he came to see it in later years. At Camp Couchiching, part of the problem derived from the coaching he received from his YMCA supervisors: "I was given to understand," he recalled in 1931, "that success in a boys' camp was measured in terms of the number of conversions and the frequency and amount of participation in testimony meetings and public prayer on the part of boys." Equally problematic was the unscientific way in which Statten himself sought to achieve these aims. It never occurred to him, for instance, that "we should evaluate the character-building values of our recreational activity." As for health objectives, Statten marveled, "We had none!" Since this rather loose approach to camping was typical for early-twentieth-century camps, hindsight must be responsible for much of Statten's self-criticism. Although he acknowledged "a gradual, but a very decided improvement in our aims and objectives" through the years, he also concluded that he and his staff lacked a clear understanding of the "specific attitudes, appreciations, skills and habits" that they wanted to develop in the boys.[20]

By establishing his own camp, Statten was free to abandon the evangelical quality of religious practice that had dominated early YMCA camps, emphasizing instead what came to be called "character education." At the same time, the Tuxis movement had convinced him of the need for clear and measurable objectives of the character development of campers. During the first four seasons at Ahmek, Statten and his staff borrowed the basic idea of the Tuxis program, scoring tent groups on the external behaviors that they believed were closely associated with the internal character traits they valued: punctuality at meals, tent tidiness, table etiquette, posture, and camp spirit. Each day, winning groups received small leather "medals" or wild goose feathers (provided by noted bird specialist Jack Miner). In time, silver cups were introduced and soon the awards system had expanded to cover "almost anything and everything," according to an early staff member. Although the bookkeeping was unwieldy, "the daily tent competition became a recognized institution within the camp."[21]

The Ahmek system changed in important ways in 1924, when Hedley S. Dimock, joined the staff as special instructor in religious education. A professor of education at the YMCA College in Chicago, Dimock appreciated Statten's attempts to establish measurable objectives for campers, but saw the award system as deeply flawed. In fact, Dimock argued, once a tent group realized that they had no chance of winning that day, they "lapsed into carelessness and indifference." Statten was convinced and discontinued the use of cups and awards after the 1924 season. (The Ahmek crest and bars, however, remained; akin to a Girl Scout sash, the crest belonged to an individual camper and served as the support for bars indicating achievement in canoeing, swimming, boxing, camp craft, and other camp activities.) He also gave Dimock permission to attempt a scientific evaluation of Ahmek's effectiveness in character building. For the next five years, Dimock and Charles E. Hendry (who had worked with Statten at Camp Tuxis and had been on the Ahmek staff from the beginning) treated the camp somewhat like a child-study laboratory, introducing a number of innovations that would put the traditional character-building mission of camp on a more scientific footing. The results of their study appeared as *Camping and Character: A Camp Experiment in Character Education*, a scholarly book first published in 1929 and reprinted twice in 1930 and again in 1949.[22]

At the heart of the assessment process was the observation of camper behavior. Counselors were given detailed instructions on how to describe their observations ("AVOID GIVING YOUR OWN OPINION AND JUDGEMENTS") and provided with specific suggestions for what to describe. The Behavior Observation Record offered twenty "suggestive items for description," each one of which had several parts. Item 3, for instance, asked, "Does he have many, few, or no companions or friends? Is he accepted as one of the group? Especially sought after as a friend? Or teased, annoyed, razzed, or bullied? Describe concretely." To be completed for each camper within the first three days of camp, and then once or twice more during the camp period, this record required a substantial commitment of time and effort on the part of the counselor. Indeed, the instructions recommended that counselors spend a portion of each evening recording the significant episodes of the day.[23]

Another key tool for assessing the overall effectiveness of camp was the Behavior Frequency Scale, which asked the counselor to assess each camper on fifty-four separate forms of behavior, noting for each whether its occurrence was Never, Seldom, Occasionally, Fairly Often, Frequent, or Extreme. Although some of the behaviors to be observed (such as "Untidy in appearance or tent" or "Practicing bad posture") were the same external signs that once had been the subject of the awards system, most focused more specifically on character traits, and particularly those that facilitated group acceptance. Positive behaviors included "considering others first," making a "friendly approach" to an "unlikable boy," making a "friendly approach to those of his group," making a "friendly approach to those of other social, economic or racial status," "contributing well considered suggestions to the thinking of the group," "showing enthusiasm for group enterprises," and "cooperating readily." Negative behaviors included "disturbing any group meeting," "hogging equipment," "hurting another's feelings," and "considering himself first." While "assuming leadership" and "displaying courage" were valued, these qualities were to be tempered by lack of conceit; "accepting recognition modestly" was specifically articulated as a positive behavior, whereas boasting, showing off, and acting superior were listed separately as distinct sins, as was "exercising authority objectionably." Dimock and Hendry also acknowledged camper sexuality, asking counselors to record whether a camper engaged in "irregular sex behavior"; they did not, however, specify what they meant by "irregular."[24]

The Behavior Frequency Scale could be used in two ways. First, it was used to assess the emotional health of individual campers, and in the most extreme cases to identify boys needing consultation with the camp psychologist. Although Ahmek did not cater particularly to problem children, camp personnel considered some form of behavior adjustment appropriate for all boys. What is more, they used application forms, letters, and personal interviews to encourage parents to think about the behavior modifications that they would like to see in their sons.[25] By quantifying camper behaviors at the beginning and end of the camp season and comparing the differences, the Behavior Frequency Scale allowed Ahmek staff to offer parents what they felt was objective evidence of the camp's effectiveness in this regard; such comparative graphs were in essence psychological versions of Mishawaka's muscle tone and posture photographs. Yet, Dimock and Hendry were equally interested in compiling behavioral data for the whole camp, aggregating it over many years, and using those results to quantify "normal" boy behavior at each stage of development. Not only was such statistical information integral to the field of child study, it also provided the scientific basis for the claims to professional expertise that Dimock and Hendry used to launch their own careers.[26]

A few of these more extreme cases were documented in *Camping and Character* as well. Freddy, for instance, had to be the center of attention: he engaged in boastful talking, he whistled before diving to ensure himself an audience, and overall displayed "a sad lack of stick-to-it-iveness." The diagnosis emphasized two points. First, Freddy was bright and attractive and tended naturally to assume the central role in any situation; his bragging and showing off were simply shortcuts to satisfying his strong desire for recognition and status. Second, Freddy's father also sought "to achieve recognition and social prestige in rather superficial and ostentatious ways," and he "worshipped" Freddy. Freddy's mother "oscillate[d] between severity as a corrective for the father's doting attitude, and indulgence as a reaction to her own severity." The method of treatment was threefold: Freddy was to stop whistling before he dove; he was to write a letter to his father saying that he was unpopular at camp, but would try to overcome it; and his counselor was to prevent him from starting any new project until he had finished the previous one. Freddy was also moved to a new tent to allow him to start fresh. The results of the treatment were not completely successful; indeed, Freddy was moved to yet a third tent before the summer was through. The only hope, Dimock concluded, were "if Freddy could be dealt with in an extra-home environment for a considerable length of time."[27]

Other cases also pointed the finger at poor parenting as the root cause of campers' behavioral difficulties. Tom suffered from hysterical homesickness because parental control had not been consistent. Albert and James, two restless, untidy, irresponsible brothers, came from a family with "four bosses": their mother, a woman of culture who was frequently away; a grandmother, who looked after them in the mother's absence; a housekeeper, who was responsible for the boys at mealtime; and their father, a successful stockbroker who returned home only on weekends and lavished on the boys gum, candy, toys, and clothes. Martin, who became enraged upon slight provocation, was "badly pampered in his eating at home." While these case studies made it clear that fathers often had a hand in creating troublesome boys, Dimock and Hendry blamed women for bad parenting. The book's summary chapter, for instance, emphasized "the desirability of getting the boy away from the female when there is evidently too much 'petticoat' government. Housekeepers, maids, and governesses in too great an abundance are not the best means for developing the social abilities and attitudes of the boy."[28]

The highly gendered nature of this discussion is familiar from the earliest years of the camp movement, but with an interesting twist. The needs of boys had always received intense professional scrutiny, perhaps because the perceived crisis of masculinity had greater resonance with the men who dominated the fields of camp directing and child psychology. Likewise, the tendency to blame mothers (or their female surrogates) for children's problems is nothing new. What is new is the tendency to put the psychological state of the child first, instead of assuming—as had camp directors of an earlier era—that a camper's emotional stability would increase with enhanced physical strength. Equally new was the application of scientific child rearing to the specifics of camp life. Rather than using amorphous concerns about the feminized home as a general rationale for the summer camp, *Camping and Character* suggested that camp could diagnose particular parental failings and prescribe individual remedies. No longer a mere consumer of expert advice on child development, the summer camp could serve as a child-study laboratory that contributed more actively to the scientific understanding of childhood.

The Ahmek system changed the nature of counselors' work in several ways. Jack Thompson, who was a seventeen-year-old counselor in training (CIT) in the summer of 1930, later recalled that "every evening after supper there was a counsellors' meeting where we discussed actual problems arising in the camp." Even as a CIT, Thompson read "and received much benefit from" two recommended texts: *Camping and Character* and *Creative Camping* (by Joshua Lieberman). For Thompson (who went on to become a clergyman) the experience was formative: "It was at Ahmek that I got my first taste of applied psychology. My earliest interests in the personalities of men were aroused at Ahmek."[29]

Perhaps more important to the daily life of campers, Ahmek's innovations proposed a new form of counselor-camper interaction. Earlier in the century, counselors at boys' camps had often been selected for their athletic prowess, and their job performance was defined primarily by their activities on the camp's playing fields or at its waterfront. While they sometimes lived with campers in their tents or cabins, they were largely seen as a passive force for good: twenty-four-hour role models of robust manliness that, it was assumed, took little special training or extra effort on their part. This older kind of counselor had been on display for campers, who were meant to look at him even as they looked up to him. At Ahmek, the camper became the object of the counselor's scrutiny. So important was this camper-directed gaze that Dimock and Hendry included it as "one of the major skills of good leadership."[30]

HOUSING THE "CAMP FAMILY"

Not every camp adopted Ahmek's Behavior Frequency Scale, but the popularity of *Camping and Character* suggests that professionally active camp directors were familiar with its methods and sympathetic to its aims. Throughout the 1930s, camp directors demonstrated this sympathy by providing settings in which counselors had the opportunity to observe closely the social interactions among their charges. Seen in this light, the elaborate cabins featured in postwar advice literature are the culmination of this sea change in camper-counselor relations.

One such setting was the unit lodge, a new camp building type associated with the unit plan popularized by the National Park Service. In organized

Figure 3.14. Norway Point Group Camp. Unit lodge, designed by E. T. Waley, 1937.

Figure 3.15. Norway Point Group Camp. Main room of unit lodge.

Figure 3.16. Camp Lincoln, Lake Hubert, Minnesota. Gopher cabin, built circa 1930.

campgrounds built in federal RDAs in the 1930s, the unit lodge was "the rallying point of a camp unit," which also included four to six "wooden tents," a counselor's cabin, and a toilet and shower structure. Since its primary function was to house rainy-day activities and evening programs, the unit lodge was essentially a large open room that provided about twenty square feet per camper in the unit. However, planners also perceived the unit lodge as "the common living room or clubroom for the campers who make up the unit," and thus insisted that a fireplace "of generous size" was its most important feature. Outdoor kitchens were an optional, although recommended, feature of the type. The lodges at Norway Point Group Camp show a typical configuration: a single large room with a fireplace at one end and a smaller screened-in kitchen beyond it (Figures 3.14 and 3.15).[31]

In some private and YMCA camps, the cabins themselves often incorporated the social function of the unit lodge. Such was the case at Camp Lincoln, the oldest boys' camp in Minnesota. For the first two decades after it was established as Camp Blake in 1909, it housed campers in long, narrow tenthouses, a few of which are extant and used for storage. Around 1930, however, Lincoln shifted to large, two-story chalet-like structures (Figure 3.16). On the ground floor, the core of the building was a social room with a corner fireplace. This was flanked on either side by sleeping rooms, each of which

Figure 3.17. Camp Warren, Eveleth, Minnesota. Intermediate cabin, built circa 1928.

Figure 3.18. Camp Warren. Plan of intermediate cabin.

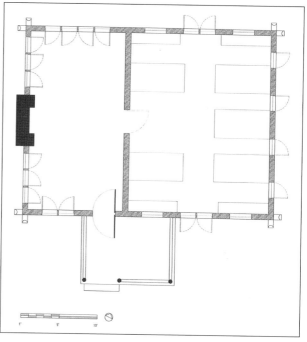

housed a counselor and seven or eight campers. Another sleeping room was located on the second floor. Similar cabins were built at Lincoln's sister camp, Camp Lake Hubert, founded in 1927.[32]

A comparable arrangement was instituted in 1928 at Camp Warren, a YMCA camp on the shores of Half Moon Lake in Minnesota. There, each of the original six log cabins contained "a living room with a fireplace, and an airy sleeping room" and was intended to house eight boys and a counselor to "preside over the cabin family" (Figures 3.17 and 3.18). In 1936 Camp Warren added a Cub Camp, a unit for younger boys from eight to eleven years of age. Although these one-room log buildings did not allow for separate living rooms, they each had a fireplace and live-in counselor to complete what brochures called "the family unit." Cabins built in 1930 at Camp Dudley included a fireplace alcove with built-in seats (Figure 3.19). Named for Princeton, Yale, and other universities (whose alumni helped pay for their construction), each cabin housed a leader, a junior leader, an aide, and six campers. Even in more modest camps, cabins included social space. Those at Camp Ojiketa, a Camp Fire Girls camp in Minnesota, were built of

dimensioned lumber and contained no fireplaces. But the front half of the cabin was devoted to a separate room for counselors and a common area for socializing.[33]

At some camps, these communal cabins augmented older sleeping cabins, rather than replacing them. In 1932, for instance, Belding Lodge was constructed at Camp Mishawaka to house ten- and eleven-year-olds, the youngest boys in camp. Now called Belding South to distinguish it from a comparable lodge built in 1950, Belding Lodge was a frame building covered with horizontal log siding and containing six sleeping rooms, each of which housed two boys and a counselor (Figure 3.20). At the center of the lodge was a communal room (called a "playroom" in brochures) fitted out with a fireplace and a rustic table and chairs (Figure 3.21). Older boys, however, continued to live in small cabins that lined the campus with military precision.[34]

It is worth noting that while these elaborate camper cabins are still in use in many camps, today they are inhabited somewhat differently. At Camp Lincoln, for instance, counselors assigned to first-floor units now sleep apart from their campers in what was originally the social room. Judging from camp-

Figure 3.20. Camp Mishawaka. Belding Lodge, built 1932, from brochure for the 1934 season.

Figure 3.21. Camp Mishawaka. Playroom at Belding Lodge, from brochure for the 1934 season.

planning literature of the 1950s, this shift seems less connected to changing perceptions of camper needs and more to a heightened awareness of the developmental needs of the young adults who worked at camps. These teenagers enjoyed a greater degree of autonomy than their prewar counterparts, and camp-planning professionals increasingly called for the "provision of some measure of privacy for the counselor."[35]

Seen against this backdrop, the elaborate cabins at camps Lincoln or Warren speak to the uneasy relationship that developed between camp and home in the first half of the twentieth century. With their porches, fireplaces, and spaces for social interaction within the cabin "family," these buildings incorporated many of the trappings of domestic architecture. Despite the inclusion of such details, these cabins were not meant to emulate the home; instead, they were intended to serve as seasonal surrogates, balancing correctives for the failings of conventional, unscientific home life. More than the result of a simple evolution in camp facilities, they were the products of changing perceptions of campers' physical and psychological needs.

SECURING HEALTHY BODIES AND SOUND MIND

Sleeping tents and cabins are ostensibly the most modest structures in any summer camp. Simple in form, they were typically built without the help of professional architects, often with the most commonplace of materials. Yet, they were rarely erected without serious reflection. At times, they were the focus of prolonged debate, much of it informed by a range of new scientific theories. Sustained initially by Victorian notions that contact with nature was inherently salubrious, tents were abandoned at many camps in the face of new ideas about the cause of disease, ideas that shifted so rapidly that other forms—particularly the tent-cabin and the wooden tent— quickly passed out of favor. More elaborate cabins not only shifted the focus to campers' psychological health, they also challenged the Victorian conviction that the mother-centered home was the best setting for raising children, especially boys.

If sleeping facilities for boys and girls differed little in form, it would be wrong to conclude either that the camp experience was the same for both sexes or that girls' camps simply followed the lead of boys' camps. Other components of the camp landscape reveal that perceived gender differences were sometimes built into the fabric of camp (as they were in sanitary facilities) and sometimes manifested in the way that camp activities were carried out (as they were in camp kitchens). In either case, physical changes in all parts of the camp landscape demonstrate that perceptions about the needs of children were in flux throughout the twentieth century, as was the very definition of childhood itself.

CHAPTER 4

Feeding an Army

Mealtime Rituals at Camp

IN 1919, THE BOYS AT CAMP RANACHQUA INTERRUPTED THEIR midday meal to turn their somewhat solemn faces toward the camera (Figure 4.1). Some of them had dark circles under their eyes, suggesting that they had not quite adjusted to sleeping on cots. Many wore the army drab favored by the Boy Scout leaders at this camp near Narrowsburg, New York. All of them sat on backless benches, facing rectangular tables covered in oil cloth and arranged in long rows under the broad roof of a rustic, open-sided dining pavilion. Once the photographer finished, they would return their attention to the contents of the white enameled dishes in front of them.

Such meals were an integral part of camp life, particularly during malnutrition scares in the 1910s, when the provision of ample, wholesome food was one of the explicit benefits of the camp experience.[1] Yet, at camps established far from running water and electricity, the challenge of providing three meals a day for dozens of campers was substantial. As camp populations grew, so did the difficulties involved in meal preparation, prompting many summer camps—including Ranachqua—to include a properly equipped kitchen in the first permanent building to grace the camp property.

Camp meals, however, were always more than an opportunity to build up scrawny campers. They were also key moments for camper socialization.

Figure 4.1. Camp Ranachqua, Harriman State Park, New York. Campers at table in the mess hall, 1919. Photograph by W. D. Hassler, New York.

Rigorously maintained mealtimes gave a clear and consistent structure to each day, even as mealtime order and routine functioned to reconnect campers with civilized human society after periods of rough-and-tumble activity in the more rugged corners of camp. These meals were ritual occasions, both in the sense that they tended to follow predictable patterns in which each participant had a clearly delineated role and also in the sense that those predictable patterns were intended to communicate, in nonverbal ways, important messages about the larger meaning of camp life. Meals were times when the camp community acted out for itself and others its own sense of its larger mission.

In short, camp meals were complex events, involving many human actors moving through several different spaces. While some of these spaces were well-defined architectural containers (like kitchens), others were created solely by human action. Both types of spaces contributed to what architectural historian Elizabeth Cromley calls "the food axis," a system of activity arenas devoted to food storage, meal preparation, eating, and cleanup.[2] By acknowledging that each meal is a chain of interlocking events, the concept of the food axis reminds us to take seriously the interconnections between seemingly disparate alimentary tasks.

In the late nineteenth century and beyond, mealtime practices took on heightened importance, as eating became (in historian John Kasson's words) "the most exquisite social test" of genteel behavior.[3] Despite the apparent contradiction of learning these behaviors in a rustic setting, meals shine a bright light on a camp's commitment to gentility and to class-inflected notions of gender roles. Especially in the early years of the camp movement, differences in mealtime rituals reveal a range in attitudes that are almost invisible in written statements about the importance of camping for boys. That those differences had begun to disappear by the 1930s is undoubtedly the result of the growing professionalization of camp directing in the period, but it also helps identify the moment when these professionals redefined the camp's role in the process of socialization. Once understood as bridges between childhood and the world of adults, American summer camps had sought to instill self-reliance and a sense of satisfaction at a job well done by maximizing camper involvement in food preparation while minimizing the use of cooking technology. By midcentury, American summer camps used a full range of kitchen technologies to distance campers from routine meal preparation, ultimately reinforcing the boundary between the realms in which adults worked and those in which children played.

The earliest private camps for boys served meals in remarkably similar settings: rough-hewn dining pavilions fitted out with deep piazzas supported by posts formed of tree trunks. Mealtime practices differed sharply, however, according to the degree of primitiveness to which they subjected campers. At one extreme was Camp Chocorua, where founder Ernest B. Balch insisted that boys do all the cooking and cleaning themselves. Balch employed no professional chef and prided himself that only tin dishes were allowed in camp. In contrast, Asquam and Pasquaney both employed professional cooks and used fine dinnerware. Pasquaney's founder, Edward S. Wilson, scoffed at the idea of "cooking one's own food (poor stuff at that!) and eating off of tin with jack knife and a two-pronged fork or no fork at *all!*" (emphasis in the original). In contrast, he advised a prospective counselor to impress upon parents that at Pasquaney "we have first class food and plenty of it and well prepared by a professional man-cook whom I pay $2.00 a day. We also eat off of *China,* and use silver-plated knives, forks, and spoons!" (emphasis in the original).[4] Wilson's attention to the details of table settings confirms his concern with maintaining new standards of gentility that had emerged in the late nineteenth century. As Kasson has pointed out, the two-tined fork (its sharp prongs made of iron, the better to fix the meat in place for cutting) and the associated practice of using the knife to put food in one's mouth had both been commonplace in the early part of the nineteenth century, but as early as the 1830s they were increasingly seen as "marks of rusticity and vulgarity." By the end of the nineteenth century, these older practices had fallen out of favor completely, and silver-plated flatware "had gone from being a luxury associated with the nobility to a ubiquitous necessity among the middle class."[5] Although Balch may have used tin dishes to evoke an old-fashioned unrefined quality, which many adherents of the new manliness had begun to reinterpret as a healthy antidote to overcivilization, for Wilson these older utensils could not be disassociated from their vulgar connotations and so were unacceptable, even at camp.

Among the camps that catered to middle-class boys, there was a great variety in the facilities for cooking and eating. At Camp Becket, meals were prepared in a kitchen attached to an open-air dining room, both housed within a rustic pavilion built in 1905, although such permanent buildings were rare in early YMCA camps (see Figure 2.7). In many others, meal preparation took

Figure 4.2. Camp Dudley, Lake Champlain, New York. Cook tent, circa 1895.

place in and around cooking and dining tents. Both facilities feature prominently in camp-planning advice published in 1902 by Edgar M. Robinson, the YMCA's international boys' work secretary, who based his recommendations on the experience of a number of successful YMCA camp leaders. As described by Robinson and as photographed at Camp Dudley in the 1890s, the cooking enclosure was a rudimentary affair (Figure 4.2). Although Robinson stated that "a shed of some kind is generally preferable to a tent for kitchen purposes," he went on to admit that "a few pieces of old canvas will serve as a roof, while the sides of the kitchen are frequently open."[6]

The technologies of cooking associated with this enclosure also varied greatly. At many camps (including Dudley), cooking was accomplished over an open fire with vessels supported on "six or eight bars of iron about four or five feet in length, either solid or made from old pipe . . . supported about eight or ten inches from the ground on stones." At other YMCA camps, iron stoves and ranges were employed, although Robinson downplayed their usefulness, noting that they were "difficult and expensive to transport."[7] His enthusiasm for portable bakers' ovens, however, was unqualified. Made of galvanized sheet iron, they were light and easily transported, especially after their cast iron coal-burning fireboxes were replaced by sheet iron fireboxes for burning wood. Another advantage for YMCA camps (whose operating expenses at this date were no more than one dollar per day per camper) was the low cost of these ovens, which could be bought secondhand either at bakeries or stove shops.[8]

Whether meals were made in cook tents or enclosed kitchens attached to dining pavilions, the responsibility for preparing food typically fell to a single cook, working with the help of campers. Although Robinson reported that "many of the small camps actually thrive on the management of amateur cooks," larger camps hired professionals.[9] Often these were African American men, whose presence preserved the all-male environment while also reinforcing the idea that some kitchen chores were beneath the dignity of white males. One former camper looked back on Camp Dudley's early history and dismissed these workers as "colored cooks without much experience," but a YMCA commentator at the time characterized the camp cook as "an aristocrat who must be treated with respect, for whom water must be pumped, errands run, and wood carried . . . a tyrant subject to no one."[10] Although offered with tongue in cheek, this comment suggests the authority that professional cooks wielded at camp. According to Robinson, camp cooks came from a variety of backgrounds. Some had been lumber camp cooks, others sea cooks, while many others had hotel or restaurant experience. By the 1910s, some camps hired white "chefs" who worked during the academic year at boarding schools and colleges; according to a 1910 brochure, cooking at Camp Becket was under the direction of James Allston, former chef at St. Margaret's School in Waterbury, Connecticut, while Camp Dudley engaged the services of Arthur M. Hall, steward of Springfield College from 1915 until his death in 1931.[11]

Even with the expertise of a professional cook, middle-class campers were deeply involved in routine meal preparation. Kitchen chores were often assigned to a small squad of campers on a rotating basis, although at many camps every camper was required to wash his own dishes at each meal. At mealtime, campers lined up, plates in hand, to receive their food as it was dished out by fellow campers, sometimes from a makeshift serving table, sometimes from the benches in the dining tent, like one photographed at a Boy Scout encampment on Hunter's Island in 1900 (Figure 4.3). After meals, campers lined up again to proceed through the dishwashing line, in which each person scraped, washed, rinsed, and dried his own dishes. Early camp literature celebrated this evidence of campers' usefulness with many pictures of boys cheerfully involved in all aspects of meal preparation: pumping water,

Figure 4.3. Boy Scout encampment, Hunter's Island, New York. Dining tent, 1912.

peeling potatoes, serving food, and washing dishes.[12] Somewhat different in character were campcraft and woodcraft lessons during which boys practiced cooking over an open flame—purportedly to equip them with the skills they needed to survive in the wilderness. In both activities, however, the line between work and play was intentionally blurred at early boys' camps, both in terms of who did the work and in terms of the spatial distinction between the areas used for cooking and eating. Food preparation was simply an integral—and highly visible—part of camp life.

On one level, this intimate involvement of male campers with food preparation—work conventionally assigned to women—seems at odds with the larger mission of the camping movement and its focus on forging a more virile mode of manhood. At another level, however, men had often accepted responsibility for cooking in the all-male environments evoked at early boys' camps—particularly in the military, at lumber camps, and on cattle ranches.[13] What is more, food preparation in certain nondomestic settings was becoming increasingly associated with middle-class, white men. Not only were restaurant and hotel kitchens increasingly the domain of a white, male professional—typically identified as a chef, rather than by the less prestigious, racially coded term *cook*—but images of men cooking over an open fire dominated depictions of all-male sociability in the late nineteenth century.[14] In *Camping in the Woods. "A Good Time Coming"* (an 1863 print issued by Currier and Ives), it is the guides who cook the day's catch, while the recreating fisherman pours himself a drink and surveys their activities (see Figure 1.15). Nonetheless, the scene celebrates a virile manliness by confirming male independence from women and their domestic influence, by underlining the self-sufficiency of these men, and by highlighting their ability to cope with the elements and even—in the case of the open fire—to command them. (Of course, the associations between manliness and cooking over an open fire still function in backyard cookouts at which Dad often "mans" the barbecue.) Equally important, the practice of giving campers kitchen duties on a rotating basis had obvious parallels with the army's practice of assigning soldiers to KP (or kitchen police) duty, a term that became common in the years before World War I. At Camp Durrell in 1906 the adult in charge of this squad was even known by the military sobriquet "officer of the day."[15] By paralleling the practices of the quintessential all-male environment, this system of organizing the labor of food preparation was perfectly consistent with the goals of early boys' camps.

When it came time to consume the meal, however, YMCA camps initially embraced a degree of gentility at odds with the metaphors of masculinity that dominated food preparation and even at odds with their own published statements. In a 1910 brochure for Camp Becket, for instance, prospective campers were warned that they "must not expect to find the dainties of the home table" at camp.[16] In *Camping for Boys,* on the other hand, Henry W. Gibson called upon his decade of experience as director of Camp Becket when he suggested that each camper be provided with a fulsome range of specialized dinnerware: "a large plate of the deep soup pattern, cereal bowl not too large, a saucer for sauce and dessert, a cup, knife, fork, table spoon, and tea spoon."[17] Although by no means as extensive as a formal dinner setting (Kasson notes, for instance, that by 1880 Reed and Barton offered as many as ten different kinds of knives, twelve kinds of forks, and twenty different spoons in each of more than a dozen flatware patterns), this setting suggests that camp food would achieve a degree of elaboration—with sauces and desserts—that went well beyond the requirements for good health.[18] With its choice of spoons, it also went well beyond the "vulgarity" associated with the antiquated practice of eating only with the knife and two-pronged fork, and might be considered the minimum needed to sustain newer middle-class standards of gentility. Likewise, Gibson's description of the camp table—"set with white oil cloth, white enamelled dishes, both serving and individual, with decorations of ferns, wild flowers or blossoms"—may have acknowledged and even celebrated the rusticity of the setting, but it also actively reinforced the importance of maintaining the material trappings of mealtime gentility.[19] Indeed, period photographs of Camp Becket show campers seated before evenly spaced place settings interspersed with specialized serving pieces—including vinegar cruets (Figure 4.4).

Equally telling are the time and attention that early camp organizers gave to the issue of table manners. In his summary of the best practices at early YMCA camps, Robinson devoted six full paragraphs to "the systematic arrangement of tables in the dining tent," dismissing the use of long tables with boys on both sides as disruptive to mealtime order. In his view, "to have a large number of boys laughing and joking together at a table, while waiters run up and down behind them shouting, 'Coffee! Coffee! Coffee! Bread! Bread! Meat! Meat!' is an unnecessary and unfortunate system of serving meals." Robinson advocated instead a number of smaller tables—one for each sleeping tent in camp—presided over by a leader who would "serve the food in approved family style." "Under this system," Robinson assured his readers, "decency and order of eating is [sic] preserved and the boys are not fed like animals at a trough."[20] Gibson was equally concerned with gentle mealtime behavior, declaring that "rough-house table manners are a disgrace to a camp even as small as six boys."[21]

Yet Robinson's condemnation of long tables confirms their use at those camps that modeled the dining experience more closely on the military mess, inspired perhaps by the actual encampments of the Great War. Camp Ranachqua is a case in point. Although less elaborate in its ornamentation than the dining pavilion at Camp Becket, this open-air dining room—with its perimeter marked by railings made of saplings and its solid roof supported by unhewn timbers—displayed many features also found in that earlier build-

Figure 4.4. Camp Becket, Becket, Massachusetts. Dining room in the pavilion, built by John E. "Pops" Gibson in 1905.

ing (see Figure 4.1). Despite such similarities, however, Ranachqua's mess hall functioned very differently, with military analogies now structuring meal-time rituals, as well as food preparation and cleanup. Of course, the very term *mess hall* was borrowed directly from the army, but so too was the arrangement of the dining space itself with long narrow tables aligned with the kitchen wall. The resulting seating arrangement facilitated food delivery by presorting campers into long queues that would lead to the serving table or serving window near the kitchen. At Camp Ranachqua, a table for leaders near the kitchen confirms that family-style dining advocated by Robinson was not practiced there.

While the military overtones of such dining arrangements were nominally in keeping with camp rhetoric, they held the potential for changing the tone of camp life in important ways. By imitating military order at mealtime, such arrangements sought not only to institute stricter control over camper behavior but also to achieve that control through external regulations, rather than depending upon the camper's internal sense of propriety. At the same time, by exposing campers to environments set up to coordinate the movements of a large number of people, the mess hall also implicitly introduced campers to the kind of rationalization that was increasingly shaping the work lives of American men—whether they labored in factories or in offices. In these mess halls, boys were encouraged to emulate adult males, but their activities were increasingly associated with routine work, rather than with the daring and heroism of the military scouts whose example had inspired Robert Baden-Powell and other early boys' workers.[22] To the extent that such arrangements treated the bodies of campers as so many interchangeable components of a large and efficient food delivery mechanism, they also undermined another important goal of the early camp movement, namely, to provide campers with a respite from "the indoor routine of city life."[23]

THE GIRL SCOUTS RESPOND

The degree to which the camping experience in general and the food axis in particular depended upon and reinforced notions about gender becomes even clearer when we consider the published advice regarding meal preparation at girls' camps. The advice offered in the Girls Scouts' 1920 *Campward Ho!* made it clear that female campers, like their male counterparts, should be intimately involved in food preparation at camp. The unidentified author's confident assertion that it is possible to feed 150 to 200 people "with only one cook and a squad of Scouts," was reinforced with multiple images of uniformed girls peeling potatoes, pumping water, and engaging in other cooking chores.[24] At the same time, the mess hall plan reproduced in the manual confirms the appeal of military metaphors and military order at Girl Scout camp—not surprising, perhaps, given the military overtones of the British Boy Scouts, which spawned both the Boy Scouts of America and the Girl Scouts (the American version of the British Girl Guides).[25] Like their male counterparts, Girl Scouts learned to cook over an open fire as part of their campcraft program.

Yet *Campward Ho!* also made it clear that Girl Scout camps were not to mimic every aspect of boys' camps. The author took particular exception to the dishwashing line in which each camper washed, rinsed, dried, and stored her own dishes. Such a system may have been easy, but it also broke "the rules being taught to Scouts as to the proper way of washing dishes: namely, to wash glass first, silver next, change the water and wash saucers, cups, plates and so forth." Not only was the dishwashing line unsanitary, it also offended the Girl Scouts' sense of the proper division of labor: "No mother would think of having each member of the family stack her dishes, take them to the sink, wash and wipe them and put them away. This method would be considered most inefficient and confusing."[26] Clearly, the Girl Scout leadership counted on the camp program to instill domestic habits that they expected girls to apply eventually in their own homes.

Such references to mothers as the ultimate authority in domestic matters suggest that the Girl Scouts embraced the various aspects of meal preparation as particularly female skills. Indeed, the amount of attention the manual devoted to the layout and equipment of the mess hall kitchen was unprecedented in camping literature and might be interpreted as an attempt to reinforce claims to female control over the kitchen. In this context, the invocation of efficiency is equally telling. On one hand, it is a reminder that this early phase of camping for girls coincided with the loss of live-in servants in middle-class households and with attempts by a new breed of female efficiency experts (chief among them Lillian Gilbreth and Christine Frederick) to teach middle-class housewives to apply principles of scientific management to the domestic sphere.[27] The new expectation that middle-class women would be more directly involved in every aspect of household labor meant that camp activities could no longer be considered generic exercises in usefulness. On the other hand, it is important to remember that the enthusiasm for efficiency had an ideological component. As architectural historian Dolores Hayden has argued, the application of so-called laborsaving technologies helped sustain conservative views of home life and women's domestic labor by undermining fledgling attempts at collective housekeeping.[28]

In line with changes taking place in middle-class homes, laborsaving technologies dominate the mess hall kitchen in *Campward Ho!* Gone is any reference to cooking over an open fire. While an integral woodshed suggests that the fuel source remained the same, the text itself emphasized the importance of a full-size range, noting that "the kitchen should be equipped with a good stove having ovens and hot water tank and be large enough to admit of holding big boilers and kettles." The same text even stated the desirability of installing a Standard Oil heater and boiler to provide piped hot water,

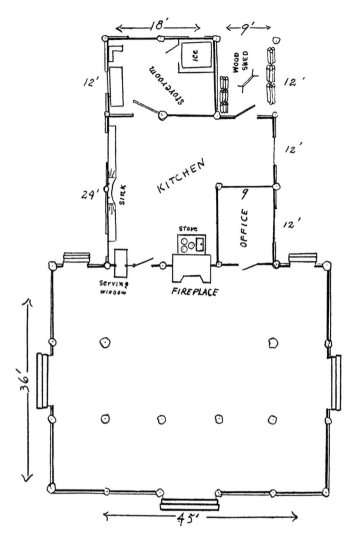

Figure 4.5. Mess hall plan for a Girl Scout camp of 150 to 200 girls, 1920. From Girl Scouts, *Campward Ho! A Manual for Girl Scout Camps*, 35.

although it also noted that such arrangements were not within the reach of most camps, as they required "a tank and power of some kind to pump up the water."[29] Yet, the kitchen plan published in *Campward Ho!* seems almost untouched by the sort of rationalization of space advocated by Frederick and other efficiency experts (Figure 4.5). Stove, sink, and serving window form a work triangle of sorts, but the inefficiency of the rest of the kitchen—particularly the way the office limits ready access to the other side of the stove—suggests that the triangle was something of a fluke. In other words, *Campward*

Ho! evoked the discourse of efficiency for rhetorical purposes, rather than to rationalize the functioning of the camp kitchen.

In short, ideas about gender had an important impact on campers' involvement with routine meal preparation at early summer camps. Although campers of both sexes were involved in similar kitchen duties, camp organizers accepted and even embraced different roles for men and women and so encouraged boys and girls to complete their kitchen tasks in different and (in their view) gender-appropriate ways and to imbue them with distinct and (they felt) gender-appropriate meanings. For boys, washing dishes at camp was something of a rite of passage, an unpleasant job that they were expected to take on cheerfully in order to demonstrate their solidarity with the group. But like the soldiers whose KP routines they emulated, male campers also understood their domestic servitude as a temporary state to be abandoned once they returned to their normal existence. In contrast, organizations like the Girl Scouts understood that meal preparation would itself come to define normality for the girls who attended their camps. Although the tasks themselves were not so different, the emphasis on order and method encouraged girls to see these domestic tasks as important in their own right and as direct practice for the daily routine of adult life.

MEALTIME RITUALS AND NEW IDEAS ABOUT CHILD DEVELOPMENT

By the 1930s, changes in camp philosophy transformed mealtime rituals along with the rest of the camp landscape. Convinced that children moved through distinct developmental phases that no amount of instruction or discipline could hurry them through, camp organizers not only adopted the decentralized unit plan, they also increasingly de-emphasized activities associated with the adult world of work. Instead of building camp program around routine food preparation, they placed renewed emphasis on activities associated with play and leisure: crafts, swimming, canoeing.

In camps that adopted the unit plan, meals were served in what was now called the dining lodge, one of the shared facilities located at the center of camp. In federal Recreational Demonstration Areas (RDAs) and the postwar camp-planning manuals that popularized their innovations, these dining lodges were T-shaped buildings, with long, narrow dining rooms set perpendicular to the kitchen wing (Figures 4.6 and 4.7). Although related to the form

Figure 4.6. Norway Point Group Camp, St. Croix River Recreational Demonstration Area (now St. Croix State Park), Minnesota. Dining lodge, designed by E. T. Waley, 1937.

Figure 4.7. Norway Point Group Camp. Plan of dining lodge. From Albert H. Good, *Park and Recreation Structures,* 3:166.

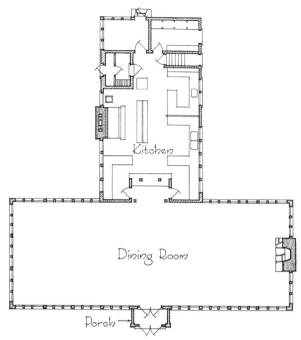

of earlier mess halls, this arrangement minimized diners' awareness of the kitchen. In part, this was achieved by reorienting the dining room away from the kitchen, a change reinforced by relocating fireplaces to the end walls. The T-shaped plan also deaccentuated the kitchen by introducing windows into the wall on the kitchen side of the dining room, an arrangement that enhanced an impression of the dining room as a freestanding structure. What is more, the introduction of separate a buffer zone between kitchen and dining areas helped ensure that kitchen sounds and smells were less likely to intrude upon the dining room.

Distinctions between the dining room and kitchen were further enhanced by formal differences. Camp dining rooms retained—and, in some cases, exaggerated—the rustic qualities of older mess halls. Indeed, camp histories often celebrate the work of local craftsmen who built the dining hall, hewing the logs for the walls and roof trusses, laying the stone for the fireplace, and forging hand-hammered light fixtures.[30] On the other side of the swinging doors, however, the kitchen was a high-tech environment. Like the school kitchen, which was also the object of professional scrutiny on the part of home

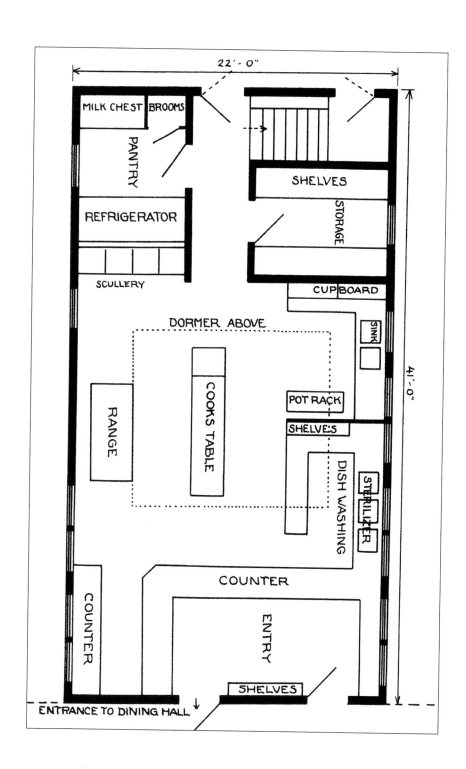

Figure 4.8. Camp Yakewi, Ashtabula County, Ohio. Camp Fire Girls kitchen layout, circa 1946. From Camp Fire Girls, *When You Plan Your Camp*, 19.

economists, the camp kitchen was planned in great detail to secure maximum efficiency, while facilitating sanitary practices aimed at protecting camper health and safety.[31] In fact, the kitchen plans reproduced in the 1930s and 1940s introduced an emphasis on rationalization that had been lacking in the kitchen layout published in *Campward Ho!* in 1920. In a kitchen plan for an organized campsite in the St. Croix River RDA in Minnesota, a prep sink is located in easy proximity to both the food storage zone and the kitchen range. In turn, this cooking area is close to the serving area, while both cooking and serving areas are close to the dishwashing alcove (see Figure 4.7). Kitchen layouts published by the Camp Fire Girls in 1946 and the Girl Scouts in 1948 were similarly zoned into storage, prep, cooking, serving, and dishwashing areas (Figure 4.8); by pulling the range and oven away from the wall, the Girl Scout plan created additional work stations—including one in the corner for a camp dietitian.

Equipment and materials further distinguished the high-tech camp kitchen from the rustic dining room. Indeed, in the 1940s, camp-planning literature advocated what was essentially a well-equipped commercial or institutional kitchen. "Hotel-type ranges," deck ovens, hot-water heaters, and electric refrigerators were all mentioned in the Girl Scout camp-planning manual, as were new fuel sources aimed at enhancing the cleanliness, comfort, and convenience of the kitchen—issues that had been of little concern in earlier cooking tents. These fuels included bottled gas, butane, fuel oil, and electricity—an unanticipated result of New Deal rural electrification campaigns. The Tennessee Valley Authority and the Rural Electrification Administration may have identified the electrification of American farms as their primary goal, but their efforts also brought electrical power lines within easy reach of camps.[32]

These new fuel sources and cooking appliances introduced to camp kitchens a level of precision necessary to meet more demanding health and sanitation standards. Whether fueled by oil or gas, dedicated hot-water heaters were needed to bring water to the 180 degrees required to disinfect dishes at the three-compartment sink (labeled "sterilizer" in the Camp Fire Girls plan); here dishes could be washed in warm soapy water, rinsed in clean water, and then immersed in 180-degree water for at least two minutes. Safe food storage called for comparable precision. While Julian Harris Salomon, the author of the Girl Scout planning manual, deemed the root cellar "a satisfactory place for the storage of vegetables," he dismissed other traditional methods for keeping food cool (including the use of springs and wells), noting that they were not reliable means for keeping food below "the safe maximum of 50 degrees." Even iceboxes were less than ideal. In their stead, Salomon advocated a range of electric refrigerators to facilitate the safe storage of different types of food: a walk-in refrigerator with separate compartments for meat and vegetables, a deep-freeze locker, and a reach-in refrigerator in the kitchen proper.[33] With their hard, reflective surfaces in industrial materials, these fixtures fundamentally altered the visual character of the kitchen, a shift that was reinforced by the switch to concrete floors (recommended both for fire protection and for easy cleaning).

These architectural changes in the dining lodge were paralleled by other revealing differences in mealtime practices. The terminology of the mess hall (with its implication that sustenance, rather than enjoyment, was the primary goal of the meal) was abandoned in favor of the gentler dining lodge (a term favored at rustic hotels where diners were expected to relish both their surroundings and the cuisine). Equally important, family metaphors reappeared, replacing military ones at every phase of the meal. Instead of being treated like interchangeable units slotted into production lines that delivered food and received dirty dishes, campers now took their meals family-style with their cabinmates. Instead of sitting with a mass of campers at long tables, they sat at small round tables of seven or eight, with parental supervision provided by their counselor. Instead of trooping individually through a cafeteria line, campers stayed seated while one of their number (called the hopper) went to the serving area to pick up platters of food for the table to share. Being hopper was a rotating job and also involved returning dirty dishes from the table to the dishwashing station. Official photographs confirm subtle changes in dining hall furnishings (including curtains, a sure sign of domestication) and the approved camper behaviors associated with them (Figure 4.9). The most significant change is the use of round tables that emphasized the unity of the cabin family, both by eliminating the head of the table (and the social hierarchy that could imply) and by facilitating eye contact among the entire group.

The rise of the dining lodge also coincided with important changes in labor organization, and especially in the tendency to remove campers from routine food preparation. While *Camp Site Development* (the 1948 Girl Scout camp-planning manual) mentioned that campers "may assist with kitchen tasks," it also emphasized the importance of restricting them to peripheral

Figure 4.9. Camp Conrad Weiser, Wernersville, Pennsylvania. Mealtime for campers and their counselor, circa 1950.

zones designed to limit their involvement with kitchen activities. One of these zones was the breezeway near the storage area, where campers could collect supplies for a cookout or an overnight trip, "without being constantly in the way of the professional cook."[34] The other was the serving area at the other end of the kitchen, where a solid counter prevented campers from trespassing into the kitchen proper, an arrangement the Camp Fire Girls also encouraged (see Figure 4.8). The high-tech kitchen was now firmly the province of paid staff, with lowly paid local youths furnishing the unskilled labor once provided free of charge by campers. More dependent on prepared foods—even frozen foods stored in the deep-freeze compartment—routine camp cooking had been stripped of all sense of adventure.

Cooking undertaken by campers as part of the camp program was now a completely separate activity that often took place in the unit lodge, the "common living room" for campers in a given unit. Architecturally, the unit lodge was a miniaturized version of the older mess hall; in both building types, for instance, the location of the fireplace and the placement of the kitchen in line with the long axis of the main room highlighted the presence of the kitchen, which was fitted out with rudimentary cooking technologies (see Figures 3.14 and 3.15). Indeed, Albert Good hinted in *Park and Recreation Structures* at a functional similarity between the two types, suggesting that "experienced camping groups may essay to cook all their meals in the outdoor kitchen [of the unit lodge]." [35]

Despite these formal similarities, however, the unit lodge came to play a very different role from that of the mess hall. Even Good had to admit that its primary function was not to facilitate routine cooking by campers, but to let them "use it on occasion for practice cooking or the novelty of preparing a meal or two, on their own." [36] Indeed, in the years after World War II, campers' cooking only rarely supplanted their regular meals. The more common pattern was for postwar camper cooking to supplement regular meals with snacks like s'mores, doughboys, or mock angel food cake, the recipes for which were published in the 1953 *Girl Scout Handbook*. [37] A far cry from the simple camp meals of earlier campcraft lessons, these delicacies relied heavily on the use of packaged foods. Skewered on or wrapped around the end of a green stick for cooking, they also lent themselves to indoor preparation in the fireplace of the unit lodge.

In one sense, the buddy burner represents the culmination of this trend in camper cooking. Intended to fuel the gypsy stove (an upended two-pound coffee can), the buddy burner was made by filling an empty tuna tin with corrugated cardboard and paraffin wax. Used by campers of both sexes on weekend camping outings throughout the postwar period, these were hardly cooking tools that youngsters could assemble quickly from nature's bounty. Nor did they encourage campers to practice future domesticity; despite the recommendation in the 1963 *Junior Girl Scout Handbook* that the buddy burner was "a good emergency fuel to have on hand if your stove at home should not work," these one-person stoves encouraged the sort of individualized approach to domestic tasks that had so bothered the author of *Campward*

Ho! forty years earlier.[38] Training campers neither for life in the wilderness nor for life at home, postwar camper cooking had been transformed into the stuff of childhood.

THE MEANING OF MEALTIME RITUALS

Cooking at camp, then, was never a simple, transparent process of supplying ample quantities of wholesome food. Rather, the food axis was a locus of struggle in which camp organizers tried to reconcile their own conflicting notions about class, gender, and, eventually, the very nature of childhood. At early boys' camps, for instance, camp organizers valued the chance to involve boys in food preparation and embraced military arrangements as appropriately manly settings in which to teach boys to do for themselves. Yet, they were often unwilling to abandon the mealtime gentility that was a defining characteristic of middle-class respectability. Put another way, the food axis was the site where camp organizers tried to negotiate the fine line between the civilized behavior that they still valued and the overcivilization that they had come to see as a threat to vital manliness.

Mealtime at girls' camps was equally complicated. Organizers may have been eager to claim kitchen activities as part of the female sphere, but they hesitated to involve girls in practices associated with the institutional kitchen—activities that did not translate easily into the kitchen of the single-family home. Indeed, camp directors embraced the technologically advanced industrial kitchens only when meal preparation had become a service adjunct to the camp's new focus on child-centered recreation.

Perhaps the very notion of technology as an ideologically neutral "service adjunct" undervalues its role in cultural institutions. After all, the industrialized kitchen did not disappear from the camper's experience of camp. Although midcentury kitchen plans kept campers behind a serving counter that prevented them from setting foot in the newly professionalized kitchen, these same plans also ensured that campers had an almost panoramic view of this industrialized environment. Everything about the new kitchen—its unfamiliar machinery, its reflective surfaces, its personnel—reminded campers that it was different from the rest of camp. Corralled in this separate realm and operated only by adults, midcentury kitchen technology reinforced in material ways the boundary between childhood leisure and adult work, and thus contributed to the larger mission of the camp.

A new, highly visible, high-tech kitchen was also a very public announcement of a camp's commitment to meeting new standards of sanitation that eventually transformed many aspects of the camp landscape. Besides the kitchen, the areas most affected were toilets and washhouses, where there was great potential for contaminating the camp water supply. In truth, however, the location and arrangement of these facilities had as much to do with cultural anxieties about gender as with science. In these very private zones of camp, youngsters learned discrete, but highly gendered, lessons about how to manage their own bodies.

CHAPTER 5

Good and Dirty?

Girls, Boys, and Camp Cleanliness

ONE SUMMER'S DAY IN ABOUT 1910, THREE BOYS GATHERED around a makeshift washstand that had been constructed from a biscuit crate and set up next to one of the tents that lined the parade ground at Camp Becket (Figure 5.1). One barefoot camper interrupted the process of brushing his teeth to smile at the camera. Another was about to wash his face (and perhaps upper body) in a small washbasin, having removed the sleeveless jersey that had left him with distinctive tan lines. His exposed garters suggested that he expected to don long trousers when he had completed his ablutions; his state of undress may explain his somewhat sheepish grin. The third boy combed his hair, studiously ignoring both the photographer and the small mirror hanging above the washstand.

Although relatively rare, photographs like this one are reminders that sanitation was a topic of considerable concern from the earliest years of organized camping. Securing an ample supply of clean water for drinking and cooking, disposing of human and kitchen waste, providing the means for campers to clean their clothes and bodies—these were issues that every camp organizer had to confront. Not only had cleanliness become the bedrock of late-nineteenth-century gentility, but medical science considered it key to the prevention of illness as well. This was particularly true as the germ theory of

Figure 5.1. Camp Becket, Becket, Massachusetts. Campers at an improvised washstand, circa 1910.

disease (first introduced to lay audiences in the 1870s) made inroads into the thinking of middle-class Americans, who by the early years of the twentieth century had developed what one later commentator dubbed "antisepticonsciousness."[1]

Convinced that their very lives depended on achieving a standard of cleanliness set by the operating room, these antisepticonscious Americans initiated wide-reaching campaigns to transform their physical environments. Hotels, Pullman sleepers, and restaurants were all touched by these efforts, but the middle-class home was the site most visibly affected by popular understandings of the germ theory.[2] Porches for sleeping and dining allowed fresh air and sunshine to sanitize rooms where the body was considered particularly vulnerable. Area rugs, sheer curtains, simple woodwork, and a prohibition on bric-a-brac were aimed at reducing the hiding places for visible house dust and invisible germs. White enamel surfaces and linoleum floors made it easy to identify areas in the kitchen that needed cleaning. But the bathroom was the locus of the greatest change, as the wooden cabinetry that disguised nineteenth-century tubs, sinks, and water closets was stripped away to expose the shape of the fixtures themselves. These fixtures (made of nonporous materials such as vitreous china and enameled iron) were white, as were the bathroom's tiled walls and floors, the better to reveal even a hint of grime. Arguably the first modern room in the American house, the early-twentieth-century bathroom imitated the hospital with its hard, white surfaces that could be kept antiseptically clean, provided the fastidious housewife availed herself of the many products marketed for her use.[3]

As standards of environmental cleanliness skyrocketed in homes and other institutional settings, however, summer camps did not simply follow suit. The issue was both philosophical and practical. Given the rural location of early summer camps, the installation of the kind of sanitary fixtures considered essential in a hygienic home was difficult, if not impossible. More important, such fixtures went against the philosophy of the camping movement, especially at boys' camps, which sought to distance male children from maternal influences and the material trappings of the feminized home. To the extent that advertisements and popular medical journalism encouraged the careful mother to accept responsibility for the hygiene of her whole family, fastidiousness itself had become feminized. Branded a mama's boy, the finicky male was an object of scorn, a figure who might be redeemed at a summer camp that did not overemphasize hygiene and the kind of personal modesty that usually accompanied it. The snapshot at the Becket washstand, for instance, reassured viewers that this camp produced boys who were willing to go barefoot and did not balk at being photographed in their underwear.

It is worth noting that issues of class and ethnicity complicate this reaction against male fastidiousness. As historian Nancy Tomes notes, being "spotless" was one strategy used by many African Americans and recent immigrants to overcome some of the more overt manifestations of racial and ethnic prejudice. Indeed, many camp organizers embraced the opportunity to introduce campers to standards of hygiene that inadequate facilities sometimes made unfamiliar in households of the urban poor. In this sense, the idea that it was acceptable for boys to be a bit dirty—even at camp—was a product of race and class privilege. [4]

Even at camps that catered to middle-class boys, camp organizers could not simply ignore hygiene altogether. Having staked their reputations on maintaining and enhancing the health of campers, they could not then subject their young charges to an environment that medical opinion and middle-class parents deemed unsanitary. (Not that these views were identical; indeed, lay audiences were often more ready to embrace the germ theory of disease than medical doctors, who had the clinical experience to question the findings of bacteriologists.) For many camping authorities the solution to their quandary lay in making a distinction between clean and dirty dirt. According to Henry W. Gibson, "Cleanliness is not the shunning of good, clean dirt, but a recognition of the fact that to pass anything from one mouth to another is a possible source of death and destruction."[5] In other words, camps needed to carve out a space for themselves somewhere between sanitary and fastidious.

A closer look at the camp landscape reveals that such a space was narrow and ever changing, in large part because the minimum threshold of sanitation crept higher and higher over the course of the twentieth century. (This trend did not affect summer camps alone, of course. It was so general a tendency that by the end of the century, some experts had begun to argue that this concern with cleanliness had gone too far; keeping children antiseptically clean compromised their ability to build effective immune systems.) Ideas about sanitation also varied with the sex and age of campers. If female campers were required to take a different approach to camp tasks that paralleled their future household duties, gender differences became even more acute when the camper's body was at stake.

Cleanliness was on the minds of camp organizers from the earliest years of the twentieth century. Eager to identify sanitary practices that would meet at least minimum standards of safety, they provided a ready audience for published advice on camp sanitation—much of it written by medical experts. But if camp directors hoped scientific expertise would simplify the process of establishing a sanitary camp, they were wrong. Despite the fact that Louis Pasteur and Joseph Lister had posited the germ theory of disease as early as the 1860s, many medical doctors held fast to the older theory that miasmas—foul and stagnant air—caused disease. What is more, when supporters of the germ theory voiced warnings about bacterial "clouds" of airborne germs, the practical distinctions between the new bacteriology and the older sanitary science were somewhat difficult to discern. In short, the germ theory of disease emerged unevenly and served, initially at least, to confound discussions about the source of disease and the best ways to combat its spread.[6]

Two early works on camp sanitation published under the auspices of the YMCA reveal just how disparate expert medical opinion could be, even in the first decade of the twentieth century. One was a long article by Elias G. Brown titled "The Sanitary Care of a Boys' Camp" that appeared in 1902 in the very first issues of the YMCA's new journal, *Association Boys*. A medical doctor who would go on to found Adirondack Camp in Glenburnie, New York, in 1904, Brown embraced a view shared by many sanitarians and germ theorists alike, namely, that disease was (in the words of Dr. Henry Hartshorne) the result of "human interference" in "the original balance of primeval nature." Thus, the camp experience itself—far from the "artificial constructions" Hartshorne blamed for causing illness—was already an important means of restoring and maintaining good health.[7] In Brown's view, all that was required was "to give nature a chance to build us up and breathe into us that fund of health and vigor which will be of so much help during the coming winter."[8] Nature, in other words, was a beneficent living entity that breathed out fresh air in order that humans might breathe it in.

Brown's conception of nature as a force for good meant that he had little advice to give regarding a camp's water supply—despite the fact that the connection between tainted water and the spread of cholera had been well established by the middle of the nineteenth century.[9] He admitted that it was essential to have ready access to water for cooking and cleaning, but ignored the possibility that water found in nature might be contaminated in any way.[10]

According to Brown, the safe disposal of human waste was also a relatively simple matter. He recommended finding a wooded site well removed from camp and out of the prevailing wind. All that was needed was a three-foot-wide trench deep enough to last the entire season. A simple rail attached to two trees and positioned over the edge of the trench provided the only seating. Undoubtedly haunted by images of filthy enclosed privies in tenement neighborhoods, he discouraged the use of a privacy fence or enclosure, and argued that an overhead covering was allowable but unnecessary. The only care required, according to Brown, was "that an inch of earth should be thrown in daily." Particularly important was that "no place nearer camp be used," as even "a little carelessness here and there in a large camp will cause disagreeable if not dangerous results."[11] In short, only human waste generated at the camp itself posed a serious threat to the water supply.

Compare this advice with that offered in Gibson's 1911 *Camping for Boys*. Although not a doctor himself, Gibson placed himself squarely in the camp of germ theorists, quoting at length from a paper by bacteriologist Charles-Edward Avery Winslow and conjuring lurid images of flies "that drink of cesspools, dine at privy vaults, eat sputum and are likely to be the most familiar guests at the dinner table . . . leaving in their tracks disease-producing germs which had adhered to their sticky feet."[12] Nature, in Gibson's view, was hardly the benign entity that Brown had envisioned, watching out for human health. Instead, the natural world was a complex environment with the potential to enhance good health as well as to damage it. Flies, after all, were a part of nature that if left unchecked could cause havoc with camp sanitation. The wind could provide fresh air, or it could disperse excreta. The summer sun could kill germs, or it could speed the decomposition of waste. What was worse, it was impossible to tell just by looking whether conditions were safe. Nature could be deceiving.

For such adherents of the germ theory of disease, the camp environment was not inherently safe and camp sanitation required great vigilance. Securing a clean water supply was a particular challenge. Despite the common conviction that running water purifies itself, Gibson (quoting Winslow) warned that "streams are particularly dangerous sources of water supply," as "a bright, clear stream . . . may be polluted at some point above." Somewhat safer were ponds, as long as they could be inspected all around for sources of

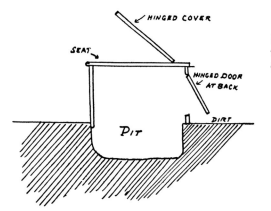

Figure 5.2. Schematic drawing for latrine with hinged lid, 1911. From H. W. Gibson, *Camping for Boys*, 29.

contamination. Better still was groundwater from a well or spring, although even these sources required constant attention to ensure protection from surface contamination from the camp's own waste water.[13]

Gibson was equally concerned with the safe disposal of human waste, advocating relatively elaborate toilet arrangements, even in temporary camps. In addition to Brown's concerns about the olfactory isolation of the toilet, he also alerted camp directors to the need to ensure that the area drained away from the camp's water supply. For an encampment of a week or more, Gibson recommended digging a trench (as Brown had described), but then building an enclosed box with hinged lids over "shaped seating" to exclude flies. The whole arrangement was to be surrounded by a six-foot canvas. In permanent camps, he called for the construction of "regular wooden closets" with covered roofs and hinged doors at the back so that the contents could be removed each week (Figure 5.2). In either case, Gibson envisioned greater attention to latrine maintenance: sprinkling dry earth in the trench after each use, applying chloride of lime to the trench each morning, scrubbing the seats with hot water and sulpho-naphthol daily, and providing a box for used toilet paper.[14]

Experts also differed in their advice on the disposal of kitchen scraps and other garbage. While Brown simply recommended emptying kitchen refuse barrels daily into a deep ditch "at some considerable distance from camp," Gibson emphasized the importance of using a covered galvanized iron pail for kitchen garbage and disposing of it "before decomposition takes place." Gibson agreed with Brown that garbage could be buried (specifying three or four inches of dirt), but a "better plan," in his view, was to burn the garbage in an incinerator. He also addressed an issue that Brown ignored completely when he advised against throwing "dirty dishwater promiscuously on the ground." Instead, there should be a trench for the purpose, which (like the latrine) would be sprinkled daily with chloride of lime.[15]

DIFFERENCES BETWEEN BOYS' AND GIRLS' CAMPS

The sanitation advice offered in early literature on girls' camps differed little from the advice for boys' camps—at least in terms of physical arrangements. For Girl Scout camps, the anonymous author of *Campward Ho!* recommended securing drinking water from a well or spring and burning kitchen garbage in a trench dug for the purpose. For toilet facilities, this author echoed Gibson's advice that temporary camps could make do with a boxed-in earthen closet, with seats fitted out with hinged covers, the whole arrangement protected by canvas. Since it was "considered a misdemeanor to throw cloths of any kind into a latrine" (a coded allusion to sanitary napkins), the only addition for girls' camps was a portable incinerator in which menstruating campers were to burn their soiled napkins. In terms of environmental precautions for camp sanitation, then, the needs of boys and girls were considered identical.[16]

Differences arose, however, when it came to the campers' roles in camp sanitation. To encourage campers to take to heart the importance of camp sanitation, Gibson advocated forming a board of health. Made up of an equal number of boys and camp leaders, this group would make a thorough round of daily inspections, "condemn everything that was unsanitary, and correct all sanitary disorders." Gibson also envisioned this board organizing a series of talks on "Sanitation and Health," and even suggested as possible topics "Flies and Filth" and "Johnnie and the Microbes." If camp organizers followed Gibson's advice to the letter, they would also have all the boys in camp write essays on these lectures.[17]

In contrast to Gibson's board of health, on which boys worked side by side with adult leaders in an emulation of the civic functions that they could be expected to take on as men, *Campward Ho!* advocated a "housekeeping squad," on which girls served under the direction of a single leader, practicing for the private duties that awaited them as wives and mothers. While much of the squad's time was involved in food preparation, the hours after breakfast were devoted to cleaning and beautifying the camp landscape: cleaning the mess hall, washhouse, latrines, campgrounds, and lanterns; burning trash; folding napkins; and filling vases with fresh flowers. Unlike the executive role played by the board of health (which first identified unsanitary conditions and then corrected them), the housekeeping squad carried out predetermined rituals of cleanliness reminiscent of the domestic rites advocated in the publications of Catharine Beecher and her successors. Not only were the time, place, and manner of their work directed by others, but the requisite tasks were also independent of any informed assessment of the site's sanitary condition. By including "fold napkins" and "clean latrines" in the same list of housekeeping chores, *Campward Ho!* reveals that sanitation at Girl Scout camps was part of a broader concern for camp order that extended well beyond the demands of good health.[18]

THE TECHNOLOGICAL RESPONSE

As much as camp directors may have hoped to keep camp sanitation simple, several factors prompted them to install more elaborate systems to provide clean water and to remove human and kitchen waste. The growing acceptance of the germ theory itself was one factor; by shedding doubt on nature's inherent goodness, it opened the door for greater human intervention in the natural environment. Increased competition between camps also played its part, as guides like those published by Porter Sargent starting in 1919 gave parents an easy way to compare facilities at hundreds of camps. In the 1920s, many states began sending health inspectors to summer camps, a practice that may have given camp directors added incentive to invest in sanitary technologies (although the impact of government health inspections is not as straightforward as it first appears).

The chemical toilet enjoyed a degree of popularity in the 1920s, offering as it did a means of meeting the demands of modern sanitation without having to install a full septic system. In 1920, Gibson had nineteen chemical toilets installed at Camp Becket. Manufactured by the Kaustine Company of Buffalo, New York, they used "an odorless crystalline sterilizer" to reduce sewage to a harmless liquid that would contaminate neither water nor soil. While such units were a great boon to camps that relied on untreated water, their aesthetics also appealed to germ theorists like Gibson. In his 1923 book, *Camp Management*, Gibson continued to support the earth closet as a "very practical" solution to waste disposal, but he described the Kaustine units in detail, emphasizing their "white china bowls, good seats, and white enamelled pipes"—the white, hard surfaces that had become the visual sig-nifiers of an antiseptic environment.[19] (Gibson remained a supporter of the Kaustine toilets into the 1930s, when he paid $197.63 to have two installed at Chimney Corners Camp, a private girls' camp that he and his wife directed after his retirement from Becket.)[20] While it is not clear how many YMCA camps followed Becket's example, three Kaustine toilets were certainly used at YMCA Camp Belknap in New Hampshire, where they were fondly chris-tened Yale, Harvard, and Dartmouth.[21]

Campward Ho! suggests that chemical toilets were used more widely. Not only did this manual recommend such facilities for Girl Scout camps, it also advocated the particular type developed for the Palisades Interstate Park: a simple structure with box seats built over a concrete-lined pit charged with water and Kaustine sterilizer. Wooden paddles attached to a five-foot length of pipe served as agitators to bring "solid matter" into contact with the Kaus-tine solution in order to facilitate decomposition. Although less elaborate and undoubtedly less expensive than Becket's manufactured units, these site-built latrines used the same chemical process and inspired a similar confi-dence; according to *Campward Ho!*, "it is not necessary to use disinfectants with this type of house."[22] By 1926, the third edition of Porter Sargent's *A Handbook of Summer Camps* listed three suppliers of sanitary systems, two of which highlighted chemical toilets in their ads.[23]

Flush toilets were also becoming more common in the 1920s, at least at camps that could afford the capital investment. Of the ninety-one private camps that paid for announcements in Sargent's 1926 *A Handbook of Sum-mer Camps*, almost 15 percent highlighted their provision of "the most mod-ern sanitation," "sanitary plumbing," or "modern conveniences." Some, like Camp Moy-Mo-Da-Yo in Cornish, Maine, made explicit the connection be-tween its modern sanitation and its "'Class A' rating from the State Board of Health." All of these camps charged between $250 and $400 for the eight-week season, with most charging more than $300.[24] In contrast, YMCA camps cost between $5 and $10 per week during that same year. At $135 for the sea-son, YMCA Camp Dudley was expensive by association standards. Even so, it was only a "generous gift" from Mrs. Hamilton M. Barksdale in 1923 that allowed Dudley to purchase a mountain spring, build a 52,000-gallon res-ervoir, and pipe water four miles to provide drinking fountains, flush toilets, and, eventually (in 1928), hot showers.[25]

The treatment of camp sanitation in camp announcements raises some interesting questions of what was driving the installation of flush toilets. As Camp Moy-Mo-Da-Yo's announcement reveals, state health inspections had become an issue. At least twelve states had instituted some form of health inspection by the mid-1920s, although some were more rigorous than others. New York amended state sanitary regulations for labor camps in 1924 to include all camps occupied by ten or more persons for a period of six days or longer; the next year three state health workers (two of them working full time) helped local health officials inspect more than five hundred camps. In Pennsylvania, health inspections were the responsibility of seven district engineers, who visited camps in the course of their regular rounds, reaching about one hundred camps a year by 1925. In contrast, voluntary inspections were the rule in Rhode Island, North Carolina, Michigan, and New Jersey; in this last case, the Department of Health inspected only twenty-eight camps between 1923 and 1925.[26]

Given responsibility for guaranteeing sanitary conditions, these inspectors tended to hold camps to a very high standard of cleanliness. In Maine, for instance, only camps that screened their dining porches against flies could receive an A rating. In a 1924 report on more than one hundred camps inspected in Massachusetts, the director of the Division of Communicable Diseases found two-thirds in "reasonably clean condition," but characterized the water supplies and sewage disposal of more than half as "questionable, poor, or definitely bad." Although sanitation regulations did not require flushing toilets, such modern conveniences made it easier to pass inspection.[27]

State health laws are not the only reason modern sanitary conveniences found their way to camp. Directors often volunteered to have their camps inspected, indicating that they valued visible, demonstrable proof of their adherence to good sanitation. While other types of toilet facilities could be made sanitary, flush toilets *looked* the part as well. That modern plumbing featured so heavily in their advertisements suggests that parents, too, accepted flush toilets as an important sign that a camp would safeguard the health of their children. At the same time, flush toilets infiltrated camps only selectively, with girls' camps being three times more likely than boys' camps to tout their modern sanitary appliances in announcements in Sargent's 1926 *A Handbook of Summer Camps*. (In contrast, boys' camps tended to skirt the issue of flush toilets; the announcement for Camp Skylark in Billerica, Massachusetts, instead promised that "sanitary conditions will bear the most critical inspection.") Thus, flush toilets and other technological responses to camp sanitation were not simply a reaction to state intervention, but were instead part of the ongoing project of summer camp: to reform gender roles while maintaining gender distinctions.[28]

In the immediate postwar period, the major camp organizations encouraged camp directors to turn to technology to solve the challenges of camp sanitation, regardless of the sex of the camper. Both the Girl Scouts and the YMCA advocated the use of drilled wells and power pumps to deliver water not only to the kitchen but to a growing range of camp facilities: infirmary, caretaker's lodge, shower house, drinking fountains, and (in some camps) swimming pool. The cost of a well and pumping equipment could be as high as $3,000 (according to the Girl Scouts' *Camp Site Development*), high enough that the Girl Scouts warned camp organizers against buying sites that required deep wells. Even when organizers could avoid the expense of a deep well, they were still encouraged to consult both a geologist and an engineer to ensure that the system was properly installed.[29]

Sewage disposal was likewise transformed in the late 1940s. In the Girl Scouts' *Camp Site Development*, Salomon acknowledged that "the old-fashioned plain privy is the cheapest and most easily maintained camp toilet facility," but recommended the flush toilet as "the most satisfactory and convenient."[30] In contrast, the Camp Fire Girls considered dry pit toilets to be temporary measures only, whereas the YMCA ignored the existence of any facility but a flushing toilet. All three organizations recommended the professionally engineered septic tank as the safest way to treat sewage.[31]

Even garbage disposal was affected by these new technologies. Once a camp installed a septic tank, for instance, it also needed a grease trap near the camp kitchen to keep grease out of the pipes and sewer lines. The balance of the garbage could be buried or burned, but campers were distanced from this unpleasant task. In the YMCA camp layout published in 1946, the garbage pit and incinerator were located on the edges of camp, well beyond the outpost cabin; easily reached by the main road, they were presumably accessed by car or truck (see Figure 1.18). The Girl Scouts went even further in isolating campers from garbage disposal, encouraging camp organizers to have it "hauled away and disposed of in a sanitary manner."[32]

If such systems had implications for the camp budget, they also affected the campers' experience. The latrine and other time-honored methods for water supply and waste removal had been cheap and easy to set up, but they needed constant vigilance and substantial camper cooperation to maintain.

In contrast, the technology-based systems advocated after World War II required professional expertise and a sizable capital investment to install, but could function with minimal camper input. Neither Gibson's board of health nor the Girl Scouts' housekeeping squad was required to keep these systems working. In the postwar camp bathroom, as in the postwar camp kitchen, adults manipulated new technologies in ways that shielded campers of both sexes from routine labor. Where early camps had helped campers (who were admittedly older adolescents) to begin the transition to adulthood, their postwar counterparts cocooned campers (who were now younger children) in a world of recreation.

CLEAN MIND IN A CLEAN BODY

While many postwar camps relieved campers of the chores required to maintain a sanitary camp environment, most put a new emphasis on facilities in which campers could keep their bodies clean—another departure from early camp practice in which the only provision for bathing was the lake or other natural body of water. The difference can be traced back to ideas about the relationship between bathing and health. In the nineteenth century, the health benefits of bathing were associated with invigorating the blood system by immersing the body in cold water. Bodily cleanliness might be desirable in polite company, but it was not considered a requisite for good health. Later, when the role of the skin was understood as a system for removing waste, a hot bath—or better yet a hot shower, which carried dirt and dead skin away from the body—became an important means of maintaining good health. At this point, the practice of immersing the body in cold water was renamed swimming and redefined as muscular exercise. These two approaches to bathing overlapped for some time, and even in the early twentieth century, reformers campaigned for the erection of public bathhouses, in which tenement dwellers could get clean by frolicking with others in large pools of tepid or cold water.[33]

Thus it was that the lake was considered an ample facility for bathing, especially at early boys' camps. Unconcerned with the camper who bathed too little, early experts worried that campers would spend too much time in the lake, losing the body heat that they equated with vitality. Brown was convinced that "some boys come home at the end of the summer actually run down from this one cause alone."[34] In *Camping for Boys*, Gibson quoted parts of Brown's warning verbatim, including his advice that boys should be encouraged to take a quick dip before breakfast and then "a good swim in the warm part of the day," a practice that many camps followed.[35] By 1923, Gibson no longer discussed swimming in connection with bathing the body, hailing it instead as "the best of all gymnastics for the involuntary muscles."[36] There is no mention, however, of any other facility where campers might clean themselves or conduct the toothbrush drills that Gibson described at length; period photographs of Camp Becket (like the one at the beginning of this chapter) reveal that toothbrushing, hair combing, and face washing took place at an improvised washstand shared by several campers at a time.

In contrast, postwar camp-planning literature put a greater emphasis on facilities for keeping campers' bodies clean. Writing for the Girl Scouts, Julian Salomon noted that "the idea that campers can be kept clean by an occasional soap scrub in the swimming-hole has been pretty well abandoned." What was required was "some place in camp where campers can get a hot cleansing bath." Since the cost of installing and maintaining hot showers in each unit was high, he recommended building a central shower house near the administrative unit, a suggestion he put into practice at Camps Bliss and Hayden (described in the Epilogue). The YMCA's postwar camp-planning manual included plans for both a central shower house (although they called it a washhouse) and a smaller version for use in each unit (Figure 5.3)—the arrangement represented in the manual's idealized layout for a camp with a capacity of 125.[37]

HYGIENE AND THE FEMALE CAMPER

The specific arrangements within these shower houses, however, varied with the sex of the campers and staff. Girls and boys were treated differently throughout the twentieth century. As early as the 1910s, for instance, the Girl Scouts typically provided a washhouse for campers' use. At some camps this was nothing more than a table covered with zinc, supplied with pitchers and basins, and protected from the elements with a tent fly. At others, the washhouse was a permanent structure, typically a rectangular building open on three sides. Camp Mary Day in Massachusetts had such a washhouse when it opened in the early 1920s. Nicknamed Tidy Tim, it had just two faucets, which campers used to fill individual washbasins; an early rendering of the camp landscape shows washbasins hanging in neat rows along one side of

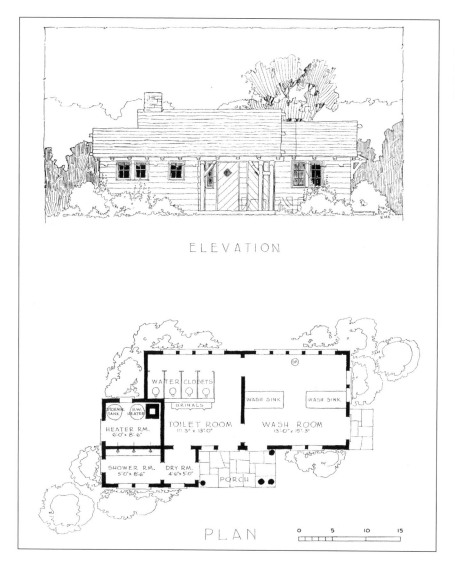

ELEVATION

PLAN

0   5   10   15

Figure 5.3. Unit washhouse for a YMCA camp, 1946. From John A. Ledlie, ed., *Layout, Building Designs, and Equipment for Y.M.C.A. Camps*, 48.

the building (see Figure 1.11). In other camps, like one pictured in *Camp-ward Ho!*, the washhouse included multiple faucets serving a long, zinc-lined trough that ran the length of the building (Figure 5.4).

Laundry facilities were another feature unique to girls' camps; although Brown had commented on the need for the occasional washing of clothes at YMCA camps, he indicated neither where clothes would be washed nor who would provide the needed labor. In contrast, female campers were

Figure 5.4. Washhouse at a Girl Scout camp, circa 1920. From Girl Scouts, *Campward Ho! A Manual for Girl Scout Camps*, 31.

encouraged to keep their clothes clean in laundry sinks typically provided in washhouses. The washhouse in *Campward Ho!* included two soapstone laundry sinks at one end and, at the other, private laundry rooms. Designated primarily for the use of counselors, these facilities were also available to campers "when given special permission"—another discreet reference to the girls' menstrual periods.[38]

This attention to menstruating female campers speaks both to early-twentieth-century worries about the bodies of adolescent girls and to the active role summer camps played in allaying those concerns. Cultural anxieties about menstruation were nothing new, of course; many cultures have taboos about contact with menstrual blood. But in the late nineteenth and early twentieth centuries, uneasiness about menstruation was exacerbated by medical doctors, who did not fully understand the biological basis of the process. Many maintained the Victorian belief that age at menarche was a moral issue; early menarche was accepted as a sign of sexual licentiousness and assumed to be common among primitive cultures from hot climates. In contrast, late menarche was associated with higher levels of civilization and with temperate climates. Thus, the bodies of adolescent girls were closely watched for reassurance that Victorian America was still civilized. Even if menarche arrived at the appropriate time, it was understood to be a critical moment at which a girl's health could be secured (if she established a regular cycle of menstruation) or destroyed (if she let education or activity get in the way of her "periodicity"). Convinced that early childbearing was detrimental to a girl's health, doctors and other middle-class Americans saw the years between menarche and marriage as a time in which a girl's purity was particularly at risk.[39]

Girls' camps addressed these concerns by providing a range of wholesome pursuits that, it was hoped, would help prolong adolescent female innocence. In addition to safeguarding the late menarche of girls from middle-class white families, camp activities were also aimed at delaying menarche in girls from families who were neither white nor middle class, thus supporting a biological change that was understood to help them achieve a higher level of civilization. At the same time, camping helped move ideas about female biology in a new direction, encouraging menstruating girls to maintain a level of physical activity that was a far cry from the Victorian prescription to retreat to the couch. The Girl Scouts even reversed the Victorian prohibition on telling girls in advance about menstruation (the fear was that such knowledge could induce menarche and so threaten the foundations of civilization itself). Through the Health Winner badge, the organization came to teach about menstruation in the 1920s, requiring a scout to learn about the physiology of the process and to have a private talk with her leader about it.[40]

Thus, the washhouses at early Girl Scout camps did not simply make provisions for menstruating girls; they were in addition an attempt to teach girls the right way to menstruate—a process that was revolutionized by the commercial availability of "sanitary" products beginning in the early years of the twentieth century. Since the use of these products was uneven (especially across generational lines within immigrant families), laundering reusable napkins made of old linen and cotton remained a necessary task well into the 1930s and 1940s.[41] Even women who used disposable napkins would need to clean clothes accidentally soiled with menstrual blood, so washing facilities continued to be important.

In providing private laundry rooms where this washing could be kept out of sight, camp washhouses facilitated the widespread adoption of "menstrual etiquette," architectural historian Rebecca Ginsburg's apt term for the cultural requirement "that women hide the fact of their periods, both in the general and in the particular, from others, especially men."[42] Of course, Victorian women of the middle class had practiced great discretion about menstruation and other bodily functions, but in the twentieth century menstrual etiquette became a cultural ideal for girls of all backgrounds. Given that young women attended camp early in their menstruating lives and that many would have experienced their first menstrual periods as campers, summer camps were well positioned to reinforce and encourage practices that girls also learned at home and at school. When a girl experienced menarche at camp, a sympathetic leader could take her aside to explain that there were ways to ensure that no one would *know*—using a napkin, disposing of it properly in the incinerator (itself concealed "in a closed box . . . in one corner of the latrine house," per the author of *Campward Ho!*), and washing her things in the *other* room, not in front of the rest of the girls.[43]

In truth, the concealment was never complete; for a camper to enter the counselors' laundry room was to admit that she had permission to cope with "special" laundry. Yet, like the coded language used in *Campward Ho!* and other camping manuals aimed at a female audience, such a protocol allowed everyone to maintain the illusion that menstruation was invisible. At the same time, the nature of the laundry itself—which squeamishness about menstrual blood made especially distasteful and which germ theorists considered dangerous—rendered private washrooms particularly important; without separate washtubs in which to soak bloodied garments, menstruating campers would certainly contaminate other girls' clothes.[44] In training girls to protect one another from their own menstrual blood, such rooms reinforced the very sensibility that gave menstrual etiquette its power in the first place.

Given these cultural imperatives, camp organizers were loath to record sanitary arrangements in any detail. But rare photographs of two washhouses at Chimney Corners Camp suggest that concerns about managing the bodies of menstruating campers extended well beyond the pages of camp-planning manuals. One image shows washing stations in an outbuilding attached to the back of the Nest, an 1804 house that had been converted to camp use in 1931; the youngest campers (those between the ages of seven and twelve) lived there, "thus avoiding the danger of trying to keep up with older girls," according to an early brochure (Figure 5.5). Although the washhouse was not equipped with running water, its individualized fittings were arranged to minimize the dangers of contact infection (a concern that had begun to dominate the thinking of germ theorists in the 1910s).[45] These included individual towel racks, soap dishes, and washbowls of white enamel (stored below the long counter that lined the perimeter of the room). Each of these basins was labeled with a girl's name, according to the memoirs of an early camper, who also recalled counselors filling the basins with water they pulled from the well.[46] The lessons implicit in the arrangement of the washhouse were made explicit in the posters lining its walls. With captions like "A clean machine

Figure 5.5. Chimney Corners Camp, Becket, Massachusetts. Washhouse at the Nest, circa 1931.

runs better. Your body is a machine. Keep it clean," and "Wash and be safer," these posters instructed campers on the links between health and hygiene.

Quite different in character was the purpose-built washhouse that served girls between the ages of thirteen and fifteen in a unit called the Eyrie (Figure 5.6). Although it, too, was fitted out with individualized washing stations in a room that had large openings on two sides, it also included an enclosed room at one end that seems to have housed the two toilets mentioned in camp records. A tall stovepipe reveals that this room was equipped with an incinerator, a device that *Campward Ho!* had deemed essential for the unobtrusive and hygienic disposal of sanitary napkins. By including the exhaust pipe in this carefully composed image, the photographer announced the incinerator's presence, but only to those who understood what it was; the photograph thus offered wordless reassurance that Chimney Corners campers would learn the right way to handle their monthly periods—once they reached the appropriate age. Indeed, the building's distance from the Nest ensured that younger girls would remain innocent of menstrual routines, perhaps a holdover of the Victorian idea that knowledge of menstruation induced menarche. While menstrual etiquette precluded the use of posters to reinforce its precepts, the building itself taught the Eagles lessons in hygiene every bit as important as those communicated to younger girls at the washhouse in the Nest.

In the postwar period, menstrual etiquette was enhanced by the provision of private toilet and shower stalls, which were widely recommended in

Figure 5.6. Chimney Corners Camp. Washhouse at the Eyrie, circa 1931.

the camp-planning manuals published by the Girl Scouts and the Camp Fire Girls. In the former, Salomon insisted that "for quite some time now, separate shower stalls for girls have not been considered a necessity," and recommended installing a single private shower stall in the section of the building designated for staff and visitors "which may be used by campers when desirable"—another coded reference to menstruation.[47] Yet only one of the two shower house plans in Salomon's *Camp Site Development* featured a gang shower, and it included a private shower booth for camper use. Given that girls had camped for decades without access to such private spaces, these shower houses were hardly a response to campers' innate sense of modesty. Instead, their careful attention to female privacy—particularly during menstruation—speaks more to the anxieties of camp organizers, who provided these settings in which campers had little choice but to enact reassuring rituals of modesty.

More telling still is the way in which these shower houses helped set a high standard for female cleanliness, both for their bodies and for their clothes. Laundry trays remained a common feature of shower houses for girls; they appeared in the dressing room in the Camp Fire Girls plan, while one of the Girl Scout plans located them in the boiler room, where they were more private and also accessible to employees (Figure 5.7). What is more, all of these shower house plans put great emphasis on the complete cleaning of the female body in the shower. Not only did the plans require campers to enter the

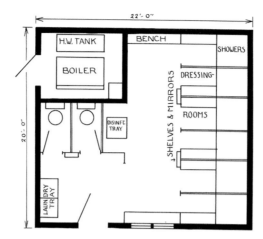

Figure 5.7. Camp Sealth, Seattle, Washington. Camp Fire Girls shower house, circa 1945. From Camp Fire Girls, *When You Plan Your Camp*, 46.

building through the dressing room (suggesting that disrobing was a prerequisite for every encounter with soap and water), but the number of showerheads outnumbered toilet stalls by at least four to one in the Girl Scout plans and by three to one in the plan published by the Camp Fire Girls.

In contrast, boys were neither encouraged to maintain privacy (except while defecating) nor expected to clean their whole bodies with any frequency. The shower houses in the YMCA manual included three areas for campers: a toilet room that included private toilet stalls and gang urinals; a washroom with large wash sinks, each of which could be used by six to eight boys at a time (a room type that had no parallel in the published plans of girls' shower houses); and a gang shower, with a communicating dry room (see Figure 5.3). In each case, the shower room was a small adjunct, with toilets outnumbering showerheads (two to one, in the central shower house). The toilet and washrooms were expansive in comparison; boys could access these large rooms through multiple doors, and there was easy communication between them. Girls may have been encouraged to clean their entire bodies, but a quick washing of the upper body at the gang sink was evidently sufficient for boys.

THE GENDERED MEANING OF CAMP CLEANLINESS

In the end, summer camp sanitation highlights the difficulties of putting science into practice. To be sure, camp organizers were eager consumers of medical advice and stood ready to reshape the smallest details of the camp environment in order to safeguard the health of their young charges. Nonetheless, increased scientific knowledge did not translate directly to clear and consistent instructions for arranging latrines or securing clean drinking water. The issue was not simply that medical doctors offered conflicting theories about the cause and transmission of disease. Rather, it was that sanitation remained closely intertwined with cultural ideals, which were highly gendered and largely impervious to scientific rationales.

Early in the twentieth century, the impact of gender ideology on sanitation was most evident in campers' involvement in the regular routines of camp maintenance. While camp directors encouraged boys to assume authority for identifying sanitary problems, they expected girls to shoulder responsibility for ameliorating them. These differences were muted only when camp directors came to embrace notions of a carefree childhood, installing sanitary technologies (flushing toilets chief among them) that relieved campers of their more labor-intensive sanitation duties.

At about the same time, a new focus on the dangers of contact infection heightened adult concerns about campers' bodies. This change, which affected girls and boys in very different ways, was no simple reflection of those concerns, however. Indeed, the menstruating bodies of adolescent girls seemed in particular need of management, and camp seemed an ideal place to introduce young women to the practices of menstrual etiquette. Ironically, the very sensibility that informed such practices made it difficult for camp organizers to engage in open discussions of a topic that was so much on their minds. Instead, they counted on their arrangement of the camp landscape to tell campers what was expected of them.

As campers moved from the private zone of the washhouse to the public arena of the council ring, they continued to encounter lessons embedded in their surroundings. Although ideas about gender had an impact on the form and use of the council ring, issues of race came to the fore. Indeed, in settings where they played at being Indian, campers learned what it meant to be white.

CHAPTER 6

Living like Savages
Tipis, Council Rings, and Playing Indian

IN 1908, SEVERAL BOYS GATHERED AROUND A CAMPFIRE ON a cool summer evening (Figure 6.1). Some sat on benches arranged in a large circle around the fire, while others circumambulated the flames, bent low, stepping to the rhythm of a skin drum played by a mustachioed man in a fringed tunic. One of the dancing boys also wore a fringed shirt, as well as a full feather headdress. Similarly dressed, one of the seated boys contemplated the scene from a roughly carved rock throne. A totem pole of sorts was situated behind the throne, not far from the frame for a tipi that stood in the shadows.

As captured on a photographer's plate, the scene was a strange mélange, for mixed among the motifs borrowed from the Plains Indians were details of early-twentieth-century life in white America; most of the boys wore kneesocks, brogues, and knickerbockers, and had cropped hair. And while the photographer's caption identified the scene as a "council & war dance," it also specified the setting as Wyndygoul, the Connecticut estate of naturalist Ernest Thompson Seton, the man beating the drum. Had they wished to do so, this band of "Indians" could have traveled by train to New York in less than an hour.

In fact, this image depicts an encampment of the Woodcraft Indians, a

Figure 6.1. Ernest Thompson Seton and Woodcraft Indians conducting a council and war dance at Wyndygoul, Cos Cob, Connecticut, 1908.

youth organization that Seton had founded in 1902 to introduce white boys to the ways of Native Americans. For many former campers, this photograph might seem to document a time-honored, perhaps even a natural, association between camping and playing Indian. But such attempts to impersonate Indians only became commonplace at American summer camps in the 1920s, and then only in very selective ways. Indeed, the use of Indian motifs varied widely in the first half of the twentieth century and depended both on white attitudes toward Native American populations and on white opinions about the needs of white children.

INDIAN, SAVAGE, CHILD

As historian Philip Deloria notes, white Americans have a long and complex history of playing Indian, one that dates as far back as the 1730s. Sometimes, whites adopted Indian dress in order to reinforce what they saw as their cultural and political distance from Britain, while at other times Indian guise served to highlight the contrast between "savage" Native Americans and the "civilized" European Americans who were colonizing their land. Initially, Indian play was overtly political, with Indian garb used as an intentionally incomplete disguise for men who flouted laws they deemed unjust. By the middle of the nineteenth century, groups like the Improved Order of Red Men used Indian motifs as the cornerstone of their fraternal rituals.[1]

The practice of playing Indian moved in new directions in the late nineteenth and early twentieth centuries, particularly in a new and widespread tendency for Native Americans themselves to play Indian. As their land and resources were taken from them, some may have felt they had little choice but to partake of the commodification of their own cultures, enacting the role of Indian in performances scripted by whites: in Buffalo Bill Cody's Wild West shows, in ethnographic displays on the Midway Plaisance at the 1893 World's Columbian Exposition in Chicago, in craft demonstrations at Fred Harvey's Hopi House on the south rim of the Grand Canyon, or in sittings for white photographers like Edward S. Curtis, who published more than 2,200 images of Native people in *The North American Indian*.[2]

Whatever reasons Native American people may have had for participating in these displays of Indian life, the stories they enacted often contributed to the larger ideological project of naturalizing the white conquest of North America. His Wild West shows, for instance, glorified Cody's bravery while also celebrating a government policy of genocide.[3] More complex were the photographs that Curtis considered objective, even scholarly, documents of authentic Indian life. But as photo historian Martha Sandweiss has demonstrated, these images simultaneously constitute an invented visual record, one that "denied the cultural complexities of the historical present." Curtis's photographs of the Plains Indians, for instance, ignored the presence of the railroad, while emphasizing activities—such as mounted war parties or ceremonial dances—that were no longer openly practiced on reservation lands. Likewise, his portrait photographs typically highlighted antiquarian costumes and captured sitters against blank backgrounds that isolated them in a timeless space. By reinforcing the idea that Indians were inherently incapable of adapting to modern culture, these selective slices of Indian life helped convince white audiences that the disappearance of Native American culture was a natural development unrelated to the cultural annihilation perpetrated by European Americans.[4]

Given their ideological purposes, these performances often focused on the Plains Indians who were offering the most active resistance to white conquest in the last decades of the nineteenth century. This is especially true of Wild West shows, which attracted enormous audiences by reenacting the Battle of the Little Big Horn and other battles from the Indian wars. As a result, the accoutrements of Plains Indian culture—especially the tipi, which featured prominently in posters for Wild West shows of the 1890s—became generic symbols of Indianness.[5]

The other new development in playing Indian was the tendency for white children to adopt Native American roles, a distinctly twentieth-century phenomenon fueled by the collision between the modern sciences of anthropology and psychology. Many anthropologists (at least before the rise of cultural anthropology spearheaded by Franz Boas) identified Indians as an inherently and thus permanently primitive people, genetically unable to participate in the process of evolution.[6] While this view contributed to the idea that Indians were a vanishing people, it also positioned Indians as the children of the human race. In the early twentieth century, psychologist G. Stanley Hall reinforced this idea of Indianness when he posited that child development recapitulated human evolution and that each child (although he meant each white child) moved through a series of developmental stages from savagery to civilization. According to Hall, white children were not only closer to Indians than they were to white adults, but their development also could be derailed if they were forced to adopt too soon the trappings of white civilization.[7]

If Hall's theories conflated the terms *child*, *savage*, and *Indian*, antimodernist sentiments helped strip savagery of some of its negative connotations. Alarmed by the enervating effects of modern urban culture, antimodernists embraced aggression—in the new sport of football, in Teddy Roosevelt's charge up San Juan Hill, in tales of knight errantry, and in the impersonation of marauding Indians—as a means of connecting modern men (and less often, women) to more authentic modes of living.[8] Thus, while whites had once equated the terms *savage* and *blood-thirsty*, antimodernists like Hall and Seton considered savagery a useful antidote to effete modernity and an integral ingredient in the protection of "robust, manly, self-reliant boyhood."[9] Savagery, in short, was a valuable weapon for resisting what Charles Fletcher Lummis (Seton's friend and fellow member of the Sequoya League) called "the maw of 'snivelization.'"[10]

Thus, playing Indian came to dominate a number of youth organizations established in the early years of the twentieth century, the best known of which was Seton's Woodcraft Indians. As the group's name suggests, woodcraft—Seton's term for a wide range of skills required to live in the woods—was a key component of the program. Making a fire with only two sticks was the most theatrical of these skills and one that Seton reveled in demonstrating. As they mastered such woodcraft skills, boys earned individual "coups," which lead to promotion to the ranks of sachem and sagamore. Organized into "tribes," they participated in Indian-inspired rituals, learned Indian lore, and practiced the kind of self-government that Seton felt was one of the most admirable aspects of Indian life.[11]

Seton's influence extended well beyond the Woodcraft Indians. In addition to inspiring his friends Luther and Charlotte Gulick to establish the Camp Fire Girls as a distaff version of the Woodcraft Indians, he played a leading role in the early years of the American version of the Boys Scouts in 1910. Although he would later complain that Robert Baden-Powell's *Scouting for Boys* included passages borrowed freely (and without attribution) from *The Birch-Bark Roll of the Woodcraft Indians*, Seton accepted the title of chief scout, positioning himself—unsuccessfully, as it turned out—to counteract the military overtones of the fledging Scouting organization.[12]

In truth, not everyone shared Seton's admiration for "the best things from best Indians."[13] As architectural historian Elizabeth Cromley has pointed out, the turn of the twentieth century was a moment when Indians (and the objects they crafted) carried a range of meanings that "reflected deeply ambivalent feelings held by predominantly white culture about the changes wrought by modernity." So, while Seton (and others) tended to see Indians as timeless and close to nature, others continued to emphasize what they interpreted as the inherently warlike qualities of Native American culture, a view that was particularly important after the bloodshed of the Civil War, when European Americans needed reassurance "that they held civilized ground." [14]

Firmly within this latter group was Daniel Beard, whose Sons of Daniel Boone encouraged modern boys to model themselves on the hardy pioneers who had battled Indian resistance as they pushed west to fulfill America's Manifest Destiny. In this scenario, Indians retained older stereotypes as bloodthirsty savages who stood in the way of progress and bore little resemblance to the noble, nature-loving people celebrated at Seton's council fires. While both men lent their support to the Boy Scouts (Beard eventually became national scout commissioner), Seton exacerbated his differences with Beard through references to "treacherous, murderous, worthless" frontiersmen. By 1915, Beard used Seton's preference for Indians over "clean and moral" pioneers to flame the nationalistic furor that prompted the ouster from the Boy Scouts of the chief scout (who lived in the United States, but retained his Canadian citizenship). [15]

In short, playing Indian at summer camp took place within a complex historical context in which "Indianness" itself was an unstable concept and in which the practices of Indian play were in flux. Indeed, these disparate modes of playing Indian—by Native Americans and by white children—became intertwined at summer camps, where antimodernist performances of Indian life often borrowed from the visual vocabulary established in Wild West shows.

THE LIMITS OF EARLY INDIAN PLAY AT SUMMER CAMP

Before World War I, references to Indian life were relatively few at most American summer camps. To be sure, several early camps took Native American names, but for every Chocorua, Pasquaney, or Mishawaka, there were dozens of other camps named for people connected with the camp's history (such as Camp Dudley, which honored Sumner Dudley, an early camp leader), for more historically distant role models (Camp Lincoln, established in 1909), for an important institutional affiliation (Groton School Camp, founded in New

Hampshire in 1893), or more prosaically for a nearby town (Camp Becket in the Berkshires).

What is more, the Indian names adopted at early summer camps were related to established place-naming practices in that they typically made reference to local landscape features. Camp Chocorua, for instance, was named for a mountain near the camp's New Hampshire site. Likewise, the founders of Pasquaney and Asquam christened their camps with the Indian terms for local natural features; Pasquaney was the Indian name for Newfound Lake, while Asquam stood on the shores of Squam Lake.[16] Even as late as 1910, Camp Mishawaka took a name that meant (or at least was understood to mean) "coming out of the woods into a clearing."[17]

This is not to say that Indian names played no part in furthering a camp's mission. The choice of the name Pasquaney, for instance, helped disguise the fact that the campsite had only recently served as the hayfield for a farm owned by the director's father. By reverting to Native American place-names, camp organizers could present the camp landscape as a wilderness environment untouched and untamed by white civilization.[18]

This association between Indians and wilderness was reinforced in other ways, particularly in field trips aimed at introducing campers to the "natural history" of the camp's locale. At Camp Mishawaka, campers who had demonstrated their proficiency in woodcraft (which brochures for 1913 and 1915 described without reference to Indian lore) were allowed to go on a number of overnight trips, including one to "the old Indian reservation on Lake Winnibigoshish." The appeal of the trip was to "see the primitive Indian, the last of his race," and to look at a host of artifacts—animate and inanimate—that were understood to hover on the brink of extinction: "the birch bark canoe, the tipi, the wigwam, the papoose, the squaw, and the medicine man." At this date, Mishawaka campers were not encouraged to take up and use any of these artifacts. Instead, these objects were valued primarily as material proof that the area is "one of the few regions in the country untouched by civilization."[19] In this scenario, Indians themselves—seemingly unable to adapt to modern life—were not highly valued, although their presence was understood to confirm the purity of the natural landscape.

Beyond these brief encounters with Native American culture, there were few full-blown attempts to play Indian at early summer camps, even at camps with Indian names. References to Indians in Henry W. Gibson's *Camping for Boys* were rare indeed and included games like Indian and white man, a "battle royal" between one team representing "white people . . . traveling over the prairie," and the other the Indians who attempt to capture the whites after they lie down to sleep for the night. Far from the antimodernist view of Indians as noble savages, such games reinforced older perceptions of Indians as sneaky and violent, while naturalizing white claims as the rightful inheritors of the North American continent. Although campers impersonated Indians during this game, they did so only fleetingly and without any expectation that they would benefit from the portrayal.[20]

Even the evening campfire and the campfire circle—an event and a site that became closely associated with playing Indian in the interwar period—drew upon a wide variety of cultural practices in the early years of the twentieth century. Camp leaders devoted little attention to describing the physical arrangement of the evening campfire, presumably because they counted on their readers' familiarity with the concept. Indeed, in the last half of the nineteenth century, images and descriptions of many kinds of campfires were widespread. There were Winslow Homer's Civil War depictions of military campfires, both in paintings and in engravings published in mass-circulation periodicals like *Harper's Weekly;* images of sportsmen's campfires in the Adirondacks, produced by artists like Arthur Fitzwilliam Tait, and reproduced in engravings by Currier and Ives in the 1850s and 1860s (see Figure 1.15); literary descriptions of Indian campfires in the novels of James Fenimore Cooper or the poetry of Rudyard Kipling; or even in bonfires that became a ritual of American collegiate life at the end of the nineteenth century.[21]

Early published advice suggests that camp leaders had many, if not all, of these sources in mind when they built fires at camp. Gibson recommended a wide range of campfire stories: "Indian legends, war stories, ghost stories, detective stories, stories of heroism, the history of fire, a talk about the stars." The music he suggested was equally varied, ranging from "college songs [that] always appeal to boys" to ballads like "My Old Kentucky Home." Even his firemaking advice embraced both the Indian method of rubbing two sticks together and the more modern technique of using a match to light kindling doused in kerosene. In short, most early camp leaders felt free to evoke several types of campfires.[22]

Having left the symbolic meaning of the campfire somewhat fluid, early-twentieth-century camp leaders were free to use the evening program to highlight aspects of the camp experience they found most significant. In early YMCA camps, for instance, the campfire was deployed to aid in the process of religious conversion. *Association Boys* served as a clearinghouse for the most effective campfire strategies, and by 1905, YMCA campfires followed a similar progression: popular songs, then patriotic songs followed by a few hymns, and finally, "when the right time has arrived," according to one account, "the leader or an assistant steps forward, and in the beautiful silence of the night, delivers a short, pointed, religious talk." Built into this program was a gradual transition from the boisterous activity of the day to a quieter moment of introspection. At the same time, because the choice of the particular songs emerged from the boys, the campfire retained an air of spontaneity that may have allowed campers to see it as an event that they initiated.[23]

Even in this early period, the fire itself was understood to impart a special quality to the evening program. At Camp Tuxis in Connecticut, one Sunday evening campfire ended with the leader's observation that camp kindles a fire in the heart of each boy that he carries back to the city to light other hearts. At the close of the campfire, "Each boy was then handed a candle and a long line was formed from the top of the hill to the cottage." The light was passed from boy to boy until "Finally the light was passed into the dark parlor of the cottage and boys filed in one by one and took their places in a semi-circle around the fire place. . . . As the leader resumed his talk he leaned over and touched the long flame to the material in the fire place, and in a moment the entire room was beautifully illuminated. As the talk proceeded and the fire died down, the intensity of feeling deepened and the testimonies given must have gladdened the very host of heaven."[24]

The passing of the sacred light from the campfire to the parlor fireplace is telling in that it upsets Victorian formulations of the relationship between gender, piety, and the domestic setting. Rather than seeing religious sentiment emanating from the woman seated at the domestic hearth (as Victorians had done), this ritual situates the origins of religious feeling in the wilder parts of nature and places responsibility for domesticating piety in male hands. Indeed, this shift is one example of a much larger fin de siècle tendency to reverse what Ann Douglas has dubbed "the feminization of American culture" that began in the first half of the nineteenth century.[25]

This willingness to invert conventional certainties was widespread—if uneven—in the early twentieth century as white, middle-class Americans struggled to define who they were and what they believed in the face of a rapidly changing world. Many doubted the value of modernity, of cultural refinement, of civilization itself. Thus, while many men and women—camp organizers among them—held fast to their negative opinions of so-called primitive Indians, others were not so sure.

WYNDYGOUL AND WOHELO: PIONEERS IN PLAYING INDIAN AT CAMP

In the early twentieth century, a handful of antimodernists began to experiment with summer camp as an ideal setting for playing Indian. Seton devised the details of the Woodcraft Indians program at summer encampments held at Wyndygoul. Likewise, the Gulicks refined the programmatic workings of the Camp Fire Girls at summer camps that they organized initially for their daughters and a few friends, but that gradually grew into full-fledged summer camps that are still in business. Together these early pioneers established modes of playing Indian that became widespread at American summer camps in the interwar period.

According to his autobiography, Seton established his first camp in order to harness the destructive energy of neighborhood boys who had vandalized his property. Located in Cos Cob, Connecticut, Wyndygoul was a 120-acre tract of farmland that Seton bought in 1900 and promptly transformed into a rustic retreat for himself and his first wife, Grace Gallatin Seton. (Convinced that he was a descendant of the Scottish Earl of Winton, Seton named his holdings for a noble estate in Scotland.) In addition to commissioning a rambling stone-and-stucco house, he remade the natural landscape, planting birch and pine trees in what had been pastures, erecting bridges to highlight the stream that fed an alder swamp he transformed into a lake, introducing waterfowl and other kinds of wildlife, and laying out nature trails throughout the wooded (and reforested) property.[26]

At one level, the estate was always part of Seton's public persona, serving as a laboratory for his work as a nature writer. It was here, for instance, that he built a hollow tree in which to conceal himself while he observed wildlife. Seton published drawings and stories that resulted from these observations, as well as detailed descriptions of the tree itself.[27] At the same time, however, the stone pillars and iron gates at the entrance announced that Wyndygoul, like other suburban estates, was intended as a private refuge, protecting the Setons (and after 1904, their daughter, Ann) from the bustle of urban life.

When local boys found that Seton's transformations had blocked their access to woods they had used for hunting, they retaliated by tearing down fences and scrawling obscenities on Seton's gates. Convinced that he could make friends with the anonymous miscreants, Seton invited all the boys at the local school to a weekend campout on his land at an Indian village he had constructed there. As incongruous as it seems to build tipis on a suburban estate with Scottish pretensions, Seton's biographer H. Allen Anderson maintains that the landscape transformations at Wyndygoul were attempts to reverse Frederick Jackson Turner's frontier thesis, by "allowing the primeval wilderness to reclaim the pastoral . . . [and thus helping] to return the West to the East." Thus, in Seton's mind, his corner of Connecticut was an ideal setting for playing Indian.[28]

On Good Friday, 1902, forty-two boys presented themselves at Wyndygoul. After a swim and a meal, they gathered around the fire to listen to tales of Indian life, stories that prepared them to accept Seton's suggestion that they should organize their campout "in the real Indian fashion." According to Seton, this included the use of Indian names (Seton himself was Black Wolf); democratic elections (for head war chief, second war chief, third war chief, and a council of twelve that included chief of the council fire, keeper of the tally, and keeper of the wampum); the adoption of a constitution (which, among other things, forbade rebellion against the council); and the agreement that boys could wear feathers on their heads (an idea that Seton credited to the boys themselves), but only if they earned each feather by winning honors in activities specified by Seton: individual athletic activities, "campercraft," and nature study. According to Seton and to participants interviewed decades later, the weekend was a great success: the vandalism ceased, the boys were set on the path to respectability, and a national movement was launched.[29]

Seton continued to host short-term encampments at Wyndygoul and later at DeWinton, a house he built in Greenwich, Connecticut, in 1915. In 1908, both Wyndygoul and its Woodcraft activities were recorded in photographs now in the collections of the Library of Congress (Figure 6.2; see also Figure 6.1). Above all, the images reveal a widespread use of Indian artifacts: tipis, totem poles, council rings, hatchets, clubs, drums, bows, and arrows. Boys did not just use Indian names while camping at Wyndygoul; they also impersonated Indians, adopting generic modes of Indian dress (wearing feather headdresses, fringed tunics, and blankets) and assuming the stony expressions of the Indians—seemingly resigned to the inevitable disappearance of their race—photographed by Curtis and others. (In truth, the blankets may

Figure 6.2. Camp of the Pocatopog Tribe at Wyndygoul, 1908.

have been primarily for the photographer's benefit or even the photographer's idea; they appear only on still figures in the most carefully composed photographs, where they could be used to cover the street clothes that several boys wear in photographs of more animated activities, such as the war dance.)

The images also suggest that boys were divided into "tribes," each of which established its own campsite, which often centered on a tipi. Although Seton reportedly scorned the ugliness of tents and encouraged the widespread use of tipis as shelters for the campers, the photographs reveal that tents were still in use in 1908, while tipis seem to have been reserved for "chiefs." At the camp of the Flying Eagles, for instance, a boy in a full feather headdress was photographed sitting alone in front of the single tipi, while other "braves" tended the fire nearby. At the camp of the Pocatopog Tribe, the photographer arranged the picture to reinforce the symbolic importance of the tipi; merging compositionally with the figure of the "chief," the tipi's large shape and light color are set apart from the smaller, darker grouping inhabited by the other members of the tribe (see Figure 6.2).[30]

The tipis at Wyndygoul reveal Seton's familiarity with the structures built by Native Americans, especially in their overall silhouettes, the prominent appearance of smoke flaps fitted out with pockets to hold the long poles that support them, the application of painted decoration, and the use of wooden pegs to join the edges of the tipi cover over the door. Even the use of canvas (which appears to be the material employed) has a precedent among Native Americans, who began using this lighter material in the late nineteenth century. Their small size and the practice of folding back the tipi cover to create a large triangular entrance (all the better to frame the figure of the "chief" sitting at the threshold) mark the tipis at Wyndygoul, however, as the products of white invention. Native American tipis were entered through small oval openings that could be covered with door flaps, and the pride of place was at the rear. More significant than these formal inaccuracies is the use of a building tradition that was foreign to the Algonquian people who had been living in the area before the arrival of Europeans and whose most common house type was the wigwam, a small, dome-shaped hut covered with bark or mat. The tipi (with its buffalo hide cover) was a distinctly western form, used by the Sioux, the Cheyenne, the Pawnee, and other warrior-hunters of the Great Plains.[31]

While the use of the tipi is consistent with Seton's policy of cultural appropriation, adopting "the best things from the best Indians," it was undoubtedly influenced by the Wild West shows, which had conflated the Plains Indians as representing all Indians in the white imagination in the late nineteenth century. To be sure, there was an ideological component of this fusion. Tipis evoked a nomadic existence and helped justify the taking of land that whites saw as unused, or at least underused, by indigenous people. At the same time, photographers like Curtis and Roland W. Reed often presented tipis as a visual echo of the Rocky Mountains, helping to reinforce the association between the tipi and the western frontier—the home of the last vestiges of a vanishing race (Figure 6.3). Not only did tipis feature prominently on Wild West posters, but show Indians were often housed in tipis as they traveled across the country as an advertising ploy. And indeed, Buffalo Bill Cody's success lay in his ability to convince eastern audiences that any piece of real estate could be transformed, at least temporarily, into the western frontier. Thus, in just the way that Seton's young neighbors had associated wearing feathers with playing Indian, they may also have seen tipis as simply the most Indian of Indian building forms. Whatever Seton's notions about the lawfulness of Indian culture, boys may have also accepted the stereotype of the Plains Indians as inherently warlike and interpreted tipis as an appealing backdrop for their more savage games of impersonation.[32]

Figure 6.3. Chief White Quiver, Piegan (Blackfeet), addressing his council, Glacier National Park, Montana, circa 1912. Photograph by Roland W. Reed.

Seton tapped into boys' interest in tipis by publishing detailed informa-tion on their construction and decoration in his early *Ladies' Home Journal* articles (1902) and then reissued the information in *The Book of Woodcraft* in 1912. Describing the construction of a ten-foot tipi "of the simplest form," these instructions were geared specifically toward boys who Seton was con-vinced would prefer this small tipi to a larger one, "as it is much handier, cheaper, and easier to make." Made of twenty-two square yards of six- or eight-ounce duck, the tipi cover would cost about five dollars, although Seton noted that it was also possible to use secondhand materials (such as an old wagon cover or a couple of old sheets) that "cost next to nothing." He even encouraged tipi-building boys not to turn up their noses at mended materials, arguing that Indian tipis were often patched "where bullets and arrows have gone through them." Through sketches and words, Seton described how to make a tipi cover (complete with smoke flaps and oval doors), how to set up the supporting poles, and how to hoist the cover into place.[33]

Seton also provided sketches of fourteen different decorative schemes that he had observed on tipis in the field. Highlighting the authenticity of the designs, Seton in some cases identified the tipi owner by name, along with the location and date of the sighting; Seton came across Hairy-Wolf's tipi, readers learn, on the upper Missouri in 1897. In fact, throughout the text, the naturalist treats tipis much as he does specimens of natural species. His anecdotes emphasize the challenges involved in tracking down and capturing each tipi's likeness in his sketchbook, while his drawing of nine tipis, divorced from their context and ranged in three rows of three, is akin to his comparative drawings of birds or flowers (Figure 6.4). Despite Seton's assertion that he "could not go among the red folk and order [a tipi] as in a department store," his text does reveal that the cash nexus facilitated his tipi-stalking. Not only did he pay the women of Hairy-Wolf's family three dollars to set up the tipi so that he could sketch it, but he also bought a tipi "ready made" from Thunder Bull, "chief of the Cheyennes."[34]

Seton himself, however, placed greater symbolic importance on the campfire that burned at the center of the council ring. As he explained in his 1912 work, *The Book of Woodcraft*, the campfire was closely associated with the very emergence of humankind. According to Seton, "When first the brutal anthropoid stood up and walked erect—was man, the great event was symbolized and marked by the lighting of the first campfire. For millions of years our race has seen in this blessed fire, the means and emblem of light, warmth, protection, friendly gathering, council." Although his language is deeply informed by evolutionary theory, Seton rejected Darwinian notions of early man as inherently competitive. In fact, like Hall and other of his antimodernist contemporaries, Seton prized the primitive and valued the campfire because he interpreted it as uniquely able to connect boys with the primitive past. Indeed, he went on to assert that "only the ancient sacred fire of wood has power

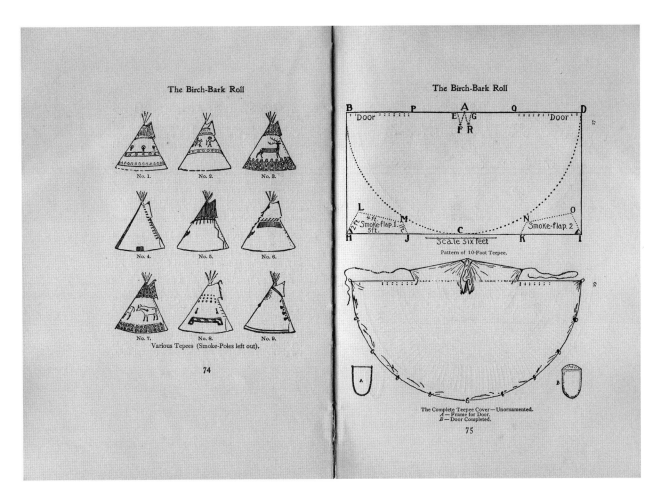

No. 1. No. 2. No. 3.

No. 4. No. 5. No. 6.

No. 7. No. 8. No. 9.
Various Tepees (Smoke-Poles left out).

74

B   P   A   Q   D
Door   Door
E   G
F   R

L   M   N   O
Smoke-flap.1.   Smoke-flap. 2.
5ft.
H   J   C   K   I
Scale Six feet
Pattern of 10-Foot Teepee.

W

A   B

The Complete Teepee Cover—Unornamented.
A—Frame for Door.
B—Door Completed.
75

Figure 6.4. Tipi design and construction, documented by Ernest Thompson Seton, 1908. From Ernest Thompson Seton, *The Birch-Bark Roll of the Outdoor Life,* 74–75.

to touch and thrill the chords of primitive remembrance. When men sit together at the campfire they seem to shed all modern form and poise, and hark back to the primitive—to meet as man to man—to show the naked soul." For Seton, then, the campfire was the portal to premodern authenticity.[35]

To unlock the magic of the campfire, Seton paid close attention to its material manifestations, including the method used for lighting the fire itself. Well known for his mastery of the Indian method of making fire by rubbing two sticks together, Seton even claimed to have set the world's record by starting a fire in this manner in thirty-one seconds. In *The Book of Woodcraft*, he provided step-by-step instructions so that every boy could follow his example. Seton also specified the use of a neat stack of horizontal logs to achieve a fire that was easy to start and that gave a steady, bright light with little heat; he objected vehemently to the high pyramid used in bonfires, as it "goes off like a flash, roasts everyone, and then goes dead."[36]

The Book of Woodcraft also provided Seton's specifications for building a "council-fire circle," the term he used to signify an Indian fire ring. As described in 1912, it was to be "a perfectly level circle twenty-four feet across . . . [with] a permanently fixed circle of very low seats," eight inches high with low backs, and additional rings of progressively higher seats in sufficient numbers to provide a fixed seat for each person in camp.[37]

Beyond these basics, Seton emphasized three qualities that accorded with his own view of Indian culture. The first was orderliness, evident not only in the precise measurements, but also in Seton's admonition that "the place should be carefully leveled and prepared, and kept always in order, for it will be used several times each day, either for councils or for games, dances, and performances." Second, Seton underscored the council ring's community orientation, noting that each band or clan in camp should make its own seat, fitted out with two loops of wire to allow them to display their standard. Finally, Seton's council ring was acutely hierarchical, including a throne for the chief to be positioned "at one side of the ring in a conspicuous place" with totem poles placed opposite.[38] For Seton, the Indian council ring was the center of camp life, and its very form reinforced the values he anticipated campers would glean from playing Indian.

In 1908, the same summer that the photographer captured the lively war dance at Wyndygoul, Luther and Charlotte Gulick expanded the scale of a camp for girls that they had started the year before for their daughters and their friends on the shores of Lake Sebago in Maine. Like Wyndygoul, Camp Gulick (as it was initially called) served as a workshop for program ideas that the Gulicks would eventually offer on a national scale in 1910 as Camp Fire Girls. Playing Indian was at the very heart of this enterprise, and the Gulicks gradually "Indianized" many aspects of camp life. Like their friend Seton, they adopted Indian names. Charlotte was known as Hiiteni, which she translated as "Life, more abundant life," while her husband took the name Timanous, or "Guiding Spirit." In about 1910, the Gulicks also gave their camp an Indian-sounding name, Wohelo, although this was a word invented by Hiiteni from the first two letters of her watchwords: Work, Health, and Love.[39]

Campers, too, were encouraged to adopt Indian personae. They took on Indian names. They braided their hair and wore headbands. They created fringed and beaded ceremonial gowns that they decorated with a vocabulary of symbols adapted from the Plains Indians, symbols that they also applied to the canoe paddles they received upon earning the Water Bug honor. They recorded each week's events in Count Books, written in the style of Longfellow's "Song of Hiawatha" and bound in brown leather. They earned "coups," with a decorated buffalo robe awarded to the camper who earned the most coups during the summer. (She kept the robe only during the winter months, bringing it back to camp the following summer to be passed on to the next winner.) They paddled war canoes and learned the Indian way of making fire at their weekly council fires.[40]

Although many of these program ideas are similar to ones Seton used at Wyndygoul, Hiiteni tailored the Wohelo activities to girls through an emphasis on crafts. Lydia Bush Brown (who had first camped at Wohelo in 1913) later explained:

> The Indian woman was the artist and craftsman of the tribe. She made the baskets and pottery. She wove the blankets and the hanging flat hammocks. And she made them beautiful with touches of decoration, because though they were made primarily for use, she also put her love and thought into the making. In this age when so much is done for the human race, Hiiteni wanted to bring back to girls the joy of making the things they used and putting in something of themselves with the decorated symbol.[41]

Despite Brown's assertions, this focus on craft was not a universal trait of Native American womanhood; indeed, there is no such thing. Rather, the notion was a product of Hiiteni's own ideals of femininity projected upon the figure of "the Indian woman." Indeed, her views resonated with those of other antimodern feminists who supported the revival of southwestern Indian pottery in the 1920s, women like Mary Austin and Mabel Dodge Luhan, who venerated what they perceived as the traditional domesticity of Pueblo women, while bemoaning the fact that modern women had (in the words of historian Margaret Jacobs) "lost the inclination to seamlessly blend home, art, and work."[42] Hiiteni's reverence for Indian craft communicates her own longing for a society in which the home conferred power and authority upon women.

Nonetheless, this difference in program emphasis also had its impact on the material expression of Indianness at Wohelo. Tipis, for instance, with their associations with Wild West shows and the bloody battles involved in taking Native lands by force, played only a small role at Wohelo; campers' memoirs make passing reference to "the Indian tepee," which suggests that

Figure 6.5. Camp Wohelo, Sebago Lake, Maine. Bluebird's Nest, 1913.

there was only one. In fact, when the Gulicks sought a romantic alternative to the tent, they turned not to Indian culture but to nature itself, housing the youngest campers in the "Bluebird's Nest," a tent built on a platform six feet off the ground (an arrangement undoubtedly inspired by the tree house that the Gulicks' teenage daughter Charlotte built for her own use in 1908; Figure 6.5).[43]

Figure 6.6. Camp Wohelo. Council fire, circa 1915.

In contrast, Wohelo campers' memories and period photographs make it clear that the weekly council ring—with its associations of community spirit—was a central component of camp life (Figure 6.6). According to Brown, the program of each council ring followed a similar pattern:

> Silently we filed up to the tennis court, our moccasined feet making no noise in the twilight woods. There we swung out in a great circle and sat cross-legged singing softly "Rolling, rolling, rolling, Keep the fire sticks quickly rolling, rolling," while Hiiteni bent over the rubbing sticks. On dry, clear evenings how quickly the spark came, but when mist rose from the lake into trees about us, it was a long time before Hiiteni stopped and carefully fed the spark with the fragrant wood-dust. Sometimes she would blow it into flame, sometimes call on one of use to blow it and light the fire. Then came "Burn, fire, burn" [a Wohelo song written by Florence Converse in 1912] and then—one never knew what, for Hiiteni had some new thing planned each week . . . Even the ceremonial was not always in the same place. It could be in the Indian tepee, or some other place in the woods. I shall never forget the time I became fire-maker. We sat in a little clearing in the woods purple with pine needles, and dark with their branches meeting overhead. Hiiteni gave me a fire-set for my own. I can see her now at that ceremony.

Written fifteen years after her first summer at camp, Brown's vivid description suggests the importance of such council fires in the life of Wohelo.[44]

While the Gulicks freely acknowledged Seton's impact on this element of camp program and especially in teaching them the Indian method of making fire, Wohelo council fires differed from those of the Woodcraft Indians in important ways. For one thing, the Gulicks themselves interpreted the Wohelo council fire not as the flame at the center of a war dance but as the flame of the domestic hearth and a reminder that (in Luther Gulick's words) "the bearing and rearing of children has always been the first duty of most women, and that must always continue to be." (They conveniently ignored the fact that child-rearing responsibilities were not universally associated with women among Native American tribes.) What is more, the Gulicks shaped the content of the event to reinforce their message. Perhaps the most obvious difference lay in the ranks conveyed at the council fire: Woodcraft Indians encouraged boys to imagine themselves as bold leaders by elevating the lowly brave to the lofty status of sachem and then sagamore; the Camp Fire Girl program as refined at Wohelo identified girls as woodgatherers, firemakers, and torchbearers, ranks that emphasized service and the duties involved in tending the hearth.[45]

The physical aspects of the council circle were also quite different. With its rock throne and permanent seating assigned by tribe, Seton's council ring used the material world to reinforce his own ideal of organizational hierarchy. In contrast, Wohelo eschewed permanent council ring fixtures and used the human ring of seated campers to demarcate the special space. The difference is significant, for it allowed Hiiteni to change the location of the council ring with ease—and thus heighten the memorable quality of what might otherwise have become a routine occurrence—as well as emphasized the inclusive nature of the event. Rather than fixing campers in their ranks around the council ring, the Wohelo council ring allowed Hiiteni to share the firemaking honors with campers and gently to expand the circle of insiders. No more authentic than what took place at Wyndygoul, this was a distinctly nonhierarchical performance of council ring activities.

Characterizing the Camp Fire Girls' seven hundred honors and badges as a "symbolic economy for female work that had no formal recompense," Deloria has interpreted this use of Indianness as a conservative move to discourage girls from seeking paid employment outside the home.[46] Nonetheless, the girls who participated in Hiiteni's council ring rituals often used their time at camp to sample new modes of living in female bodies: shedding restrictive clothing, hiking long distances, paddling canoes, sweating profusely, and generally developing a strong sense of self-worth. Many Wohelo alumnae reminisce about the life lessons they learned at camp and the skills that carried them along life paths that sometimes included graduate school and leadership roles, as well as marriage and motherhood. In other words, playing Indian could mean different things to different people. Thanks to this loose fit between action and interpretation, Indian motifs came into widespread use at American summer camps.

SETON AND THE INTERWAR BOOM IN INDIAN PLAY AT CAMP

Beginning in the 1910s, Seton did a great deal to encourage white children to play Indian at camp. As his own relationship with the Boy Scouts deteriorated, he began promoting Woodcraft activities with renewed vigor, opening the organization to girls, adopting the name Woodcraft League, issuing revised (and gender-specific) editions of *The Birch-Bark Roll* in 1918 and 1920, and presiding over a large number of colorful Grand Council ceremonies that served as his most effective recruiting tool. Although he often hosted such events at Wyndygoul (and, later, DeWinton), his diaries reveal that he also maintained a busy travel schedule in the summer months, visiting camps for a few days at a time in order to initiate new Woodcraft tribes or to reenergize existing organizations. In some years, his schedule was grueling, as in 1918, when he visited six camps between mid-May and mid-August, three of them in a twelve-day period that found him at home for only a single night between each trip. And while he visited a number of camps in New England and the Adirondacks (including Camp Becket in 1916 and Camp Dudley in 1913, 1917, and 1921), he also traveled farther afield, making several visits to the Culver Woodcraft Camp in Indiana, and as well as taking trips to Tennessee in 1914, Colorado in 1917, Wyoming in 1919, and Missouri and Ontario (where he visited Camp Ahmek) in 1922. A frequent (and much sought after) speaker at conferences for camp leaders, Seton was able to bring the Woodcraft message to a wide number of camp professionals in a relatively short time. Although Seton's papers make no mention of the financial arrangements involved in these trips, Taylor Statten's biographer notes that Seton received a per diem salary of twenty dollars during the ten days he spent at Ahmek.[47]

Seton's diary entries describing these visits are cryptic, but he makes it clear that they evolved over time. In the early 1910s, he tended to spend most of his time with campers, imparting both natural history and Indian lore. On a 1913 trip, for instance, he arrived on Saturday evening at Kamp Kiamesha in New Jersey and immediately held an Indian council. On Sunday he spent "All day with boys. Took a long hike up mountain," and departed again Monday morning at five o'clock. Later that summer he made a longer five-day sojourn to Camp Dudley, which included an Indian council at which he taught campers the "Caribou Dance[,] Scalp Dance[,] Sweat Lodge[,] last greatest success." Gradually, however, Seton began to focus his energies on Indian lore and especially on activities calculated to perpetuate the Woodcraft spirit after he left. Thus, he devoted greater attention to instructing camp leaders in Indian dances, often bestowing upon them Indian names that could serve as ongoing reminders of their initiation into Indian ways. On a 1917 visit to Camp Chief Ouray in Colorado, for instance, Seton "taught Mrs. Herrick the Snake Dance," and renamed her "Na-Chanti or Heart in Hand" before he left.[48]

Even more important, Seton began to spend his time at camp making the accoutrements of Woodcraft rituals, objects that he could leave behind to recall his lessons. Sometimes these were small items, like a drum Seton made at Camp Greenkill in 1915 from a lardpail and a calf skin, or the spears he made for tilting during his 1917 trip to Camp Chief Ouray. But more often than not, the primary souvenir that Seton left behind was the council ring itself. Indeed, by 1915, his diary is full of entries recording his involvement in the site selection, construction, and dedication of summer camp council rings. "In camp—worked on a new council ring" (at Camp Inkwod, June 21, 1915); "We made a council ring and at night had a short council" (at Camp Becket, June 30, 1915); "Selected Council Ring . . . Planned Council Ring (at Culver Woodcraft Camp, July 22 and 24, 1916); "Council Ring finished at last" (at Camp Chief Ouray, July 24, 1917); "Fixed up my old Council Ring" (on a return visit to Camp Dudley, May 20, 1920); and "At Adirondack Camp found Elias Brown dead, his wife running the camp. Built and dedicated a fine new Council Ring" (at Adirondack Camp, July 8, 1921).[49]

By all accounts, Seton was a mesmerizing speaker, whose visits had a profound impact on campers and camp directors, often inspiring long-term involvement with Indian lore. At Camp Dudley, for instance, Seton's visit in 1913 inspired the practice of putting on a grand Indian pageant, a practice that continued for many years. Using a script written by Melvil Dewey (inventor of the Dewey Decimal System and a founder of the nearby Lake Placid Club), Dudley campers attempted to reenact the peace pact among the Six Nations of the Iroquois. Performed for an audience that included members of the general public, this pageant emphasized dramatic effect over historical accuracy. To the "hypnotic" beat of the tom-tom, "Indians" in paint and

Figure 6.7. Camp Dudley, Westport, New York. Indian pageant, early 1920s.

feathers emerged from the woods to take their place in front of six tipis arranged in a semicircle; standing in six straight lines reminiscent of a drill formation, the players enacted Seton's ideals of Indian order and hierarchy (Figure 6.7). The tension of the piece hinged on the confrontation between Hadius, the war god, and the spirits of the earth, moon, corn, and sun, who pleaded for peace. For a moment it looked as if Hadius's war dance and his appeal to the masculinity of the braves ("Shall we weakly yield to women . . . now be men and bravely follow") would sway the Six Nations to war. But after a prayer to the Great Spirit, there was a flash and a cloud of smoke and the war pole was changed from red to white, a sign that peace was the right course. A peace dance followed, and the performance culminated in a huge peace fire that illuminated the woods.

Although Dewey's script included a vigorous war dance (which remained a touchstone of most performances of Indianness for white men and boys), the spirits of peace checked imminent hostilities, which were—significantly—not aimed at whites. Peaceful Indians also featured prominently in other pageants of this period, including the Hiawatha Pageant at Camp Charlevoix in

Michigan; directed by Professor J. Raleigh Nelson of the University of Michigan and performed before hundreds of visitors each year, its highlight was Father Marquette smoking the Pipe of Peace. A far cry from early camp games that encouraged campers to impersonate bloodthirty savages, these pageants emphasized the nobility of Native Americans, presenting them as people to be admired and emulated. Campers may have donned feathers and fringed shirts only temporarily, but they were meant to carry the lessons of Indian culture with them for the rest of their lives.[50]

By about 1920, Seton's antimodernist message had affected all aspects of the way in which Indian motifs were deployed at camps, including camp-naming practices. Not only did many of the camps founded during in the 1920s camp-building boom adopt Indian names, but those names were also less likely to be linked to the geography of the camp's locale. Instead, directors were more likely to introduce Indian names that evoked their aspirations either for the camp or for campers. Camp Ahmek is a case in point. Founded in 1921, Ahmek drew its name from the Ojibwe word for "beaver," while founding director Taylor Statten was known at camp as Gitchiahmek (or "Great Beaver"). When Statten and his wife, Ethel Statten, established a sister camp to Ahmek three years later, they called it Wapmeo, or "Bluebirds of Happiness." Ethel herself was known as Tonakela, evidently an Ojibwe word meaning "you first." Organization camps were likewise attracted to aspirational Indian names in the 1920s. In Minnesota alone, the Camp Fire Girls established Camp Tanadoona ("Lives out of Doors") in 1924 and Camp Ojiketa ("Sweetness of Life") in 1926, while the St. Paul YMCA established Camp Widjiwagan (Ojibwe for "Comradeship") in 1929. The Minneapolis YMCA was a pioneer in this approach to Indian names, calling its camp on Green Lake Icaghowan (from the Sioux phrase for "to grow everywhere") at least as early as 1916. But in the 1920s, the organization expanded on this practice, calling newly established camps Menogyn (again meaning "to grow everywhere," but this time rendered in Ojibwe) and Ihduhapi (the Sioux word for "carry your own burden").[51]

THE ROLE OF INDIAN GUIDES

Seton's camp visits also helped generate a great demand for the services of Indian guides, experts responsible for introducing campers to purportedly authentic Indian lore. In some cases, these guides were themselves Native

Figure 6.8. Medomak Camp, Washington, Maine. "Our Indian's Cabin," from brochure for the 1933 season.

Americans who lived at camp for the season. One such guide—identified only as "our Indian"—was pictured in the 1933 brochure for Medomak Camp, sitting on the steps of his log cabin (Figure 6.8); as two white men look on, seated campers listen in rapt attention to tales of "his forefathers who roamed these forests in the days before the white man came." No longer depicted as a static figure presented solely as an antiquarian object of the camper's gaze (as was the reservation Indian in earlier Mishawaka brochures), this man is pictured in modern dress, actively engaging with campers.[52]

Images from other camp brochures suggest that the presence of such Indian guides threatened established racial hierarchies. A 1930s brochure from the Culver Woodcraft Camp, for instance, includes several images of a figure identified only as "a real Indian Chief." Consisting of full feather headdress, ornamented vest, beaded bracelets, loincloth, fringed leggings, and moccasins, the chief's traditional clothing contrasts sharply with the modern military dress of Culver's campers, triggering white interpretations of Indians as isolated from the process of cultural evolution, permanently stuck in a primitive state. And while some images show the standing chief instructing campers in archery (evidence that many established camp activities were given an Indian flavor in the interwar period), the brochure's full-page cover photo reverses the power relationship between Indian and white (Figure 6.9). Seated on the ground among the most familiar artifacts of Indian life—a drum, a bow and arrows, and a second feather headdress—the chief leans back on one arm to look up at the young white boy who stands over him, leaning on a paddle painted with Indian symbols. Two tipis in the background suggest

Figure 6.9. Culver Woodcraft Camp, Culver, Indiana. Indian chief and camper, from cover of brochure for the 1936 season.

that this encounter takes place—symbolically at least—in Indian territory. While the brochure promises that the white boy will learn much from the Indian at the Culver Woodcraft Camp, it also reassures parents, campers, and camp directors themselves that his racial heritage—supported by the military might evoked in his camp uniform—will allow him to maintain the superior position.[53]

Other camps avoided the ideological difficulties of integrating a Native American man into the life of the camp by hiring what might be called "white Indians." These were men—like Seton—who had lived among Native Americans for some length of time and felt they could claim both an in-depth knowledge of Indian cultures and a spiritual affinity with Indian life. Not content to describe Indian practices in cold, analytical terms, white Indians invariably engaged in elaborate performances of Indianness. Typically they assumed Indian names, which, they hastened to point out, Native American friends had bestowed upon them. They donned Indian garb, manipulated Indian artifacts, and enacted Indian rituals. At most camps, they encouraged campers to do the same, thus using an oral tradition to pass along Indian lore, a practice that enhanced their reputations for authenticity.

One of the most interesting of these white Indians was Julian Harris Salomon, who went on to become the leading camp planner of the post–World War II era. Born in Norwich, Connecticut, in 1896, Salomon grew to young manhood during the early decades of the twentieth century, when competing organizations for boys were cropping up everywhere. Salomon was an avid participant, organizing a chapter (called a "fort") of the Sons of Daniel Boone in 1909, joining the first Boy Scout Troop in Brooklyn, New York (where his family had moved), in 1910, and achieving the rank of Eagle Scout in 1913. Although he does not seem to have officially joined the Woodcraft Indians, he wrote to Seton after reading the serialization of *Two Little Savages* in the *Ladies' Home Journal*, thus securing an invitation to Wyndygoul, where he enjoyed "some great days . . . [and] got [his] first chance to sleep in a real Indian tipi."[54]

Throughout the 1910s, Salomon spent his summers working as a camp counselor, eventually joining the staff of the Culver Woodcraft Camp, where he again encountered Seton when Black Wolf visited Indiana in 1921. In 1922, Salomon began his career as a Boy Scout executive, first in Terre Haute, and then in Rockland County, Maryland, positions that gave him responsibility for directing summer camps and (in the case of Camp Krietenstein in

Indiana) for camp planning as well. By the mid-1920s, he began to raise his profile within the camping profession nationally both through his service to the Camp Directors Association (and later to its successor organization, the American Camping Association) and by accepting teaching positions in a variety of camp leadership courses. In 1936, Salomon joined the staff of the National Park Service, designing the organized campgrounds built at Recreational Demonstration Areas and writing the camp-planning sections of *Park and Recreation Structures*. This experience provided him with the credentials to launch his career as a professional camp planner, a vocation he pursued with vigor into the 1960s.[55]

From his youngest days, Salomon developed an interest in Indian lore, first as the result of passing encounters with members of the Mohegan tribe living near his boyhood home in Norwich and later consolidated by his acquaintance with a young western Indian known as Winthrop, whom Salomon's father employed as a gardener. According to an autobiographical sketch Salomon wrote in 1928, Winthrop made the six-year-old Salomon his first bow and arrow, took him on tramps through the woods, and showed him how to swing from tree to tree in order to "break a trail when being pursued." Once the family moved to Brooklyn, young Salomon made frequent visits to the Indian exhibitions at the Natural History Museum in New York, where (according to his own account) he spent time with staff ethnologists who demonstrated Indian dance steps for him.

Throughout the 1910s, Salomon used his Indian interests to develop camping programs and in 1920 collaborated with another young scout leader on the production of an Indian pageant that won first prize in the International Scout Contests at the first International Boy Scout Jamboree held in London. He may have overstated the impact of the pageant on the Boy Scouts (claiming that the organization's use of Indian lore was a "direct result" of the pageant's success), but there is no doubt that Salomon's Indian interests enhanced his own career in working with boys. The pageant brought him to the attention of General Leigh R. Gignilliat, who invited him to work at Culver Woodcraft Camp—a position that led in turn to his first job as a scout executive. Likewise, his early involvement in leadership training courses hinged on his knowledge of Indian lore.

During the 1920s, Salomon sought out firsthand experiences with Native Americans: "camping" with the Blackfeet, tramping through Pueblo country, and "visiting" Indians in the highlands of central Mexico. While such trips ostensibly gave him an opportunity to learn authentic Indian practices, they also became (at least in Salomon's later accounts) treasured confirmation of the superiority of Salomon's knowledge of "the old Indian ways." Indeed, Salomon liked to recall that the Blackfeet whose reservation he visited had only heard accounts of making a fire by rubbing two sticks together, but had never seen it done. When Salomon demonstrated, the Blackfeet (who had previously only tolerated his presence) "welcomed [him] as a member of the group," conferring upon him the name Apota, or "Firemaker."

By the end of the decade, Salomon consolidated his role as an "Indian expert" through the publication of his four-hundred-page *Book of Indian Crafts and Indian Lore*, which offered how-to information for making and using popular Indian artifacts (including war bonnets, war shirts, moccasins, tipis, wigwams, bows, and arrows), as well as tips on firemaking, dance steps, and Indian names. One chapter was called "Producing an Indian Pageant." Hailed as an indispensable guide for Scouts and Camp Fire Girls, the tome also attracted the attention of camp directors. According to one enthusiastic reviewer, it belonged on every camp director's shelf "next to the Bible."[56]

During these same years, Salomon also began a career as a professional Indian guide known as Soaring Eagle (Figure 6.10). Dressed in elaborate Indian garb, he offered "American Indian Entertainments" that purported to admit viewers "to the real life of the red man." Although he often performed for adult audiences (once sharing the stage with Seton at a meeting of the Brooklyn Chamber of Commerce), Salomon also advertised "other programs . . . especially prepared for schools, scouts, and camps." In fact, according to a promotional pamphlet issued in about 1930, Salomon's "summers are largely spent visiting camps as an entertainer and teacher of Indian crafts." The pamphlet's long list of testimonials (headed by one from Seton) reveals that he spoke both at individual camps (including Camps Ponemah and Miramichi, and Tanager Lodge) and at workshops for camp leaders, including one held at the Teachers College at Columbia University.[57]

Salomon saw himself as a destroyer of Indian stereotypes, particularly "the ideal savage of the would-be philanthropic sentimentalist" and "the bathless barbarian who has whooped through so many pages of fiction." Instead, he sought to emphasize the humanity of Native Americans by demonstrating that the Indian was "a man, subject to the same passions and infirmities as ourselves." Nonetheless, his entertainments reinforced antimodernist tropes, in which the Indian was "an inheritor of old cultures and of wise, poetic and

Figure 6.10. Julian Harris Salomon dressed as Soaring Eagle, circa 1930.

beautiful customs and beliefs, marvelously harmonious with his temperament and environment." What is more, Soaring Eagle's interpretation of Indian life "as it existed in the Long Ago," reinforced the belief that "the real life of the red man" was a thing of the past. [58]

Thus, Salomon's performances were not merely colorful and entertaining (although, by all accounts, they were that); they were also ideologically charged. By freezing Indian culture in "the Long Ago," they helped distance white audiences from hostilities against Native Americans, military actions that had taken place—many of them—within the lifetime of Salomon's parents. By emphasizing a generic "Indian" culture, they ignored the cultural specificity connected with the actual lives of Native Americans and denied the modern realities of reservation life. In all these ways, such enactments helped excuse white audiences of responsibility for political action in the present.

Judging from the testimonials printed in the promotional brochure, audiences embraced both the spectacle and the ideological content of Soaring Eagle's performances. Fay Welch, director of Tanager Lodge, marveled at Salomon's ability to hold an audience of more than 150 "completely spellbound." J. Wilford Allen, director of Camp Ponemah, concurred but also commented on the larger issues: "You [Salomon] certainly have a real missionary spirit in endeavoring to bring before the people some of the departing glories of a vanishing race. I wish the real thing, as you show it, could be taught in every school in our land."[59] Not only did Allen find Soaring Eagle's entertainment perfectly consistent with the idea that Native Americans were an endangered species, as it were, he also accepted Soaring Eagle's performance as perfectly authentic, a satisfying substitute for the original that blunted somewhat the sense of loss he might otherwise have experienced when faced with the disappearance of a culture he admired.

INDIANIZING THE SUMMER CAMP LANDSCAPE

In a setting like the summer camp, where feathers and beads were the only outward signs that a white man had assumed an Indian persona, the material aspects of Native American culture were crucial for imparting an Indian flavor to camp activities. Although Indian-inspired structures were available in the early twentieth century, they became widespread only in the 1920s and 1930s, including attempts to re-create landscape features that had been used by the native people of the particular region. Salomon, for instance, encouraged the readers of *The Book of Indian Crafts and Indian Lore* to build one wigwam or more "as part of the Indian village in your summer camp." The wigwam was easy to make, and because it had been "rather neglected by us for the better known tipi in our pictures and books," it was also in greater need of preservation. Indeed, Salomon was convinced that white campers could play an important role in this preservation project, especially "in the

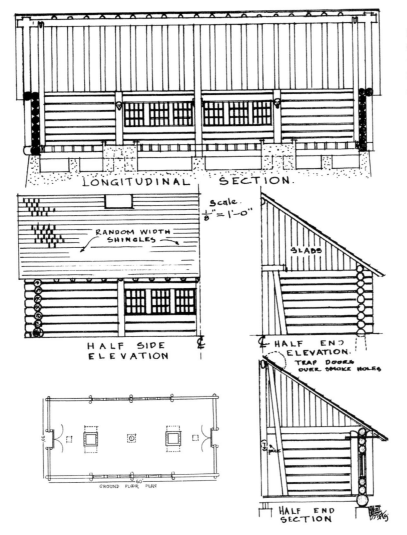

Figure 6.11. Camp Delmont, Montgomery County, Pennsylvania. Unami Big House, 1918. From Boy Scouts of America Department of Camping, *Camp Site Development Plans,* 40.

East, [where] all of the materials the Indians used in wigwam construction can still be found," and where campers could thus build "exact reproductions of this type of Indian home."[60]

Likewise, Camp Delmont, a Boy Scout camp in Pennsylvania, constructed in the 1920s what was called the Unami Big House (Figure 6.11). Designed to emulate the ceremonial structure used for the harvest rituals of the Delaware, the Delmont Big House was a large rectangular structure built of horizontal logs set into posts on the long sidewalls, with vertical slabs used as infill above the plate in the end gables. Except for the provision of windows in the long walls, the Delmont version followed the form of the original quite closely, with the longitudinal axis marked by end doors, a central post, and two fire-pits situated below smoke holes in the roof.

The meaning of these forms, however, was lost completely. While the Delaware Big House was oriented east-west to symbolize the journey from birth to death, descriptions of the Camp Delmont Big House (published in *Camp Site Development Plans* in 1927) made no mention of the building's orientation. Nor did they comment upon the importance of the number 12 in Delaware cosmology, a number evoked in the twelve days of the harvest ritual and in the twelve masks carved on interior posts.[61] Although the Boy Scout text identified the building as a ceremonial structure, the specific content of the ceremony was up for grabs, as long as the boys contributed the decoration and thus took a personal interest in the Big House: "Pictures, leather, bead and handicraft work, taxidermy specimens and any other striking object to which may be attached a history or legend, will add to the atmosphere of the building." Implicit in this description is the sense that the Indian legends taught here were not inherently meaningful—indeed, they might even be made up on the fly and attached to a taxidermy specimen. Instead, their importance is measured in their ability to enchant campers:

> When council fires burn on the ceremonial altars, the smoke issuing from the smoke holes in the roof (just as it did when the Indians gathered in their "Big Houses")[,] the eager faces of the boys that encircle the large room, enthralled with the program, will prove to any council the tremendous part that such a romantic building can play in the education of the boy.[62]

If few such Big Houses appeared on the grounds of American summer camps, it may have been because the log construction (which scholars now confirm may have been influenced by Swedish immigrants) did not seem suitably Indian to white eyes.[63]

Despite readily available information about wigwams and Big Houses, tipis remained the favorite form of Indian building at American summer camps. Camp directors could obtain tipis in a number of ways, including buying them outright from commercial purveyors of mass-produced Indian-themed goods. One of the first merchants to tap into the market was George H. Chappell Jr., of Westwood, New Jersey, whose 1908 advertisement on the back cover of *The*

Figure 6.12. Chimney Rock Camp, Lake Lure, North Carolina. Tipi in the Indian Village, from brochure for the 1934 season.

Birch-Bark Roll announced that he could supply tipis, as well as bows, bow-strings, arrows, arrowheads, feathers, scalps, spears, wampum, fire sticks, and *"everything needed* for forming or maintaining a camp on these lines" (emphasis in the original). Or camp directors could make tipis, by following either Seton's instructions (which were readily available in a new edition of *The Book of Woodcraft* issued in 1921) or Salomon's (which appeared in a 1925 *Boys' Life* article, in *Camp Site Development Plans* in 1927, and in his own *Book of Indian Crafts and Indian Lore*). While not substantially different in content from Seton's tipi-making instructions, Salomon's provided more detailed information on the construction process, encouraged white children to invent decorative designs of their own, and illustrated his instructions with several images of tipis made by Boy Scouts.[64]

In addition to confirming that many camp directors succumbed to the desire to introduce tipis into the camp landscape, camp brochures of the interwar period also reveal that the appeal of the form was almost purely symbolic. Tipis did not, for instance, serve as sleeping accommodations as they had at Seton's early encampments at Wyndygoul; modern concerns for campers' health made such uses unthinkable. Instead, they were part background, part prop for a range of woodcraft activities. At Culver Woodcraft Camp, Salomon staged an Indian pageant against a backdrop of six tipis, while "a seventh was erected during the action, in order that the audience might see how a tipi was set up." At many other camps, however, a single example was considered sufficient. At Chimney Rock Camp, for instance, a lone tipi next to a small council ring was potent enough symbolically to signify an entire "Indian Village," where members of the Woodcraft League followed the program outlined in Seton's *Birch-Bark Roll* (Figure 6.12). Tipis, in other words, could function as a form of landscape shorthand for antimodernist interpretations of Native American life that emphasized living lightly on the land in harmony with the environment.[65]

Yet, tipis did not always carry such antimodernist connotations. At Camp Mishawaka they served as the symbolic headquarters for the chiefs of the Sioux and the Chippewa, the "tribes" pitted against one another in intracamp athletic competitions (Figure 6.13). In this context, they symbolized aggression and warfare, a meaning reinforced by their position overlooking the campus, which itself was transformed into a symbolic battleground when campers played a version of capture the flag they called Scalping.[66]

Tribally based organizations became widespread in the interwar period, although their activities highlight the complex impact of volumes such as

Figure 6.13. Camp Mishawaka, Grand Rapids, Minnesota. Headquarters of the Big Chiefs, from brochure for the 1929 season.

Figure 6.14. Medomak Camp. Camper performing a war dance, from the brochure for the 1933 season.

Salomon's *Book of Indian Crafts and Indian Lore*. On one hand, such resources provided camp directors with easy access to a great deal of factual information about the range of North American Indian tribes and the diversity of their cultural practices. In this way, these books may have facilitated the process by which the directors of Medomak Camp in Maine, for instance, settled upon geographically dispersed Mohawks, Delawares, Senecas, and "Navahoes" as the names for their camp tribes.[67] On the other, Salomon's book—with its early chapters titled "War Bonnets and Head-dresses" and "War Shirts, Leggins, and Women's Costume"—did little to dislodge popular conceptions of the Indian as warrior.[68] At camps like Medomak, the ultimate performance of Indianness in the interwar period remained the war dance (Figure 6.14). Indeed, by symbolically pitting geographically distant Native American groups against one another, camp tribes actually reinforced the misconception that all Indian people were inherently warlike. Removing white protagonists from this mode of Indian play also erased white actions as a factor in Indian aggression.

THE INDIAN COUNCIL RING

Both the term *council ring* and the form advocated by Seton were in widespread use at camps of all kinds in the 1920s. *Camp Site Development Plans* (published by the Boy Scouts in 1927) included a hypothetical layout for a divisional camp, in which each division would focus on activities associated

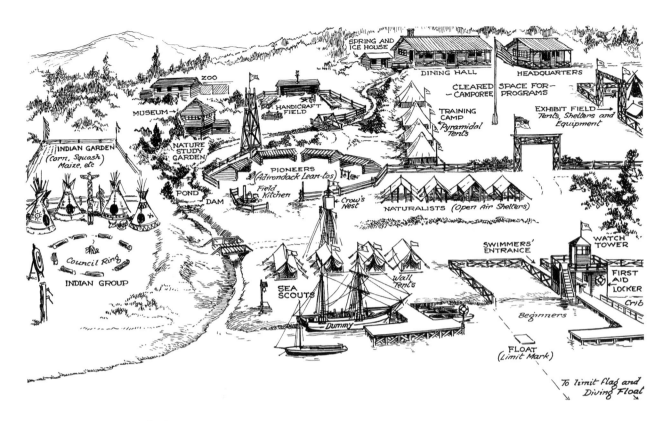

Figure 6.15. Boy Scout Camp division plan, showing tipis and council ring, 1927. From Boy Scouts of America Department of Camping, *Camp Site Development Plans*, 3.

with a different theme (Figure 6.15). The Indian group at the far left included a simplified but clearly labeled council ring. The same publication included the plan of Camp Siwanoy, where even the schematic depiction suggested Seton's influence by hinting at logs stacked in the approved manner and a rudimentary ritual axis created by the entrance (see Figure 1.3).[69]

Although the form of the campfire circle was becoming somewhat standardized in the interwar period, its symbolic meaning was still open to debate, particularly concerning issues of gender.[70] Seton, for instance, explained his program in the following terms: "Realizing that *manhood, not scholarship*, is the first aim of education, we have sought out those pursuits which develop the finest character, the finest physique, and . . . which in a word, *make for manhood*" (emphasis in the original).[71] Two years later, Seton's friend Charles A. Eastman (Ohiyesa)—himself a highly assimilated Santee Sioux raised by traditional Dakota people and then educated at Dartmouth and Boston University medical school—also emphasized what he saw as the natural connection between the campfire and manhood. In his 1914 book, *Indian Scout Talks: A Guide for Boy Scouts and Camp Fire Girls*, Eastman wrote: "As fire is the symbol of enthusiasm, energy, and devotion, and is with the Indians a strictly masculine emblem, it is fit that the young men gather about it before going upon a journey or 'war-path.'" While he described evening ceremonies for Boy Scouts centered on the fire, Eastman's version of "The Maiden's Feast" was a noontime ritual focused on "the 'Sacred Stone,' a rudely heart-shaped or pyramidal boulder, which has been touched lightly with red paint."[72] Other tribes might contest this interpretation, and so could the Gulicks, for whom there seemed to be an equally natural connection between the camp fire (which they associated with domesticity) and femininity.

These differences in interpretation coexisted throughout the interwar period and may have had some impact on where the council ring was located. In boys' camps, for instance, there was a tendency to situate the council ring in clear view, as we have already seen at Camp Siwanoy. At Camp Wigwam, three council rings were in use by 1930, two of which were in very visible locations: one was on the edge of the camp's main clearing, which with a totem pole and a tipi formed "the camp emblem"; the other near the middle of camp was on axis with the theater and a natural amphitheater, for ceremonials that involved all campers (see Figure 1.10). The third was set near the nature museum and arts and crafts studio, useful adjuncts for the teaching of Indian lore at this council ring.

In contrast, the council rings of girls' camps tended to be either hidden from view or divested of their hierarchical arrangements. At Camp Mary Day, the council bowl, as it was called, was on the margins of the camp grounds, but close to the craft house, a location that may have suggested itself because of the heavy use of Indian-inspired crafts used in council ring ceremonies (see Figure 1.11). Camp brochures for Camp Alanita for Girls in northern Alabama hint at the distant location of the council ring used for their "weekly 'pow-wows'" when they mention "memories of the trail up the hills at night, lighted only by the dancing flashlights."[73] In contrast, the preliminary layout for Camp Ojiketa, a Camp Fire Girl camp in Minnesota, included two campfire locations, each at the hub of a half-circle of camper cabins (Figure 6.16). While obviously visible from the main part of camp, they lacked the chief's throne or any other indication of a ritual axis, suggesting that these were less for ceremonial use and more for intimate gatherings.

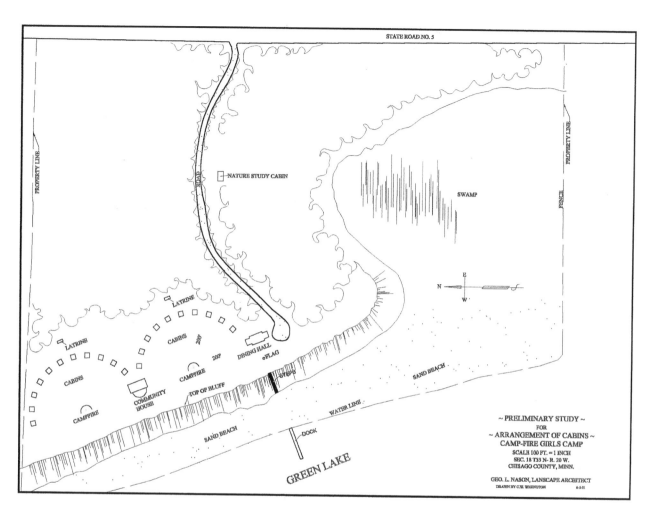

STATE ROAD NO. 5

PROPERTY LINE

PROPERTY LINE

FENCE

NATURE STUDY CABIN

SWAMP

ROAD

E

N

W

S

LATRINE

LATRINE

CABINS

200'

200'

DINING HALL

oFLAG

CABINS

CAMPFIRE

COMMUNITY HOUSE

TOP OF BLUFF

STEPS

SAND BEACH

CAMPFIRE

SAND BEACH

WATER LINE

DOCK

GREEN LAKE

~ PRELIMINARY STUDY ~
FOR
~ ARRANGEMENT OF CABINS ~
CAMP-FIRE GIRLS CAMP
SCALE 100 FT. = 1 INCH
SEC. 18 T33 N- R. 20 W.
CHISAGO COUNTY, MINN.

GEO. L. NASON, LANSCAPE ARCHITECT
DRAWN BY C.W. WORINGTON   6-5-31

Figure 6.16. Camp Ojiketa, Chisago County, Minnesota. Preliminary study of site plan, designed by landscape architect George L. Nason in 1931.

In many ways, the debates about the gendered meaning of the Indian campfire took the focus off its racial implications. As cultural studies scholar Shari Huhndorf has argued, antimodernist celebrations of Native American cultures did nothing to challenge European American domination and instead left "stereotyped visions of Native life intact and the radically unequal relations between European American and Native American unquestioned." In encouraging campers to find their authentic selves by temporarily adopting Indian ways, summer camps urged white children to see themselves as the rightful inheritors to North America, thus downplaying the violence involved in the conquest of Indian lands and erasing white responsibility for that violence. Undoubtedly, individual campers played Indian at the summer camp council ring with the best of intentions, but the Indian campfire nonetheless reinforced white privilege.[74]

PLAYING INDIAN IN DECLINE

In the postwar period, many American summer camps de-emphasized playing Indian. This is not to say that Indian motifs disappeared entirely, as some practices (including camp "tribes") had become firmly entrenched in many camp traditions. What is more, mass-produced craft materials tended to highlight Indian motifs, albeit in highly inauthentic forms. Many postwar campers recall making lanyards of brightly colored gymp (a plastic produced by the Pyrotex Corporation of Leominster, Massachusetts) or using the same material to stitch together imitation leather wallets prestamped with Indian motifs. But campers' performances of Indianness were less prolonged, less complete, and less public. Indian pageants and other opportunities for white children to play Indian were rapidly becoming a thing of the past, as were the tipis and other landscape features that supported them.[75]

The campfire circle remained an important part of the camp landscape, but camp-planning professionals increasingly stripped it of its Indian associations, a process that began in the late 1930s. This is particularly apparent in Albert Good's influential *Park and Recreation Structures*, published by the National Park Service in 1938. Illustrated in the second volume was a campfire circle at Lassen Volcanic National Park in northern California, in a familiar arrangement of low log seats around a ring of stone for the fire (Figure 6.17). Although the forms were familiar from Seton's writings, the meanings attached to them were quite different. Not only was the term *council ring* de-emphasized, but the text itself also avoided any mention of Native American parallels. Quite to the contrary, Good asserted that in planning the campfire circle "there are no fixed principles, no time-revered traditions to be pressed," and he encouraged camp planners instead to select "surroundings that suggest . . . the glories of Nature unmodified."[76] The campfire circle, then, was being construed now as an extension of the natural environment, devoid of previous cultural connections. Elsewhere in the publication a layout for an organized camp showed the council ring banished to the edges of the camp landscape (see Figure 1.17).

This de-Indianized campfire circle dominated the flood of camp-planning

Figure 6.17. Lassen Volcanic National Park, California.
Campfire circle, circa 1935. From Albert H. Good, *Park
and Recreation Structures,* 2:200.

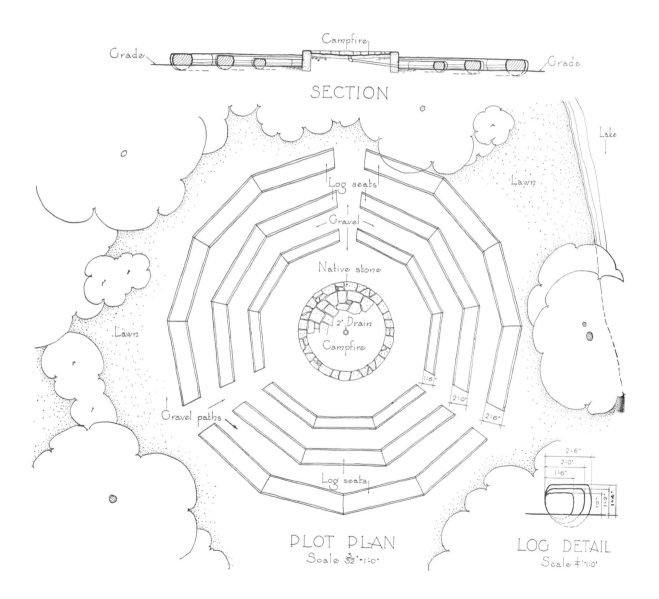

Figure 6.18. Campfire circle for a YMCA camp, 1946. From John A. Ledlie, ed., *Layout, Building Designs, and Equipment for Y.M.C.A. Camps,* 45.

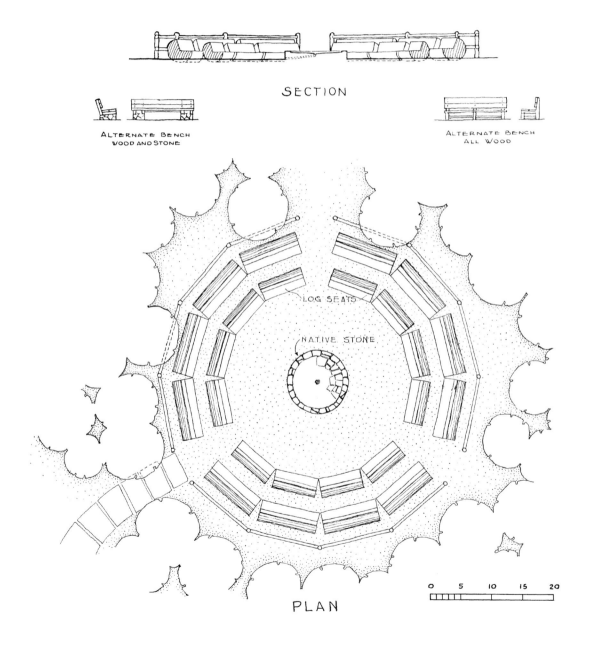

SECTION

ALTERNATE BENCH
WOOD AND STONE

ALTERNATE BENCH
ALL WOOD

LOG SEATS

NATIVE STONE

PLAN

0   5   10   15   20

literature that emerged at the end of World War II. When the YMCA published *Layout, Building Designs, and Equipment for Y.M.C.A. Camps* in 1946, it included a council ring modeled very closely on the National Park Service example, described as "an attractive setting for special ceremonial programs of the camp," without any allusion to Indian cultural practices (Figure 6.18). On the idealized camp layout included in the same publication, the council ring was located in the woods, out of sight from the rest of camp, divorced from the visible symbolic role it played in the interwar period (see Figure 1.18). In Salomon's 1948 *Camp Site Development*, the council ring was included on the layout for a two-unit tent camp, but not in the master plan for a larger camp. Nowhere did the text give the specifications for a permanent campfire area. The council ring was similarly absent from the Camp Fire Girls' 1946 *When You Plan Your Camp*.[77]

The stripping of Indian associations from the campfire circle is a complex phenomenon driven by multiple forces. Deloria has argued that at any given moment the particular ways in which whites played Indian is connected to the status of actual Native American people who assumed important roles in "assisting, confirming, co-opting, challenging, and legitimating the performative tradition of aboriginal American identity."[78] However, the particular mode of playing Indian considered here highlights changes taking place within the context of North American summer camps, changes that bring us back to a consideration of the camp as a site for the remaking of American childhood.

Among them is the emergence of camp directing as a profession, which had a decisive impact on how camp leaders assessed their own effectiveness. Especially after the establishment of the American Camping Association in 1935, camp directors came to base their professional status on their quantifiable impact on campers—such as improving their posture and muscle tone—and less on intangible qualities of their own character—for example, a deep knowledge of Indian lore. Indeed, in the postwar period camp directors also signaled their professional aspirations by distinguishing themselves more self-consciously from campers. Early in the twentieth century, the head of the camp had been called a leader, someone who led campers by example, showing them how to light a fire without matches, for instance. Forty years later, the head of the camp was a director, someone who supervised a paid staff from an administration building connected to the dining lodge.

These changes had an impact on campfire activities themselves. Indian ceremonials enacted around the council ring had often been highly scripted performances, but ones in which campers played important roles. In the late 1930s, advice literature began to focus instead on elaborate campfire spectacles that the camp director could produce for the amazement of the camper. Henry W. Gibson, still a force in the summer camp movement, published *Recreational Programs for Summer Camps* in 1938. Although he briefly mentioned a rubbing-stick fire (albeit without any reference to Indian practices), he described in greater detail what he called a "fire from heaven," in which the campfire was to be lit by a flaming wad of kerosene-soaked burlap sent shooting down a wire stretched between the fire circle and a tree. Even more daring was the tunnel fire, in which kerosene-soaked burlap was pulled quickly by cable through a tunnel of boards in order to light the campfire in "a mysterious manner."[79] Far from involving the camper directly, these campfires depended for their effectiveness on the campers' complete ignorance of the preparations.

THE CULTURAL WORK OF PLAYING INDIAN

In short, there was nothing natural about the use of Indian motifs at American summer camps. Early in the twentieth century, camp leaders used Indian names and field trips to Indian sites to underline the conceptual distance between the camp landscape and the civilized realms of campers' everyday lives, but they rarely encouraged campers to think of themselves as Indians. Only in the interwar period did large numbers of campers impersonate Indians directly, with the aid of Indian artifacts that ranged in size from the arrowhead to the council ring. Although motivated in part by the desire to reconnect campers with primitive impulses threatened by modern existence, these performances also completed other ideologically charged tasks. By encouraging campers from many different ethnicities to don a shared identity that they could all shed at will, playing Indian helped create a shared sense of whiteness among European American children. Equally important, by reinforcing the connections between Indians and the primitive past, even most respectful performances of Indianness contributed to the sense that "true" Indian culture had all but disappeared and thus helped sustain a larger cultural project that treated the white domination of North America as a fait accompli.

In the postwar period, the use of Indian motifs without acknowledging their Indian roots was perhaps the logical extension of this cultural project— a suggestion that Indian-white relations were a nonissue in the modern world.

Indeed, when camp professionals discussed race after World War II, they did so exclusively in terms of the summer camp's potential to ameliorate relationships between white and African American youths.[80] The status of contemporary Indians and their political rights had been rendered largely invisible in mainstream American culture, as at American summer camps.

Even when playing Indian at camp was at its peak in the interwar years, camp organizers never said that their purpose was to reinforce particular ideas about race, whether to underline a sense that European Americans were the rightful inheritors of the North American continent or to bolster racial hierarchies that favored whites; some may not have entertained such ideas. Yet by arranging the cultural landscape to encourage particular kinds of performances on the part of their young charges, they helped support such racial hierarchies, even if they did so at something other than a conscious level.

The purpose of reading the camp landscape in this way is to acknowledge that the work of maintaining racial inequities often involves people who are acting with the best of intentions. This is one of the things that makes racism so hard to recognize and so difficult to eradicate. Equally important, such a reading highlights the central role the cultural landscape often plays in allowing people simply not to notice the inequalities that structure their daily lives. In short, the cultural landscape has been given responsibility for communicating some of the summer camp's most powerful messages.

Summer Camps, Modern Architecture, and Modern Life

IN 1955, THE PROFESSIONAL JOURNAL *ARCHITECTURAL FORUM* published a glowing article about Camp Bliss, a new summer camp for girls in Fishkill, New York, owned and operated by the Herald Tribune Fresh Air Fund. The text highlighted the decentralized layout provided by "Veteran Camp Planner" Julian Harris Salomon, while the images and their extensive captions celebrated the architectural designs of Edward Larrabee Barnes, a Harvard-trained architect who, at age forty, was beginning to make a name for himself as a designer of modern houses. According to the article's anonymous author, the camp's "program of intimate groups . . . is well in advance of most camp practice. Its architecture is even further ahead."[1]

Indeed, Barnes's designs were explicitly modern, in that they were based on a distinctly avant-garde vision of architecture in which structural logic and continuous space were key components. The dining hall was a large square room with a steeply pitched roof supported on "ingenious tilted A-trusses [that] free the tall space of tie rods and clutter, [and] come together with a fine knife-sharp edge."[2] The gable end was filled with large expanses of glass that provided a view of the lake, as well as glimpses of the tree tops evoked in the building's truss work (Figure E.1). Sharing a family resemblance with the dining hall were the village halls (what other camps called unit lodges) in the

Figure E.1. Camp Bliss, Sharpe Reservation, Fishkill, New York. Interior of dining hall, designed by Edward Larrabee Barnes, 1953–54. Photograph by Ben Schnall.

Figure E.2. Camp Bliss. Village hall, designed by Edward Larrabee Barnes, 1953–54. Photograph by Ben Schnall.

Figure E.3. Camp Bliss. Camper tents, designed by Edward Larrabee Barnes, 1953–54. Photograph by Ben Schnall.

Figure E.4. Camp Bliss. Infirmary, designed by Edward Larrabee Barnes, 1953–54. Photograph by Ben Schnall.

dispersed residential units (Figure E.2). Unlike the dining hall, these were true A-frames (with roof rafters stretching from the ridgeline to the floor), a form just beginning to be associated with vacation homes in California and on the ski slopes of Vermont.[3] Similar in form were Barnes-designed tent platforms with lateral walls that canted out at the top; panels in the topmost part of these walls were hinged at the bottom, allowing them to swing into the tent for increased ventilation (Figure E.3).

Although different in character from these program buildings, the administrative buildings were also informed by modern ideas about structure and planning. The director's house, infirmary, and staff houses were all low, flat-roofed buildings, constructed of common lumber, and stained dark brown (Figure E.4). Designed on multiples of a 9'-9" × 12'-20" bay, each was fitted out with a perimeter gallery to provide external circulation and maximize flexibility. Instead of conventional exterior walls, these buildings featured non-load-bearing curtain walls that allowed the introduction of a water-drainage crack between the wall and the gallery floor.[4]

Although this article and a follow-up piece published in 1957 encouraged readers to marvel at the way that "modern design is found in many unusual places," even "camping in the woods," modern buildings were becoming increasingly common at postwar summer camps.[5] Barnes himself went on to design many more, most for the Fresh Air Fund and situated on the same tract of land, the Sharpe Reservation, in Fishkill. In addition to using his Bliss tent designs at Camps Anita and Coler (essentially extensions to Camp Bliss and now considered a single entity, known colloquially as Camp ABC), the fund hired him in 1954 to design two additional buildings at the girls' camps: Mary Louise Lodge, a winterized building that served as a counselors' retreat during the summer and as the base for weekend camping excursions during the rest of the year (Figure E.5); and the Great Lodge, an open-air building with a massive fireplace designed to function like a large version of a village hall. Within two years, Barnes had also designed the Ogden Reid Boathouse on Deer Lake, a facility intended to serve all the camps at Sharpe (Figure E.6).[6]

Figure E.5. Camp Bliss. Mary Louise Lodge, designed by Edward Larrabee Barnes, 1954–55. Photograph by Ben Schnall.

Figure E.6. Sharpe Reservation. Ogden Reid Boat House, designed by Edward Larrabee Barnes, 1954–55. Photograph by Ben Schnall.

By the end of the decade, the Barnes office had started work on two other camps at the site: Camp Hayden (a boys' camp where Richard R. Moger was the Barnes associate in charge) and Camp Hidden Valley (a coeducational camp that accommodated children with physical challenges).[7]

Barnes, however, was not alone in applying the principles of modernism to summer camps. By the time Salomon published a revised edition of *Camp Site Development* in 1959, he was able to include several modern buildings that had recently been commissioned by Girl Scout councils in Maryland, Illinois, Missouri, and Hawai'i.[8] Among them was a fanciful tipi-esque dining hall built for the Anne Arundel County council in Maryland. Roofed with a thin shell cone supported by compression rings and tension rods, the building was designed to be assembled economically by amateurs. Featuring a flue that could be lowered over the central fireplace for campfire ceremonies, this building helped establish a national reputation for the firm of Rogers, Taliaferro and Lamb (now known as RTKL).[9]

In many respects, summer camps were ideal venues for architects to explore architectural modernism, which always encompassed more than the

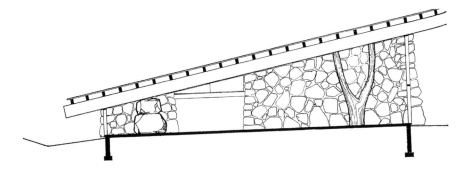

Figure E.7. Camp Hayden, Sharpe Reservation, Fishkill, New York. Dining hall section, designed by Edward Larrabee Barnes (Richard R. Moger, associate in charge), circa 1958.

machine aesthetic and its heavy reliance on industrially produced materials. Imbued with the Enlightenment's faith in the importance of starting from first principles, modern architects were intent on getting back to basics in architectural form, function, and structure. To the extent that they agreed with Swiss-born architect Le Corbusier that "great architecture . . . is the immediate product of human instinct," they embraced the "primitive builder" as their paragon.[10]

In this sense, the simple programs of camp buildings (especially tents and village halls) appealed to modern architects who identified the essence of architecture as the drive to meet fundamental human needs: shelter from the rain, natural light, and good ventilation. Likewise, these architects were particularly well positioned to give material expression to the summer camp's association with primitivism. Some even saw camp commissions as a chance to design with natural materials only partly processed by human skill. At Camp Hayden, for instance, the dining hall roof rested on a central laminated beam supported at one end by massive boulders and at the other by the Y-shaped trunk of a large tree (Figure E.7).

At the same time, other modern concerns—with enhancing close connections between indoors and out, creating visual interest without ornamentation, and using commonplace materials—meshed well with the requirements of the summer camp landscape. *Camping Magazine* profiled the camp in November 1955, noting with approval Barnes's contention that "camp architecture should not form a barrier *against* nature; it should be an expression *of* nature" (emphasis in the original).[11] The Fund undoubtedly appreciated the fact that Barnes worked "without exceeding his modest budget," designing "a full complement of buildings that blend with the surrounding wilderness."[12]

To read the buildings at Camp Bliss solely in terms of architectural modernism is to miss much of their significance, however. Like the many other camps discussed in this book, Camp Bliss is connected to larger trends that affected modern life in twentieth-century North America, including the tendency to manufacture wilderness environments from formerly productive lands. Located seventy-five miles north of New York City, the Sharpe Reservation on which Camp Bliss stands had once been agricultural land; in the nineteenth century it had supported a number of farms, as well a factory that produced baskets used in nearby vineyards. In 1932, Dr. William Sharpe bought one thousand acres to serve as a wilderness retreat, a place where he could escape from the pressures of his surgery practice in New York City. By the late 1940s, he had decided to donate the land to a charitable organization and settled upon the Fresh Air Fund, which offered free camping vacations to poor children of all races from New York City.[13]

Fund officers embraced the donation as an opportunity to make dramatic changes in their camping program. Rather than continue to support eight different campsites in New York and Connecticut, the fund began to consolidate its camping operations on this single, massive site; additional donations allowed the fund to buy adjacent land, and by 1960 the Sharpe Reservation comprised some three thousand acres.[14] An initial master plan, developed by Salomon, called for five small camps around an artificial lake (Deer Lake, started in 1952).[15] By 1959, those plans had expanded to include a second body of water (Beaver Lake) and a total of six camps.

Likewise, the layout of Camp Bliss and its sister camps was an elaboration of the unit plan idea implemented in New Deal Recreational Demonstration Areas and explicated in *Park and Recreation Structures* and a host of postwar camp-planning manuals (Figure E.8). Like those RDAs, Bliss provided campers with intimate social groupings that engaged them in age-appropriate activities. The major difference at the Sharpe Reservation was that each camp catered to the kind of narrow age group served by an RDA unit (a change that allowed the fund to serve a much larger number of campers). At the same time, the campstead represented a new level of social organization that was larger than the tent, but smaller than what the RDA called a unit and what the fund called a village. In this sense, the cultural landscape at Camp Bliss speaks to a distinctly modern view of childhood as a series of

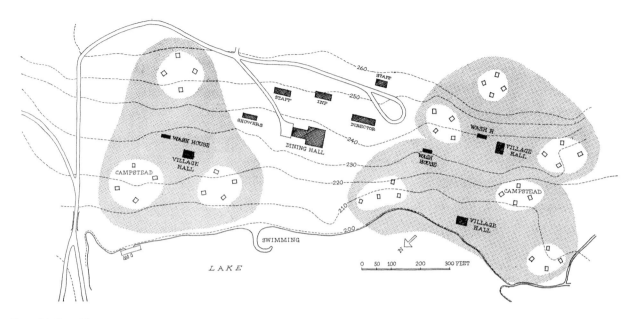

Figure E.8. Camp Bliss.
Site plan, circa 1955.

discrete developmental phases, each with its own scientifically determined needs and interests.

At the same time, many other aspects of the Bliss landscape contributed to the larger cultural project of reinforcing the idea of childhood as a special time by highlighting the distinction between the play spaces used by children and the workplaces inhabited by adults. These differences are particularly acute at Bliss (and at Camp Hayden as well), where the buildings devoted to program activities were large and rather romantic evocations of tents (or, in Hayden's case, caves), while the administrative buildings were modest, one-story structures. According to *Architectural Forum*, the service buildings at Camp Bliss "borrow[ed] the coolness and adult practicality of a Japanese house."[16] Barnes's panoramic representations of the Bliss landscape (published in *Architectural Forum*) underline the extent to which he intended these service buildings to fade into the background.

Likewise, the Bliss dining hall helped reinforce the boundaries between children and adults by minimizing diners' awareness of the kitchen. The square plan of the dining hall proper helped convey the impression that this room was a freestanding pavilion, while the A-trusses reinforced that sensation by highlighting the room's center aisle; this arrangement called attention to the glazed gable end and its natural vistas (the view published in *Archi-*

tectural Forum) or to the massive fireplace, while distracting attention from the low, lateral wall that led to the kitchen (Figure E.9). What is more, the kitchen's low ceilings helped reduce its exterior appearance.

Finally, despite their modern forms, the buildings at Camp Bliss also worked to reinforce the underlying antimodernism that continued to pervade summer camp discourse, and especially the sense that the modern world did not provide the best setting for children to live in their natural, somewhat savage, state. *Architectural Forum* articles on Camp Bliss commented on Barnes's pursuit of antimodernist goals with particular clarity, characterizing the Bliss buildings as a "family of friendly wigwams scattered along a lake," designed "with a handful of fresh primitive shapes."[17] Seven years later, the same journal noted that "the effect throughout" Camp Hayden was "of primitive materials put together by hand," and it described the dining hall as "one enormous cavelike room." This latter article made a direct connection between this primitiveness and the architect's understanding of the camp's mission with a quote attributed to Barnes himself: "A city boy at Hayden knows right away he's in the country, in touch with the land."[18] Featuring an image of two boys scaling the rock face of the dining hall chimneystack, the story also implied that the gender of the campers played a role in Barnes's choice of a "rugged" version of the primitive at Camp Hayden (Figure E.10).

In short, if we focus too closely on modern aesthetics, we can sometimes lose sight of the many other ways that the cultural landscape has helped define the contours of modern life. American summer camps—even those untouched by architectural modernism—were shaped by modern conceptions of children and childhood, which emphasized reforming gender roles while reinforcing racial hierarchies. What is more, these institutions did their best to shape campers themselves into boys and girls who would develop into men and women who would thrive in a modern world that championed the values of a white middle class. Summer camps may have positioned themselves in opposition to the fast pace and artificiality of modern life, but the cultural landscape reveals that these manufactured versions of the wilderness implicitly worked to support and maintain modern culture.

Figure E.10. Camp Hayden. Exterior detail of dining hall. Photograph by David Hirsch.

ACA Accredited Residential Camps Established before 1960

(Based on American Camping Association directory, 2000)

	Location	Affiliation	Gender	Year
ALABAMA				
Alpine Camp for Boys	Mentone	Private	Boys	1959
Camp Chandler	Wetumpka	YMCA	Coed	1929
Camp Colemen	Trussville	Girl Scouts	Girls	1925
Camp Cosby	Alpine	YMCA	Coed	1922
Camp DeSoto	Mentone	Private	Girls	1916
Camp Fletcher	Bessemer	Camp Fire	Coed	1926
Camp Skyline Ranch	Mentone	Private	Girls	1947
Children's Fresh Air Farm	Birmingham	Presbyterian	Coed	1923
Cottaquilla	Anniston	Girl Scouts	Girls	1948
Kamp Kiwanis	Ecelectic	Girl Scouts	Girls	1959
Laney for Boys	Mentone	Private	Boys	1959
North Alabama Youth Senior Camp	Blountsville	Woodmen of the World	Boys/Girls	1959
Scoutshire Woods	Citronelle	Girl Scouts	Girls	1944
Winnataska	Pell City	Boy Scouts	Coed	1918
ALASKA				
Birchwood Camp	Chugiak	Private	Coed	1959
Camp Li-Wa	Fairbanks	Private/Christian	Coed	1959
Togowoods	Wasilla	Girl Scouts	Girls	1958
Victory Bible Camp	Palmer	Private/Christian	Coed	1947

	Location	Affiliation	Gender	Year
ARIZONA				
Camp Wamatochick	Prescott	Camp Fire	Coed	1924
Friendly Pines Camp	Prescott	Private	Coed	1941
Maripai	Prescott	Girl Scouts	Girls	1934
Orme Summer Camp	Mayer	Private	Coed	1929
Sky Y Camp	Prescott	YMCA	Coed	1938
Tonto Rim American Baptist Camp	Payson	Baptist	Coed	1950
Triangle Y Ranch Camp	Oracle	YMCA	Boys/Girls/Coed	1949
ARKANSAS				
Camp Aldersgate	Little Rock	Methodist	Coed	1947
Joseph Pfeifer Kiwanis Camp	Little Rock	Kiwanis	Coed	1929
CALIFORNIA				
All Nations Camp	Wrightwood	Private	Boys/Coed	1917
All Peoples Christian Center	Los Angeles	Private/Christian	Coed	1949
Alpine Conference Center	Blue Jay	Private	Coed	1957
Azalea Trails Camp	Idylwild	Girl Scouts	Girls	1940
Bar 717 Ranch Camp Trinity	Hayfork	Private	Coed	1930
Bearskin Meadow Camp	Kings Canyon National Park	Private	Coed	1938
Big Bear Lake	Los Angeles	Presbyterian	Coed	1939
Bloomfield	Malibu	Private	Boys/Girls/Coed	1953
Bothkin	Fairfax	Girl Scouts	Girls	1950
Camp Alonim	Simi Valley	Private	Boys/Girls/Coed	1951
Camp Arbolado	Angelus Oaks	YMCA	Boys/Girls/Coed	1925
Camp Armstrong	Occidental	Christian Youth Organization	Coed	1950
Camp Arrowhead	Lake Arrowhead	Lutheran	Girls/Coed	1955
Camp Augusta	Nevada City	Private	Coed	1931
Camp Big Bear	Big Bear Lake	YMCA	Boys/Girls/Coed	1938
Camp Bluff Lake	Big Bear Lake	YMCA	Boys/Girls	1948
Camp Conrad Chinnock	Los Angeles	Private	Boys/Girls/Coed	1958
Camp Crescent	Los Angeles	Private	Boys/Girls/Coed	1957
Camp Edwards	Angelus Oaks	YMCA	Coed	1927
Camp Hollywoodland	Hollywood	Private	Girls/Coed	1925
Camp Joan Mier	Malibu	Private	Boys/Girls/Coed	1960
Camp Jones Gulch	La Honda	YMCA	Coed	1934
Camp Krem Camping Unlimited	Boulder Creek	Private	Coed	1957
Camp Lakota	Frazier Park	Girl Scouts	Girls	1949
Camp Marston and Raintree Ranch	Julian	YMCA	Coed	1921
Camp Max Strauss	Glendale	Private/Jewish	Coed	1938
Camp Medocino	Fort Bragg	Boys & Girls Club	Coed	1930
Camp Menzies	Arnold	Girl Scouts	Girls	1947
Camp Minaluta	Nevada City	Camp Fire	Coed	1928
Camp Oakes Greater Long Beach	Big Bear City	YMCA	Coed	1954
Camp Oakes West County Family	Big Bear City	YMCA	Coed	1960
Camp Osito Rancho	Big Bear Lake	Girl Scouts	Girls	1937
Camp Pacific Academy by the Sea	Carlsbad	Army, Navy Academy	Boys/Girls/Coed	1943

	Location	Affiliation	Gender	Year
Camp Paivika	Crestline	Private	Boys/Girls/Coed	1947
Camp Round Meadow	Fawnskin	YMCA	Coed	1925
Camp Stevens	Julian	Episcopal	Coed	1952
Camp Sugar Pine	Camp Connell	Girl Scouts	Girls	1950
Camp Ta Ta Pochon	Angelus Oaks	YMCA	Coed	1923
Camp Tatapochen	Alhambra	YMCA	Coed	1923
Camp Tecuya	Frazier Park	Private	Girls	1952
Camp Wasewagan	Angelus Oaks	Camp Fire	Coed	1936
Camp Wastahi	Boulder Creek	Camp Fire	Boys/Girls/Coed	1925
Catalina Island Camps	Two Harbors	Private	Coed	1926
Cherith at Sky Meadows	Angelus Oaks	Private	Boys/Girls/Coed	1946
Cherry Valley	Avalon	Private	Boys/Girls/Coed	1920
Circle V Ranch	Santa Barbara	Private	Coed	1945
City Team Camp May Mac	Felton	Private/Christian	Coed	1935
Cloverleaf Ranch	Santa Rosa	Private	Boys/Girls/Coed	1947
Costanoan	Cupertino	Private	Boys/Girls/Coed	1954
Cottontail Ranch Club	Calibases	Private	Coed	1957
Cub Resident Camp Mataquay	Julian	Boy Scouts	Boys	1938
Douglas Ranch Camps	Carmel Valley	Private	Boys/Girls	1925
El Camino Pines	Frazier Park	Private/Christian	Coed	1958
El-O-Win	Shaver Lake	Girl Scouts	Girls	1959
Enchanted Hills Camp	Napa	Private	Coed	1947
Forest Home Indian Village and Adventure Mountain	Forest Falls	Private	Coed	1938
Fox	Avalon	YMCA	Boys/Girls/Coed	1926
Gold Arrow Camp	Lakeshore	Private	Coed	1933
Griffith Park Boys Camp	Los Angeles	Private	Boys	1920
Harker Summer Programs	San Jose	Private	Coed	1956
Harold F. Whittle	Fawnskin	YMCA	Coed	1958
Helendade Scout Reservation	Running Springs	Boy Scouts	Boys	1960
Hidden Falls Camp	Soquel	Girl Scouts	Girls	1957
Hidden Villa Summer Camp	Los Altos Hills	Private	Coed	1945
Idyllwild Arts Summer Program	Idyllwild	Private	Coed	1948
Jack Hazard	Dardanelle	YMCA	Boys/Girls/Coed	1924
Jameson Ranch Camp	Glenville	Private	Coed	1935
Kennolyn Camps	Soquel	Private	Boys/Girls/Coed	1946
LA County 4-H Summer Camp	Crestine	4-H	Coed	1946
Lake Arrowhead Forest Lawn Scout Reservation	Cedar Glen	Boy Scouts	Boys	1949
Lazy J Ranch Camp	Malibu	Private	Coed	1945
Luther Village Camp Yolijwa	Oak Glen	Private/Christian	Boys/Girls/Coed	1957
Mariastella	Wrightwood	Private/Christian	Girls	1946
Montecito Sequoia Family Vacation Camp	Kings Canyon National Park	Private	Coed	1946
Mount Hermon's Redwood Camp	Mount Hermon	Private	Coed	1921
Mountain Meadow Ranch	Susanville	Private	Coed	1955
Mt Crags Camp	Calabasas	Salvation Army	Coed	1939
Ojai Valley Summer School and Camp	Ojai	Private	Coed	1943

	Location	Affiliation	Gender	Year
Oliver	Descanso	Private	Boys/Girls/Coed	1953
Pilgrim Pines Camp and Conference Center	Yucaipa	Private/Christian	Boys/Girls/Coed	1944
Pine Valley Bible Conference Association	Pine Valley	Private/Christian	Coed	1947
Plantation Farm Camp	Cazadero	Private	Boys/Girls/Coed	1952
Pythian Youth Camp	Kings Canyon National Park	Private	Coed	1946
Ramah in California	Ojai	Private/Jewish	Coed	1956
Shalom Institute Camp and Conference Center	Malibu	Private/Jewish	Coed	1951
Shasta Camp Cherith	Emigrant Gap	Private/Christian	Boys/Girls	1959
Skylake Yosemite Camp	Wishon	Private	Coed	1945
Skylark Ranch	San Jose	Girl Scouts	Girls	1953
Stanley Ranch Camp	Castaic	Private	Coed	1945
Tahquitz	Angelus Oaks	Private	Boys	1959
Tautona Girl Scouts	Angelus Oaks	Girl Scouts	Girls	1945
Tawonga	Groveland	Private	Coed	1926
Thousand Pines Christian Camp and Conference Center	Crestline	Baptist	Boys/Girls/Coed	1939
UCLA Uni Camp	Los Angeles	Private	Coed	1935
Unalayee	Callahan	Private	Coed	1949
Voorhis Viking	Mammoth Lakes	Boys & Girls Club	Boys/Coed	1929
Waltons Grizzly Lodge	Portola	Private	Coed	1926
Wawona	Wawona	Private	Coed	1929
Westminster Woods	Occidental	Presbyterian	Boys/Girls/Coed	1946
Wilshire Boulevard Temple Camps and Conference Center	Malibu	Private/Jewish	Coed	1952
Wintaka	Running Springs	Camp Fire	Boys/Girls	1958
Wolahi	Julian	Camp Fire	Boys/Girls/Coed	1933
Wylie Woods Presbyterian Conference Center	Los Angeles	Presbyterian	no information available	1949

COLORADO

	Location	Affiliation	Gender	Year
Adventure Unlimited Ranches	Buena Vista	Private	Coed	1955
Blue Mountain Ranch	Florissant	Private	Boys/Girls/Coed	1947
C Bar T Trail Ranch	Bellvue	Private	Coed	1958
Camp Chief Ouray of the Rockies	Granby	YMCA	Coed	1907
Camp Santa Maria del Monte	Shawnee	Catholic	Coed	1930
Camp Shady Brook	Sedalia	YMCA	Boys/Girls	1948
Cheley Colorado Camps	Estes Park	Private	Boys/Girls	1921
Children's Diabetes Camp	Ward	Private	Coed	1957
Colorado Camp Cherith	Greeley	Private	Girls	1950
Eagle Lake Camp	Colorado Springs	Private/Christian	Boys/Girls/Coed	1957
Easter Seals Colorado Rocky Mountain Village	Empire	Private	Coed	1951
Flying G Ranch	Sedalia	Girl Scouts	Girls	1945
Geneva Glen Camp	Indian Hills	Private	Coed	1922
J Bar CC Ranch Camp	Elbert	Private	Coed	1953

	Location	Affiliation	Gender	Year
Rainbow Trail Lutheran Camp	Hillside	Lutheran	Coed	1957
Sanborn Western Camps	Florissant	Private	Boys/Girls	1948
Shwayder Camp of Temple Emanuel	Idaho Springs	Private/Jewish	Coed	1948
Sky High Ranch	Woodland Park	Private	Girls	1952
Templed Hills Camp and Retreat Center	Woodland Park	Private/Christian	Coed	1955
Tomahawk Ranch	Bailey	Girl Scouts	Girls	1953

CONNECTICUT

	Location	Affiliation	Gender	Year
Aspetuck	Weston	Private	Girls	1939
Awosting Chinqueka	Bantam	Private	Boys/Girls	1900
Bucks Rock Camp	New Milford	Private	Coed	1943
Camp Claire	Lyme	Private/Christian	Coed	1916
Camp Hazen	Chester	YMCA	Coed	1920
Camp Jewell Outdoor Center	Colebrook	YMCA	Boys/Girls/Coed	1901
Camp Laurelwood	Madisong	Private	Coed	1937
Camp Mohawk	Litchfield	YMCA	Girls	1919
Camp Sloane	Lakeville	YMCA	Coed	1928
Camp Wah-Nee	Torrington	Private	Coed	1930
Camp Washington	Lakeside	Private	Coed	1917
Camp Woodstock	Woodstock Valley	YMCA	Coed	1922
Center Church Camp Asto Wamah	Columbia	Private/Christian	Boys/Girls/Coed	1910
Easter Seal Camp Hemlocks	Hebron	Private	Coed	1950
Girl Scout Laurel Resident Camp	Lebanon	Girl Scouts	Girls	1955
Incarnation Center	Ivoryton	Private/Christian	Coed	1886
KenMont and KenWood Camps	Kent	Private	Boys/Girls	1924
Maria Pratt	Torrington	Girl Scouts	Girls	1947
S J Ranch	Ellington	Private	Girls	1956
Windham Tolland 4-H Camp	Pomfret Center	4-H	Coed	1954

DELAWARE

	Location	Affiliation	Gender	Year
Children's Beach House	Lewes	Private	Coed	1936

FLORIDA

	Location	Affiliation	Gender	Year
Camp Challenge	Sorrento	Private	Boys/Girls	1960
Camp Crystal Lake	Starke	Private	Coed	1948
Camp Wewa	Apopka	YMCA	Coed	1920
Dorothy Thomas	Riverview	Girl Scouts	Girls	1954
Florida WMU Camps	Marianna	Baptist	Girls	1946
Lake Aurora Christian Assembly	Lake Wales	Private/Christian	Coed	1947
Montgomery Presbyterian Center	Starke	Presbyterian	Coed	1957
Scoutcrest Camp	Odessa	Girl Scouts	Girls	1940
Welaka	Jupiter	Girl Scouts	Girls	1959

GEORGIA

	Location	Affiliation	Gender	Year
Athens YMCO Camp for Girls	Clarkesville	YMCO	Girls	1925
Calvin Center	Hampton	Presbyterian	Coed	1960
Camp Concharty	Shiloh	Girl Scouts	Girls	1956

	Location	Affiliation	Gender	Year
Camp Juliette Low	Cloudland	Private	Girls	1922
Camp Kiwanis	Danielsville	Kiwanis	Coed	1951
Camp Lookout	Rising Fawn	Methodist	Coed	1956
Camp Low	Savannah	Girl Scouts	Girls	1957
Camp Martha Johnson	Lizella	Girl Scouts	Girls	1925
Camp Mikell	Toccoa	Episcopal	Coed	1941
Camp Tanglewood	Martinez	Girl Scouts	Girls	1946
Camp Timber Ridge	Mableton	Girl Scouts	Girls	1924
Camp Toccoa	Toccoa	Camp Fire	Coed	1927
Glisson	Dahlonega	Methodist	Boys/Girls	1925
Pine Acres	Acworth	Girl Scouts	Girls	1960

HAWAI'I

	Location	Affiliation	Gender	Year
Camp H. R. Erdman	Waialua	YMCA	Boys/Girls/Coed	1926
Camp Sloggett	Lihue	YMCA	Coed	1937
Homelani	Waialua	Salvation Army	Boys/Girls/Coed	1942

IDAHO

	Location	Affiliation	Gender	Year
Alice Pittenger	McCall	Girl Scouts	Girls	1940
Camp Cross	Coeur D'Alene	Episcopal	Boys/Girls/Coed	1923
Camp Lutherhaven	Coeur D'Alene	Lutheran	Boys/Girls/Coed	1945
MiVoden Summer Camp and Retreat Center	Hayden Lake	Private/Christian	Coed	1940
Sweyolakan	Coeur D'Alene	Camp Fire	Boys/Girls/Coed	1922
Ta-Man-A-Wis	Swan Valley	Girl Scouts	Girls	1957

ILLINOIS

	Location	Affiliation	Gender	Year
4-H Memorial Camp	Monticello	4-H	Coed	1946
Algonquin	Algonquin	Private	Boys/Girls/Coed	1907
Camp Cedar Point	Makanda	Girl Scouts	Girls	1953
Camp Duncan	Ingleside	YMCA	Boys/Girls/Coed	1921
Camp Henry Horner	Ingleside	Private/Jewish	Coed	1907
Camp Little Giant	Carbondale	Private	Boys/Girls/Coed	1953
Camp Shaw-Waw-Nas-See	Manteno	4-H	Coed	1957
Camp Tuckabatchee	Ottawa	Private	Coed	1927
Camp Widjiwagan	Springfield	Girl Scouts	Girls	1936
Carew	Makanda	Presbyterian	Coed	1952
Chicago Youth Centers Camp Rosenthal	Dowagiac	Private	Coed	1956
Dean	Big Rock	Girl Scouts	Girls	1947
Easter Seal Summer Camp	Yorkville	Private	Coed	1949
Farm and Ranch Campus at The Center	Palos Park	Private	Coed	1936
Hastings Lake Camps	Lake Villa	YMCA	Coed	1922
Lutheran Outdoor Center	Oregon	Lutheran	Coed	1927
Medill McCormick Outdoor Program Center	Stillman Valley	Girl Scouts	Girls	1940
Ondessonk	Ozark	Catholic	Boys/Girls/Coed	1959

	Location	Affiliation	Gender	Year
Tapawingo	Metamora	Girl Scouts	Girls	1957
Triangle D Camp for Children with Diabetes	Ingleside	Private	Boys/Girls/Coed	1949

INDIANA

	Location	Affiliation	Gender	Year
Boys & Girls Club Camp	Noblesville	Boys & Girls Club	Boys/Girls/Coed	1913
Bradford Woods Outdoor Education Camping Center	Martinsville	Private	Coed	1955
Camp Alexander Mack	Milford	Private/Christian	Coed	1924
Camp Crosley	North Webster	YMCA	Coed	1921
Camp John Warvel	Milford	Private	Boys/Girls	1955
Camp Lawrence	Merriville	Christian Youth Organization	Coed	1959
Camp Livingston	Bennington	Private/Jewish	Coed	1920
Camp Millhouse	South Bend	Private	Coed	1937
Camp Potawotami	South Milford	YMCA	Boys/Girls/Coed	1919
Camp Pycoa	Brownstown	Presbyterian	Boys/Girls/Coed	1953
Camp Rancho Framasa	Nashville	Christian Youth Organization	Coed	1946
Camp Tecumseh	Brookston	YMCA	Coed	1924
Culver Summer Camps	Culver	Private	Coed	1902
Ella J. Logan	Syracuse	Girl Scouts	Girls	1928
Gnaw Bone Camp	Nashville	Private	Girls	1943
Happy Hollow Children's Camp	Nashville	Private	Coed	1951
Henry F. Koch	Cannelton	Girl Scouts	Girls	1941
Howe Military School Summer Camp	Howe	Private	Boys	1925
Jameson	Indianapolis	Private	Boys/Girls/Coed	1928
Lutherwald	Howe	Lutheran	Coed	1955
Ruth Lilly Outdoor Center	St. Paul	YMCA	Coed	1946
Sycamore Valley Girl Scout Camp	Lafayette	Girl Scouts	Girls	1950
Waycross Camp	Morgantown	Episcopal	Coed	1957

IOWA

	Location	Affiliation	Gender	Year
Abe Lincoln	Blue Grass	YMCA	Coed	1922
Aldersgate United Methodist Camp	Villisca	Methodist	Coed	1957
Camp Tanglefoot	Clear Lake	Girl Scouts	Girls	1947
Camp Wapsie	Coggon	YMCA	Coed	1918
Camp Wa-Shawtee	Hamburg	Girl Scouts	Girls	1960
Camp Wyoming	Wyoming	Presbyterian	Coed	1960
Conestoga	New Liberty	Girl Scouts	Girls	1946
Des Moines YMCA Camp	Boone	YMCA	Boys/Girls/Coed	1919
East Iowa Bible Camp	Deep River	Private/Christian	Coed	1944
Forest Lake	Bloomfield	Baptist	Boys/Girls	1951
Foster	Spirit Lake	YMCA	Boys/Girls	1912
Hantesa	Boone	Camp Fire	Coed	1919
Ingham Okoboji Lutheran Bible Camps	Milford	Lutheran	Boys/Girls/Coed	1924
Iowa 4-H Education and Natural Resources	Madrid	4-H	Coed	1950
Lakota Camp	Dayton	Girl Scouts	Girls	1960

	Location	Affiliation	Gender	Year
Little Cloud	Epworth	Girl Scouts	Girls	1950
L-Kee-Ta	Danville	Girl Scouts	Girls	1945
Lutheran Lakeside Camp	Spirit Lake	Lutheran	Boys/Girls/Coed	1960
Riverside Lutheran Bible Camp	Story City	Lutheran	Boys/Girls/Coed	1943
Wesley Woods Camp and Retreat Center	Indianola	Methodist	Boys/Girls/Coed	1956

KANSAS

	Location	Affiliation	Gender	Year
Camp Wood	Elmdale	YMCA	Coed	1915

KENTUCKY

	Location	Affiliation	Gender	Year
Bear Creek Aquatic Camp	Benton	Girl Scouts	Girls	1940
Camp Ernst	Burlington	YMCA	Coed	1928
Camp Piomingo	Brandenburg	YMCA	Coed	1938
Cedar Ridge	Louisville	Private	Boys/Girls/Coed	1960
Loucon Training and Retreat Center	Leitchfield	Methodist	Boys/Girls/Coed	1951
Pennyroyal	Utica	Girl Scouts	Girls	1956

LOUISIANA

	Location	Affiliation	Gender	Year
Covington	Covington	Girl Scouts	Girls	1927
Marydale	St. Francisville	Girl Scouts	Girls	1947
Wawbansee	Simsboro	Girl Scouts	Girls	1946

MAINE

	Location	Affiliation	Gender	Year
Agassiz	Poland	Private	Coed	1935
Alford Lake Camp	Hope	Private	Girls/Coed	1907
Androscoggin	Wayne	Private	Boys	1907
Camp Agawam	Raymond	Private	Boys	1919
Camp Arcadia	Casco	Private	Girls	1916
Camp Cedar	Casco	Private	Boys	1954
Camp Fernwood	Poland	Private	Girls	1921
Camp Jordan	Ellsworth	Private	Coed	1908
Camp Lawroweld	Weld	Private	Coed	1948
Camp Mechuwana	Winthrop	Methodist	Coed	1948
Camp Natarswi	Millinocket	Girl Scouts	Girls	1936
Camp Runoia	Belgrade Lakes	Private	Girls	1907
Camp Samoset	Casco	Private	Boys	1944
Camp Takajo	Naples	Private	Boys	1947
Camp Walden	Denmark	Private	Girls	1916
Camp Waziyatah	Waterford	Private	Coed	1922
Camps Newfound and Owatonna	Harrison	Private	Boys/Girls	1914
Caribou for Boys	Waterville	Private	Boys	1922
Chewonki	Wicasset	Private	Boys/Coed	1915
Cobbossee	Winthrop	Private	Boys	1902
Darrow Wilderness Trip Camp	Grand Lake Stream	Private	Coed	1957
Encore Coda	Sweden	Private	Coed	1950
Forest Acres Camp for Girls	Fryeburg	Private	Girls	1927
Four Winds	Sargentville	Private	Girls	1946

	Location	Affiliation	Gender	Year
Indian Acres Camp for Boys	Fryeburg	Private	Boys	1924
JCC Camp Kingswood	Bridgton	Private	Coed	1948
Kamp Kohut	Oxford	Private	Coed	1907
Kawanhee	Weld	Private	Boys	1921
Kingsley Pines Camp	Raymond	Private	Coed	1929
Kippewa for Girls	Monmouth	Private	Girls	1957
Laurel	Readfield	Private	Coed	1949
Laurel South	Casco	Private	Coed	1921
Manitou	Oakland	Private	Boys	1947
Mataponi	Naples	Private	Girls	1950
Matoaka for Girls	Smithfield	Private	Girls	1951
Med-O-Lark Camp	Washington	Private	Coed	1920
Modin	Belgrade	Private	Coed	1922
Nashoba North	Raymond	Private	Coed	1933
New England Camp Cherith	Alfred	Private/Christian	Girls	1945
New England Music Camp	Sidney	Private	Coed	1937
O-AT-KA	Sebago	Private	Boys	1906
Pinecliffe	Harrison	Private	Girls	1917
Sebago	Sebago Lake	Salvation Army	Boys/Girls/Coed	1957
Skylemar	Naples	Private	Boys	1948
Tapawingo Camp	Sweden	Private	Girls	1919
Timanous	Raymond	Private	Boys	1917
Tripp Lake Camp	Poland	Private	Girls	1911
Vega	Kents Hill	Private	Girls	1936
The Wavus Camps	Jefferson	Private	Coed	1922
Wawenock	Raymond	Private	Girls	1910
Wekeela for Boys & Girls	Canton	Private	Coed	1922
Wigwam	Waterford	Private	Boys	1910
Wildwood	Bridgton	Private	Boys	1953
Winnebago	Kents Hill	Private	Boys	1919
Winona Camps for Boys	Bridgton	Private	Boys	1908
Wohelo Luther Gulick Camps	South Casco	Private	Girls	1907
Wyonegonic	Denmark	Private	Girls	1902

MARYLAND

	Location	Affiliation	Gender	Year
Airy	Thurmont	Private	Boys	1924
Camp Conowingo	Conowingo	Girl Scouts	Girls	1956
Camp Glyndon	Reistertown	Private	Boys/Girls/Coed	1952
Camp Letts	Edgewater	YMCA	Coed	1906
Camp Pecometh	Centreville	Private/Christian	Coed	1946
Camp Puhtok	Monkton	Salvation Army	Coed	1942
Camp Saint Charles	Rock Point	Private	Boys	1951
Camp Tockwogh	Worton	YMCA	Coed	1938
Camp Wright	Stevensville	Epsicopal	Coed	1930
Carroll County 4-H Center	Westminster	4-H	Coed	1960
Chesapeake Center	Port Deposit	Private/Christian	Coed	1955
Echo Hill Camp	Worton	Private	Coed	1944
Elks Camp Barrett	Annapolis	BPO Elks	Coed	1952

	Location	Affiliation	Gender	Year
Fairlee Manor Recreation and Education Center	Chestertown	Private	Boys/Girls/Coed	1954
Greentop	Sabillasville	Private	Coed	1937
Grove Point	Earleville	Girl Scouts	Girls	1948
Habonim Dror Camp Moshava	Street	Private/Jewish	Coed	1935
Harford County 4-H Camp	Street	4-H	Coed	1921
Louise	Cascade	Private/Jewish	Girls	1922
Mar-Lu-Ridge	Jefferson	Private/Christian	Coed	1959
Western Maryland 4-H Center	Swanton	4-H	Boys/Girls/Coed	1956

MASSACHUSETTS

	Location	Affiliation	Gender	Year
Atwater	North Brookfield	Private	Boys/Girls	1921
Avoda	Middleboro	Private/Jewish	Boys	1927
Bauercrest	Amesbury	Private	Boys	1931
Belvoir Terrace Fine Performing Arts Center	Lenox	Private	Boys	1954
Bement Camp and Conference Center	Charlton Depot	Episcopal	Boys/Girls/Coed	1948
Burgess/Hayward	Sandwich	YMCA	Boys/Girls/Coed	1928
Camp Becket	Becket	YMCA	Boys	1903
Camp Bonnie Brae	East Otis	Girl Scouts	Girls	1919
Camp Frank A. Day	East Brookfield	YMCA	Coed	1916
Camp Greylock for Boys	Becket	Private	Boys	1916
Camp Hi-Rock	Mount Washington	YMCA	Boys/Girls/Coed	1948
Camp Howe	Hawthorne	4-H	Coed	1928
Camp Leslie	Georgetown	4-H	Coed	1939
Camp Marshall and Massachusettes 4-H Home	Spencer	4-H	Coed	1931
Camp Middlesex	Ashby	4-H	Coed	1940
Camp Mishnoah	Holland	Private	Girls	1928
Camp Romaca	Hinsdale	Private	Girls	1929
Camp Rotary	Lynn	Rotary Club	Coed	1921
Camp Wonderland	Sharon	Salvation Army	Boys/Girls/Coed	1924
Cape Cod Sea Camps Monomoy and Wono	Brewster	Private	Coed	1922
Chimney Corners Camp	Becket	YMCA	Girls	1931
Clara Barton Diabetes Camp	North Oxford	Private	Girls/Coed	1932
Crane Lake Camp	West Stockbridge	Private/Jewish	Coed	1922
Danbee for Girls	Hinsdale	Private	Girls	1950
East Boston Camps	Westford	Private	Boys/Girls/Coed	1937
Eisner Camp for Living Judaism	Great Barrington	Private/Jewish	Coed	1958
Elliott P. Joslin Camps	Charlton	Private	Boys	1948
Farley Outdoor Education Center	Mashpee	4-H	Coed	1934
Good News	Forestdale	Private/Christian	Boys/Girls/Coed	1935
Green Eyrie	Harvard	Girl Scouts	Girls	1925
Horizons for Youth	Sharon	Private	Coed	1938
Lapham	Ashby	Private	Coed	1938
Lenox	Lee	Private	Boys/Girls	1918
Mah-Kee-Nac	Lenox	Private	Boys	1929

	Location	Affiliation	Gender	Year
Morgan Memorial Fresh Air Camp	South Athol	Private	Coed	1906
New England Keswick	Monterey	Private/Christian	Coed	1941
Pembroke	Pembroke	Private	Girls	1936
Ramah in New England	Palmer	Private/Jewish	Coed	1954
Springfield Boys Club Camp	Brimfield	Boys Club	Coed	1920
Taconic	Hinsdale	Private	Coed	1932
Watitoh	Becket	Private	Coed	1937
Wildwood	Gardner	Private	Coed	1950
Winadu	Pittsfield	Private	Boys	1927
Wind in the Pines Girl Scout Center	Plymouth	Girl Scouts	Girls	1929
Wing Duxbury Stockade	Duxbury	Private	Boys/Girls	1936
Wingate Kirkland	Yarmouth	Private	Coed	1957
Winnekeag	Ashburnham	Private/Christian	Boys/Girls/Coed	1951

MICHIGAN

	Location	Affiliation	Gender	Year
Anna Behrens	Greenville	Girl Scouts	Girls	1960
Au Sable	Grayling	Seventh-day Adventist	Coed	1948
Camp Algonquin	Hastings	YMCA	Coed	1947
Camp Arbutus-Hayo-Went-Ha for Girls	Traverse City	YMCA	Girls	1914
Camp Beechpoint	Allegan	Private	Coed	1959
Camp Copneconic	Fenton	YMCA	Coed	1915
Camp Daggett	Petoskey	Private	Coed	1925
Camp Eberhart	Three Rivers	YMCA	Boys/Girls/Coed	1909
Camp Hayo-Went-Ha	Central Lake	YMCA	Boys	1904
Camp Kidwell	Bloomingdale	4-H	Coed	1949
Camp Manitou Lin	Middleville	YMCA	Coed	1913
Camp Metamora	Metamora	Girl Scouts	Girls	1936
Camp Narrin	Ortonville	Girl Scouts	Girls	1946
Camp Newaygo NCCS	Newaygo	Private	Boys/Girls/Coed	1926
Camp Nissokone	Oscoda	YMCA	Boys	1914
Camp O'Fair Winds	Columbiaville	Girl Scouts	Girls	1930
Camp Ohiyesa	Holly	YMCA	Coed	1918
Camp Pendalouan	Montague	YMCA	Coed	1924
Camp Pinewood	Twin Lake	YMCA	Boys/Girls/Coed	1925
Camp Playfair	Lexington	Girl Scouts	Girls	1947
Camp Roger	Rockford	Private	Coed	1941
Camp Shawadasee	Lawton	Girl Scouts	Girls	1956
Camp Walden	Cheboygan	Private	Boys/Girls/Coed	1959
Camp Wathana	Holly	Camp Fire	Coed	1926
Camp Westminster on Higgins Lake	Roscommon	Private/Christian	Boys/Girls/Coed	1925
Cavell Metro Detroit	Lexington	YMCA	Girls	1914
Cedar Campus	Cedarville	Private/Christian	Coed	1954
Circle Pines Center	Delton	Private	Coed	1938
Covenant Point Bible Camp	Iron River	Private/Christian	Coed	1926
Crystalaire	Frankfort	Private	Coed	1921
CYO Boys' Camp	Carsonville	Catholic Youth Organization	Boys	1946
CYO Camp for Girls	Port Sanilac	Catholic Youth Organization	Girls	1950

	Location	Affiliation	Gender	Year
Deer Trails	Harrison	Private	Girls	1938
Echo Grove Camp and Conference Center	Leonard	Salvation Army	Boys/Girls/Coed	1921
Fortune Lake Lutheran Camp	Crystal Falls	Lutheran	Coed	1929
Fowler Center	Mayville	Private	Boys/Girls/Coed	1957
Greenwood Presbyterian Camp	Gowen	Presbyterian	Boys/Girls/Coed	1952
Greenwoods Camp for Boys	Decatur	Private	Boys	1935
Henry	Newaygo	Presbyterian	Coed	1937
Huron Forest Camp Cherith	Oscoda	Private/Christian	Boys/Girls	1941
Indian Trails Camp	Grand Rapids	Private	Coed	1953
Lake Ann Baptist Camp	Lake Ann	Baptist	Coed	1948
Lake of the Woods Camp for Girls	Decatur	Private	Boys/Girls	1935
Leelanau Kohahana Camps	Maple City	Private/Christian	Boys/Girls	1921
Little Pine Island Camp	Comstock Park	Salvation Army	Coed	1925
Maplehurst	Kewadin	Private	Coed	1955
Miniwanca	Shelby	American Youth Foundation	Boys/Girls	1925
Mystic Lake Camp	Lake	YMCA	Coed	1926
Oak Hills Camp	Harrison	Girl Scouts	Girls	1949
Pine Ridge Bible Camp	Cedar Springs	Private/Christian	Coed	1946
Presbyterian Camps	Saugatuck	Presbyterian	Boys/Girls/Coed	1899
Sancta Maria	Gaylord	Catholic	Boys	1933
Sea Gull	Charlevoix	Private	Girls	1955
Storer Camps	Jackson	YMCA	Boys/Coed	1918
Tannadoonah	Vandalia	Camp Fire	Boys/Girls/Coed	1929
Van Buren Youth Camp	Bloomingdale	Private	Coed	1950

MINNESOTA

	Location	Affiliation	Gender	Year
Big Sandy Camp and Retreat Center	McGregor	Private/Christian	Coed	1959
Bovey	Solon Springs	Private	Coed	1950
Camp Birchwood	La Porte	Private	Boys/Girls	1959
Camp Buckskin	Ely	Private	Coed	1959
Camp Chippewa for Boys	Cass Lake	Private	Boys	1935
Camp Christmas Tree	Mound	YMCA	Coed	1958
Camp Foley	Pine River	Private	Coed	1925
Camp Greenwood	Buffalo	Girl Scouts	Girls	1925
Camp Ihduhapi	Loretto	YMCA	Coed	1930
Camp Kamaji	Cass Lake	Private	Girls	1914
Camp Lakamaga	Marine on St. Croix	Girl Scouts	Girls	1927
Camp Lake Hubert for Girls	Lake Hubert	Private	Girls/Coed	1927
Camp Lincoln for Boys	Lake Hubert	Private	Boys/Coed	1909
Camp Menogyn	Grand Marais	YMCA	Boys/Girls	1922
Camp Miller	Sturgeon Lake	YMCA	Boys/Girls/Coed	1898
Camp Olsen	Longville	YMCA	Coed	1954
Camp Onomia	Onamia	Private/Christian	Coed	1949
Camp Pepin	Stockholm	YMCA	Coed	1934
Camp Trowbridge	Vergas	Camp Fire	Boys/Girls/Coed	1929
Camp Voyageur	Ely	Private	Boys	1951
Camp Warren	Eveleth	YMCA	Boys/Girls	1928

	Location	Affiliation	Gender	Year
Camp Widjiwagan	Ely	YMCA	Boys/Girls	1929
Catholic Youth Camps	McGregor	Catholic	Coed	1946
Courage	Maple Lake	Private	Coed	1955
Covenant Pines Bible Camp	McGregor	Private/Evangelical Christian	Coed	1954
Eden Wood	Eden Prairie	Private	Coed	1958
Emmaus	Menahga	Private/Christian	Coed	1934
Grindstone Lake Bible Camp	Sandstone	Private/Evangelical Christian	Coed	1932
Kooch-I-Ching	International Falls	Private	Boys	1924
Lake of the Woods Bible Camp	Baudette	Private/Christian	Coed	1934
Laketrails Base Camp	Oak Island	Private	Coed	1952
Luther Crest Bible Camp	Alexandria	Private/Christian	Boys/Girls/Coed	1945
Minne-Wa-Kan	Cass Lake	Private/Christian	Coed	1944
Mishawaka for Boys and Girls	Grand Rapids	Private	Boys/Girls	1910
National TTT Summer Camp	Eden Valley	National TTT Society	Girls	1951
North Central Camp Cherith	Frazee	Private/Christian	Boys/Girls	1947
Shetek Lutheran Ministries	Slayton	Lutheran	Coed	1947
Singing Hills	Waterville	Girl Scouts	Girls	1952
Tanadoona	Excelsior	Camp Fire	Coed	1924
Thunderbird for Boys	Bemidji	Private	Boys	1946
Wilderness Canoe Base	Grand Marais	Private/Christian	Boys/Girls/Coed	1956

MISSISSIPPI

	Location	Affiliation	Gender	Year
Camp Henry Pratt	Columbus	YMCA	Coed	1926
Camp Lake Stephens	Oxford	Methodist	Boys/Girls/Coed	1946
Camp Wahi	Brandon	Girl Scouts	Girls	1949
Hopewell Camp and Conference Center	Oxford	Presbyterian	Coed	1949

MISSOURI

	Location	Affiliation	Gender	Year
Camp Cedarledge	Pevely	Girl Scouts	Girls	1927
Camp Fiddlecreek	Gray Summit	Girl Scouts	Girls	1956
Camp Finbrooke	Rogersville	Private	Girls	1950
Camp Lakewood	Potosi	YMCA	Coed	1947
Camp Shawnee	Waldron	Private	Coed	1953
Camp Wakonda	Ash Grove	YMCA	Coed	1953
Camp Wyman	Eureka	Kiwanis	Boys/Girls/Coed	1898
Mihaska	Bourbon	Salvation Army	no information available	1948
Mintahama	Joplin	Girl Scouts	Girls	1946
Mo-Kan Camp	Kansas City	Salvation Army	Boys/Girls/Coed	1920
Oakledge	Warsaw	Girl Scouts	Girls	1947
Prairie Schooner	Kansas City	Girl Scouts	Girls	1947
Sherwood Forest Camp	Lesterville	Private	Boys/Girls	1937
Taum Sauk	Lesterville	Private	Boys/Girls/Coed	1946
Woodland	Albany	Girl Scouts	Girls	1948

MONTANA

	Location	Affiliation	Gender	Year
Christikon	McLeod	Lutheran	Coed	1951

	Location	Affiliation	Gender	Year
NEBRASKA				
Camp Kitaki	Louisville	YMCA	Boys/Girls	1903
Camp Maha	Omaha	Girl Scouts	Girls	1945
Floyd Rogers	Omaha	Private	Coed	1931
Gene Eppley Camp Retreat	Omaha	Salvation Army	Boys/Girls/Coed	1944
NEVADA				
Foxtail	Las Vegas	Girl Scouts	Girls	1953
NEW HAMPSHIRE				
Bear Hill Camp	Allenstown	4-H	Coed	1936
Berea	Bristol	Private/Christian	Boys/Girls/Coed	1945
Brookwoods Deer Run	Alton	Private/Christian	Boys/Girls/Coed	1944
Camp Allen for Individuals with Disabilities	Bedford	Lions/Kiwanis	Coed	1931
Camp Belknap	Wolfeboro	YMCA	Boys	1903
Camp Bernadette	Wolfeboro	Private/Christian	Girls	1953
Camp Birchmont	Wolfeboro	Private	Boys/Girls/Coed	1951
Camp Calumet Lutheran	West Ossipee	Lutheran	Coed	1960
Camp Fatima	Gilmanton IW	Private/Christian	Boys/Coed	1949
Camp Foss	Barnstead	YMCA	Girls	1923
Camp Hale	Center Sandwich	Private	Boys	1900
Camp Huckins	Freedom	YMCA	Girls	1928
Camp Kenwood and Evergreen	Potter Place	Private	Boys/Girls	1930
Camp Lawrence	Laconia	YMCA	Boys	1907
Camp Marist	Center Ossipee	Private	Boys	1949
Camp Merriwood	Orford	Private	Girls	1949
Camp Mi-Te-Na	Alton	YMCA	Boys	1913
Camp Nokomis	Laconia	YMCA	Girls	1952
Camp Robin Hood	Freedom	Private	Boys/Girls	1927
Camp Squanto	West Swanzey	Private/Christian Evangelical	Coed	1957
Camp Tecumseh	Center Harbor	Private	Boys	1903
Camp Winaukee	Moultonboro	Private	Boys	1920
Camp Yavneh	Northwood	Private/Jewish	Coed	1944
Camp Young Judaea	Amherst	Private/Jewish	Coed	1939
Fleur-De-Lis Camp	Fitzwilliam	Private	Girls	1929
Glen Brook	Marlborough	Private	Coed	1946
Happy T Ranch	Rumney	Private/Christian Evangelical	Coed	1957
Kingswood Camp	Piermont	Private	Boys	1909
Menotomy	Meredith	Girl Scouts	Girls	1923
Merrowvista	Ossipee	American Youth Foundation	Coed	1924
Moosilauke	Orford	Private	Boys	1904
North Woods and Pleasant Valley Camps	Mirror Lake	YMCA	Boys/Girls	1929
Pemigewassett	Wentworth	Private	Boys	1908
Robindel for Girls	Center Harbor	Private	Girls	1951
Runels/Machagamee	Pelham	Girl Scouts	Girls	1930

	Location	Affiliation	Gender	Year
Takodah	Richmond	YMCA	Boys/Girls/Coed	1921
Tel Noar	Hampstead	Private/Jewish	Coed	1946
Tevya	Brookline	Private/Jewish	Coed	1940
Tohkomeupog	East Madison	Private	Boys	1932
Wabasso	Bradford	Girl Scouts	Girls	1956
Wa-Klo	Jaffrey	Private	Girls	1938
Walt Whitman	Piermont	Private	Coed	1948
Waukeela	Eaton Center	Private	Girls	1922
Wicosuta	Bristol	Private	Girls	1920
Wikaya	Richmond	YMCA	Boys	1921
William Lawrence Camp	Center Tuftonboro	Private	Boys	1913

NEW JERSEY

	Location	Affiliation	Gender	Year
Appel Farm Arts and Music Center	Elmer	Private	Boys/Girls/Coed	1960
Baptist Camp Lebanon	Lebanon	Baptist	Coed	1949
Beisler Camping and Retreat	Port Murray	Lutheran	Boys/Girls/Coed	1952
Camp Bernie	Port Murray	YMCA	Coed	1957
Camp Cedar Knoll	Millville	Baptist	Coed	1950
Camp Ockanickon and Matollionequay	Medford	YMCA	Boys/Girls/Coed	1906
Camp Ralph S. Mason	Hardwick	YMCA	Coed	1900
Camp Sussex	Sussex	Private	Boys/Girls/Coed	1923
Dark Waters	Medford	Quaker	Coed	1928
Fairview Lake	Newton	YMCA	Boys/Girls/Coed	1915
Happiness Is Camping	Blairstown	Private	Coed	1958
Inawendiwin Program Center	Tabernacle	Girl Scouts	Girls	1950
Kiddie Keep Well	Edison	Private	Coed	1924
Lou Henry Hoover	Middleville	Girl Scouts	Girls	1953
Merry Heart Easter Seal	Hackettstown	Easter Seal	Coed	1949
Nejeda	Stillwater	Private	Boys/Girls	1957
Presbyterian Camp and Conference Center	Johnsonburg	Presbyterian	Coed	1959
Sacajawea	Newfield	Girl Scouts	Girls	1950
Star Lake Camp	Bloomingdale	Salvation Army	Coed	1923
Sun 'N Fun Arc Gloucester Resident Camp	Williamstown	Private	Coed	1957
Trail Blazer Camps	Montague	Private	Boys/Girls	1887
Vacamas Programs for Youth	West Milford	Private	Boys/Girls/Coed	1924

NEW MEXICO

	Location	Affiliation	Gender	Year
Brush Ranch Camps for Girls and Boys	Tererro	Private	Boys/Girls	1956
Camp Tall Pines	Mayhill	Girl Scouts	Girls	1958
Philmont Scout Ranch	Cimarron	Boy Scouts	Boys	1938

NEW YORK

	Location	Affiliation	Gender	Year
Amahami	Deposit	Girl Scouts	Girls	1929
Baco for Boys Che-Na-Wah for Girls	Minerva	Private	Boys/Girls	1923

	Location	Affiliation	Gender	Year
Berkshire Hills Emanuel Camps	Copake	Private	Coed	1931
Blue Bay	East Hampton	Girl Scouts	Girls	1947
Brant Lake Camp	Brant Lake	Private	Boys	1916
Camp Aldersgate	Brantingham	Methodist	Coed	1948
Camp Bristol Hills	Canandaigua	Private	Coed	1931
Camp Chateaugay	Merill	Private	Coed	1946
Camp Cory	Penn Yan	YMCA	Coed	1921
Camp Cummings	Brewster	Educational Alliance	Coed	1955
Camp Dudley	Westport	YMCA	Boys	1885
Camp Eagle Island	Saranac Lake	Girl Scouts	Girls	1938
Camp Echo	Burlington	Private	Boys/Girls/Coed	1924
Camp Edey	Bayport	Girl Scouts	Girls	1945
Camp Hilltop	Hancock	Private	Coed	1924
Camp Jeanne d'Arc	Merrill	Private	Girls	1922
Camp Li-Lo-Li	Randolph	Private	Boys/Girls/Coed	1953
Camp Lokanda	Glen Spey	Private	Coed	1937
Camp Na-Sho-Pa	Bloomingburg	Private	Boys/Girls/Coed	1937
Camp Onyahsa	Jamestown	YMCA	Coed	1898
Camp Pontiac	Copake	Private	Coed	1922
Camp Schodack	Holland	Girl Scouts	Girls	1957
Camp Scully	Wynantskill	Catholic	Coed	1920
Camp Seneca Lake	Penn Yan	Private/Jewish	Coed	1939
Camp Seven Hills	Holland	Girl Scouts	Girls	1930
Camp Stella Maris	Livonia	Private/Christian	Coed	1926
Camp Victory Lake	Hyde Park	Seventh-day Adventist	Coed	1950
Camp Wabasso	Redwood	Private	Coed	1950
Camp Wakoda	Central Valley	Girl Scouts	Girls	1924
Camp Weona	Gainesville	YMCA	Coed	1897
Camp Whitman on Seneca Lake	Dresden	Private	Coed	1952
Camps of Greater NY	Huguenot	YMCA	Coed	1924
Casowasco Conference Center	Moravia	Methodist	Coed	1946
Cherith of Western New York	Hunt	Private/Christian	Girls/Coed	1946
Chingachgook on Lake George	Kattskill Bay	YMCA	Coed	1913
Chipinaw	Swan Lake	Private	Coed	1926
Clearpool Education Center	Carmel	Private	Coed	1901
Deerfoot Lodge	Speculator	Private/Christian	Boys	1930
Delta Lake Bible Conference Center	Rome	Private/Christian	Coed	1890
Echo Lake	Warrensburg	Private	Coed	1945
Epworth	High Falls	Methodist	Coed	1959
Flint	Riverhead	4-H	Coed	1924
Forest Lake Camp	Warrensburg	Private	Boys/Girls	1926
Fresh Air Fund Camp	Fishkill	Private	Boys/Girls/Coed	1948
Frost Valley	Claryville	YMCA	Coed	1901
Girls' Vacation Fund	East Windham	Private	Girls	1935
Hidden Valley	Montour Falls	4-H	Coed	1945
Kamp Kiwanis	Taberg	Kiwanis	Boys/Girls/Coed	1930
Kennybrook	Monticello	Private	Coed	1941
Kingswood	Hancock	Methodist	Coed	1958

	Location	Affiliation	Gender	Year
Lake Chautauqua	Bemus Point	Lutheran	Boys/Girls/Coed	1937
Lakeland	Franklinville	Private/Jewish	Coed	1910
Lakota	Wurtsboro	Private	Coed	1930
Long Point Camp	Penn Yan	Salvation Army	Coed	1953
Lourdes Camp	Skaneateles	Private	Coed	1921
Ma-He-Tu	Bear Mountain	Lutheran	Girls	1937
Monroe	Monroe	Jewish	Coed	1941
North Country Camps	Keeseville	Private	Boys/Girls	1920
Nothern Frontier	North River	Private	Boys	1946
Olmsted	Cornwall-on-Hudson	Private	Boys/Girls/Coed	1901
Point O'Pines Camp for Girls	Brant Lake	Private	Girls	1957
Pok-O-Mac Cready	Willsboro	Private	Boys/Girls	1905
Presbyterian Center at Holmes	Holmes	Presbyterian	Coed	1946
Quinipet	Shelter Island Heights	Methodist	Coed	1947
Ramapo Anchorage Camp	Rhinebeck	Private	Coed	1923
Raquette Lake Camps	Raquette Lake	Private	Boys/Girls	1916
Regis-Applejack	Paul Smiths	Private	Coed	1946
Rising Sun at Redhook	Rhinebeck	Private	Boys	1930
Rochester Sunshine Camp	Rush	Rotary Club	Boys/Girls	1922
Rock Hill Camps	Mahopac	Girl Scouts	Girls	1922
Scatico	Elizaville	Private	Boys/Girls	1921
Scope Peconic Dunes Camp	Peconic	Private	Coed	1930
Sequoia	Rock Hill	Private	Coed	1930
Sky Lake of Wyoming Conference	Windsor	Methodist	Coed	1947
Surprise Lake Camp	Cold Spring	Private	Coed	1902
Talooli	Pennellville	Camp Fire	Boys/Girls/Coed	1945
Tapawingo	Speculator	Private/Christian	Girls	1959
Tel Yehudah	Barryville	Private/Jewish	Coed	1948
Treetops	Lake Placid	Private	Coed	1921
Turner	Salamanca	Catholic	Coed	1923
University Settlement Beacon Camps	Beacon	Private	Coed	1910
Wabenaki	Southfields	Southfields	Coed	1949
Walden	Diamond Point	Private	Coed	1935
Wendy	Wallkill	Girl Scouts	Girls	1931
Wilbur Herrlich	Patterson	Private/Christian	Boys/Girls/Coed	1922

NORTH CAROLINA

	Location	Affiliation	Gender	Year
Blue Star Camps	Hendersonville	Private/Jewish	Coed	1948
Broadstone	Banner Elk	Private	Coed	1952
Camp Arrowhead	Tuxedo	Private	Boys	1937
Camp Carolina				
Backcountry Adventure	Brevard	Private	Boys	1924
Camp Hanes	King	YMCA	Coed	1927
Camp Judaea	Hendersonville	Private/Jewish	Coed	1960
Camp Merri Mac	Black Mountain	Private/Christian	Girls	1950
Camp Merrie Woode	Sapphire	Private	Girls	1919
Camp Sea Gull	Arapahoe	Private	Boys	1948
Camp Tekoa	Hendersonville	Methodist	Coed	1949

	Location	Affiliation	Gender	Year
Cheerio	Glade Valley	YMCA	Boys/Girls/Coed	1960
Chestnut Ridge	Efland	Methodist	Coed	1959
Cliff Payne Youth Camp	Randleman	WOW	Coed	1954
Don Lee	Arapahoe	Methodist	Coed	1950
Eagle's Nest Camp	Pisgah Forest	Private	Coed	1922
Graham	Henderson	Girl Scouts	Girls	1956
Greenville	Cedar Mountain	YMCA	Coed	1912
Gwynn Valley	Brevard	Private	Coed	1935
Holston Presbytery Camp and Retreat Center	Banner Elk	Presbyterian	Boys/Girls/Coed	1955
Illahee	Brevard	Private	Girls	1921
Johns River Valley Camp	Collettsville	Private/Christian	Coed	1936
Kanata	Wake Forest	YMCA	Coed	1954
Kanuga for Boys and Girls	Hendersonville	Private/Christian	Coed	1928
Keyauwee Program Center	Sophia	Girl Scouts	Girls	1945
Mary Atkinson	Selma	Girl Scouts	Girls	1958
Millstone Center	Ellerbe	4-H	Coed	1939
Mitchell	Swansboro	4-H	Coed	1956
Occoneechee	Mill Spring	Girl Scouts	Girls	1956
Presbyterian Point	Clarksville	Girl Scouts	Girls	1955
Quaker Lake Camp	Climax	Quaker	Boys/Girls/Coed	1940
Ridgecrest Summer Camps	Ridgecrest	Private/Christian	Boys/Girls	1929
Rockbrook Camp for Girls	Brevard	Private	Girls	1921
Rockmont for Boys	Black Mountain	Private/Christian	Boys	1956

NORTH DAKOTA

	Location	Affiliation	Gender	Year
Camp Sioux	Arvilla	Private	Coed	1952

OHIO

	Location	Affiliation	Gender	Year
Akron Camp	Akron	Rotary Club	Coed	1924
Aldersgate	Carrollton	Methodist	Coed	1948
Asbury	Hiram	Methodist	Coed	1948
Butterworth	Maineville	Girl Scouts	Girls	1930
Camp Allyn	Batavia	Private	Coed	1921
Camp Burton	Burton	Baptist	Coed	1955
Camp Campbell Gard	Hamilton	YMCA	Coed	1926
Camp Cheerful	Strongsville	Private	Coed	1940
Camp Christopher	Bath	Catholic Youth Organization	Coed	1924
Camp Kern	Oregonia	YMCA	Boys/Girls/Coed	1910
Camp Libbey	Defiance	Girl Scouts	Girls	1936
Camp Noah	Clinton	YMCA	Boys/Girls/Coed	1929
Camp O'Bannon	Newark	Private	Coed	1922
Camp Ohio	St Louisville	4-H	Coed	1928
Camp Oty Okwa	South Bloomingville	Private	Coed	1942
Camp Swoneky	Oregonia	Salvation Army	Coed	1958
Camp Wise	Chardon	Private/Jewish	Coed	1907
Centerville Mills	Chagrin Falls	YMCA	Coed	1902
Crowell Hilaka	Richfield	Private	Girls	1937

	Location	Affiliation	Gender	Year
Falcon	Carrollton	Private	Coed	1959
Fort Hill	Hillsboro	Private/Christian	Coed	1948
Geneva Hills Center	Lancaster	Presbyterian	Coed	1959
George L. Forbes	Highland Hills	Private	Coed	1933
Great Trails	Malvern	Girl Scouts	Girls	1951
Greenwood Lake Camp	Delaware	Salvation Army	Coed	1932
Hidden Hollow Camp	Bellville	Private	Boys/Girls/Coed	1940
Highbrook Lodge	Chardon	Private	Boys/Girls/Coed	1928
Hiram House Camp	Moreland Hills	Private	Coed	1896
Ho Mita Koda	Newbury	Private	Boys/Girls	1929
Joy Outdoor Education Center	Clarksville	Private	Coed	1938
Lutheran Memorial Camp	Fulton	Lutheran	Coed	1948
Molly Lauman	Lucasville	Girl Scouts	Girls	1929
Mowana	Mansfield	Lutheran	Coed	1941
Ohio Camp Cherith	Madison	Private/Christian	Boys/Girls	1949
Otterbein	Logan	Methodist	Coed	1943
Red Oak Camp	Kirtland	Private	Boys	1947
Roosevelt Firebird	Bowerstown	Private	Boys/Girls	1918
Sheldon Calvary Camp	Conneaut	Episcopal	Coed	1936
Stonybrook	Waynesville	Girl Scouts	Girls	1953
Timberlane	Wakeman	Girl Scouts	Girls	1959
Triple S Camp	Sugar Grove	Private	Coed	1947
Wakatomika	Utica	Girl Scouts	Girls	1942
Wanake	Beach City	Methodist	Coed	1944
Whip-Poor-Will	Morrow	Girl Scouts	Girls	1936
Whitewood	Windsor	4-H	Coed	1940
Wildwood Christian Education Center	Milford	Presbyterian	Boys/Girls/Coed	1960
Wilson Outdoor Center	Bellefontaine	YMCA	Coed	1918
Woodland Altars	Peebles	Private/Christian	Coed	1960

OKLAHOMA

	Location	Affiliation	Gender	Year
Camp Classen	Davis	YMCA	Coed	1941
Camp Takatoka	Chouteau	YMCA	Boys/Girls	1913
Hudgens	McAlester	Baptist	Boys	1960
New Life Ranch	Colcord	Private/Christian	Coed	1958
Nunny-Cha-Ha	Davis	Baptist	Girls	1956
Waluhili	Chouteau	Camp Fire	Boys/Girls/Coed	1949

OREGON

	Location	Affiliation	Gender	Year
Arrowhead	Lake Oswego	Girl Scouts	Girls	1948
Camp Cleawox	Florence	Girl Scouts	Girls	1929
Camp Collins	Gresham	YMCA	Coed	1926
Camp Howard	Corbett	Catholic Youth Organization	Coed	1953
Camp Latgawa	Eagle Point	Methodist	Coed	1954
Camp Low Echo	Klamath Falls	Girl Scouts	Girls	1945
Camp Magruder	Rockaway	Methodist	Coed	1945
Camp Silver Creek	Sublimity	YMCA	Boys/Girls/Coed	1938

	Location	Affiliation	Gender	Year
Camp Westwind	Otis	YMCA	Boys/Girls/Coed	1936
Easter Seals Camping Program	Corbett	Easter Seals	Coed	1952
Gales Creek Camp for Diabetic Children	Forest Grove	Private	Coed	1952
Kilowan	Dallas	Camp Fire	Coed	1933
Mt. Hood Camp	Government Camp	Kiwanis	Coed	1933
Namanu	Sandy	Camp Fire	Coed	1924
Suttle Lake	Sisters	Methodist	Coed	1918
Tamarack	Sisters	Private	Boys/Girls/Coed	1935

PENNSYLVANIA

	Location	Affiliation	Gender	Year
Allegheny	Stoystown	Methodist	Coed	1948
Archbald	Kingsley	Girl Scouts	Girls	1920
Black Rock Retreat	Quarryville	Private/Christian	Coed	1954
B'nai B'rith Perlman	Starlight	Private/Jewish	Coed	1954
Bryn Mawr Camp	Honesdale	Private	Girls	1921
Camp Allegheny	Ellwood	Salvation Army	Coed	1945
Camp Cayuga	Honesdale	Private	Coed	1957
Camp Conrad Weiser	Wernersville	YMCA	Coed	1948
Camp Eder	Fairfield	Private/Christian	Coed	1957
Camp Fitch	North Springfield	YMCA	Boys/Girls/Coed	1914
Camp Green Lane	Green Lane	Private	Coed	1946
Camp Harmony	Hooversville	Private/Christian	Coed	1924
Camp Henry Kaufmann	Bolivar	Girl Scouts	Girls	1957
Camp Joseph and Betty Harlam	Kunkletown	Private/Jewish	Boys/Girls/Coed	1958
Camp Lake Como	Lake Como	YMHA/YWHA	Coed	1920
Camp Lee Mar	Lackawaxen	Private	Coed	1953
Camp Lembac	North Springfield	Presbyterian	Coed	1947
Camp Lohikan in the Pocono Mountains	Lake Como	Private	Coed	1957
Camp Nazarene	Lahaska	Baptist	Coed	1958
Camp Poyntelle Lewis Village	Poyntelle	Private/Jewish	Coed	1949
Camp R	Rockwood	Catholic Youth Organization	Coed	1940
Camp Sandy Cove	White Haven	Private/Christian	Boys/Girls/Coed	1950
Camp Skycrest	Hawley	YMCA	Coed	1945
Camp Speers Eljabar	Dingmans Ferry	YMCA	Coed	1948
Camp Starlight	Starlight	Private	Coed	1947
Camp Sunshine	Thornton	Private	no information available	1934
Camp Susquehannock for Boys	Brackney	Private	Boys	1905
Camp Wayne	Preston Park	Private	Boys/Girls	1921
Camp Weequahic	Lakewood	Private	Coed	1953
Camp William Penn	East Stroudsburg	Private	Boys/Girls	1953
Camps Milford	Milford	YMHA/YWHA	Coed	1920
Canadensis	Canadensis	Private	Coed	1941
Chen-A-Wanda	Thompson	Private	Coed	1939
The College Settlement Camps	Horsham	Private	Coed	1922
Crestfield	Slippery Rock	Presbyterian	Coed	1948
Crystal Lake Camps	Hughesville	Christian Scientist	Coed	1949

	Location	Affiliation	Gender	Year
Echo Trail	Felton	Girl Scouts	Girls	1953
Elliott	Volant	Girl Scouts	Girls	1960
Equinunk Blue Ridge	Equinunk	Private	Boys/Girls	1920
Furnace Hills	Denver	Girl Scouts	Girls	1948
Golden Slipper Camp	Stroudsburg	Private	Coed	1948
Gretna Glen Camp	Lebanon	Methodist	Coed	1948
Habonim Dror Camp Galil	Ottsville	Private/Jewish	Coed	1946
Haycock Camping Ministries	Kintnersville	Private/Christian	Boys/Coed	1960
Heinz House Camp	Ellwood City	Private	Boys/Girls/Coed	1926
Indian Head Camp	Honesdale	Private	Coed	1940
Indian Run	Glenmoore	Girl Scouts	Girls	1933
Innabah	Spring City	Methodist	Boys/Girls/Coed	1929
Kon-O-Kwee	Fombell	YMCA	Coed	1925
Kweebec	Schwenksville	Private	Coed	1935
Lake Greeley Camp	Greeley	Private	Boys/Girls/Coed	1957
Ligonier Camp and Conference Center	Ligonier	Private/Christian	Coed	1914
Lutherlyn	Prospect	Lutheran	Coed	1948
Mont Lawn Camp	Bushkill	Private/Christian	Boys/Girls/Coed	1894
Mosey Wood	White Haven	Girl Scouts	Girls	1939
Moshava	Honesdale	Private/Jewish	Coed	1945
Nawakwa	Arendtsville	Lutheran	Coed	1929
Netimus	Milford	Private	Girls	1930
Nock-A-Mixon	Kintnersville	Private	Coed	1938
Onas	Ottsville	Private	Coed	1922
Oneka	Tafton	Private	Girls	1908
Paradise Farm Camps	Downington	Private	Coed	1875
Pine Forest Camp	Greeley	Private	Coed	1931
Pinemere Camp	Stroudsberg	Private/Jewish	Coed	1942
Pocono Plateau	Cresco	Methodist	Boys/Girls/Coed	1946
Pocono Ridge	South Sterling	Private	Coed	1957
Ramah in the Poconos	Lake Como	Private/Jewish	Coed	1950
Redwing	Renfrew	Girl Scouts	Girls	1923
Saginaw	Oxford	Private	Boys/Girls	1930
Seneca Hills Bible Conference	Franklin	Private/Christian	Coed	1936
Sequanota	Jennerstown	Lutheran	Boys/Girls/Coed	1947
Sesame Rockwood Camps	Blue Bell	Private	Coed	1954
Shohola	Greeley	Private	Boys	1943
Streamside Camp and Conference Center	Stroudsberg	Private/Christian	Boys/Girls/Coed	1942
Susque	Trout Run	Private/Christian	Boys/Girls	1947
Swatara	Bethel	Private/Christian	Coed	1943
Tohikanee	Quakertown	Girl Scouts	Girls	1953
Towanda	Honesdale	Private	Coed	1923
Trail's End Camp	Beach Lake	Private/Jewish	Coed	1947
Tweedale	Oxford	Girl Scouts	Girls	1930
Tyler Hill Camp	Tyler Hill	Private	Coed	1955

	Location	Affiliation	Gender	Year
Variety Club Camp and Developmental Center	Worcester	Private	Coed	1949
Westminster Highlands Camp	Emlenton	Presbyterian	Coed	1957
Wood Haven	Pine Grove	Girl Scouts	Girls	1954

RHODE ISLAND

	Location	Affiliation	Gender	Year
Aldersgate	North Scituate	Methodist	Coed	1945
Canonicus Camp and Conference Center	Exeter	Baptist	Coed	1948
Fuller	Wakefield	YMCA	Coed	1887

SOUTH CAROLINA

	Location	Affiliation	Gender	Year
Bishop Gravatt Center	Aiken	Episcopal	Coed	1947
Burnt Gin Camp	Wedgefield	Private	Coed	1945
Camp Chatuga	Mountain Rest	Private	Coed	1956
Congaree Program Center	Lexington	Girl Scouts	Girls	1949
McCall Royal Ambassador Camp	Sunset	Baptist	Boys	1960
Robert M. Cooper Leadership Center	Summerton	4-H	Boys/Girls/Coed	1935
St. Christopher Camp and Conference Center	Johns Island	Private/Christian	Boys/Girls/Coed	1938
Thunderbird	Lake Wylie	YMCA	Boys/Girls	1936
Wabak	Marietta	Girl Scouts	Girls	1948

SOUTH DAKOTA

	Location	Affiliation	Gender	Year
NeSoDak Bible Camp/Klein Ranch	Waubay	Lutheran	Coed	1942
Outlaw and Atlantic Mountain Ranches	Custer	Lutheran	Coed	1958

TENNESSEE

	Location	Affiliation	Gender	Year
Buffalo Mountain Camp and Retreat Center	Jonesborough	Methodist	Coed	1949
Camp Hazlewood	Springville	Girl Scouts	Girls	1959
Camp Lindahl	Mt. Juliet	Easter Seals	Boys/Girls/Coed	1959
Camp Marymount	Fairview	Catholic	Boys/Girls	1942
Camp Montvale	Maryville	YMCA	Coed	1949
Camp Sky-Wa-Mo	Bluff City	Girl Scouts	Girls	1947
Camp Thunderbird	Chattanooga	Private/Christian	Coed	1950
Circle YI Ranch	La Vergne	Youth Incorporated	Coed	1945
Clyde Austin Center	Greeneville	4-H	Coed	1949
Clyde M. York Center	Crossville	4-H	Boys/Girls/Coed	1949
Ocoee	Ocoee	YMCA	Coed	1923
Tanasi	Andersonville	Girl Scouts	Girls	1954
Wesley Woods	Townsend	Methodist	Coed	1959

TEXAS

	Location	Affiliation	Gender	Year
Agnes Arnold	Conroe	Girl Scouts	Girls	1944
Boothe Oaks	Sweetwater	Girl Scouts	Girls	1952
Briarwood Retreat Center	Argyle	Lutheran	Coed	1959

	Location	Affiliation	Gender	Year
Camp Carter	Forth Worth	YMCA	Coed	1948
Camp Chrysalis	Kerrville	Lutheran	Coed	1949
Camp El Har	Dallas	Private/Christian	Coed	1937
Camp Flaming Arrow	Hunt	YMCA	Coed	1927
Camp Grady Spruce	Graford	YMCA	Boys/Girls/Coed	1949
Camp Kiwanis	Amarillo	Girl Scouts	Girls	1928
Camp Stewart for Boys	Hunt	Private	Boys	1924
Camp Texlake	Spicewood	Girl Scouts	Girls	1942
Casa Mare	Seabrook	Girl Scouts	Girls	1958
Cho-Yeh Camp and Conference Center	Livingston	Presbyterian	Boys/Girls/Coed	1947
El Tesoro	Granbury	Camp Fire	Coed	1934
Heart O'The Hills Camp	Hunt	Private/Christian	Girls	1953
Hermann Sons Youth Camp	Comfort	Order of the Sons of Hermann	Boys/Girls	1954
La Jita	Utopia	Girl Scouts	Girls	1948
Lutherhill Camp and Retreat Center	La Grange	Lutheran	Boys/Girls/Coed	1954
Mitre Peak	Fort Davis	Girl Scouts	Girls	1947
Prude Ranch Summer Camp	Fort Davis	Private	Coed	1951
Rockey River Ranch	Wimberley	Private	Boys/Girls	1951
Sky Ranch	Van	Private/Christian	Coed	1955
Sweeney	Gainesville	Private	Boys/Girls/Coed	1947
Texas Lions Camp	Kerrville	Lions Club	Boys/Girls	1949
Timberlake	Azle	Girl Scouts	Girls	1945
Val Verde	McGregor	Camp Fire	Coed	1948
Young Judaea Retreat and Conference Center	Wimberley	Private/Jewish	Coed	1953

UTAH

	Location	Affiliation	Gender	Year
Camp Trefoil Ranch	Provo	Girl Scouts	Girls	1946

VERMONT

	Location	Affiliation	Gender	Year
Abnaki	North Hero	YMCA	Boys	1901
Aloha	Fairlee	Private	Girls	1905
Aloha Hive	Fairlee	Private	Girls	1915
Betsey Cox	Pittsford	Private	Girls	1952
Billings	Fairlee	Private	Coed	1906
Brown Ledge Camp	Colchester	Private	Girls	1926
Camp Catherine Capers	Wells	Private	Girls	1952
Camp Hochelaga	South Hero	YMCA	Girls	1919
Camp Sangamon	Pittsford	Private	Boys	1922
Camp Waubanong	Brattleboro	4-H	Coed	1924
Downer Camp	Sharon	4-H	Coed	1945
Farnsworth	Thetford	Girl Scouts	Girls	1909
Farwell for Girls	Newbury	Private	Girls	1906
Indian Brook	Plymouth	Quaker	Girls	1940
Keewaydin Camps	Salisbury	Private	Boys	1894
Killooleet	Hancock	Private	Coed	1927

	Location	Affiliation	Gender	Year
Kiniya	Colchester	Private	Girls	1919
Lanakila	Fairlee	Private	Boys	1922
Lochearn Camp for Girls	Post Mills	Private	Girls	1916
Tamarack Farm	Plymouth	Quaker	Coed	1951
Timberlake	Plymouth	Quaker	Boys	1939
Wapanacki	Hardwick	Girl Scouts	Girls	1938

VIRGINIA

	Location	Affiliation	Gender	Year
Baker	Chesterfield	Private	Coed	1957
Bethel	Fincastle	Private/Christian	Coed	1927
Bretheren Woods Camp and Retreat Center	Keezletown	Private/Christian	Coed	1958
Camp Blue Ridge	Montebello	Seventh-day Adventist	Coed	1957
Camp Civitan at Triple C Lodge	Chesapeake	Private	Coed	1960
Camp Hanover	Mechanicsvile	Presbyterian	Coed	1957
Camp Happyland	Richardsville	Salvation Army	Coed	1946
Camp Kum-Ba-Yah	Lynchburg	Private	Coed	1950
Camp May Flather	Mount Solon	Girl Scouts	Girls	1932
Camp Mount Shenandoah	Millboro Springs	Private	Girls	1927
Camp Potomac	Leesburg	Girl Scouts	Girls	1948
Camp Skimino	Williamsburg	Girl Scouts	Girls	1955
Camp Virginia	Goshen	Private	Boys	1928
Carysbrook	Riner	Private	Girls	1923
Easter Seal West	New Castle	Easter Seal	Coed	1957
Highroad Program Center	Middleburg	Methodist	Coed	1949
Holiday Lake Educational Center	Appomattox	4-H	Coed	1941
Jamestown Educational Center	Williamsburg	4-H	Coed	1928
Ma Wa Va Camp Cherith	Madison	Private	Coed	1959
Presbyterian Point	Clarksville	Presbyterian	no information available	1955
Southwest Virginia Educational Center	Abingdon	4-H	Boys/Girls	1958
Virginia Elks Youth Camp	Millboro	Elks Club	Boys/Girls	1949

WASHINGTON

	Location	Affiliation	Gender	Year
Burton	Vashon Island	Private	Coed	1909
Camp Colman	Lakebay	YMCA	Boys/Girls/Coed	1912
Camp Dart-Lo	Spokane	Camp Fire	Coed	1945
Camp Firwood	Bellingham	Private/Christian	Coed	1954
Camp Huston	Gold Bar	Episcopal	Coed	1928
Camp Orkila	Seattle	YMCA	Boys/Girls/Coed	1906
Camp Sealth	Vashon Island	Camp Fire	Boys/Girls/Coed	1920
Camp Seymour	Gig Harbor	YMCA	Coed	1906
Cascade Camp Cherith	Belfair	Private/Christian	Boys/Girls	1947
Don Bosco	Camation	Catholic Youth Organization	Boys/Girls/Coed	1950
Four Winds and Westward Ho	Deer Harbor	Private	Coed	1927
Hidden Valley Camp	Granite Falls	Private	Boys/Girls/Coed	1947
Killoqua	Stanwood	Camp Fire	Coed	1941
Lake Wenatchee Camp	Leavenworth	YMCA	Coed	1928
Miracle Ranch	Port Orchard	Private/Christian	Boys/Girls/Coed	1960

	Location	Affiliation	Gender	Year
Parsons	Brinnon	Boys Scouts	Boys	1918
River Ranch	Carnation	Girl Scouts	Girls	1952
Robbinswold	Lilliwaup	Girl Scouts	Girls	1928
Roganunda	Naches	Camp Fire	Girls/Coed	1923
Singing Wind	Toledo	Private	Boys/Girls	1958
St. Albans	Belfair	Girl Scouts	Girls	1935
Sunset Lake	Wilkeson	Private/Christian	Coed	1957
Volasuca Volunteers of America	Sultan	Private	Coed	1941
Zanika Lache	Leavenworth	Camp Fire	Coed	1932

WEST VIRGINIA

	Location	Affiliation	Gender	Year
Bluestone Conference Center	Hinton	Presbyterian	Coed	1953
Camp Alleghany	Lewisburg	Private	Girls	1922
Camp Greenbrier	Alderson	Private	Boys	1898
Camp Horseshoe	St. George	YMCA	Boys/Girls/Coed	1940
White Rock	Capon Bridge	Girl Scouts	Girls	1945

WISCONSIN

	Location	Affiliation	Gender	Year
Alice Chester	East Troy	Girl Scouts	Girls	1924
Birch Trail	Minong	Private	Girls	1959
Camp Birchrock	Rhinelander	Camp Fire	Coed	1947
Camp Black Hawk	Elton	Girl Scouts	Girls	1956
Camp Chi	Lake Delton	Private/Jewish	Coed	1921
Camp Evelyn	Plymouth	Girl Scouts	Girls	1948
Camp Forest Springs	Westboro	Private/Christian	Coed	1958
Camp Gray	Reedsburg	Catholic	Coed	1956
Camp Icaghowan	Amery	YMCA	Coed	1909
Camp Jorn	Manitowish Waters	YMCA	Coed	1953
Camp MacLean	Burlington	YMCA	Coed	1941
Camp Manito Wish	Boulder Junction	YMCA	Boys/Girls	1919
Camp Minikani	Hubertus	YMCA	Coed	1919
Camp Nawakwa	Cornell	Girl Scouts	Girls	1926
Camp Ojibwa	Eagle River	Private	Boys	1928
Camp Ramah in Wisconsin	Conover	Private/Jewish	Coed	1947
Camp Singing Hills	Elkhorn	Girl Scouts	Girls	1954
Camp Timberlane for Boys	Woodruff	Private	Boys	1960
Camp Wawbeek	Wisconsin Dells	Easter Seal	Coed	1938
Chalk Hills Camp	Wausaukee	Girl Scouts	Girls	1940
Chippewa Bay	New Auburn	Girl Scouts	Girls	1958
Chippewa Ranch Camp	Eagle River	Private	Girls	1946
Clearwater Camps	Minocqua	Private	Girls	1933
Covenant Harbor Bible Camp and Retreat	Lake Geneva	Private/Christian	Coed	1947
Eau Claire Camp Manitou	New Auburn	YMCA	Coed	1915
Edwards Camp	East Troy	YMCA	Coed	1929
Ehawee	Mindoro	Girl Scouts	Girls	1951
Happy Hollow III Crossroads	Elkhorn	Girl Scouts	Girls	1959
Harand Camp of the Theatre Arts	Beaver Dam	Private	Coed	1955

	Location	Affiliation	Gender	Year
Helen Brachman	Almond	Private	Coed	1906
Herzl Camp	Webster	Private/Jewish	Coed	1946
Holiday Home Camp	Williams Bay	Private	Coed	1887
Honey Rock Camp	Three Lakes	Private/Christian	Boys/Girls/Coed	1951
House in the Wood	Delavan	Private	Coed	1910
Kawaga for Boys	Minocqua	Private	Boys	1915
Lake Lucerne Camp and Retreat Center	Neshkoro	Methodist	Boys/Girls/Coed	1947
Lake Wapogasset Lutheran Bible Camp	Amery	Lutheran	Coed	1948
Luther Point Bible Camp	Grantsburg	Lutheran	Coed	1946
Lutherdale Bible Camp	Elkhorn	Lutheran	Coed	1944
Needlepoint Daypoint	Hudson	Private	Coed	1957
Nicolet for Girls	Eagle River	Private	Girls	1944
North Star Camp for Boys	Hayward	Private	Boys	1945
Northwoods	Mason	Girl Scouts	Girls	1957
Olin Sang Ruby Union Institute	Oconomowoc	Private	Coed	1951
Osoha	Boulder Junction	Private	Girls	1921
Pottawatomie Hills	East Troy	Girl Scouts	Girls	1927
Red Pine Camp for Girls	Minocqua	Private	Girls	1937
Towering Pines Camp	Eagle River	Private	Boys	1945
U-Nah-Li-Ya	Suring	Private	Coed	1937
Union League Boys and Girls Clubs Camp	Salem	ULBGC	Coed	1924
Wakonda	Oxford	Seventh-day Adventist	Coed	1927
We-Ha-Kee	Winter	Catholic	Girls	1923
Wisconsin Lions Camp	Rosholt	Lions Club	Coed	1956
Wonderland Camp	Camp Lake	Salvation Army	Boys/Girls/Coed	1903
Woodland for Girls	Eagle River	Private	Girls	1940

WYOMING

	Location	Affiliation	Gender	Year
Teton Valley Ranch Camps	Kelly	Private	Boys/Girls	1939

NOTES

INTRODUCTION

1. Estimates for camp attendance come from the American Camping Association (recently renamed the American Camp Association; ACA), the largest association serving the organized camping industry. According to the ACA Web site, "over ten million young people benefited from a summer camp experience" in 2001, while between 1995 and 2003 there were nationwide enrollment increases of 8 to 10 percent annually. If this trend continues, camp enrollments will top fourteen million in 2006. *Fact Sheet*, American Camping Association, http://www.acacamps.org/media/factsheet. htm. Accessed 19 March 2003.

2. For turn-of-the-century ideas about nature's physical and social benefits for urban children, see Cranz, *The Politics of Park Design*, 61–68.

3. McKay, *The Quest of the Folk*, chapter 1, especially 34–35.

4. For nineteenth-century American schools, see Upton, "Lancasterian Schools, Republican Citizenship, and the Spatial Imagination of Early Nineteenth-Century America"; Cutter, "Cathedral of Culture"; Gulliford, *America's Country Schools*, especially 34–61 and 159–229. For Sunday schools, see Boyer, *Urban Masses and Moral Order in America, 1820–1920*, chapter 3. For twentieth-century schools, and particularly their connections with architectural modernism (although not in the United States), see Saint, *Towards a Social Architecture;* Dudek, *Kindergarten Architecture*. For early-twentieth-century playgrounds in public parks, see Cranz, *The Politics of Park Design*, chapter 2. For children's reading rooms, see Van Slyck, *Free to All*, 173–216.

5. Gutman and de Coninck-Smith, Introduction to *Designing Modern Childhoods*.

6. Beam, *Winslow Homer's Magazine Engravings*, 19.

7. Macleod, *Building Character in the American Boy*, 32–36; Nasaw, *Children of the City*, 138–57.

8. This idea was put forward in historian Frederick Jackson Turner's frontier thesis, first

articulated in 1893 and developed in a number of publications, including *The Frontier in American History* (1920).

9. Rotundo, *American Manhood*, 251–55; Shi, "Ernest Thompson Seton and the Boy Scouts"; Hantover, "The Boy Scouts and the Validation of Masculinity."

10. Gibson, *Camping for Boys*, 7, 9.

11. Cavallo, *Muscles and Morals*; Macleod, *Building Character in the American Boy*.

12. Lears, *No Place of Grace*, 302–4.

13. For the impact of antimodernism on the home, see Robertson, "House and Home in the Arts and Crafts Era"; May, "Progressivism and the Colonial Revival."

14. Miller, "Girls in Nature/The Nature of Girls," 16–73.

15. Roosevelt voiced his concern about race suicide in "Social Evolution," in *American Ideals*, 226–27. See also Bederman, *Manliness and Civilization*, 200–206.

16. Deloria, *Playing Indian*.

17. Tennant, "Complicating Childhood"; Downs, *Childhood in the Promised Land*; Martino and Wall, eds., *Cities of Childhood*; see also Van Slyck, "Summer Camps," in *Encyclopedia of Children and Childhood in History and Society*.

18. Mishler, *Raising Reds*, 83, 86.

19. Joselit and Mittelman, eds., *A Worthy Use of Summer*, 14–28.

20. Balmer, *Mine Eyes Have Seen the Glory*, 92–108.

21. Graham, *Our Kind of People*, 52–54.

22. Adler, "Adventure in Democracy"; Webb, "Color-blind Summer Camps," 493.

23. May, *Homeward Bound*. Among other things, May argues that the baby boom was not simply a response to postwar affluence or a retreat into private life (as some scholars have posited), but a means of expressing citizenship and very much connected to larger political debates.

24. Sargent, *A Handbook of Summer Camps*.

25. Wack, *The Camping Ideal*, 9.

26. Scott, "Follow Up Camp Results," 131.

27. Playground and Recreation Association of America, *Camping Out*, 9–10.

28. The figure is Salomon's own estimate. "Camp Planner Can 'Think Like a Child.'"

29. "Man O' War Middy," *Camping* 3 (January 1928), 6; "Camping's Recommended Dealers," *Camping* 3 (February 1928), 4; "'Fulton Quality' Tents for Your Summer Camp," *Camping* 3 (March 1928), 9; Condé Nast advertisement, *Camping* 4 (February–March 1929), 5; Pope and Cottel Co. advertisement for sectional buildings, *Camping* 4 (February–March 1929), 9.

30. Eells, *History of Organized Camping*, 101–2, 110–13.

31. Elin Lindberg, "Camp and Camping History, 1912–1953," typescript, 1956 (GSUSA).

32. Cromley, "Transforming the Food Axis," 9.

33. Jacobson, *Whiteness of a Different Color*, especially chapters 2 and 3.

34. In addition to these seven thousand resident camps, the American Camp Association estimates that there are five thousand day camps. *Fact Sheet*, American Camping Association, http://www.acacamps.org/media_center/view.php?file=camp_trends_trend_fact_sheet.html. Accessed 21 June 2005.

35. Many YMCA officials lent their energies to the founding of the Boy Scouts, including Edgar G. Robinson, who served as the YMCA's first international secretary of boys' work between 1901 and 1922, while simultaneously fulfilling the role of executive secretary of the fledgling Boy Scouts for some months in 1910. Likewise, Luther Halsey Gulick, first secretary for physical work for the International Committee of the YMCA, also established Camp Wohelo in Maine, a private camp for girls, where he and his wife, Charlotte Vetter Gulick, worked out the program for another new youth organization, Camp Fire Girls. The Gulicks, in turn, were greatly influenced by the thinking of Ernest Thompson Seton, who had sponsored camps for his

Woodcraft Indians, an organization that was eventually subsumed into the Boy Scouts.

36. See, e.g., Kahn, *Sleepaway*.

1. PUTTING CAMPERS IN THEIR PLACE

1. Heaton (1875–1951) is best known as supervising architect of the Cathedral of Saint Peter and Saint Paul (Washington Cathedral), but he also designed several camp buildings. In addition to his work at Camp Letts, he designed buildings for Kamp Kahlert, a camp sponsored by the Washington, D.C., YWCA, and Camp Goodwill, which provided summer outings in Washington's Rock Creek Park for indigent mothers and children. Drawings for all of these camp projects are preserved in the Prints and Photographs Division of the Library of Congress (ADE - UNIT 822).

2. Cronon, *Nature's Metropolis*, especially 46–54; Turner is quoted on page 54.

3. John Muir, *Alaska Fragment* (1890), in *Bartlett's Familiar Quotations*, 15th ed. (Boston: Little, Brown, 1980), 637.

4. Terrie, *Forever Wild*, 92. Jacoby, *Crimes Against Nature*, 200–202.

5. Bermingham, *Landscape and Ideology*, 9.

6. "Camp Mishawaka: The Entrance to Health and Happiness," brochure for the 1934 season, 5 (Mishawaka).

7. The myth of Paul Bunyan was first published in 1914 in an advertising pamphlet titled *Paul Bunyan and His Big Blue Ox*, issued by the Red River Lumber Company. See also Benét, *The Reader's Encyclopedia*, 147.

8. Gibson, *Camping for Boys*, 27.

9. Maynard, "'An Ideal Life in the Woods for Boys,'" 9.

10. "The C. E. Cobb Camps, Denmark, Maine," notice for the 1934 season, Camp Wyonegonic. See *Bridgton, Maine, 1768–1994*, 598, 599, and 656–57.

11. "Camp Lincoln, Camp Lincoln Prep, Summer Camps for Boys," brochure for the 1937 season, 31 (MHS).

12. "Camp Mishawaka: A Summer Camp for Boys—in the Wilds of Minnesota," brochure for the 1913 season, 21 (Mishawaka).

13. "Camp Becket for Boys," brochure for the 1910 season, 14 (Kautz).

14. "Camp Mary Day, Newton Girl Scout Camp," brochure for the 1924 season, n.p. (PTGSC).

15. "Camp Mary Day, Newton Girl Scout Camp," brochure for the 1933 season, n.p. (PTGSC).

16. "Camp Histories," *Colonial Patchwork* (March–April 1977), n.p. (PTGSC).

17. For turn-of-the-century ideas about nature's physical and social benefits for urban children, see Cranz, *The Politics of Park Design*, 61–68.

18. Hall is credited with coining the term *adolescence*, which is also the title of his best-known work, *Adolescence: Its Psychology and Its Relations to Physiology, Anthropology, Sociology, Sex, Crime, Religion and Education*. See also Ross, *G. Stanley Hall*, and Bederman, *Manliness and Civilization*, chapter 3.

19. Cronon, *Nature's Metropolis*, 31.

20. Rotundo, *American Manhood*, 251–55.

21. George M. Beard, *American Nervousness: Its Causes and Consequences* (New York, 1881), 3; quoted in Bederman, *Manliness and Civilization*, 85.

22. Bederman, *Manliness and Civilization*, 88.

23. Ibid., 16–23.

24. Macleod, *Building Character in the American Boy*, 48, 268.

25. Ibid., 136–41.

26. Hall, "Feminization in School and Home," 10240.

27. Hale is quoted in Gibson, *Camping for Boys*, 38.

28. Hall, *Adolescence*, 2:619. Roosevelt voiced his concern about race suicide in "Social Evolution," in *American Ideals*, 226–27. These ideas are

discussed at length in Bederman, *Manliness and Civilization*, 200–206.

29. DeVries, *The Campfire Girls as Detectives*, 13–20.

30. Camp Fire Girls, *The Book of the Camp Fire Girls*, 8.

31. Deloria, *Playing Indian*, 113.

32. Bederman, *Manliness and Civilization*, 25.

33. Gibson, *Camping for Boys*, 26.

34. Maynard, "'An Ideal Life in the Woods for Boys,'" 6, 8, 10, and 12.

35. Ibid., 15–16.

36. Charlotte Gulick wrote these words in a 1909 letter to potential campers. The letter is reproduced in full in Hewson, *Wohelo Down through the Years*, 15–16.

37. "Report of the Y.M.C.A. Camp Conference," 205.

38. Osborn, *Camp Dudley*, 17–27.

39. Unlike Becket's layout, however, U.S. Army camps did not give mess halls parade-ground frontage, which was reserved for more important administrative buildings. See Hoagland, "Village Constructions," 223.

40. Gibson, *Camping for Boys*. My sense of the book's importance was confirmed when I found that the first edition I bought online had come from the personal library of Charles R. Scott, first president of the Camp Directors Association of America.

41. Schneller, "The Complete Story of Camp Mishawaka," c. 1925, typescript in the L. G. Schneller papers 2, 14 (MHS); Camp Fire Girls, *The Book of the Camp Fire Girls*, 46; Girl Scouts, *Campward Ho!*

42. "Camp Becket for Boys," brochure for the 1910 season, 10 (Kautz).

43. Girl Scouts, *Campward Ho!*, 94–96.

44. Gibson, *Camping for Boys*, 24, 39.

45. Osborn, *Camp Dudley*, 19, 22–23. Maynard, "'An Ideal Life for Boys in the Woods,'" 10–11.

46. Examples of these books include Cheley, *The Boy Scout Trail Blazers*; Bates, *The Khaki*

Boys at Camp Sterling*; and Randall, *Army Boys in France*.

47. Rotundo, *American Manhood*, 62; also quoted in Maynard, "'An Ideal Life for Boys in the Woods,'" 6.

48. Susan Miller's dissertation details these war efforts, noting that they foundered on the rocks of public disapproval when they took girls out of the domestic sphere. Miller, "Girls in Nature/The Nature of Girls," 16–73. The Girl Scout song is quoted on 88.

49. Wack, *The Camping Ideal*, 9, 11, 15.

50. Miller, "Girls in Nature/The Nature of Girls," 105–6.

51. Department of Camping, *Camp Site Development Plans*, 1.

52. "Camp Alleghany," brochure for the 1934 season, 6 (Gutman).

53. Quoted in Macleod, *Building Character in the American Boy*, 133.

54. Miller, "Girls in Nature/The Nature of Girls," 156–57.

55. "Blazing Trail Camp," brochure for the 1931 season, n.p. (Gutman).

56. Gilborn, *Adirondack Camps*, 58–59.

57. The exterior form of this museum is modeled directly on a lookout lodge in the Rocky Mountains that appeared in Wick, *Log Cabins*. Wick was a Buffalo-based architect trained at Cornell and the Massachusetts Institute of Technology; his book was the first devoted exclusively to log houses. See also Perdue, "Designing Wildness," chapter 8.

58. It is possible that Beard had some impact on this choice. After all, he was on the organizing committee and served as national scout commissioner for thirty years, but according to Macleod, the position was largely a ceremonial one. What is more, the publication of log buildings in *Camp Site Development Plans* came about twenty years after Beard's first association with the Boy Scouts.

59. Gilborn points out that "lean-to" and "open camp" are often incorrectly used as synonyms, when in fact "open camp" should be an umbrella

term for a range of forms, only one of which is the lean-to. Gilborn, *Adirondack Camps*, 40–48.

60. Barnhill, *Wild Impressions*, 87.

61. "Camp Durrell for Boys," brochure for the 1912 season, 9 (Kautz).

62. Boy Scouts of America Department of Camping, *Camp Site Development Plans*, 16, 19.

63. "Blazing Trail Camp," brochure for the 1933 season, n.p. (Gutman).

64. Carr, *Wilderness by Design*, 275–76, 293–95.

65. Julian H. Salomon, interview by S. Herbert Evison, 1 November 1971, tape number 111, transcript, 24 (Bancroft).

66. McClelland, *Building the National Parks*, 7. McClelland offers a succinct summary of NPS landscape naturalization techniques in her introduction (1–8) and discusses their application to RDAs on 414–20.

67. Ibid., 418.

68. Maier's advice is quoted in Carr, *Wilderness by Design*, 281–82.

69. Good, *Park and Recreation Structures*, 1:4. Salomon confirmed his authorship of the section on camp planning in his 1971 interview with S. Herbert Evison.

70. Good, *Park and Recreation Structures*, 3:109.

71. Concerned that the text did not reflect well on the Girl Scouts, the Girl Scouts of the USA withheld permission to publish this site plan, as well as six other building plans from Salomon's *Camp Site Development*.

72. Ledlie, *Layout*, 6.

73. Ledlie, "Consultation on Camping," 2.

74. Ledlie, *Layout*, 9–10.

75. Girl Scout Camp Bureau memo of August 1945; retyped text of Philip N. Youtz, AIA, "Camp Buildings and Equipment," *Give and Take*, March 1931 (GSUSA).

76. "Camp Becket for Boys," brochure for the 1910 season, 14 (Kautz).

77. For a description of an early counselor train-

ing program, see "Camp Lincoln, Camp Lincoln Prep, Summer Camps for Boys," brochure for the 1937 season (MHS).

78. Cross, *Kids' Stuff*, 135.

79. Adams, "The Eichler Home," 169–70.

2. FUN AND GAMES

1. Meeting minutes of the Girl Scouts Camp Committee, 14 September 1926 (GSUSA).

2. According to Henry W. Gibson, for instance, "Boys need to get away from the schoolroom and books, and may I say the martyrdom of examinations, high marks, promotions and exhibitions!" Gibson, *Camping for Boys*, 9.

3. Sutton-Smith, "Does Play Prepare the Future?" 137.

4. Sheehy, "American Angling"; Gilmore, "'Another Branch of Manly Sport."

5. Many scholars have noted the difficulty of defining leisure, especially given that many people pursue as recreation what others do for work. Grier, "Are We Having Fun Yet?" 1–2; Gelber, *Hobbies*, 36–38.

6. Shapiro, *Child's Garden*, 24–25.

7. Cavallo, *Muscles and Morals*, 76–84.

8. Ibid., 32–34.

9. Gelber also points out, however, that many hobbies simultaneously affirmed workplace values by ensuring that hobbyists were not idle during their leisure time. He quotes John Clarke and Chas Cruchter's apt phrase "the Protestant leisure ethic" to describe the tendency toward worklike leisure. Gelber, *Hobbies*, 2–3, 11, 37.

10. Both the Cleveland study and the violence of boys' play are discussed in Mergen, "Toys and the Culture of Childhood," 97, 101. The cultural politics of the nickelodeon are discussed in Nasaw, "Children and Commercial Culture," 22–24.

11. Although this perception of urban space as inappropriate for children's play developed at the end of the nineteenth century, it was still in place at the end of the twentieth century, according to

geographer Owain Jones, who notes that parents allow children greater freedom to play in spaces that adults perceive as pure—such as a rural village. Jones, "Melting Geography," 32–36. The report of the Society for the Prevention of Cruelty to Children is quoted in Nasaw, "Children and Commercial Culture," 15.

12. West, *Growing Up in Twentieth-Century America*, 20.

13. Although laws prohibiting unaccompanied children from attending movies were on the books in most states by the second decade of the twentieth century, they had little effect on the numbers of children who patronized nickelodeons—estimated at 500,000 to 600,000 daily in 1910. Nasaw, "Children and Commercial Culture," 17–18.

14. The published advice to children combined age-old activities, like tops, as well as newer contraptions like rubber-band-powered airplanes. Mergen, "Toys and the Culture of Childhood," 97.

15. These include the Woodcraft Indians, Sons of Daniel Boone, Knights of King Arthur, Girl Pioneers of America, and the Beehive Girls. The Knights of King Arthur was a church-based boys' group founded by William Byron Forbush. Macleod, *Building Character in the American Boy*, 112. The Girl Pioneers and Beehive Girls were both incorporated into Juliette Low's Girl Scouts, Inc. Tedesco, "Making a Girl into a Scout," 23.

16. Zelizer, *Pricing the Priceless Child*, 49–55.

17. PAA organizers were particularly dubious of foreign-born parents. According to Cavallo, one of the play director's tasks was to serve as "a countermodel for children whose immigrant fathers were neither especially successful nor much admired in their new country." Cavallo, *Muscles and Morals*, 2, 36–38, 40–45.

18. Wood, "Objectives in Outings and Camps for Boys," 114–15. In the 1920s and 1930s, Wood went on to become a leading advocate for opening the YMCA to women and girls. Hopkins, *History of the Y.M.C.A. in North America*, 564–65.

19. "Report of the Private Camp Conference," 190.

20. Osborn, *Camp Dudley*, 31.

21. Statten, "Twenty-Five Years of Camping," 1.

22. "Report of the Private Camp Conference," 190.

23. Robinson, "Association Boys' Camps," 99.

24. "A Summer Camp as Developed by the New York Boys' Club," 218.

25. Robinson, "Association Boys' Camps," 94–95

26. "Report of the Private Camp Conference," 191–93.

27. Streightoff, "Summer Camps," 133.

28. Robinson, "Association Boys' Camps," 98. Scott, "Wawayanda," 101–2.

29. "Report of the Private Camp Conference," 192–93.

30. West, *Growing Up in Twentieth-Century America*, 21–22.

31. Wood, "Objectives in Outings and Camps for Boys," 116.

32. "Report of the Y.M.C.A Camp Conference," 207–8.

33. "Report of the Private Camp Conference," 196, 198.

34. Ibid., 196–97.

35. W. Barksdale Maynard, "'An Ideal Life in the Woods for Boys,'" 24.

36. "Report of the Private Camp Conference," 196.

37. "Camp Jeanne d'Arc: The Catholic Camp for Girls," brochure from the 1928 season, 17 (Jeanne d'Arc).

38. "This Interesting Data from Camp Wawayanda," 101.

39. Robinson, "Association Boys' Camps," 101, 103.

40. Scott, "Wawayanda," 102, 105.

41. Robinson, "Association Boys' Camps," 105.

42. Ibid.

43. Quoted in DeLuca, *Our Loyal Band*, 37, 50, 60–61.

44. "Report of the Private Camp Conference," 187–89.

45. Such schedules appear in "Camp Becket for Boys," brochure for the 1910 season, 10 (Kautz); "Camp Durrell for Boys," brochure for the 1912 season, 10 (Kautz); and "Camp Mishawaka, A Summer Camp for Boys—in the Wilds of Minnesota," brochure for the 1913 season, 6 (Mishawaka).

46. While scholars still believe that there are gender differences in the propensity to collect, they maintain that girls are the more avid collectors. Gelber, *Hobbies*, 95–99.

47. Gibson, "Camps Durrell and Becket," 120; Kaighn, "Camp Dudley," 120.

48. Gelber, *Hobbies*, 200–204.

49. "Report of the Private Camp Conference," 194.

50. Kaighn, "Camp Dudley," 115; "Report of the Y.M.C.A. Camp Conference," 209.

51. "Report of the Private Camp Conference," 194.

52. Gelber contrasts "domestic masculinity" with "masculine domesticity"—another early-twentieth-century development in which men worked with their wives on domestic projects that degendered the home. Gelber, *Hobbies*, 205–7, 217.

53. "Report of the Private Camp Conference," 195.

54. "Shoelaces to Kayaks to Nature—Growth of Crafts at Wawayanda," *Wawayanda Whirlwind, Fiftieth Anniversary Number* (December 1951), 8 (Kautz).

55. "Camp Becket for Boys," brochure for the 1910 season, 11 (Kautz). As Steven Gelber points out, pyrography was less a departure from Victorian craft than its rough surfaces suggest; "The objects themselves, however, were the usual mix of boxes, whatnot shelves, bookends, wall plaques, match safes, picture frames, taborets, and so forth." Gelber, *Hobbies*, 194.

56. Dietrich-Smith, "Cultural Landscape Report," 101.

57. Predating the establishment of the Negro League, the Cuban Giants were organized in 1885 by Stanislaus Kostka "Cos" Govern, C. S. Massey, and Frank P. Thompson, headwaiter at the Argyle Hotel in the resort town of Babylon, Long Island, where early games were played to entertain hotel guests. In 1886, they were featured entertainers at Henry Flagler's Hotel Ponce de León in St. Augustine, Florida. The team played its last season in 1899. http://www.nlbpa.com/1887_cuban_giants.html. Accessed 20 June 2003.

58. Osborn, *Camp Dudley*, 66.

59. Ibid., 69.

60. Quoted in Cavallo, *Muscles and Morals*, 60.

61. Ibid., 94.

62. Gibson, *Camping for Boys*, 209–10.

63. Ibid., 210–11.

64. Osborn, *Camp Dudley*, 70; Scott, "Camp Wawayanda," 98.

65. Gibson, *Camping for Boys*, 210.

66. "Camp Becket for Boys," brochure for the 1910 season, 4 (Kautz).

67. Gibson, "Camps Durrell and Becket," 118.

68. "Camp Arcadia," brochure for the 1921 season, 7 (Gutman).

69. "Camp Mishawaka, A Summer Camp for Boys—in the Wilds of Minnesota," brochure for the 1913 season, 6 (Mishawaka).

70. Scott, "Camp Wawayanda," 92–93.

71. Gibson, "Camps Durrell and Becket," 118.

72. Camp Dudley, brochure for the 1908 season, 4–5 (Dudley).

73. "Proposed Recreational Educational Building, Camp Becket," undated flyer (Becket).

74 . Osborn, *Camp Dudley*, 84; Jennifer Martin, Camp Merrie-Woode, National Register of Historic Places Registration Form, 1995, section 7, page 9 (NRHP).

75. Good, *Park and Recreation Structures*, 3:146.

76. "Camp Mishawaka," brochure for the 1932 season, 21 (Mishawaka).

77. "Camp Mishawaka," brochure for the 1934 season, 25 (Mishawaka).

78. McKay, *The Quest of the Folk*, 12–13.

79. "Blazing Trail Camp," brochure for the 1933 season, n.p. (Gutman).

80. Whisnant, *All That Is Native and Fine*, 157–61.

81. "Rockbrook Camp for Girls," brochure for the 1924 season, 24 (Rockbrook).

82. "Rockbrook Camp for Girls," brochure for the 1935 season, n.p. (Rockbrook).

83. Fuller, "Beautiful Articles Are Made on Camp Looms," *Hillaway Wave* 6 (12 August 1934), 4 (MHS).

84. Boy Scouts of America Department of Camping, *Camp Site Development Plans*, 28, 31.

85. Dietrich-Smith, "Camp Hayo-Went-Ha," 61.

86. Gibson, *Camp Management*, 109, 115.

87. Quoted in DeLuca, *Our Loyal Band*, 50.

88. Good, *Park and Recreation Structures*, 3:145–46.

89. Kaighn, "Camp Dudley," 116.

90. Zelizer, *Pricing the Priceless Child*, 3.

91. Kaighn, "Camp Dudley," 116.

92. Dulles, *The American Red Cross*, 248–50. Mays, "The History of the Water Safety Program of the American National Red Cross," 61.

93. Zelizer, *Pricing the Priceless Child*, 50–52.

94. Dulles, *The American Red Cross*, 249.

95. Rebec and Gaeddert, "The History of The American National Red Cross, Volume VII, The Development of First Aid, Life Saving, Water Safety and Accident Prevention" (Washington, D.C.: The American National Red Cross, 1950), 74; typescript preserved in Records of the American National Red Cross, Group 3 (1935–46), 494.2 General History of the ANRC (Monographs), 7–10, Box 767 (Red Cross).

96. Lundell, *Fires of Friendship*, 29–30.

97. Edwin H. Carroll, assistant national director, First Aid and Life Saving, to A. L. Schafer, 28 July 1931, Records of the American National Red Cross, Group 2 (1917–34), Series number 549, Box 576 (Red Cross).

98. Harry A. Kenning, Report on visit to Camp Burton, 9–11 July 1928, Records of the American National Red Cross, Group 2 (1917–34), Series number 549, Box 576 (Red Cross).

99. R. S. Eaton to H. F. Enlows, 4 November 1934, Records of the American National Red Cross, Group 2 (1917–34), Series number 549, Box 576 (Red Cross).

100. W. E. Longfellow, Report of visit to the Boy Scout Training Camp for Camp Directors and Water Front Men at Camp Bert Adams, 15–20 April 1929, and W. E. Longfellow, Report of visit to the Camp Directors' Conference for YMCA of New Jersey and Pennsylvania, 8 May 1930, Records of the American National Red Cross, Group 2 (1917–34), Series number 549, Box 576 (Red Cross).

101. Rebec and Gaeddert, "The History of The American National Red Cross, Volume VII," 74.

102. Mays, "History of the Water Safety Program," 71.

103. The crib illustrated in the Girl Scout camp-planning manual of 1920 was based on a type used at camps in Palisades Interstate Park. Girl Scouts, *Campward Ho!*, 81.

104. Ibid., 83.

105. Good, *Park and Recreation Structures*, 3:144.

106. The introduction of the buddy system was not always easy. When Longfellow visited Camp Menatoma in 1934, he found that "a great deal of opposition had been taking place, to the installation of the buddy plan. Too much restriction bored the youngsters and they wrote home to their parents about it." W. E. Longfellow, Report of visit to Camp Menatoma, 19 August 1934, Records of the American National Red Cross, Group 2 (1917–34), Series number 549, Box 576 (Red Cross).

107. Mergen, "Toys and the Culture of Childhood," 100.

108. Ibid., 101.

109. Girl Scouts, *Campward Ho!*, 108–9.

110. Camp Fire Girls, *Handbook for Leaders of Camp Fire Girls*, 163.

111. Koch, "Girls Build Log Cabin and Make

Its Simple Furniture," *Hillaway Wave* 3 (29 July 1931), 1 (MHS).

112. Camp Fire Girls, *Handbook for Leaders of Camp Fire Girls*, 127–28.

113. Drawing on Judith Butler's work, Gagen's emphasis is on the urban playground of the Progressive Era as a spatial mechanism for managing "the alignment of certain gender performances with certain sexualized bodies." Gagen, "Playing the Part." Cavallo offers an alternative interpretation of the relationship between baseball as played on Progressive Era playgrounds and gendered notions of citizenship, arguing that the personality type of the ideal team player was "a blend of those masculine and feminine traits that play organizers thought essential for individual stability and social order." Cavallo, *Muscles and Morals*, especially chapter 5.

114. Camp Fire Girls, *Handbook for Leaders of Camp Fire Girls*, 109–10.

115. Graham, *Working at Play in Summer Camps*, 23, 47–54.

116. Ibid., 54, 95–98, 103–6, 112–13.

117. This information on Salomon's career appeared in "Camp Planner Can 'Think Like a Child.'"

3. HOUSING THE HEALTHY CAMPER

1. The details of the Moody Fresh Air homes are briefly described by G. P. Rockwell, superintendent of Fresh Air Work, on the inside front cover of an album of photographs that Rockwell took between 1903 and 1905. The album is preserved in Moody Church records at the Billy Graham Archives, Wheaton College.

2. Lears, *No Place of Grace*, 107–16.

3. For Victorian concerns about the health risks posed by the body asleep, see Barker, *The Bedroom and Boudoir*.

4. Leonard G. Schneller, "The Complete Story of Camp Mishawaka," 14, 26–27, typescript in the L. G. Schneller papers, c. 1925 (MHS).

5. Girl Scouts, *Campward Ho!*, 12.

6. Edwards, *Taylor Statten*, 30; Osborn, *Camp Dudley*, 30–31.

7. Peck, "Things Learned in Seventeen Consecutive Seasons in One Boys' Camp"; Gibson, *Camping for Boys*, 42–48.

8. "Camp Mishawaka, A Summer Camp for Boys—in the Wilds of Minnesota," brochure for the 1913 season, 8–9 (Mishawaka).

9. Schneller, "The Complete Story of Camp Mishawaka," 59–60 (MHS).

10. "The Improvement Shown in Eight Weeks at Camp Mishawaka," flyer attached to the Camp Mishawaka brochure for the 1935 season (Mishawaka).

11. Playground and Recreation Association of America [PRAA], *Camping Out*, 58–59. This formula was cited as "the generally accepted standard" by the camp-planning adviser to the Girl Scouts and the National Park Service; see Salomon, "Space Requirements in Sleeping Cabins," 14.

12. PRAA, *Camping Out*, 424–26.

13. Schneller, "The Complete Story of Camp Mishawaka," 28 (MHS). Publishing detailed architectural drawings in order to boost claims to professional status is a long-standing tradition, particularly in the building trades; see Upton, "Pattern Books and Professionalism," 107–50.

14. Ramsdell, "Designing a Boys' Camp in the Minnesota Woods," 414. Ramsdell rendered the camp's name I-Cag-Ho-Wan, perhaps to suggest the correct pronunciation.

15. Gibson, *Camp Management*; PRAA, *Camping Out*, 62; Boy Scouts of America Department of Camping, *Camp Site Development Plans*, 18.

16. Salomon, "Space Requirements in Sleeping Cabins," 14–15; Good, *Park and Recreation Structures*, 3:173.

17. Good, *Park and Recreation Structures*, 3:173.

18. Although Hall saw recapitulation as a human process, his analysis was particularly influential in debates of masculinity and may have indirectly fueled some aspects of the late-twentieth-

century men's movement, with its meetings in the woods and its rituals—and their trappings—modeled on Native American practices.

19. Edwards, *Taylor Statten,* 28–49, 65–73.

20. Statten, "Twenty-Five Years of Camping," 1–2.

21. Dimock and Hendry, *Camping and Character,* 96–97.

22. Ibid., 99. Edwards, *Taylor Statten,* 100–101.

23. Dimock and Hendry, *Camping and Character,* 153–55.

24. Ibid., 170.

25. Ibid., 18–24.

26. Dimock and Hendry went on to organize the Institute for Character Education in the Summer Camp, which sponsored at least eight annual meetings before 1937. The report of the eighth meeting is Hendry's *Appraising the Summer Camp.*

27. Dimock and Hendry, *Camping and Character,* 188–92. The authors do not specify how they came to their conclusions about Freddy's parents (or the other parents they mention in the book). In an earlier chapter, they mention that "parents visiting camp also make possible the eliciting of the more intimate and therefore more valuable data on the boy's behavior adjustment needs" (19), but they might have also made deductions from campers' descriptions of their home lives.

28. Ibid., 21–22.

29. Lundell, *Fires of Friendship,* 19.

30. Many camp directors with professional aspirations decried these hiring criteria, but their repeated complaints suggest that the practice continued. Dimock and Hendry, *Camping and Character,* 156.

31. Good, *Park and Recreation Structures,* 3:143.

32. For the early history of Camp Blake, see Leslie, *Centennial History of Nisswa,* 57. For a somewhat breathless appreciation of Camp Lincoln's rustic furniture and fittings, see Platou, "The Lure of an Ideal Camp," 78–81.

33. "Camp Warren," brochure for the 1928 season, 4, and "Camp Warren," brochure for the 1941 season (MHS). See also Wiley and Lehmann, *Builders of Men,* 310.

34. "Camp Mishawaka," brochure for the 1935 season, 9–11 (MHS).

35. Miller, "Camp Housing as a Factor in Good Camping," 22. For the development of postwar youth culture, see Mintz and Kellogg, *Domestic Revolutions,* 199–201.

4. FEEDING AN ARMY

1. For concerns about malnutrition in the 1910s, see Levenstein, *Revolution at the Table,* 112–20.

2. Cromley, "Transforming the Food Axis," 9.

3. Kasson, *Rudeness and Civility,* 182.

4. Wilson is quoted in Maynard, "'An Ideal Life in the Woods for Boys,'" 21.

5. Kasson, *Rudeness and Civility,* 189–91.

6. Robinson, "Association Boys' Camps," 85.

7. Ibid., 92.

8. Operating expenses for YMCA camps were published in "Association Boys' Camps Reported in 1901." Of the sixty-one camps that included information on their operating costs, only one, in Evanston, Illinois, spent one dollar per camper per day, whereas another, in Paris, Illinois, spent only twenty cents per camper per day.

9. Robinson, "Association Boys' Camps," 93.

10. Osborn, *Camp Dudley,* 48; Streightoff, "Summer Camps," 131–32.

11. "Camp Becket for Boys," brochure for the 1910 season, 3 (Kautz); Osborn, *Camp Dudley,* 12.

12. The best sources for images of male campers involved in food preparation are articles published in *Association Boys:* Gibson, "Camps Durrell and Becket," and Robinson, "The Experimental Woodcraft Camp." Comparable images for girls are to be found throughout Girl Scouts, *Campward Ho!*

13. Mercier, "Montanans at Work."

14. For the gendered, racial hierarchy in professional kitchens, see Levenstein, *Revolution at the Table*, 14–15.

15. Gibson, "Camps Durrell and Becket," 116.

16. "Camp Becket for Boys," brochure for the 1910 season, 3 (Kautz).

17. Gibson, *Camping for Boys*, 52.

18. Kasson, *Rudeness and Civility*, 189.

19. Gibson, *Camping for Boys*, 52.

20. Robinson, "Association Boys' Camps," 86–87.

21. Gibson, *Camping for Boys*, 52.

22. For Baden-Powell's interest in turning military scouting into a game for boys, see Macleod, *Building Character in the American Boy*, 133–36.

23. Wood, "Objectives in Outings and Camps for Boys," 113.

24. Girl Scouts, *Campward Ho!*, 37.

25. For militarism in British scouting, see Springhall, "The Boy Scouts, Class and Militarism in Relation to British Youth Movements, 1908–1930." See also Warren, "Sir Robert Baden-Powell, the Scout Movement and Citizen Training in Great Britain, 1990–1920," and Springhall's response, "Baden-Powell and the Scout Movement before 1920: Citizen Training or Soldiers for the Future?"

26. Girl Scouts, *Campward Ho!*, 45.

27. Published in the same year as *Campward Ho!* was Christine Frederick's influential domestic advice manual, *Household Engineering*.

28. Hayden, *The Grand Domestic Revolution*, 264–65.

29. Girl Scouts, *Campward Ho!*, 34–36.

30. A case in point is Kirby Lodge, at Camp Widjiwagan, a YMCA camp on Burntside Lake in northern Minnesota. Completed in 1949, the lodge was the product of professional design expertise, but the name most closely associated with the building is that of Robert Zimmermann, who supervised the log work that gives the dining room its distinctive character. The lodge was initially designed by an architect from Virginia, identified in camp records only as Mr. Aldrich, and then later redesigned (to reduce the size and cost of the project) by the St. Paul architectural firm of Ingemann and Bergstedt. Ericsson and Shepard, *Widjiwagan*, 56–59.

31. The physical transformation of the school kitchen is celebrated in Bryan, *The School Cafeteria*, especially chapter 9.

32. In many ways, camp electrification paralleled patterns of farm electrification identified by David Nye. Early in the century, for instance, the few summer camps that had access to electricity generated their own power. Only after the New Deal redefined electricity as "a definite necessity" (to use President Franklin D. Roosevelt's words) and helped establish a wide-reaching rural power grid did the use of electricity become more commonplace at camp.

While some commentators had seen the use of electricity as inimical to the mission of summer camp (as some had worried that electric power would undermine the virtues of farm life), both farmers and camp organizers came to embrace the adoption of new technologies as a way of improving rural life—without changing its essential character. By equalizing the domestic working conditions in rural and urban homes, Nye contends, rural electrification fueled the spread of suburbia and thus played a role in the eradication of the agrarian countryside, which intensified the perceived need for summer camps in the postwar period. Nye, *Electrifying America*, chapter 7.

33. Salomon, *Camp Site Development*, 57–58, 61–62.

34. Ibid., 58.

35. Good, *Park and Recreation Structures*, 3:143.

36. Ibid.

37. Girl Scouts, *Girl Scout Handbook*, 280–81.

38. Girl Scouts, *Junior Girl Scout Handbook*, 120.

5. GOOD AND DIRTY?

1. William W. Bauer, "Antisepticonscious America," *American Mercury* 28 (July 1933): 323–26, quoted in Tomes, *The The Gospel of Germs*, 158–59. For the connections between cleanliness and gentility, see Bushman, *The Refinement of America*, 41–42.

2. Practices that seem unremarkable today—providing a new cake of soap in its original wrapper in hotel rooms or refilling water glasses at the table in a restaurant—date from this period. Tomes, *The Gospel of Germs*, chapter 7 and especially 166–77.

3. The history of the domestic bathroom is well documented, particularly in Ogle, *All the Modern Conveniences*; Blaszczyk, *Imagining Consumers*, 171–76; and for the British context, Eveleigh, *Bogs, Baths, and Basins*.

4. Tomes, *The Gospel of Germs*, 192–93.

5. Gibson, *Camping for Boys*, 25–26.

6. Tomes, *The Gospel of Germs*, 34–38, 57–62.

7. Henry Hartshorne, *Our Homes* (Philadelphia: Presley Blakiston, 1880), 9, quoted in Tomes, *The Gospel of Germs*, 57–58. Hartshorne was the first professor of hygiene at the University of Pennsylvania Medical School.

8. Brown, "The Sanitary Care of a Boys' Camp," 100.

9. Tomes, *The Gospel of Germs*, 29.

10. Brown, "The Sanitary Care of a Boys' Camp," 111.

11. Ibid., 111–12.

12. Gibson, *Camping for Boys*, 30.

13. Ibid., 32–33.

14. Ibid., 28–29.

15. Brown, "The Sanitary Care of a Boys' Camp," 112–13; Gibson, *Camping for Boys*, 30–31.

16. Girl Scouts, *Campward Ho!*, 142–47.

17. Gibson, *Camping for Boys*, 34–36.

18. According to Dolores Hayden, Beecher elevated domestic tasks "to a level of frenzied holiness as the rites of the 'home church' of Christ" in order to support the idea that women wielded authority in the domestic sphere equivalent to that wielded by men (including Beecher's father and seven brothers) in the pulpit. While subsequent authors may not have had precisely the same religious motivation, they did maintain the practice of organizing housework into daily, weekly, and seasonal rituals. Hayden, "Catharine Beecher and the Politics of Housework."

19. Gibson, *Camp Management*, 57–59.

20. "Chimney Corners Camp, Value of Land, Buildings, and Equipment, Becket, Mass.," n.d., n.p. (Chimney Corners).

21. "Belknap Factoids," http://www.campbelknap.org/pages/factoids.htm. Accessed 7 May 2006.

22. Girl Scouts, *Campward Ho!*, 146–48.

23. Dail Steel Products Company of Lansing, Michigan, offered Wolverine Chemical Toilets; King & Company of Boston did not specify the manufacturer of its "odorless chemical toilet closets." Sargent, *A Handbook of Summer Camps*, 657.

24. The paid announcements (547–604) offer more detailed information than the brief paragraphs that Porter and his staff wrote on the hundreds of private camps included in the guide. Boy Scout camps (96–128), Girl Scout camps (128–135), Camp Fire Girl camps (136–143), YMCA camps (144–61), and YWCA camps (162–63) were listed individually with addresses and fees, but not described. Sargent, *Handbook of Summer Camps*.

25. By 1934, the screened privy (like the one recommended in Gibson in 1909) that had once served Dudley campers was considered "far from satisfactory." Osborn, *Camp Dudley*, 49–50.

26. Sargent, *Handbook of Summer Camps*, 41–42.

27. Ibid., 41.

28. Ibid., 580.

29. Ledlie, *Layout, Building Designs, and Equipment for Y.M.C.A. Camps*, 25; Salomon, *Camp Site Development*, 14–15.

30. Salomon, *Camp Site Development*, 24, 27, 29–30.

31. Camp Fire Girls, *When You Plan Your Camp*, 8; Ledlie, *Layout, Building Designs, and Equipment for Y.M.C.A. Camps*, 23.

32. Salomon, *Camp Site Development*, 30–33.

33. Lupton and Miller, *The Bathroom, the Kitchen and the Aesthetics of Waste*, 18–19; Bushman and Bushman, "The Early History of Cleanliness in America"; Glassberg, "The Public Bath Movement in America."

34. Brown, "The Sanitary Care of a Boys' Camp," 119.

35. Gibson, *Camping for Boys*, 20, 205.

36. Ibid., 93, 119.

37. Salomon, *Camp Site Development*, 38, 46.

38. Girl Scouts, *Campward Ho!*, 38.

39. Brumberg, *The Body Project*, 7–11.

40. Ibid., 11–18, 46.

41. Ibid., 41–47.

42. Ginsburg, "'Don't Tell, Dear,'" 365–66.

43. Girl Scouts, *Campward Ho!*, 146.

44. Brumberg, *Body Project*, 38.

45. Tomes, *The Gospel of Germs*, 237–39.

46. "Camp," an unattributed memoir of life at Chimney Corners Camp in 1931, n.d, n.p. (Chimney Corners).

47. Salomon, *Camp Site Development*, 46.

6. LIVING LIKE SAVAGES

1. Deloria, *Playing Indian*.

2. Scholars from a range of disciplines have studied sites where Native Americans were involved in interpreting their culture for the entertainment and edification of white audiences. Rather than dismissing such performances as inauthentic (although this they surely were), the most sophisticated of these treatments have used Edward Said's theory of Orientalism to link the social construction of Indianness with the social construction of whiteness. Huhndorf, *Going Native*; Gidley, *Edward S. Curtis and the North American Indian, Incorporated*; Curtis, *The Plains Indian Photographs of Edward S. Curtis*; Finger, *Cherokee Americans*; Kasson, *Buffalo Bill's Wild West*; Parezo and Troutman, "The 'Shy' Cocopa Go to the Fair."

3. As Joy Kasson argues, reenactments of the Battle of the Little Big Horn (introduced as the grand finale of the Wild West Show in 1893) were particularly complex cultural phenomena in that they enhanced the show's claim to historical significance, "gave advocates of expansionism a martyr . . . [to] justify their cause," positioned Cody as Custer's successor in the work of conquest, and helped Americans process their feelings about the Civil War in ways that "helped make war imaginatively appealing again." Kasson, *Buffalo Bill's Wild West*, 113–14, 244–48.

4. In addition to situating Curtis's work within an ideological tradition that saw Native Americans as a vanishing race, Sandweiss also positions it within a tradition of public and commercial photography in which words—lectures, captions, and other texts—were central to giving the images meaning. Sandweiss, "Picturing Indians."

5. In the early decades of the twentieth century, tipis appeared in postcards from the Grand Canyon; in Asheville, North Carolina, a Cherokee man dressed as a Sioux warrior in a 1935 parade aimed at attracting tourists to the Eastern Band's reservation in the Smoky Mountains. In the 1935 parade, Cherokee Goingback Chiltoskey rode on horseback dressed as a Sioux warrior, although he later admitted to historian John Finger that he had never before been on a horse. Finger, *Cherokee Americans*, 98–99. For Wild West Show posters featuring tipis, see Kasson, *Buffalo Bill's Wild West*, 87, 148, 192, 197.

6. As early as 1894, Boas offered a critique of evolutionary ethnology and particularly its tendency to conflate the achievement of civilization with an aptitude for civilization. He elaborated his ideas on race in *The Mind of Primitive Man*, first published in 1911 and again in revised form in 1939. Dippie, *The Vanishing American*, 281–83.

7. For Hall's conflation of children, savagery, and Indians, see Deloria, *Playing Indian*, 106–7.

8. Although Jackson Lears does not touch on white appropriation of Indian motifs in the early twentieth century—emphasizing instead a fin de siècle fascination with the Middle Ages as the childhood of the human race—his analysis of anti-modernism's "worship of force" and its idealization of "premodern mental simplicity" can also encompass the phenomenon of "playing Indian." Lears, *No Place of Grace*, 107–17, 144–49.

9. Ernest Thompson Seton, "The Boy Scouts in America," *Outlook* (July 1910), 633, quoted in Deloria, *Playing Indian*, 107.

10. Charles Fletcher Lummis, letter to Edgar L. Hewett, 7 January 1927, quoted in Hewett, "Lummis the Inimitable."

11. The Woodcraft program is described in Seton, *The Birch-Bark Roll of the Woodcraft Indians*, 54–63, and in Macleod, *Building Character in the American Boy*, 130–32. See also Morris, "Ernest Thompson Seton and the Origins of the Woodcraft Movement," 183–94; Anderson, "Ernest Thompson Seton and the Woodcraft Indians"; Deloria, *Playing Indian*, 95–108. Even this cursory overview of the Woodcraft program reveals some of the contradictions inherent in Seton's views of Native Americans. On one hand, he tended to ignore the cultural differences between tribal groups, forging them into his own amalgam of generic "Indian" practices. At the same time, he refused to accept the dominant ideology that saw Indians as a vanishing race inherently inferior to whites. Instead, he felt more sympathetic to the aims of the Sequoya League, founded in 1901 by a group of reform-minded whites intent on securing better treatment for Native Americans. Indeed, Seton seems to have seen the larger aims of the Woodcraft Indians as twofold: to use Indian culture to reinvigorate white boyhood and to encourage white boys to support Indian reform by teaching them to appreciate real Indians. His involvement with the Sequoya League is discussed in Anderson, *The Chief*, 133.

12. Seton's impact on the Gulicks is discussed in Deloria, *Playing Indian*, 111, and Anderson, *The Chief*, 166–69; official histories of the Camp Fire Girls reveal Seton's ongoing interest in the organization, which included hosting training sessions for Guardians (as Camp Fire Girl leaders were called) at DeWinton, his Greenwich estate. Buckler, Fiedler, and Allen, *Wo-He-Lo*, 121–22. For Seton's contentious relationship with the Boy Scouts, see Macleod, *Building Character*, 147–51, 156, and Anderson, *The Chief*, 151–75.

13. Seton, *Trail of an Artist-Naturalist*, 384.

14. Cromley, "Masculine/Indian," 268.

15. Seton's conflicts with Beard are treated in Macleod, *Building Character*, 239, and Anderson, *The Chief*, 158–60; they are highlighted in Deloria, *Playing Indian*, 95–102.

16. Maynard, "'An Ideal Life in the Woods for Boys,'" 6, 8, 10.

17. Mishawaka's director Steve Purdum provided the translation in 1996; significantly, no camp brochures include information about the camp's Indian name. Beginning in the late 1920s, brochures do translate the name of Lake Pokegama as "The Lake of the Far Stretching Arm," although a more accurate translation (according to Purdum) is "path off the main path." "Camp Mishawaka: A Summer Camp for Boys," brochure for the 1929 season, 10 (Mishawaka).

18. Maynard, "'An Ideal Life in the Woods,'" 10.

19. "Camp Mishawaka, 'Safety and Health First,'" brochure for 1915 season, 20 (Mishawaka).

20. Gibson, *Camping for Boys*, 217.

21. For Homer's Civil War engravings, see Goodrich, *The Graphic Art of Winslow Homer*, and Beam, *Winslow Homer's Magazine Engravings*. For images of sportsmen's fires in the Adirondacks, see Barnhill, *Wild Impressions*. Rudyard Kipling evoked the Indian campfire in "The Feet of the Young Men" (1897). For collegiate bonfires, see Horowitz, *Campus Life*.

22. Gibson, *Camping for Boys*, 124–25.

23. Streightoff, "Summer Camps," 133–34. The year before, another article described a very similar program held at Camp Tuxis in Connecticut. Cobleigh and Smith, "Some Interesting Things about Camp Tuxis," 122–23.

24. Cobleigh and Smith, "Some Interesting Things about Camp Tuxis," 122–23.

25. Douglas, *The Feminization of American Culture*.

26. Although Seton described the house as "an inexpensive cabin," Wyndygoul was a substantial Tudoresque house on which (according to his biography) he spared no expense. Seton, *Trail of an Artist-Naturalist*, 377. Descriptions of Seton's landscape changes at Wyndygoul in this and subsequent paragraphs are drawn from Anderson, *The Chief*, 106–9, and from Lucinda H. MacKethan, "The Setons at Home: Organizing a Family Biography," http://www.nhc.rtp.nc.us/biography/mackethan.htm. Accessed March 2004.

27. Seton documented the construction and use of his hollow tree in a series of ten "bulletins" published in *Country Life in America* between November 1908 and April 1909. The first of these was "Making a Hollow Tree and What Came of It: Bulletin 1," *Country Life in America* 15 (November 1908), 47, 84.

28. Anderson, *The Chief*, 106.

29. This early campout and the events leading up to it are described in Anderson, *The Chief*, 138–41. For Seton's version, see Seton, *Trail of an Artist-Naturalist*, 376–85.

30. Seton seems to have been particularly offended by the military connotations of tents. Anderson, *The Chief*, 141.

31. Nabokov and Easton, *Native American Architecture*, 150–73.

32. Cody even transformed parts of Europe into the western frontier by superimposing sketches of tipis over a photograph of the interior of the Roman Colosseum, an image that was published in an 1893 program booklet for the Wild West Show. Kasson, *Buffalo Bill's Wild West*, 111–12.

33. Seton, *The Book of Woodcraft*, 469–70.

34. Ibid., 468, 474–78.

35. Ibid., 5.

36. Ibid., 191.

37. Ibid., 182–83.

38. Ibid., 183.

39. Hewson, *Wohelo Down through the Years*, 20, 22, 31, 53, 120.

40. Ibid., 18, 30, 36–38, 61, 70, 82; Buckler, Fiedler, and Allen, *Wo-He-Lo*, 13–18.

41. Lydia Bush Brown writing in 1928, quoted in Hewson, *Wohelo Down through the Years*, 43.

42. Jacobs, *Engendered Encounters*, 169–70.

43. Hewson, *Wohelo Down through the Years*, 25, 43, 84–85.

44. Lydia Bush Brown writing in 1928, quoted in Hewson, *Wohelo Down through the Years*, 43.

45. Gulick is quoted in Buckler, Fiedler, and Allen, *Wo-He-Lo*, 22.

46. Deloria, *Playing Indian*, 113.

47. Seton diaries, vol. 22: 18, 127; vol. 23: 123, 126; vol. 24: 32, 37–41, 85–95, 164–66; vol. 25: 48, 100, 110, 150, 154–57. Seton's diaries are preserved in the Natural History Museum in New York, although photocopies are also available in the Seton Memorial Library on the Philmont Scout Ranch in Cimarron, New Mexico. Edwards, *Taylor Statten*, 88.

48. Seton diaries, vol. 22: 8, 18; vol. 24: 39, 41 (Seton).

49. Seton diaries, vol. 23: 38, 42, 123, 126; vol. 24: 41; vol. 25: 100, 110 (Seton).

50. Thomas Hale et al., *Camp Dudley*, 34–35. "Camp Charlevoix," brochure for the 1930 season, 14 (Gutman).

51. Edwards, *Taylor Statten*, 84, 98; Lundell, *Summer Camp*, 28, 34; Ericsson and Shepard, *Widjiwagan*, 6; Wiley and Lehmann, *Builders of Men*, 303, 306, 311.

52. "Medomak Camp," brochure for the 1933 season, 3 (Gutman).

53. "Culver Woodcraft Camp," brochure for the 1936 season, 13 (Gutman).

54. This outline of Salomon's career derives chiefly from two autobiographical sketches: an untitled text focusing on his interest in Indian culture written for *Harper's* in connection with the publication of *The Book of Indian Crafts and Indian Lore* in 1928, and another titled "Camping Experience of Julian Harris Salomon," which is undated, but written in about 1973. I am grateful to Richard B. Salomon for providing copies of these and other primary sources documenting his father's fascinating career.

55. For Salomon's postwar camp-planning career, see "Fresh Air Camp Is Lauded by 'Architectural Forum'"; "Camp Planner Can 'Think Like a Child,'"; "Civilized Camps Are Dull to Youngsters" (Salomon).

56. The Bible comment is from an unnamed reviewer for *Camper and Hiker* magazine quoted in a promotional flyer issued by Harper and Brothers, publishers of *The Book of Indian Crafts and Indian Lore* (Salomon). Other endorsements were provided by Daniel C. Beard, L. L. McDonald (Boy Scouts national camp director), M. W. Stirling (of the Smithsonian Institution), and J. Stevenson Hill (identified as executive manager, Camp Fire Girls National Headquarters).

57. "American Indian Entertainments," promotional brochure for Julian Harris Salomon, or "Soaring Eagle," n.d., n.p. (Salomon).

58. Ibid.

59. Ibid.

60. Salomon, *The Book of Indian Crafts and Indian Lore*, 150–51.

61. Nabokov and Easton, *Native American Architecture*, 87–89.

62. Boy Scouts of America Department of Camping, *Camp Site Development Plans*, 39.

63. Nabokov and Easton, *Native American Architecture*, 87.

64. Seton, *Birch-Bark Roll*, back cover; Seton, *Book of Woodcraft*, 468–78; Salomon, "The Indian Tipi"; Boy Scouts of America Department of Camping, *Camp Site Development Plans*, 42; Salomon, *Book of Indian Crafts*, 130–47.

65. Salomon, *The Book of Indian Crafts and Indian Lore*, 369; Chimney Rock Camp brochure for the 1934 season, n.p. (Gutman).

66. Although Mishawaka campers were organized into tribes as early as 1915 (and perhaps as early as 1911), tipis used as headquarters for the big chiefs seem to have made their first appearance in the late 1920s; they were pictured in "Camp Mishawaka, A Summer Camp for Boys," brochure for the 1929 season, 34 (Mishawaka). Scalping was still being played on the Mishawaka campus during my visit in the summer of 1998.

67. "Medomak Camp," brochure for the 1933 season, 19 (Gutman).

68. Salomon, *The Book of Indian Crafts and Indian Lore*, especially chapters 2 and 3. For the stereotype of the Indian as perpetual warrior, see Hill, "Developed Identities," 155–57.

69. Boy Scouts of American Department of Camping, *Camp Site Development Plans*, 3, 6.

70. In her study of the use of Indian materials in the domestic interiors of European Americans, Elizabeth Cromley notes that "the gendering of Indian objects was fluid" and especially dependent on context. Spears—so often associated with the masculine realm of warfare—could be feminized when used to support curtains in a "cozy corner" of a middle-class house. Cromley, "Masculine/Indian," 270.

71. Seton, *Book of Woodcraft*, 5.

72. Eastman, *Indian Scout Talks*, 138, 147. A physician and YMCA youth worker, Eastman was also a founding member of the Society of American Indians, a Pan-Indian organization established in 1911. *Native America in the Twentieth Century: An Encyclopedia* (New York: Garland, 1994), s.v. "Pan-Indianism." Although we might expect Eastman's Indian heritage to allow him to speak with some authority on these issues, Philip Deloria has pointed out that being a "real" Indian often complicated the cultural situation of figures like Eastman. At one level, he was an embodiment of Indian culture. At another level, especially when self-con-

sciously enacting Indian culture for non-Indians, Eastman also—in Deloria's formulation—"imitated non-Indian imitations of Indians." Thus, like Seton, Eastman was an interpreter of Indian culture, and one whose interpretation could be refuted. Deloria, *Playing Indian,* 122–23.

73. "Camp Alanita for Girls," brochure for the 1927 season, 17 (Gutman).

74. Huhndorf, *Going Native,* 4–5.

75. The text and illustrations from a 1955 Pyrotex brochure on how to make a lanyard with gymp are reprinted in Kahn, *Sleepaway,* 97–98.

76. Good, *Park and Recreation Structures,* 2:197.

77. Ledlie, *Layout, Building Designs, and Equipment for Y.M.C.A. Camps,* 44.

78. Deloria, *Playing Indian,* 8–9.

79. Gibson, *Recreational Programs for Summer Camps,* 5–6.

80. For examples of the postwar tendency to define interracial camping as an experience for whites and African Americans, see Patrick, "A New Kind of Camp"; Webb, "Color-blind Summer Camps."

EPILOGUE

1. "Architecture Goes Camping," 135.

2. Ibid., 136.

3. Some of the earliest A-frames were built in northern California, notably by Wally Reemelin (a mechanical engineer with an interest in art and architecture) in Berkeley in 1948–49 and by architect John Campbell, whose A-frame Leisure House could be constructed from kits first marketed in

1951. Henrik Bull designed an A-frame ski cabin at Stowe, Vermont, in 1953. Chad Randl, *A-Frame,* chapter 3.

4. The construction details of these buildings were featured in John L. Spring, "The 'Big Piece' Way to Build."

5. "Architecture in the Rough," 121.

6. Ibid., 120–23.

7. "Two Camps Designed for Summer Fun"; "Oneness of Form and Material."

8. Salomon, *Camp Site Development,* 2nd ed., 80, 106, 109–10, 118, 120–21.

9. "Recreation Buildings." Mary Corbin Sies, Isabelle Gournay, and Erica Schultz, Girl Scout Lodge, Camp Woodlands, Anne Arundel County (1953–54), National Register level documentation prepared for the Maryland Historical Trust, The Modern Movement in Maryland Survey, Phase Two, December 2005, 7.1 (NRHP).

10. Le Corbusier (Charles-Édouard Jeanneret), *Vers une Architecture* (Paris, 1926) 53–55, quoted in Rykwert, *On Adam's House in Paradise,* 16.

11. "Portrait of a New Camp—1955," 18.

12. "Architecture in the Rough," 121.

13. "Notes for a History of the Fresh Air Fund: Part 3 (1947–1957)," n.d., 5 (FAF).

14. Ibid., 4; Fresh Air Fund, *Annual Report for 1960* (FAF).

15. Fresh Air Fund, *Annual Report for 1952,* 14 (FAF).

16. "Architecture Goes Camping," 137.

17. Ibid., 135.

18. "Two Camps Designed for Summer Fun," 93.

BIBLIOGRAPHY

Adams, Annmarie. "The Eichler Home: Intention and Experience in Postwar Suburbia." In *Gender, Class, and Shelter: Perspectives in Vernacular Architecture, V,* edited by Elizabeth Collins Cromley and Carter L. Hudgins, 164–178. Knoxville: University of Tennessee Press, 1995.

Adler, Louise. "Adventure in Democracy." *Recreation* 39 (June 1945): 121, 165.

Anderson, H. Allen. *The Chief: Ernest Thompson Seton and the Changing West.* College Station: Texas A&M University Press, 1986.

————. "Ernest Thompson Seton and the Woodcraft Indians." *Journal of American Culture* 8 (1985): 43–50.

"Architecture Goes Camping." *Architectural Forum* 103 (July 1955): 134–39.

"Architecture in the Rough." *Architectural Forum* 107 (October 1957): 120–23.

"Association Boys' Camps Reported in 1901." *Association Boys* 1 (June 1902): 122–23.

Balmer, Randall. *Mine Eyes Have Seen the Glory: A Journey into the Evangelical Subculture in America.* New York: Oxford University Press, 1993.

Barker, Lady Mary Anne. *The Bedroom and Boudoir.* London: Macmillan, 1878.

Barnhill, Georgia B. *Wild Impressions: The Adirondacks on Paper.* Blue Mountain Lake, N.Y.: Adirondack Museum; Boston: Godine, 1995.

Bates, Captain Gordon. *The Khaki Boys at Camp Sterling.* New York: Cupples and Leon, 1918.

Beam, Philip C. *Winslow Homer's Magazine Engravings.* New York: Harper and Row, 1979.

Bederman, Gail. *Manliness and Civilization: A Cultural History of Gender and Race in the United States, 1880–1917.* Chicago: University of Chicago Press, 1995.

Benét, William Rose. *The Reader's Encyclopedia.* New York: Thomas Y. Crowell, 1965.

Bentley, W. H. "The House That Jack Built." *Camping Magazine* 12 (February 1940): 19, 24.

Bermingham, Ann. *Landscape and Ideology: The English Rustic Tradition, 1740–1860.*

Berkeley and Los Angeles: University of California Press, 1986.

Birns, Beverly, and Sarah Hall Sternglanz. "Sex-Role Socialization: Looking Back and Looking Ahead." In *Social and Cognitive Skills: Sex Roles and Children's Play*, edited by Marsha B. Liss, 235–51. New York: Academic Press, 1983.

Blaszczyk, Regina Lee. *Imagining Consumers: Design and Innovation from Wedgwood to Corning*. Baltimore: The Johns Hopkins University Press, 2000.

Bledstein, Burton J. *The Culture of Professionalism: The Middle Class and the Development of Higher Education in America*. New York: Norton, 1976.

Boy Scouts of America Department of Camping. *Camp Site Development Plans*. [New York]: Boy Scouts of America, 1927.

Boyer, Paul. *Urban Masses and Moral Order in America, 1820–1920*. Cambridge, Mass.: MIT Press, 1978.

Bridgton, Maine, 1768–1994: An Updated Bicentennial History. Bridgton, Maine: Bridgton Historical Society, 1993.

Brown, Elias G. "The Sanitary Care of a Boys' Camp." *Association Boys* 1 (April 1902): 48–51; (June 1902): 110–21.

Brown, Virginia Pounds, and Katherine Price Garmon. "Early Camps at Winnataska." *Alabama Review* 44 (1991): 285–309.

Brumberg, Joan Jacobs. *The Body Project: An Intimate History of American Girls*. New York: Vintage Books, 1997.

Bryan, Mary de Garmo. *The School Cafeteria*. New York: Crofts, 1940.

Buckler, Helen, Mary F. Fiedler, and Martha F. Allen, eds. *Wo-He-Lo: The Story of Camp Fire Girls, 1910–1960*. New York: Holt, Rinehart and Winston, 1961.

Bushman, Richard L. *The Refinement of America: Persons, Houses, Cities*. New York: Knopf, 1992.
———, and Claudia L. Bushman. "The Early His-tory of Cleanliness in America." *Journal of American History* 74 (March 1988): 1213–38.

Camp Becket In-the-Berkshires, 1903–1953. Boston: YMCA of Massachusetts and Rhode Island, 1953.

Camp Fire Girls. *The Book of the Camp Fire Girls*. New York: Camp Fire Girls, 1913; 10th printing, 1922.
———. *Handbook for Leaders of Camp Fire Girls*. New York: Camp Fire Girls, 1935.
———. *When You Plan Your Camp*. New York: Camp Fire Girls, 1946.

"Camp Planner Can 'Think Like a Child.'" *Grand Rapids (Mich.) Press*, 30 August 1959.

Carnes, Mark C., and Clyde Griffen, eds. *Meanings for Manhood: Constructions of Masculinity in Victorian America*. Chicago: University of Chicago Press, 1990.

Carr, Ethan. *Wilderness by Design: Landscape Architecture and the National Park Service*. Lincoln: University of Nebraska Press, 1998.

Cavallo, Dominick. *Muscles and Morals: Organized Playgrounds and Urban Reform, 1880–1920*. Philadelphia: University of Pennsylvania Press, 1981.

Cheley, F. H. *The Boy Scout Trail Blazers*. New York: Barse and Hopkins, 1917.

"Civilized Camps Are Dull to Youngsters." *Atlanta Journal and Constitution*, 23 April 1967, 8–E.

Cobleigh, Irving, and Harvey L. Smith. "Some Interesting Things about Camp Tuxis." *Association Boys* 3 (June 1904): 107–30.

Cranz, Galen. *The Politics of Park Design: A History of Urban Parks in America*. Cambridge, Mass.: MIT Press, 1982.

Cromley, Elizabeth C. "Masculine/Indian." *Winterthur Portfolio* 31 (Winter 1996): 265–80.
———. "Transforming the Food Axis: Houses, Tools, Modes of Analysis." *Material History Review* 44 (Fall 1996): 8–22.

Cronon, William. *Nature's Metropolis: Chicago and the Great West*. New York: Norton, 1991.

Cross, Gary. *Kids' Stuff: Toys and the Changing*

World of American Childhood. Cambridge, Mass.: Harvard University Press, 1997.

Curtis, Edward S. *The Plains Indian Photographs of Edward S. Curtis*. Lincoln: University of Nebraska Press, 2001.

Cutler, William W., III. "Cathedral of Culture: The Schoolhouse in American Educational Thought and Practice since 1820." *History of Education Quarterly* 29 (Spring 1989): 1–40.

Deloria, Philip J. *Playing Indian*. New Haven, Conn.: Yale University Press, 1998.

DeLuca, Dave. *Our Loyal Band: The Story of the First 100 Years of YMCA Camp Becket*. Becket, Mass.: Becket-Chimney Corners YMCA, 2003.

DeVries, Julianne. *The Campfire Girls as Detectives*. [New York]: World Syndicate, 1933.

Dietrich-Smith, Deborah. "Cultural Landscape Report: Camp Hayo-Went-Ha." n.p.: State YMCA of Michigan, 1999.

Dimock, Hedley S., ed. *Character Education in the Summer Camp, II: Report of Institute Held at the Y.M.C.A. College, Chicago, April 17–20, 1931*. New York: Association Press, 1931.

———, ed. *Putting Standards into the Summer Camp: Report of Seventh Annual Camp Institute under Joint Auspices of George Williams College and Chicago Camping Association, March 20–22, 1936*. New York: Association Press, 1936.

———, and Charles E. Hendry. *Camping and Character: A Camp Experiment in Character Education*. New York: Association Press, 1929.

Dippie, Brian W. *The Vanishing American: White Attitudes and U.S. Indian Policy*. Middletown, Conn.: Wesleyan University Press, 1982.

Douglas, Ann. *The Feminization of American Culture*. New York: Knopf, 1977.

Downs, Laura Lee. *Childhood in the Promised Land: Working-Class Movements and the Colonies de Vacances in France, 1880–1960*. Durham, N.C.: Duke University Press, 2002.

Dudek, Mark. *Kindergarten Architecture: Space for the Imagination*. London: Spon Press, 1996.

Dulles, Foster Rhea. *The American Red Cross: A History*. New York: Harper and Brothers, 1950.

Eastman, Charles A. *Indian Scout Talks: A Guide for Boy Scouts and Camp Fire Girls*. 1914. Reprint, Boston: Little, Brown, 1920.

Edwards, C. A. M. *Taylor Statten: A Biography*. Toronto: Ryerson Press, 1960.

Eells, Eleanor. *History of Organized Camping: The First 100 Years*. Martinsville, Ind.: American Camping Association, 1986.

Ericsson, Dwight, and John Shepard. *Widjiwagan: A History from 1929 to 1989*. St. Paul: Camp Widjiwagan, YMCA of Greater St. Paul, 1994.

Etaugh, Claire. "Introduction: The Influence of Environmental Factors on Sex Differences in Children's Play." In *Social and Cognitive Skills: Sex Roles and Children's Play*, edited by Marsha B. Liss, 1–19. New York: Academic Press, 1983.

Eveleigh, David J. *Bogs, Baths, and Basins: The Story of Domestic Sanitation*. Stroud, UK: Sutton, 2002.

Finger, John R. *Cherokee Americans: The Eastern Band of Cherokees in the Twentieth Century*. Lincoln: University of Nebraska Press, 1991.

Frederick, Christine. *Household Engineering: Scientific Management in the Home*. Chicago: American School of Home Economics, 1920.

"Fresh Air Camp Is Lauded by 'Architectural Forum.'" *New York Herald Tribune*, 5 July 1955.

Gagen, Elizabeth. "Playing the Part: Performing Gender in America's Playgrounds." In *Children's Geographies: Playing, Living, Learning*, edited by Sarah L. Holloway and Gill Valentine, 213–29. London: Routledge, 2000.

Gelber, Steven M. *Hobbies: Leisure and the Culture of Work in America*. New York: Columbia University Press, 1999.

Getz, Gail M. "The Great Escape: Camping in the Nineteenth Century." *Pennsylvania Heritage* 11 (1985): 18–25.

Gibson, H. W. *Camp Management: A Manual for Camp Directors*. Cambridge, Mass.: Murray, 1923.

————. *Camping for Boys*. New York: Association Press, 1911.

————. "Camps Durrell and Becket." *Association Boys* 5 (June 1906): 113–27.

————. *Recreational Programs for Summer Camps*. New York: Greenberg, 1938.

Gidley, Mick. *Edward S. Curtis and the North American Indian, Incorporated*. Cambridge: Cambridge University Press, 1998.

Gilborn, Craig. *Adirondack Camps: Homes Away from Home, 1850–1950*. Blue Mountain Lake, N.Y.: Adirondack Museum; Syracuse, N.Y.: Syracuse University Press, 2000.

Gilmore, Russell S. "'Another Branch of Manly Sport': American Rifle Games, 1840–1900." In *Hard at Play: Leisure in America, 1840–1940*, edited by Kathryn Grover, 93–111. Amherst: University of Massachusetts Press; Rochester, N.Y.: Strong Museum, 1992.

Ginsburg, Rebecca. "'Don't Tell, Dear': The Material Culture of Tampons and Napkins." *Journal of Material Culture* 1 (1996): 365–75.

Girl Scouts. *Campward Ho! A Manual for Girl Scout Camps*. New York: Girl Scouts, 1920.

————. *Girl Scout Handbook: Intermediate Program*. New York: Girl Scouts of the United States of America, 1953.

————. *Junior Girl Scout Handbook*. New York: Girl Scouts of the United States of America, 1963.

Glassberg, David. "The Public Bath Movement in America." *American Studies* 20 (1979): 5–21.

Goldstein, Jeffrey H., ed. *Toys, Play, and Child Development*. Cambridge: Cambridge University Press, 1994.

Good, Albert H. *Park and Recreation Structures*. 3 vols. Washington, D.C.: National Park Service, 1938.

Goodrich, Lloyd. *The Graphic Art of Winslow Homer*. New York: Museum of Graphic Art; Washington, D.C.: Smithsonian Institution Press, 1968.

Graham, Abbie. *The Girls' Camp: Program-Making for Summer Leisure*. New York: Womans Press, 1933.

————. *Working at Play in Summer Camps*. New York: Womans Press, 1941.

Graham, Lawrence Otis. *Our Kind of People: Inside America's Black Upper Class*. New York: HarperCollins, 1999.

Grant, Julia. *Raising Baby by the Book: The Education of American Mothers*. New Haven, Conn.: Yale University Press, 1998.

Grier, Katherine C. "Are We Having Fun Yet?" In *Hard at Play: Leisure in America, 1840–1940*, edited by Kathryn Grover, 1–7. Amherst: University of Massachusetts Press; Rochester, N.Y.: Strong Museum, 1992.

Groth, Paul. *Living Downtown: The History of Residential Hotels in the United States*. Berkeley and Los Angeles: University of California Press, 1994.

Grover, Kathryn, ed. *Hard at Play: Leisure in America, 1840–1940*. Amherst: University of Massachusetts Press; Rochester, N.Y.: Strong Museum, 1992.

Gulliford, Andrew. *America's Country Schools*. Washington, D.C.: Preservation Press, 1984.

Gutman, Marta, and Ning de Coninck-Smith, eds. *Designing Modern Childhoods: History, Space, and the Material Culture of Children*. New Brunswick, N.J.: Rutgers University Press, forthcoming.

Hale, Thomas, John Jones, Martyn Keeler, and William J. Schmidt, eds. *Camp Dudley: The First Hundred Years*. [Westport, N.Y.]: Camp Dudley, 1984.

Hall, G. Stanley. *Adolescence: Its Psychology and Its Relations to Physiology, Anthropology, Sociology, Sex, Crime, Religion and Education*. 2 vols. New York: Appleton, 1904.

————. "Feminization in School and Home." *World's Work* 16 (May 1908): 10237–44.

Hantover, Jeffery P. "The Boy Scouts and the Validation of Masculinity." *Journal of Social Issues* 34 (1978): 184–95.

Hayden, Dolores. "Catharine Beecher and the Politics of Housework." In *Women in American Architecture: A Historic and Contemporary Perspective*, edited by Susana Torre, 40–49. New York: Whitney Library of Design, 1977.

———. *The Grand Domestic Revolution: A History of Feminist Designs for American Homes, Neighborhoods, and Cities*. Cambridge, Mass.: MIT Press, 1981.

Hendry, Charles E., ed. *Appraising the Summer Camp: Report of the Eighth Annual Camp Institute under Joint Auspices of George Williams College and the Chicago Camping Association, April 9–11, 1937*. New York: Association Press, 1937.

Hewett, Edgar L. "Lummis the Inimitable." *Papers of the School of American Research*, n.s., 35 (1944): 1–14.

Hewson, Charlotte Gulick. *Wohelo Down through the Years: Memories of Camping at the Luther Gulick Camps 1907–1930*. South Casco, Maine: Wohelo Press, 2000.

Hill, Richard W., Sr., "Developed Identities: Seeing the Stereotypes and Beyond." In *Spirit Capture: Photographs from the National Museum of the American Indian*, edited by Tim Johnson, 139–60. Washington, D.C.: Smithsonian Institution Press, 1998.

Hoagland, Allison K. "Village Constructions: U.S. Army Forts on the Plains, 1848–1890." *Winterthur Portfolio* 34 (Winter 1999): 215–37.

Holloway, Sarah L., and Gill Valentine, eds. *Children's Geographies: Playing, Living, Learning*. London: Routledge, 2000.

Hopkins, C. Howard. *History of the Y.M.C.A. in North America*. New York: Association Press, 1951.

Horowitz, Helen Lefkowitz. *Campus Life: Undergraduate Cultures from the End of the Eighteenth Century to the Present*. New York: Knopf, 1987.

Hundorf, Shari M. *Going Native: Indians in the American Cultural Imagination*. Ithaca, N.Y.: Cornell University Press, 2001.

Inness, Sherrie A., ed. *Delinquents and Debutantes: Twentieth-Century American Girls' Cultures*. New York: New York University Press, 1998.

Jacobs, Margaret D. *Engendered Encounters: Feminism and Pueblo Cultures, 1879–1934*. Lincoln: University of Nebraska Press, 1999.

Jacobson, Matthew Frye. *Whiteness of a Different Color: European Immigrants and the Alchemy of Race*. Cambridge, Mass.: Harvard University Press, 1998.

Jacoby, Karl. *Crimes against Nature: Squatters, Poachers, Thieves, and the Hidden History of American Conservation*. Berkeley and Los Angeles: University of California Press, 2001.

Johnson, C. Walton. "The Camp of the Future." *Camping Magazine* 8 (October 1936): 9, 25.

Johnson, Tim, ed. *Spirit Capture: Photographs from the National Museum of the American Indian*. Washington, D.C.: Smithsonian Institution Press, 1998.

Jones, Owain. "Melting Geography: Purity, Disorder, Childhood and Space." In *Children's Geographies: Playing, Living, Learning*, edited by Sarah L. Holloway and Gill Valentine, 29–47. London: Routledge, 2000.

Joselit, Jenna Weissman, and Karen S. Mittelman, eds. *A Worthy Use of Summer: Jewish Summer Camping in America*. Philadelphia: National Museum of American Jewish History, 1993.

Kahn, Laurie Susan. *Sleepaway: The Girls of Summer and the Camps They Love*. New York: Workman, 2003.

Kaighn, R. P. "Camp Dudley." *Association Boys* 4 (June 1905): 109–24.

Kaiser, Harvey H. *Great Camps of the Adirondacks*. Boston: Godine, 1982.

Kasson, John F. *Rudeness and Civility: Manners in Nineteenth-Century Urban America*. New York: Hill and Wang, 1990.

Kasson, Joy S. *Buffalo Bill's Wild West: Celebrity,*

Memory, and Popular History. New York: Hill and Wang, 2000.

Kaynor, Fay Campbell. "The Golden Era of Private Summer Camps." *Vermont History News* 41 (1990): 46–50.

Keller, Betty. *Black Wolf: The Life of Ernest Thompson Seton*. Vancouver: Douglas and McIntyre, 1984.

Kohlstedt, Sally Gregory. "Collectors, Cabinets and Summer Camp: Natural History in the Public Life of Nineteenth-Century Worcester." *Museum Studies Journal* 2 (Fall 1985): 10–23.

Lears, T. J. Jackson. *No Place of Grace: Antimodernism and the Transformation of American Culture, 1880–1920*. New York: Pantheon, 1981.

Ledlie, John A. "Consultation on Camping." *Association Boys' Work Journal* 12 (March 1945): 2–3, 5.

———, ed. *Layout, Building Designs, and Equipment for Y.M.C.A. Camps*. New York: Association Press, 1946.

Leslie, Earl C. *Centennial History of Nisswa*. [Minnesota: s.n.], 1986.

Levenstein, Harvey A. *Revolution at the Table: The Transformation of the American Diet*. New York: Oxford University Press, 1988.

Lieberman, Joshua. *Creative Camping: A Coeducational Experiment in Personality Development and Social Living, Being the Record of Six Summers of The National Experimental Camp of Pioneer Youth of America*. New York: Association Press, 1931.

Liss, Marsha B., ed. *Social and Cognitive Skills: Sex Roles and Children's Play*. New York: Academic Press, 1983.

Longstreth, Richard. *City Center to Regional Mall: Architecture, the Automobile, and Retailing in Los Angeles, 1920–1950*. Cambridge, Mass.: MIT Press, 1997.

———. *The Drive-In, the Supermarket, and the Transformation of Commercial Space in Los Angeles, 1914–1941*. Cambridge, Mass.: MIT Press, 1999.

Lowrey, Nathan S. "Tales of the Northern Maine Woods: The History and Traditions of the Maine Guide." *Northeast Folklore* 28 (1989): 69–110.

Lundell, Liz, ed. *Fires of Friendship: Eighty Years of the Taylor Statten Camps*. Toronto: Taylor Statten Camps, 2000.

———. *Summer Camp: Great Camps of Algonquin Park*. Toronto: Stoddart, 1994.

Lupton, Ellen, and J. Abbott Miller. *The Bathroom, the Kitchen and the Aesthetics of Waste*. Cambridge, Mass.: MIT List Visual Arts Center, 1992.

Macleod, David I. *Building Character in the American Boy: The Boy Scouts, YMCA, and Their Forerunners, 1870–1920*. Madison: University of Wisconsin Press, 1983.

Malatzky, David M., ed. *The History of Camp Ranachqua (1917–1937)*. New York: Greater New York Councils, Boy Scouts of America and Ten Mile River Scout Museum, 2001.

———. *Summer Camp! The History of the New York City Boy Scout Summer Camps, from Hunter's Island to Ten Mile River, 1910–2002*. New York: Greater New York Councils, Boy Scouts of America and Ten Mile River Scout Museum, 2002.

Martino, Stefano de, and Alex Wall, eds. *Cities of Childhood: Italian Colonies of the 1930s*. London: Architectural Association, 1988.

Mason, Bernard S. "Plans for a Council Ring." *Camping Magazine* 9 (April 1937): 12–13, 29–30.

May, Bridget. "Progressivism and the Colonial Revival: The Modern Colonial House, 1900–1920." *Winterthur Portfolio* 26 (Summer/Autumn 1991): 107–22.

May, Elaine Tyler. *Homeward Bound: American Families in the Cold War Era*. New York: Basic Books, 1988.

Maynard, W. Barksdale. "'An Ideal Life in the Woods for Boys': Architecture and Culture in the Earliest Summer Camps." *Winterthur Portfolio* 34 (Spring 1999): 3–29.

Mays, Margaret Annie. "The History of the Water Safety Program of the American National Red Cross." DPE diss., Springfield College, 1973.

McClelland, Linda Flint. *Building the National Parks: Historic Landscape Design and Construction*. Baltimore: The Johns Hopkins University Press, 1998.

McKay, Ian. *The Quest of the Folk: Antimodernism and Cultural Selection in Twentieth-Century Nova Scotia*. Montreal and Kingston: McGill-Queen's University Press, 1994.

Mechling, Jay. *On My Honor: Boy Scouts and the Making of American Youth*. Chicago: University of Chicago Press, 2001.

Mercier, Laurie K. "Montanans at Work: Camp Cooks in Montana." *Montana* 39 (1989): 70–75.

Mergen, Bernard. "Toys and the Culture of Childhood." In *Small Worlds: Children and Adolescents in America, 1850–1950*, edited by Elliott West and Paula Petrik, 86–106. Lawrence: University Press of Kansas, 1992.

Meyer, Carter Jones, and Diana Royer, eds. *Selling the Indian: Commercializing and Appropriating American Indian Cultures*. Tucson: University of Arizona Press, 2001.

Miller, Susan A. "Girls in Nature/The Nature of Girls: Transforming Female Adolescence at Summer Camp, 1900–1939." PhD diss., University of Pennsylvania, 2001.

Miller, Willis W. "Camp Housing as a Factor in Good Camping." *YMCA Business Administration* 108 (April 1951): 21–22.

Mintz, Steven, and Susan Kellogg. *Domestic Revolutions: A Social History of American Family Life*. New York: Free Press, 1988.

Mishler, Paul C. *Raising Reds: The Young Pioneers, Radical Summer Camps, and Communist Political Culture in the United States*. New York: Columbia University Press, 1999.

Morris, Brian. "Ernest Thompson Seton and the Origins of the Woodcraft Movement." *Journal of Contemporary History* 5 (1970): 183–94.

Moses, L. G. *Wild West Shows and the Images of American Indians, 1883–1933*. Albuquerque: University of New Mexico Press, 1996.

Nabakov, Peter, and Robert Easton. *Native American Architecture*. New York: Oxford University Press, 1989.

Nasaw, David. "Children and Commercial Culture: Moving Pictures in the Early Twentieth Century." In *Small Worlds: Children and Adolescents in America, 1850–1950*, edited by Elliott West and Paula Petrik, 14–25. Lawrence: University Press of Kansas, 1992.

———. *Children of the City: At Work and at Play*. Garden City, N.Y.: Anchor Press/Doubleday, 1985.

Neubauer, John C. "Plans for a Block House." *Camping Magazine* 12 (October 1940): 15.

Nye, David E. *Electrifying America: Social Meanings of New Technology*. Cambridge, Mass.: MIT Press, 1990.

Ogle, Maureen. *All the Modern Conveniences: American Household Plumbing, 1840–1890*. Baltimore: The Johns Hopkins University Press, 1996.

"Oneness of Form and Material." *Progressive Architecture* 44 (December 1963): 107–17.

Osborn, Minnott A., ed. *Camp Dudley: The Story of the First Fifty Years*. New York: Huntington Press, 1934.

Parezo, Nancy J., and John W. Troutman, "The 'Shy' Cocopa Go to the Fair," in *Selling the Indian: Commercializing and Appropriating American Indian Cultures*, ed. Carter Jones Meyer and Diana Royer, 3–43. Tucson: University of Arizona Press, 2001.

Paris, Leslie M. "The Adventures of Peanut and Bo: Summer Camps and Early-Twentieth-Century American Girlhood." *Journal of Women's History* 12 (Winter 2001): 47–76.

———. "Children's Nature: Summer Camps in New York State, 1919–1941." PhD diss., University of Michigan, 2000.

Patrick, Thomas W. "A New Kind of Camp." *Parents' Magazine* 21 (May 1946): 42, 134–38.

Peck, George G. "Things Learned in Seventeen Consecutive Seasons in One Boys' Camp." *Association Boys* 1 (April 1902): 51–53.

Perdue, Martin Clay. "Designing Wildness: Rustic Wooden Architecture in the United States, 1830–1915." PhD diss., University of Virginia, forthcoming.

Phillips, Laura A. W., and Deborah Thompson. *Transylvania: The Architectural History of a Mountain County*. Brevard, N.C.: Transylvania County Joint Historic Preservation Commission, 1998.

Platou, Elaine C. "The Lure of an Ideal Camp." *Keith's Beautiful Homes Magazine* (August 1926): 78–81.

Playground and Recreation Association of America. *Camping Out: A Manual on Organized Camping*. New York: Macmillan, 1924.

"Portrait of a New Camp—1955." *Camping Magazine* (November 1955): 18–20.

Ramsdell, Charles H. "Designing a Boys' Camp in the Minnesota Woods." *Parks and Recreation* 15 (March 1932): 413–15.

Randall, Homer. *Army Boys in France*. New York: George Sully, 1918.

Randl, Chad. *A-Frame*. New York: Princeton Architectural Press, 2004.

"Recreation Buildings: Girl Scout Lodge." *Progressive Architecture* 38 (August 1957): 121–23.

"Report of the Private Camp Conference." *How to Help Boys* 3 (July 1903): 183–204.

"Report of the Y.M.C.A. Camp Conference." *How to Help Boys* 3 (July 1903): 204–18.

Robertson, Cheryl. "House and Home in the Arts and Crafts Era: Reforms for Simpler Living." In *"The Art That Is Life": The Arts and Crafts Movement in America, 1875–1920*, edited by Wendy Kaplan, 336–57. Boston: Museum of Fine Arts, 1987.

Robinson, Edgar M. "Association Boys' Camps." *Association Boys* 1 (June 1902): 65–121.

———. "The Experimental Woodcraft Camp." *Association Boys* 9 (June 1910): 116–29.

Roosevelt, Theodore. *American Ideals*. New York: G. P. Putnam's Sons, 1897, 1927.

Ross, Dorothy. *G. Stanley Hall: The Psychologist as Prophet*. Chicago: University of Chicago Press, 1972.

Ross, Patricia M., and Diane M. White. *Cedar Hill Memories: The Warren Family and Girl Scouts in Waltham, Massachusetts*. Boston: Patriots' Trail Girl Scouts Council, 1996.

Rotundo, E. Anthony. *American Manhood: Transformations in Masculinity from the Revolution to the Modern Era*. New York: Basic Books, 1993.

———. "Boy Culture: Middle-Class Boyhood in Nineteenth-Century America." In *Meanings for Manhood: Constructions of Masculinity in Victorian America*, edited by Mark C. Carnes and Clyde Griffen, 15–36. Chicago: University of Chicago Press, 1990.

Rykwert, Joseph. *On Adam's House in Paradise: The Idea of the Primitive Hut in Architectural History*. 2nd ed. Cambridge, Mass.: MIT Press, 1981.

Saint, Andrew. *Towards a Social Architecture: The Role of School-Building in Post-War England*. New Haven, Conn.: Yale University Press, 1987.

Salomon, Julian Harris. *The Book of Indian Crafts and Indian Lore*. 1928. Reprint, Mineola, N.Y.: Dover, 2000.

———. *Camp Site Development*. New York: Girl Scouts of the U.S.A., 1948.

———. *Camp Site Development*. 2nd ed., rev. and enl. New York: Girl Scouts of the U.S.A., 1959.

———. "The Indian Tipi." *Boys' Life* 15 (September 1925): 13.

———. "Space Requirements in Sleeping Cabins." *Camping Magazine* 8 (May 1936): 14–15.

Sanders, J. Edward. *Safety and Health in Organized Camps*. New York: National Bureau of Casualty and Surety Underwriters, 1931.

Sandweiss, Martha A. "Picturing Indians: Curtis in Context." In Edward S. Curtis, *The Plains In-*

dian *Photographs of Edward S. Curtis*, 13–38. Lincoln: University of Nebraska Press, 2001.

Sargent, Porter. *A Handbook of Summer Camps: An Annual Survey*. 3rd ed. Boston: Porter Sargent, 1926.

Scott, Charles R. "Follow Up Camp Results." *Association Boys* 3 (June 1916): 131.

———. "Wawayanda: The New Jersey Boys' Camp." *Association Boys* 6 (June 1907): 87–110.

Seton, Ernest Thompson. *The Birch-Bark Roll of the Woodcraft Indians*. New York: Doubleday, Page, 1908.

———. *The Book of Woodcraft*. Garden City, N.Y.: Garden City Publishing, 1912, 1921.

———. *Trail of an Artist-Naturalist*. New York: Charles Scribner's Sons, 1940.

Shapiro, Michael Steven. *Child's Garden: The Kindergarten Movement from Froebel to Dewey*. University Park: Pennsylvania State University Press, 1983.

Sheehy, Colleen J. "American Angling: The Rise of Urbanism and the Romance of the Rod and Reel." In *Hard at Play: Leisure in America, 1840–1940*, edited by Kathryn Grover, 77–92. Amherst: University of Massachusetts Press; Rochester, N.Y.: Strong Museum, 1992.

Shepard, Augustus D. "Camp Architecture." *Camping Magazine* 4 (February 1932): 12–14.

Shi, David E. "Ernest Thompson Seton and the Boy Scouts: A Moral Equivalent of War?" *South Atlantic Quarterly* 84 (Autumn 1985): 379–81.

Spring, John L. "The 'Big Piece' Way to Build." *Popular Science* (December 1954): 153–57.

Springhall, J. O. "Baden-Powell and the Scout Movement before 1920: Citizen Training or Soldiers for the Future?" *English Historical Review* 102 (1987): 934–42.

———. "The Boy Scouts, Class and Militarism in Relation to British Youth Movements, 1908–1930." *International Review of Social History* 16 (1971): 125–58.

Statten, Taylor. "Twenty-Five Years of Camping." In *Character Education in the Summer Camp, II: Report of Institute Held at the Y.M.C.A. College, Chicago, April 17–20, 1931*, edited by Hedley S. Dimock, 1–9. New York: Association Press, 1931.

Streightoff, Frank H. "Summer Camps." *Association Boys* 4 (June 1905): 128–34.

"Subtleties of the Camp Environment." *Camping Magazine* 5 (April 1933): 11–14.

"A Summer Camp as Developed by the New York Boys' Club," *Work with Boys* 12 (July 1912): 215–18.

Sutton-Smith, Brian. "Does Play Prepare the Future?" In *Toys, Play, and Child Development*, edited by Jeffrey H. Goldstein, 130–46. Cambridge: Cambridge University Press, 1994.

———. *Toys as Culture*. New York: Gardner Press, 1986.

———, and B. G. Rosenberg. "Sixty Years of Historical Change in the Game Preferences of American Children." *Journal of American Folklore* 74 (1961): 17–46.

Tedesco, Laureen. "Making a Girl into a Scout: Americanizing Scouting for Girls." In *Delinquents and Debutantes: Twentieth-Century American Girls' Cultures*, edited by Sherrie A. Inness, 19–39. New York: New York University Press, 1998.

Tennant, Margaret. "Complicating Childhood: Gender, Ethnicity, and 'Disadvantage' within the New Zealand Children's Health Camps Movement." *Canadian Bulletin of Medical History* 19 (2002): 179–99.

Terrie, Philip G. *Forever Wild: Environmental Aesthetics and the Adirondack Forest Preserve*. Philadelphia: Temple University Press, 1985.

———. "Urban Man Confronts the Wilderness: The Nineteenth-Century Sportsman in the Adirondacks." *Journal of Sport History* 5 (Winter 1978): 7–20.

"This Interesting Data from Camp Wawayanda." *Association Boys* 2 (June 1903): 100–101.

Tomes, Nancy. *The Gospel of Germs: Men, Women, and the Microbe in American Life*. Cambridge, Mass.: Harvard University Press, 1998.

"Two Camps Designed for Summer Fun." *Architectural Forum* 117 (July 1962): 91–93.

Turner, Eugene A., Jr. *One Hundred Years of YMCA Camping*. Chicago: YMCA of the USA, 1985.

Upton, Dell. "Lancasterian Schools, Republican Citizenship, and the Spatial Imagination of Early Nineteenth-Century America." *Journal of the Society of Architectural Historians* 55 (September 1996): 238–53.

———. "Pattern Books and Professionalism." *Winterthur Portfolio* 19 (Summer/Autumn 1984): 107–50.

Van Slyck, Abigail A. "Connecting with the Landscape: Campfires and Youth Culture at American Summer Camps, 1890–1950." In *Designing Modern Childhoods: History, Space, and the Material Culture of Children /An International Reader*, edited by Marta Gutman and Ning de Coninck-Smith. New Brunswick, N.J.: Rutgers University Press, forthcoming.

———. *Free to All: Carnegie Libraries and American Culture, 1890–1920*. Chicago: University of Chicago Press, 1995.

———. "Housing the Happy Camper." *Minnesota History* 58 (Summer 2002): 68–83.

———. "Kitchen Technologies and Mealtime Rituals: Interpreting the Food Axis at American Summer Camps, 1890–1950." *Technology and Culture* 43 (October 2002): 668–92.

———. "Summer Camps." In *Encyclopedia of Children and Childhood in History and Society*, edited by Paula S. Fass, 3:798–800. New York: Macmillan Reference, 2003.

———. "Summer Camps." In *Encyclopedia of World Environmental History*, edited by Shepard Krech III, J. R. McNeill, and Carolyn Merchant, 3: 1171–74. New York: Routledge, 2003.

———, and Annmarie Adams. "Children's Spaces." In *Encyclopedia of Children and Childhood in History and Society*, edited by Paula S. Fass, 1: 187–94. New York: Macmillan Reference, 2003.

Wack, Henry Wellington. *The Camping Ideal: The New Human Race*. New York: Red Book Magazine, 1925.

Warren, Allen. "Sir Robert Baden-Powell, the Scout Movement and Citizen Training in Great Britain, 1990–1920." *English Historical Review* 101 (1986): 376–98.

Webb, Kenneth B. "Color-blind Summer Camps." *Nation* 168 (30 April 1949): 493–95.

West, Elliott. *Growing Up in Twentieth-Century America: A History and Reference Guide*. Westport, Conn.: Greenwood Press, 1996.

———, and Paula Petrik, eds. *Small Worlds: Children and Adolescents in America, 1850–1950*. Lawrence: University Press of Kansas, 1992.

Whisnant, David E. *All That Is Native and Fine: The Politics of Culture in an American Region*. Chapel Hill: University of North Carolina Press, 1983.

Wick, William S. *Log Cabins: How to Build and Furnish Them*. New York: Forest and Stream Publishing, 1889.

Wiley, S. Wirt, and Florence Lehmann. *Builders of Men: A History of the Minneapolis Young Men's Christian Association, 1866–1936*. Minneapolis: [YMCA], 1938.

Wood, Walter M. "Objectives in Outings and Camps for Boys." *Association Boys* 6 (June 1907): 111–17.

Zelizer, Viviana A. *Pricing the Priceless Child: The Changing Social Value of Children*. New York: Basic Books, 1985.

INSTITUTIONAL ARCHIVES

American National Red Cross Records, National Archives (Red Cross)

Bancroft Library, University of California at Berkeley (Bancroft)

Billy Graham Center Archives, Wheaton College, Wheaton, Illinois (Graham)

Fresh Air Fund Archives, New York (FAF)

Girl Scouts of the U.S.A. Archives, New York (GSUSA)

Gutman Library, Harvard University (Gutman)

Kautz Family YMCA Archives, University of Minnesota (Kautz)

Library of Congress (LC)

Minnesota Historical Society (MHS)

National Register of Historic Places, National Park Service, Department of the Interior (NRHP)

Patriots' Trail Girl Scout Council, Waltham, Massachusetts (PTGSC)

Schlesinger Library, Radcliffe College (Schlesinger)

Seton Memorial Library, Philmont Scout Ranch, Cimarron, New Mexico (Seton)

Social Welfare History Archives, University of Minnesota (SWHA)

ARCHIVES OF INDIVIDUAL CAMPS

Big Sandy Camp, McGregor, Minnesota (Big Sandy)

Camp Ahmek, Algonquin Park, Ontario (Ahmek)

Camp Arcadia, Casco, Maine (Arcadia)

Camp Becket, Becket, Massachusetts (Becket)

Camp Dudley, Westport, New York (Dudley)

Camp Green Cove, Tuxedo, North Carolina (Green Cove)

Camp Greenwood, Buffalo, Minnesota (Greenwood)

Camp Illahee, Brevard, North Carolina (Illahee)

Camp Jeanne d'Arc, Merrill, New York (Jeanne d'Arc)

Camp Kamaji, Cass Lake, Minnesota (Kamaji)

Camp Lakamaga, Marine, Minnesota (Lakamaga)

Camp Lake Hubert, Lake Hubert, Minnesota (Lake Hubert)

Camp Lincoln, Lake Hubert, Minnesota (Lincoln)

Camp Merrie-Woode, Sapphire, North Carolina (Merrie-Woode)

Camp Miller, Sturgeon Lake, Minnesota (Miller)

Camp Mishawaka, Grand Rapids, Minnesota (Mishawaka)

Camp Mondamin, Tuxedo, North Carolina (Mondamin)

Camp Ojiketa, Chisago City, Minnesota (Ojiketa)

Camp Tanadoona, Excelsior, Minnesota (Tanadoona)

Camp Wapomeo, Algonquin Park, Ontario (Wapomeo)

Camp Warren, Eveleth, Minnesota (Warren)

Camp Widgiwagan, Minnesota (Widgiwagan)

Camp Wilderness, Park Rapids, Minnesota (Wilderness)

Catholic Youth Camp, McGregor, Minnesota (CYC)

Chimney Corners Camp, Becket, Massachusetts (Chimney Corners)

Covenant Pines Bible Camp, McGregor, Minnesota (Covenant Pines)

Grindstone Lake Bible Camp, Sandstone, Minnesota (Grindstone)

Luther Gulick Camps, South Casco, Maine (Gulick)

Rockbrook Camp, Brevard, North Carolina (Rockbrook)

Sharpe Reservation, Fishkill, New York (Sharpe)

Wyonegonic, Denmark, Maine (Wyonegonic)

PERSONAL PAPERS

Julian H. Salomon papers, in the possession of Richard B. Salomon (Salomon)

From the Prints and Photographs Division, Library of Congress: 1.1, 1.7, 1.14, 2.14, 3.5, 4.1, 4.3, 6.1, 6.2.

Courtesy of the Becket–Chimney Corners YMCA: 1.2, 2.7, 2.11, 2.13, 2.22, 3.3, 4.4, 5.1, 5.5, 5.6.

Courtesy of William W. Rockwell Collection, Pasquaney Archives, Concord, New Hampshire: 1.4.

Courtesy of Wohelo—The Luther Gulick Camps: 1.5, 6.5, 6.6.

Courtesy of Camp Dudley, YMCA, Inc.: 1.6, 2.2, 2.10, 2.16, 6.7.

Courtesy of Special Collections, Monroe C. Gutman Library, Harvard Graduate School of Education: 1.9 (used with permission of Camp Alleghany); 1.10 (used with permission of Camp Wigwam); 1.16 (used with permission of Medomak Camp); 2.8 (used with permission of Camp Arcadia); 2.19;

6.8 (used with permission of Medomak Camp); 6.9 (used with permission of Culver Woodcraft Camp); 6.12; 6.14 (used with permission of Medomak Camp).

Courtesy of Girl Scout Museum at Cedar Hill, Patriots' Trail Girl Scout Council: 1.11.

Courtesy of the Adirondack Museum: 1.15.

Courtesy of YMCA of the USA and Kautz Family YMCA Archives, Andersen Library, University of Minnesota: 1.18; 2.4; 2.5 (used with permission of Camp Hazen); 2.6; 2.26; 3.8 (used with permission of Camp Icaghowan); 3.13; 3.19 (used with permission of Camp Dudley); 4.2 (used with permission of Camp Dudley); 4.9 (used with permission of Camp Conrad Weiser); 5.3; 6.18.

Courtesy of Camp Mishawaka: 2.1, 2.9, 2.23, 3.6, 3.7, 3.20, 3.21, 6.13.

Courtesy of Chocorua Island Chapel Association: 2.3.

Courtesy of Rockbrook Camp: 2.18.

From Moody Church Collection, Billy Graham Center Archives, Wheaton College: 3.1, 3.2.

Courtesy of Camp Fire USA: 4.8, 5.7.

Courtesy of the National Museum of the American Indian, Smithsonian Institution: 6.3. Photograph by Roland W. Reed. P22456.

Courtesy of Philmont Museum–Seton Memorial Library, Boy Scouts of America, Cimarron, New Mexico: 6.4. A gift of Mrs. Julia M. Seton.

Courtesy of Richard B. Salomon: 6.10.

Courtesy of the Frances Loeb Library, Harvard Graduate School of Design: E.1, E.2, E.3, E.4, E.5, E.6, E.10.

Drawings by Allison Park: 3.12, 3.18, 6.16.

Reprinted with permission from *Parks & Recreation* magazine, National Recreation and Park Association (2005): 3.9.

The following photographs were taken by the author: 1.12, 2.12, 2.15, 2.17, 2.20, 2.21, 2.24, 2.25, 3.11, 3.14, 3.15, 3.16, 3.17, 4.6.

INDEX

Baden-Powell, Robert, 134, 172, 263n22; on undermined manhood, 9–10

Balch, Ernest B., 127

Barksdale, Mrs. Hamilton M., 155

Barnes, Edward Larrabee, 222, 224; design by, 214–20; modernism and, 218–19

Baseball, 40, 42, 43, 45, 50, 51, 59, 89, 94; citizenship and, 62, 63; fields for, 79, 93; girls and, 90, 91; organized by adults, 61–63; as ritual of community, 61–62

Bathing, 158–59

Beard, Adelia, 23, 46

Beard, Daniel Carter, 46, 268n56; Boy Scouts and, 173; Seton and, 266n15; Sons of Daniel Boone and, 23

Beard, George M., 9, 26, 256n58

Beard, Lina, 23, 46

Bederman, Gail, 9, 11

Beecher, Catherine, 59, 154, 264n18

Behavior, 43; assessing, 114; bad parenting and, 115; controlling, 134; dining hall/mess hall, 134, 141; normal, 115

Behavior Frequency Scale, 114–15, 117

Behavior Observation Record, 113

Belding Lodge, 120, 121

Bermingham, Ann, 4

Big House. *See* Unami Big House

Birch-Bark Roll of the Woodcraft Indians, The (Seton), 172, 183, 189, 203; advertisement in, 201–2

Black Wolf. *See* Seton, Ernest Thompson

Blazing Trail Camp, 25, 29, 74

Bluebird's Nest, 186

Boas, Franz, 171, 265n5

Bodies: cleaning, 147, 158–59, 164–66; documentation of, 103–4

Book of Indian Crafts and Indian Lore, The (Salomon), 197, 199, 204, 268n54; tipis and, 202

Book of the Camp Fire Girls, The, 11, 16

Book of Woodcraft, The (Seton), 181; on campfires, 182, 183–84; on tipis, 202

"Booming of the Logs, The" (Kimball), 5

Boys' camps: feminized homes and, 148; girls'

camps and, 11; primitiveness of, 23; rationale for, 10; recreational freedom at, 48–52

Boy Scout camps, xxviii, 125, 129, 130; division plan for, 204–5; nature museum, 26, 77; tents at, 101; waterfront layout at, 86–87

Boy Scouts of America, xxiii, xxxi, 134, 172; daily program by, 17; Department of Camping, 20; founding of, 9, 46; International Boy Scout Jamboree, 196; Salomon and, 93, 195, 197; tipis by, 202; waterfront layouts and, 87; YMCA and, 254n35. See also *Boys' Life; Camp Site Development Plans*

Boy Scout Training Camp for Camp Directors and Water Front Men, 84–85

Boys' Life, xxviii, 202

Brigham, Mrs. Kenneth H., 32

British Boy Scouts, 134

British Girl Guides, 134

Brown, Elias G., 190; on loafing, 58; on nature/health, 150; sanitation and, 150, 151, 152–53; swimming and, 158–59

Brown, Lydia Bush, 185, 187

Buddy system, 88, 260n106

Buffalo Bill's Wild West Show, xxv, 51, 170–71, 173, 180, 185

Buildings, 72–73; administrative, 34, 217; camp landscape and, 64, 80; multipurpose recreation, 64, 65; nature study, 72, 77–78, 77, 78; private camp, 64, 100, 118; single-purpose recreation, 79–80; winterized, 35; YMCA camp, 64, 65, 67

Bunyan, Paul, 5, 255n7

Cabins: camper, 25, 120, 122; canvas, 106; communal, 118–22; counselor, 118, 120; craft, 74, 75, 76, 77; decentralization of, 81; health and, 105–6, 108–10; log, 25, 74, 75, 76–78, 77, 78, 94, 193; sleeping, 110, 111, 118–22; tents and, 110

Camp ABC, 218

Camp Ahmek: applied psychology at, 116–17; changes at, 113; counselors at, 117; observations at, 110–16; naming of, 192; Seton at, 189

Camp Alanita for Girls, 206

drinking water, 153; on garbage disposal, 153; on hygiene, 164; on kitchens, 136–37, 140; on labor-saving technology, 135; on menstruation, 163; on sanitation, 154; on toilets, 155; on washhouses, 161; on waterfronts, 85

Camp Warren, 25; cabins at, 25, 119, 122; Cub Camp at, 119; Kirby Lodge, 263n30

Camp Wawayanda, 32; baseball at, 63; buildings at, 65, 67; crafts at, 61; private devotions at, 54

Camp Widjiwagan, 192, 263n30

Camp Wigwam, 23; council ring at, 206; site plan for, 22–23

Camp Winona, 7

Camp Wohelo, 13; Bluebird's Nest, 186; council fire at, 187, 188; council ring at, 187, 188; naming of, 184; playing Indian at, 177–89; "shack" at, 13–14

Camp Wyonegonic, 7

Camp Yakewi: kitchen layout for, 139, 140

Camp-y camps, 41–42, 81

Canadian Camping Association, 112

Canadian Standard Efficiency Tests (CSET), 111–12

Catalina Island: YMCA camp at, 15

Cavallo, Dominic, 47, 261n113

CDA. *See* Camp Directors Association

CDAA. *See* Camp Directors Association of America

Chapels, open-air, 53–57

Chappell, George H., Jr., 201–2

Character: camping and, xxii, 110–17

Chautauquas, xxix, 4

Chefs and cooks, 129, 131

Chicago YMCA, 32–33, 47

Child development, 42; mealtime and, 137–38, 140–44; play and, 43–44

Childhood, 123, 224; adult anxieties about, xxi–xxiii, 8–9; inventing, xxi; purity of, 45; social construction of, xxi, xxxii, 123, 144

Child labor legislation, xxii–xxiii

Child psychology, 110, 116

Child space/time: reorganization of, 46

Child study, 44, 99, 113, 115, 116

Chimney Corners Camp: Eyrie, 164, 165; Kaustine toilets at, 155; menstrual routines at, 164; Nest,

163, 164; Treasure Trove, 78; washhouse at, 163–64, 165

Chimney Rock Camp, 76, 203; craft cabin at, 76

Citizenship, xxii, 62, 254n23; gendered notions of, 90–91, 261n113; promoting, 47

Civilization, 10, 177; camp landscape and, 212; gender differentiation and, 11; social evolution of, 9; wilderness and, 3

Class: camp landscape and, xxxiv; tensions, xxi. *See also* Middle-class children; Middle-class identity

Cleanliness, 147, 149; antisepticonsciousness and, 148; environmental, 148; gendered meanings of, 166–67; gentility and, 264n1; rituals of, 154; showers and, 165; standards of, xxxvii, 156. *See also* Sanitation

Cobb, Charles, 7

Cody, William F. "Buffalo Bill," 170–71, 180, 265n3, 267n32

Collecting, 45, 59, 259n46

Converse, Florence, 187

Cooking, xxxvi; at boys' camps, 129–31, 144; at girls' camps, 134–37, 144; manliness and, 131; technology for, 128, 143; water for, 147

Cooks: black, 62; chefs and, 129, 131; professional, 129, 142

Cook tents, 128, 129

Cooper, James Fenimore, 175

Cottages, 38, 105–6; summer, 4; tent-, 106

Council fires, 168, 173, 184, 185, 187, 188. *See also* Campfires

Council rings, xxxvii, 23, 178, 182, 184, 204–8, 212; at boys' camps, 206; camp life and, 187; gender and, 167; at girls' camps, 206, 207; laying out, 190, 211; location of, 188, 206, 208. *See also* Seton, Ernest Thompson

Counselors, 36, 92, 119; cabins for, 120, 122; campers and, 116, 117

Cox, L. D., 41

Craft houses, 31, 81

Crafts, 61, 73, 77, 94; culture of, 74; girls and, 89–90, 185; log cabins and, 76; Native Americans and, 185. *See also* Manual training

ABIGAIL A. VAN SLYCK holds the Dayton Chair in Art History and directs the Architectural Studies Program at Connecticut College. She is the author of *Free to All: Carnegie Libraries and American Culture, 1890–1920*. She has served as president of the Vernacular Architecture Forum and on the national board of the Society of Architectural Historians.

DATE DUE